K. B. MADSEN

THEORIES OF MOTIVATION

A comparative study of modern theories of motivation

Fourth edition

THE KENT STATE UNIVERSITY PRESS
and
MUNKSGAARD
1968

Library of Congress Catalog Card Number 68-22338

THE KENT STATE UNIVERSITY PRESS
Kent, Ohio 44240

or

MUNKSGAARD
47, Prags Boulevard
DK-2300 Copenhagen S, Denmark

PRINTED IN HOLLAND BY HOOIBERG, EPE

PREFACE TO THE 4th EDITION

This is a book about *theories* of motivation. Therefore, the reader who is mainly interested in the experimental and other empirical *facts* about motivation should consult other books which deal more directly with empirical research in motivation. This book deals only *indirectly* with facts as the empirical basis for the theories presented.

This books contains a *comparative study* of theories of motivation. This constitutes the main difference between it and many other books about 'Theories' (especially such well-known works as: *Hilgard and Bower*'s: 'Theories of Learning' and *Hall and Lindzey*'s: 'Theories of Personality', both of which contain presentations of theories, some of which are also dealt with in this book).

Although the book covers a period of 3–4 decades, there is *no* historical description of the evolution of motivational psychology. Thus this book is not a work in the history of psychology, but rather must be classified under another 'metascientific' discipline, the *philosophy of science*, and especially under the subdiscipline called '*meta-theory*'.

As a philosophy-of-science-study of psychological theories this book may be of interest to both *philosophers* and *psychologists* (to graduate students as well as scientists). The philosopher may regard the book as an *application* of his science to psychological theories. The *psychologist* may regard the book as a survey of the complicated and confusing field of motivational theories, and perhaps gain deeper insight into the problems of constructing theories, which is very important for a modern scientist.

It is at least the present author's hope that *this* book will contribute to the creation of or reinforce interest in scientific theories—the most complex product of the human race. The author's interest in the topic was awakened by his greatest teacher, the Danish philosopher and professor, dr. phil. h.c. *Jørgen Jørgensen.*

In the present (4th) edition (which is about to be translated into Czech, Spanish and Polish) there is a new introductory chapter plus supplements to several chapters, which bring the study of the 20 theories up-to-date. There are—in Chapter 16—comments on other books too. But the many new theories appearing in recent years cannot be dealt with satisfactorily within the framework of this book.

Therefore, the author is writing a *new* book containing a comparative study of 10 new theories ('Modern Theories of Motivation').

The translation of *this* edition has been supervised by *John T. Bruce,* M.A.

Copenhagen
May, 1967.

K. B. Madsen
Professor of General Psychology
The Royal Danish School of
Educational Studies.
Copenhagen NV.

CONTENTS

PART I THE CONCEPTUAL FRAME-OF-REFERENCE: META-THEORETICAL PSYCHOLOGY, A BRANCH OF THE SCIENCE OF SCIENCE

PART II ANALYSIS OF THEORIES

PART III COMPARISON OF THE THEORIES

Part I

THE CONCEPTUAL FRAME-OF-REFERENCE: META-THEORETICAL PSYCHOLOGY A BRANCH OF THE SCIENCE OF SCIENCE

'— there is nothing so practical as a good theory'

K. LEWIN

Chapter 1

Meta - Science

—the Science of Science—
and its application to psychology

Introduction. Everything can be the object of a scientific study—even science itself. This book is a contribution to such a scientific study of one science, psychology. Therefore, we will devote the first Chapter to a general discussion of the science of science or '*meta-science*'.

Meta-science has not yet evolved into a systematic organized science. It exists only as separate disciplines inside several sciences. The disciplines are:

1. The philosophy of science.
2. The history of science.
3. The psychology of science.
4. The sociology of science.

We will discuss these disciplines separately and, finally we will try to organize them into a systematic science of science.

The Philosophy of Science

General. The oldest science of science is the 'mother-science', *philosophy*. But not all philosophy is about science. There are: 'a philosophy of morality', 'a philosophy of religion', 'a philosophy of the arts, 'a philosophy of education', and so on. But a main part of modern philosophy can be called '*the philosophy of science*'. This is a part of meta-science, and is well established with its own journals and several textbooks, handbooks and monographs. The philosophy of science can be divided further into three subdisciplines:

'The philosophy of science = { 1. Epistemology; 2. Methodology; 3. Meta-theory }

Epistemology. Among these disciplines 'epistemology'—or 'theory of knowledge'—is the oldest and most fundamental. It deals with the fundamental problems of all knowledge—pre-scientific as well as scientific. It tries to answer questions such as: What is knowledge? What is truth? What are the conditions for obtaining true knowledge?, and so on. In the course of time several schools of philosophy have tried to answer these questions with their peculiar theories of knowledge, such as 'rationalism', 'empiricism', criticism', 'positivism', 'pragmatism', 'operationism', 'logical empiricism', 'Oxford-philosophy', etc. Many of the modern philosophies of sciences can be united under the label '*analytical philosophy*', as they see the task of philosophy as *analyzing* concepts, propositions and theories (in opposition to the older philosophy, which saw the task of philosophy mainly as *synthesizing* all available knowledge into a comprehensive 'worldsystem').

Methodology. This subdiscipline deals with the *empirical methods* of science. It describes and analyzes the problems about such methods as general observation, experimentation, case-studies, testing, measuring, etc. There are several papers and books about this subject matter in general—and about the methods of psychology in particular. Among these the works of *Andrews* (1948), *Bjørkman* (1962), *Brown and Ghiselli* (1955) and *Hyman* (1964) may be noted. Sometimes 'methodology' is used in a comprehensive way including the next discipline, too. But the difference is, that methodology deals with the *empirical* methods, while meta-theory deals with the *theoretical* methods: the methods of constructing theories.

Meta-theory. From what is already said you can understand, that 'meta-theory' is 'the theory of theories'[1]). This sub-discipline deals with the 'products of science': scientific theories, which perhaps are the most complex products of the most complex organisms on the earth. As theories are complex systems of words and sentences it could also be said, that meta-theory deals with the vocabulary (concepts) and language (theories) of science (cf. Mandler and Kessen 1959).

The role of theory in science is in modern times stressed by the philosophical school named: '*logical Empiricism*'. As the name of this school indicates, they hold that theory is second only to empirical observation. The role of theory in science can also be illustrated by the sequence:

$$\text{Observation} \rightarrow \text{theory} \rightarrow \text{observation.}$$

The first arrow indicates what is called 'induction': a generalization from empirical observation to general formulations of 'hypotheses', which explain the observation. The second arrow indicates the so-called 'deduction': logical specification from general formulations to specific descriptions of observations. These observations are said to be 'predicted' from the theory. We will go much deeper into this theory of theories in Chapter 2. That Chapter is based for the most part on works of philosophers who could be united under the broad label 'analytical philosophers': *Ayer*, *Bergman*, *Braithwaite*, *Brodbeck*, *Campel*, *Carnap*, *Feigl*, *Hempel*, *Jørgensen*, *Kaila*, *Ness*, *Neurath*, *Popper*, *Reichenback*, *Russel*, *Ryle*, *Scriven* and many others

---

[1]) The author should here like to introduce a new term as a substitute for 'meta-theory' namely the term: '*systematology*'; the study of scientific systems ('theories', 'models' etc.).

who are indicated in the list of references (after Chapter 4).

The philosophers belonging to logical empiricism have been most interested in studying theories within mathematics and physics. And they are more or less implicitly of the opinion, that all scientific theories ought to be like mathematical-physical theories. In other words: their concepts, definitions and theories about theories can be described as 'normative'.

A more purely descriptive approach to meta-theory is found in a Scandinavian meta-theory called '*discourse analysis*'. It was formulated by *H. Törnebohm* (1952, 1955, 1957) and applied to psychology by *Carl Lesche* (1960).

While the logical empiricists study scientific theories by comparing them with logical or mathematical systems, the discourse analysts make 'case-studies' of theories and describe them in their own ways.

A similar purely descriptive approach to meta-theory was independently formulated by another Scandinavian philosopher, *Arne Ness* (1936, 1962).

The approach to meta-theory in this book is a combination of the different analytical approaches: The 20 theories are analyzed mainly in accordance with the meta-theory of logical empiricists. But the author has combined the ideas of logical Empiricism with ideas of some psychologists—especially *Tolman*, *Lewin*, *Spence*, and *S. Koch.*

The comparison of theories in the last part of this book is completely the author's own work—for better or for worse.

The Philosophy of Psychology. We have now discussed the philosophy of science in general. But this book is devoted especially to the '*philosophy of psychology*' which is the application of the philosophy of science to the science: psychology. Besides this application there are of course similar applications of the philosophy of science to other sciences, and so we have 'the philosophy of mathematics', 'the philosophy of physics', etc.

Perhaps physics and psychology are the two sciences which have attracted most philosophical attention. Many philosophers and psychologists are engaged in the study of the philosophy of psychology. The American Psychological Association has now a division for 'philosophical psychology' which may be more or less identical with 'the philosophy of psychology'.

The same division of the philosophy of science into three subdisciplines can be made with the philosophy of psychology, and we then have the following subdisciplines:

The philosophy of psychology = {
1. Epistemology of psychology
2. Methodology of psychology
3. Meta-theory of psychology

Among these subdisciplines the third has our special interest as this book belongs to '*the meta-theory of psychology*' or '*meta-theoretical psychology*' as it also could be designated[2]). It is here formally defined as '*the meta-theoretical study of psychological theories*'. This meta-theoretical study is made as a *purely empirical or descriptive study: an analysis and comparison of (psychological) theories, which results in a description and classification of the theories.*

The frame-of-reference or tools for the analysis are presented in the first part of this book. In the second part we present results of the analysis of 20 theories, while in the third part we describe the comparison of the theories. We have chosen theories of motivation as the special object for our meta-theoretical study, because motivation plays a central role in modern psychology. Many of the theories could as well be characterized as theories of learning or theories of personality, as they in fact are comprehensive and general psychological theories. But we have especially analyzed their concepts and hypotheses about motivation.

As mentioned earlier many philosophers and psychologists are interested in the philosophy of psychology. Perhaps it is so, that philosophers are mainly interested in the epistemology of psychology. Among these philosophers are *Bergman*, *Feigl*, *Jørgensen*, *Kaila*, *Ness*, *Peters*, *Russell*, *Ryle* and *Scriven*. Many psychologists are interested in the methodology of psychology and the meta-theory of psychology. We can mention only a few, who are indicated in the list of references: *Brunswik*, *Griffith*, *Hebb*, *Hilgard*, *Hull*, *Kantor*, *Koch*, *Lewin*, *Marx*, *Pratt*, *Rosenthal*, *Spence*, *Stevens*, *Tolman*, *Turner* and *Wolman*.

It is of course difficult to draw a sharp boundary between these subdisciplines, as well as between the whole philosophy of science and the other discipline, the history of science to which we now turn.

The History of Science

General. The second discipline belonging to meta-science is '*the history of science*'. It is the only discipline which is developed to a degree comparable to the philosophy of science. History is almost as old as philosophy, and the two disciplines of these sciences dealing with science are the oldest disciplines constituting meta-science.

It is difficult to draw a sharp boundary between these two disciplines, as between the other disciplines. It is most difficult to distinguish methodology and meta-theory on the one side and the history of science on the other side, especially if the meta-theory is of the purely descriptive sort—as it is in this book. The difference lies mainly in the fact, that the history of science describes the chronological order of the scientific production, and tries to *explain* the scientific development. In other words: it is especially the (historical) *explanations* which make the difference between the history of science, which is both descriptive and explanatory and the philosophy of science which is purely descriptive.

The history of science can be divided into subdisciplines in accordance with the sciences, the history is dealing with. Thus we have 'the history of philosophy',

---

[2]) Or in accordance with our new term: 'systematology of psychology'.

'the history of physics', and so on. Among these subdisciplines belongs naturally the history of psychology.

The History of Psychology. There has in the last decade been a growing interest in the history of psychology. It is perhaps a symptom of psychology's growing to a mature state, that psychologists are interested in the past development of their science.

The 'grand old man' in the history of psychology is *E. G. Boring*, who also has dealt with the other meta-scientific disciplines. Besides his books you can find in the list of references the books of *Esper* (1965), *Garrett* (1941), *Murphy* (1951), *Peters* (1953), *Postman* (1962), *Razran* (1965), *Tegen* (1949), *Watson* (1963), *Woodworth* (1964) and *Wolman* (1960).

There are many works which belongs both to the history of psychology and the next discipline, we are going to discuss, 'the psychology of science'. This is specially the case with biographical studies of famous scientists. The most well-known case of a historical and psychological study of a scientist is perhaps *Ernest Jones's* (1962) biography of *Sigmund Freud.*

The Psychology of Science

General. A complete science of science or meta-science must include a discipline called '*the psychology of science*', because science is a result of human behavior. This discipline for the moment only exists in the form of shattered investigations. But in its full development it must come to include the same disciplines as psychology does—all applied to science as the object. We then have the following subdisciplines:

'The psychology of science' = { 1. The general psychology of science.
2. The differential psychology of science.
3. The social psychology of science.

We will discuss the content of these subdisciplines and mention some of the investigations already made.

The General Psychology of Science. Scientific *activity* is mainly observation and creative thinking. Therefore, the general psychology of science must be a special part of the general psychology of *perception* and *thinking*. In recent years there has been a growing interest in creative thinking—both artistic, technical and scientific thinking. But many of the investigations have been more with the creative personality which belongs to the next subdiscipline. A bibliography on 'creativity in research in the physical sciences' was compiled by *Benton* (1961).

Scientific activity must, just as all behavior, be motivated. The special motivation for scientific activity is, therefore, a possible object of study for the general psychology of science[3]).

[3]) A recent book, which is 'a critical examination of the psychology of science and scientists' is: Abraham H. Maslow: The Psychology of Science (N.Y. 1966).

The Differential Psychology of Science. This is the psychological study of the special scientific *personality* (and intelligence-structure). There have been some studies in this field. They are of two slightly different types:

a. '*Case-studies*' of single—often famous—scientists. This type af study has much in common with general *biographical* studies. Besides the mentioned biography of Freud by Ernest Jones, we can mention *Amon's* (1962) and *Hays's* (1962) studies of Hull's 'Notebooks'.
b. '*Group-studies*' of a group of scientists often employing tests and other objective methods. While the first mentioned type often are longitudinal studies, this type is often 'cross-sectional'. One of these group-studies is that of *Anna Roe* (1953). Also *Terman* (1959) has among his approximately 1500 intelligent children compared those who became scientists with, those who did not.

The Social Psychology of Science. Much modern scientific research is accomplished as teamwork, and, therefore, the group-conditions and group-relationships and the leadership in the group are important for the research-work. As group-behavior is the object for social psychology, there must be a '*social psychology of science*'. This subdiscipline of the psychology of science has been cultivated by the American psychologist *Donald C. Pelz* (see Pelz (1958, 1964)). He has studied the different kinds of leadership and the different forms of contact in research-team-work, and found what its influence was on the productivity of group-members.

With the social psychology of science we are in the border-area of the last meta-scientific discipline, but we must first deal with a special application of the psychology of science.

The Psychology of Psychology. As the other meta-scientific disciplines the psychology of science also can be divided into subdisciplines according to the special science—or group of scientists, which are the object of the psychological study. We then have:

'the psychology of mathematics',
'the psychology of physics'
'the psychology of biology',
'the psychology of psychology',
etc.

The examples of research in the psychology of science mentioned have been concerned with almost all areas of science. But especially E. Jones's biography of Freud is a good example of a piece of 'psychology of psychologists'. Another example is *David P. Campell's* (1965) investigation of the vocational interests of presidents of the American Psychological Association, and *P. H. Kriedl's* (1949) investigation of the vocational interests of psychologists in general.

The Sociology of Science

General. The development of modern science depends much on the society to which it belongs: it depends on financial facilitation or inhibition, etc. Besides, this modern science is organized into institutions and professions, and the scientific development is dependent on information and communication in the society in general and in the professional organization especially. There is a Scandinavian investigation of the co-operation between scientists (Valpola and Törnudd, 1963).

All these phenomena are the object for a '*sociology of science*'. This meta-scientific discipline is of course connected with the other meta-scientific disciplines, and there are borderzones between them. We have just mentioned that the social psychology of science must have a border-zone in common with the sociology of science. And there is also a border-zone between the sociology of science and the history of science. This border-zone is the description of the contemporary conditon of a science in a special country or area. It could perhaps be called '*the geography of science*'.

The Sociology of Psychology. As the other meta-scientific disciplines the sociology of science can be divided into subdisciplines according to the science studied. Then we have: 'the sociology of mathematics', 'the sociology of physics' and so on. And among these of course '*the sociology of psychology*'. Some research has been done within this discipline. The American Psychology Association has taken the initiative and sponsored two research projects. One is reported on in *K. E. Clark's*: 'America's psychologists: A survey of a growing profession' (1957). The other is an as yet unfinished project on scientific information exchange among psychologists. (See the preliminary report from 1964).

A systematic integration of meta-scientific disciplines

General. We have now analyzed the different existing meta-scientific disciplines. There are not any other disciplines developed at the moment—at least not known to the author, and he cannot think of any other possible meta-scientific disciplines.

But now we come to the problem: what are the systematic relationships between the disciplines? We will try to draw a model for an integration of the disciplines into a *systematic meta-science*. We will make this integration on the basis of a conception of the *tasks of sciences*. In accordance with the general opinion among contemporary scientists the tasks of sciences are: *description*, *explanation* (and *prediction*[4])). We will now see how these tasks are distributed among the meta-disciplines.

1. '*The philosophy of science* has the task of analyzing and *describing* the sciences. This task is further divided between the subdisciplines in the following way:

a. *Epistomology* has the task of analyzing the fundamental problems of all scientific knowledge and *describing* the solutions of these problems by formulations of the *basic propositions* (principles, axioms, workinghypotheses, etc.), which are

---

[4]) Prediction is logical, identical with explanation; it is only the time-perspective, which is different and makes prediction more difficult.

the more or less explicit starting point for the sciences.

b. *Methodology* has the task of analyzing and *describing* the *emperical methods* of the sciences.

c. *Meta-theory*[5]) has the task of analyzing and *describing* the *theories* of the *sciences.*

Summaryzing we could say, that the philosophy of science has the task of giving a *systematic description* of the sciences, which can form the basis for the description given in the other disciplines.

2. *The history of science* also has the task of describing the sciences. But this description must be a description of the development of the sciences, in other words: a *cronological or historical description.* But besides this, the history of science has the task of *explaining* (and perhaps: predicting) the historical development of the sciences. Perhaps one could roughly characterize historical explanations as '*ideographic*' or 'single-case-explanations'. This is different from the '*nomothetic*' or general-law-explanations, which we find in the remaining two meta-scientific disciplines.

3. *The psychology of science* also has the task of *describing* and *explaining* (perhaps predicting) sciences. But the psychological description must, of course, be a description of scientific *activity* as a kind of *behavior*. And the description of the men of science, must be a description of the *scientific personality*.

Besides these descriptions there can be *explanations* of the scientific *activity* in accordance with *general* psychological concepts, hypotheses and theories; and there can be explanations of the *development* of the scientific personality in accordance with the concepts, hypotheses and theories in *differential* psychology (of personality and intelligence).

As mentioned earlier a *combination* of historical and psychological descriptions and explanations can be *made* in the *biographical* studies of famous scientists.

4. *The sociology of science* also has the tasks of *describing* and *explaining* sciences. But the description must, of course, be a sociological description, which is a description in accordance with sociological concepts (group, organisation, institution, society, profession, class, communication, etc.); and explanations (and perhaps predictions) are made in accordance with sociological hypotheses as theories.

As mentioned earlier there are also border-zones between sociology and the psychology of science (*the social psychology* of sciences) and between sociology and the history of sciences (the 'geography' of science).

We can illustrate this systematic integration of meta-scientific disciplines by a diagram (p. 19).

Meta-scientific Psychology. We have now analyzed and integrated the whole of meta-science. As the meta-scientific disciplines are so intimately interrelated, it is possible to combine them in one study of a particular science—or of a part of a

---

[5]) or rather 'systematology'.

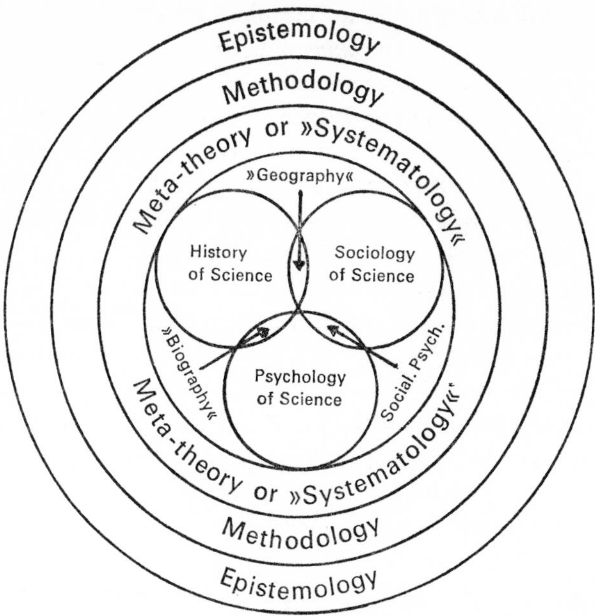

A diagram representing the systematic organisation of the different disciplines constituting the *Meta-science.*

science. We then have the following '*combined meta-scientific disciplines*': 'Meta-scientific mathematics', 'meta-scientific physics', 'meta-scientific chemistry', 'meta-scientific biology', 'meta-scientific psychology', etc.

We can make an explication of the content of the combined meta-scientific disciplines applied to psychology:

'Meta-scientific Psychology' =

1. The philosophy of psychology.
   a. The epistemology of psychology.
   b. The methodology of psychology.
   c. The meta-theory of psychology.
2. The history of psychology.
3. The psychology of psychology.
4. The sociology of psychology.

'*Meta-scientific psychology*' can formally be defined as '*the combined meta-scientific* (philosophical, historical, psychological and sociological) *study of psychology*'. The term 'meta-scientific psychology' could perhaps be shortened to 'meta-psychology", and similar in the other sciences: 'meta-mathematics', meta-physics', etc. Unfortunately, the term 'meta-physics' is still in use with an out-dated meaning: 'a speculative philosophy of nature', which supplements the physics for an all-round world-system. And the term 'meta-psychology' was used in yet another way by Freud. In other words: the old meaning af 'meta-' is 'philosophical supplements to a science', while the modern meaning of 'meta-' is 'science dealing with'. In order to prevent confusing these two meanings of 'meta-', we *recommend always using 'meta-scientific', when the meaning is 'science dealing with'*.

There have of course been some combined meta-scientific studies of psychology. One of the 'grand old men' in this science is *E. G. Boring*, who not only has made historical studies of psychology, but has also contributed philosophical, psychological and sociological studies 'see Boring (1961 and 1963)). Another allround meta-scientific psychologists is *Sigmund Koch*. Besides several papers and sections of books, he has been the editor of the great work sponsored by the American Psychological Association: 'Psychology—A study of a science' (see *Koch* (1959–63)). This latter work, which is not yet finished, is based upon a questionnaire sent to all the contributing psychologists. In this questionnaire they are asked to answer meta-scientific questions about philosophical matters (especially, methodological and meta-theoretical) as well as about historical, psychological and sociological subjects. Koch has discussed the questionnaire and made preliminary summaries in six volumes. He is at the moment writing the 7th volume, which is designed to be a comprehensive exposition of this extensive and intensive meta-scientific study of psychology. This volume will be the first comprehensive allround and systematic exposition of 'meta-scientific psychology'—and perhaps of any meta-science.

Shattered through this monumental work there are many contributions related to the subject matter of this book. Especially, one might single out a meta-scientific study of 'motivation in learning' by E. R. Hilgard (see S. Koch, vol. V, 1963).

Another meta-scientific book has appeared since the first edition of this book. It is 'Allgemeine Psychologie'—'2. Band: Motivation' edited by *H. Thomae* (1965). There are many systematic and thorough meta-scientific analysis of several concepts and theories (but no over-all comparison). Many American books about motivation of course appeared since the first edition of this book. But most of these are expositions of the particular authors' own theories of motivation (which will be analyzed in Chapter 16 of this book); or they are general textbooks of motivational psychology (which also will be briefly discussed in Chapter 16). The American book, which is most like this, is *Cofer and Appley*: '*Motivation, Theory and Research*' (1964), which also will be analyzed in Chapter 16.

It is now possible to give a precise pre-view of *this* book: It is a *meta-theoretical* study of psychological theories (mainly) about *motivation*. The theories are from the period 1930–1966. The sequence of theories is chronological and there is a very brief historical introduction to each theory. The basis for the analysis of the theories is laid down in the following Chapters: 2–4. Then follows in Chapters 5–16 a meta-theoretical *analysis* of 20 theories, while Chapters 17–19 take up the meta-theoretical *comparison* of the theories (which perhaps is the most unique feature of this book). It ends with a suggestion for synthesis in Chapter 20.

Chapter 2

Scientific Theories

Scientists have more and more accepted that the goal of science is to construct one or more theories which *systematize* the descriptions of results of experiments and other observations, whereby it will be possible to *explain* the observations already made and to *predict* new ones. It may therefore be practical to give a brief presentation in this chapter of the philosophy of theories in general[1]); in the first section the logical relations or *syntax* of the theories will be discussed, and in the next section the actual epistemological relations or *semantics* of the theories will be dealt with. The following chapter will discuss the special problems concerning psychological theories.

THE SYNTAX OF THE THEORIES

Definition of Theory

The term 'theory' has a general and a special meaning. The general meaning of '*theory*' is '*any descriptive and/or explanatory systems of symbols*'. Most scientific 'theories' outside physics are theories in this general sense of the word, and in the following 'theory' will be used with this general meaning if nothing else is said.

Axiomatization

'*Theory*', when used with its special meaning, means '*an axiomatized deductive system.*' This description is used when the statements (or formulas) of the theory have been arranged or systematized in *primary statements* (also: axioms, postulates, premisses, or principles) and *secondary statements* (also: consecutive statements, consequences, conclusions, or theorems). The secondary statements can be transformed or *deduced* from the primary (or other secondary) statements in accordance with the logical rules for conclusion or transformation. The primary statements

---

[1]) This presentation is mainly based upon the works given in the bibliography after Chapter 4.

are the presuppositions of the theory from which the secondary statements of the theory in question can be explained, but the primary statements must be assumed or postulated. They may, however, be explained by a deduction from the primary statements of another theory.

The statements consist of words (or terms), which can partly be *undefined* and partly *defined* words, combined in sentences according to common linguistic or special rules of syntax.

Most often the undefined words are abstract or hypothetical terms which are defined by means of less abstract terms and finally by empirical terms. The contrary can also happen, as observable terms can be used as undefined terms. The first method has the advantage—according to *Carnap*—that it provides better possibilities for constructing a system of hypotheses or 'laws' (i. e. a 'theory') in which the abstract terms are only defined implicitly through the axioms; whereas the second method gives better possibilities for empirical control of the individual abstract terms.

In physics the first method is used the most, as the axiomatization of a theory has great advantages. First the presuppositions of the theory are formulated *explicitly* and can then be made the object of analysis and maybe revision. Next it is often possible to deduce from the theory *more consequences* than those it should explain, and this may provide possibilities for *predicting* new consequences.

Symbolization

A theory, especially an axiomatized theory, can consist of 'artificial' symbols or *signs*, either mathematical or logical signs. Such a '*deductive (axiomatized) system of signs*' is called '*a calculus*'. It might be treated as a 'meaningless' game of signs, the rules of which allow the combination of signs into formulas and transformation into new formulas.

The advantage of using a calculus rather than a deductive system formulated in every-day language is that deduction is easier to control and that it can be done faster and more mechanically (in some cases it may even be done by machines).

Calculus is either purely mathematical, or logical, constructed without intention of application, but later used or '*interpreted*' for symbolizating an axiomatized theory. A calculus may also be constructed as a symbolic 'translation' of a certain axiomatized theory. In both cases rules for the interpretation of the empirical terms must be given, the so-called *co-ordinating definitions*. Finally we may have *partly symbolized* deductive theories where the symbolic presentation serves the purpose of avoiding ambiguities which cannot be avoided with everyday language.

Formalization

The co-ordinating definitions which indicate the relation between a calculus and an axiomatized theory are given in the *meta-theory* of the theory, a theory of the theory in question. Besides these, the meta-theory of a theory must include: 1) a list of the undefined signs of the theory; 2) a list of *syntactical rules*, i.e. rules for construction of statements (formulas or sentences); 3) a list of *the transformation-rules* of the theory i. e. rules for transformation or deduction. When a theory is in accordance with the rules of syntax and transformation of its meta-theory, it is said to be 'consistent', or '*formally true*.' Besides these rules, which all are concerned with the *form* of the theory, a complete meta-theory must include some *semantic* rules. These will be discussed very summarily in the next part of the chapter.

A theory is said to be '*formalized*' when its meta-theory is explicitly and completely formulated. If a theory is *neither* formalized, *nor* symbolized, the syntactical (and semantic) rules of everyday language are presupposed; if a theory is not formalized, but symbolized, the syntactical (and semantic) rules of general mathematics and/or logic are presupposed.

Axiomatization, symbolization, and formalization are independent of each other, but as a rule they occur in the given order. When nothing else is mentioned in the following, an 'axiomatized theory' will stand for 'a theory which is only axiomatized', while a 'symbolized theory' stands for 'a theory which is axiomatized and symbolized'. The term 'deductive theory' will be used as a generic term for all the classes of theories just mentioned.

THE SEMANTICS OF THE THEORIES

Semantic Function

If a system of symbols is to be usable as a means of communication it must have a *semantic function*, i.e. the words of the system must have 'meaning' and the statements must be 'true' to as high a degree as possible. Therefore it is not sufficient that a theory is consistent (or formally true); if it is to be used for description and explanation it must also be empirically true (or probable).

The Meaning of Words

That a word has '*meaning*' means that it *represents*, or symbolizes something which is different from the word itself (a phenomenon, an object, or a relation) to one or more individuals. That which the word represents is called its '*designatum*.' Thus 'meaning' can briefly be defined as 'the relation between a word and its designatum'. It is, however, impossible to discuss all the difficult problems concerning 'meaning' and 'truth' here. Only those which are of most importance for psychological theories will be made the object of closer analysis.

Not all words in a sentence have a meaning, as some words, *the logical invariables*, have the sole function of giving the sentence its logical or syntactical form.

Some of the other words in the sentence are called concrete or—in scientific theories—*empirical terms.* These words have a *'direct meaning'*, i.e. they can through a definition indicate an *observable designatum.*

There are also words which are called abstract, or—in scientific theories—theoretical, or *hypothetical terms*[2]). They have *no* direct meaning. Therefore their function in scientific theories has often been discussed, because an uncritical use of them makes a scientific theory an uncontrollable meta-physical system. Extreme empirists have therefore tried to avoid them, but this is impossible if it is also desired, besides description of observations, to give explanations and predictions. Attempts have therefore been made to control their use by means of reductive (operationistic, or conditional) definitions, i. e. definitions which in the form: 'If..., then... = ...,' indicate the conditions of observations which must be present if the hypothetical term is to be used.

Many philosophers (among others Bertrand Russel and R. Carnap) have maintained that it is not only practical, but also possible to define all hypothetical terms by reductive definitions. Others, on the other hand, have maintained that it might be practical, but that it is not yet possible. Finally some (among others L. W. Beck (106) and R. B. Braithwaite (13)) have maintained that it is not even practical to limit the hypothetical terms to those which can be reductively defined, as the 'fruitfulness' of the theory in question ist hereby reduced, because they can only explain observations which are already described, but not predict new ones. The hypothetical terms in the theory should be sufficiently defined in the primary statements (the postulates, the axioms) which may, among other things, be considered a kind of implicit definition of these terms so that they only indirectly get meaning through their function in the theory. Thus all discussion about their 'existence' is useless or absurd (and meta-physical). *R. B. Braithwaite* writes (13, p. 68):

'A definition of the theoretical terms, would thus sacrifice one of our principal objects in constructing a scientific theory, that of being able to extend it in the future, if way opens, to explain facts about new things by incorporating the theory in a more general theory having a wider field of application.'

Others have, however, a more *realistic* attitude, as for example *Feigl* (25) and *Jørgen Jørgensen*, and the latter writes (p. 168 in (118)):

'We describe these of us independent constant connections and variations of phenomena as *laws of nature* which express the of us independent (objective) relations between objects. They may, as far as I can see, be considered direct *copies* of objective relations between objects, and through them we can in a sense know something about the *inter-relations* of the objectives.'

In Chapter 3 this problem of hypothetical terms will be further discussed in connection with psychological theories.

---

[2]) The classification: empirical and hypothetical terms, corresponds rather well to the classification: *descriptive* and *explanatory* terms.

The Truth of Statements

It is a necessary, but not sufficient requirement that all words in a statement —except the logical invariables—have a direct or indirect meaning, if the sentense is to be true. *Empirical truth*—contrary to formal truth, or consequence—is not absolute, but *relative*. Even the most simple statements, the so-called *protocol statements*, cannot be absolutely, empirically true or false. Their '*empirical truth*' is the same as 'lingustically correct description of a fact', (an observed object, phenomenon, or event). But even to establish the linguistic 'accuracy' of a description is something which must be discussed in relation to certain accepted linguistic standards. And as regards the more *general statements*, '*empirical truth*' means the same as '*probability*,' or 'possibility of deducing a large or small number of true protocol statements.' The more true protocol statements we can deduce from a general statement, the higher is its degree of probability.

Thus 'empirical truth' is controlled with empirical methods (observation and experiment) as opposed to formal truth, or consequence, which is checked through an analysis of the agreement of the deductions with the rules of transformation. This difference is, however, only superficial, as agreement with the rules of transformation is not sufficient if the theory is not to be only a meaningless game of signs, but is to be used for description and explanation. One must also check whether the rules of transformation are such that it is really possible to reach empirically true conclusions (theorems, etc.) by deduction from empirically true premisses (primary statements, postulates, etc.). This can be checked through an empirical control of the conclusions. This experience-control has been accomplished with the regard to the classical-logical rules in the course of time, and the rules have been learned through common usage with the result that they seem 'evident' now; but the rules of transformation of newly constructed logical and mathematical calcula must be empirically controlled if they are to be interpreted. In other words, *formal* truth must also in the end be controlled with *empirical* methods if it appears in scientific theories and not only in meaningless calcula, which only have to be consistent. (This has especially been stressed by Jørgen Jørgensen (40) and C. L. Hull (35).

Empirical control is thus very essential for scientific theories and distinguishes them both from *meta-physical* constructions of systems of symbols, and from *purely formal games of signs*[3]).

Protocol Statements

Previously 'protocol statements' have been called the most simple statements, whose truth consisted in the linguistically correct description of a fact, and which were used to check the truth of more general statements. (The details of these problems will not, however, be discussed here). There has been some discussion

[3]) The definition and theories of truth given here are based upon logical empirism, which amongst other things synthesizes the classical theories of truth: the theory of evidence, coherence, and correspondence, the last being stressed most (cf. G. H. von Wright (105)).

in modern epistemology about how the statements which were to be called protocol statements should be formulated. However, two opinions have been defended. *The phenomenologists* maintained that the protocol statements should be '*phenomenological statements*', i. e. 'statements describing an individual's experience of a single phenomenon at a certain time'; *the physicalists*, on the other hand, maintained that the protocol statements ought to be '*physicalistic statements*', i. e. 'statements describing a property of an individual object at a certain time.' This was particularly necessary if a common scientific language was desired, as all scientific terms should be reducable to physicalistic statements. After much discussion the philosophers have now nearly agreed that which kind of statements are chosen as protocol statements, i. e. as 'basis of experience' depends purely upon *convention.*

Scientific Hypotheses

As scientific hypotheses are more or less general statements they can, according to the above, neither be absolutely empirically true, or false, but *they are more or less probable.* Their degree of probability is checked by empirical control of the deduced protocol statements. But if the scientific hypotheses are arranged in a deductive theory, their degree of probability is also dependent upon the degree of probability of the other hypotheses, so that the probability of a deductive theory is empirically controlled as a whole. If a scientific hypothesis gives false protocol statements it need not necessarily be rejected. If it is desirable to keep that particular hypothesis because it appears as a hypothesis in other theories, it is possible to alter other hypotheses in the theory. This phenomenon has caused some philosophers to consider scientific hypotheses as 'conventions' or 'maxims'; but according to *Braithwaite* it is not incompatible with the conception of scientific hypotheses as being simply generalizations, because the conventional feature is a consequence of the arrangement of the hypotheses in a deductive system. *In summary it can be said about scientific hypotheses (and theories) that they can neither be accepted as absolutely true, nor can they be rejected as absolutely false, but it must be possible to control empirically their degree of probability.*

If a scientific hypothesis possesses such a degree of probability that it for some time is accepted as being true by the majority of scientists, it is called a '*scientific law*'.

Statistical Laws

Since the development of the statistical laws of atomic physics there has been a great deal of discussion about these laws among physicists and philosophers. Some have considered them temporary, transitional phenomena which can later be reduced to general deterministic laws. *Einstein* shares this conception, and he writes for example as follows:

'some physicists, among them myself, cannot believe that we must abandon actually and forever, the idea of direct representation of physical reality in space and time, or that we must accept the view that events in nature are analogous to a game of change' (113)

Others (for example *Niels Bohr* (107)) have maintained that two essentially different kinds of scientific laws will have to be accepted in the future. The opinion that *the statistical laws are the primary scientific laws,* and the deterministic laws are special borderline cases of statistical laws (namely statistical hypotheses with the probalities O and 1) has also been defended. Thus R. B. Braithwaite writes (13) p. 116:

'But now that the most advanced of the sciences in the most sophisticated and far-reaching of its theories postulates an irreducibly statistical form of explanation, it will be unreasonable for a philosopher of science to ignore the special problems presented by statistical hypotheses. On the contrary, it will be safer for the philosopher to take statistical hypotheses as being the normalcy, and to regard universal (i. e. non-statistical) hypotheses as being extreme cases of statistical hypotheses when the proportions in question are 100 or 0%.'

This last possible conception of the relation between statistical and deterministic laws is also defended by Gösta Carlsson (18), and I also consider it the most rational and probable conception especially because the modern scientific conception of deterministic hypotheses, or 'laws' has completely eliminated the meta-physical (anthropomorphical and teleological) elements of the classical conception of 'causal relation', so that 'a causal relation' now can be defined as 'a constant (functional) relation' formulated in a qualitative or quantitative *deterministic* hypothesis. This last mentioned conception makes it possible to predict events exactly and completely—contrary to a *statistical* hypothesis which only makes it possible to predict, exactly and completely, *the average* of a larger number of events, because the relation dealt with is more or less variable. As far as I can se, *there is then only a difference in degree between deterministic and statistical hypotheses, a difference in degree of probability* because of the greater or smaller constancy or variance of the relations in question[4]).

Scientific Models

Another problem which is often discussed in modern epistemology and theoretical science is the use of *models* in science.

The term 'model' has many different meanings in science. The original meaning of the word was 'illustrative presentation of a theory'. This illustrative presentation could be three-dimensional or two-dimensional. Its purely psychological function was to visualize something which was very abstract, thus giving not only a more satisfactory experience of 'understanding', but also assisting in the process of thinking and thereby in revising the theory (cf. Carnap (110)). The relation between the model and the theory must (in this sense) be described as an anlogy-relation, or rather: an isomorphy-relation. The same is true about the relation

---

[4]) This statement is also in accordance with those made by *M. Blegvad* and *G. Rasch* in 'The Problem of Causality' (Nordisk Sommeruniversitet, 1951).

between the model and the subject area which the theory discusses. But as only a similarity in structure exists between the model and the theory (and 'reality') we are in danger of making the error of transferring non-structured, qualitative characteristics of the model to the theory and 'reality'.

Lately 'model' has also been used for the 'general outline of a proposed theory' or 'a potential theory'. This meaning may overlap the first one, as an illustrative model may have been formed *before* the actual theory was constructed.

'Model' may also mean 'mathematical model,' which is, as far as I can see, tantamount to 'calculus' used in the sense formerly defined.

Finally 'model', can be used, very inaccurately, as equalling 'theory', in psychology as in other sciences. In the following the original usage ('model' = 'illustrative presentation') will be used[5]).

Summary

The contents of this very brief chapter can be summarized in the following description of scientific theory in general:

A theory is a descriptive and explanatory *system of symbols.* It is called a *deductive* system if it possesses at least one of the following characteristics: *axiomatization* (arrangement of the statements in primary statements and secondary, deduced statements); *symbolization* (replacement of terms and statements with signs and formulas, maybe arranged in a logical-mathematical formula system, *a calculus*); *formalization* (an explicit formulation of the presuppositions of the theory, its meta-theory).

In scientific theories the words must have '*meaning*' and the sentences (the hypotheses) must be empirically true or *probable*; this is checked with empirical methods (observation and experiment). Some of the words, *the hypothetical terms*, can, however, only indirectly have meaning, and the probability of some of the statements (the primary ones) can only be controlled indirectly through their deduced, secondary hypotheses and the deduced *protocol statements* of these hypotheses. The protocol statements can be both phenomenological (dealing with experiences of phenomena) or physicalistic (dealing with things and their characteristics).

Scientific hypotheses ('laws') can be *statistical* or non-statistical, '*deterministic.*' The deterministic hypotheses may be considered extreme cases of statistical hypotheses (with a probability of 0 or 1). 'Models' may be regarded as illustrative presentations of a theory.

The importance of the theories lies partly in intellectual satisfaction, partly in the increased possibilities for making practical use of the results of science which they offer.

---

[5]) After this was written and the bibliography completed a series of articles has been published in 'The British Journal for the Philosophy of Science' (especially vol. IV, no. 15 and 16) on models in physics and psychology. They have, however, not made it necessary to alter the above description.

Chapter 3

Psychological Theories

Following the brief examination of the philosophy of scientific theories in general in the previous chapter, a more detailed examination of the philosophy of psychological theories in general (i. e. 'Meta-Theoretical Psychology') will be presented here. The subsequent chapters, will deal with individual psychological theories of motivation. To ease the comparison this chapter will begin with an examination of logical problems and the deal with the epistemological problems concerning psychological theories.

THE SYNTAX OF PSYCHOLOGICAL THEORIES

The Level of Development of Psychological Theories

Most psychological theories are not yet deductive theories, but only 'theories' in the more general sense of the word: 'descriptive and explanatory system of symbols.' The not-yet-deductive theories can briefly be characterized as '*classifying theories*' meaning 'systems of symbols which describe, classify, and maybe explain an group of phenomena'. The most essential feature of these theories is that they classify the phenomena on the basis of a description. In some classifying theories explanations are also given, but the explanatory hypotheses have not been arranged in a deductive system. (If they were, the theory should no longer be described as a classifying theory, but as a deductive system).

The classifying theories can—according to *Parsons* and *Shils* (94)—be divided into 1) *ad hoc classifying systems* consisting of a classification in arbitrarily chosen classes without inter-relations just as in common-sense classifications, and 2) *categorical systems* consisting of a system of inter-related classes. Most psychological systems have reached this level of development.

Parsons and Shils continue their classification of theories according to level of development, forming two more classes: theoretical systems, and empirical-theoretical systems, both of which, according to the terminology used here, must be characterized as deductive systems. The difference between them is not, however, a difference in the logical form of the theories, but an epistemological difference (viz. a difference in the conditions under which the probability of the theories can be controlled; the theoretical systems are controlled in standardized situations in laboratories whereas the other systems are controlled by means of situations in everyday life). Thus Parson and Shils have confused logical and epistemological classifications.

Axiomatization of Psychological Theories

It is practical to axiomatize theories; it might even be asserted that it is more necessary in psychology than in physics, as it is more necessary that the presuppositions of the theory are formulated explicitly in axioms or postulates when the number of probable hypotheses is small. This is for example maintained by *L. Bloomfield (8) p. 48:*

'In the sciences that deal with man there is little enough that we have even learned to observe. It is all the more desirable that we lay bare our situation and our doubts by the frank survey of the postulational method.'

Still, there is a big difference between axiomatization of physical and psychological theories, and this has especially been stressed by *K. W. Spence* (85). Axiomatization in physics is mainly a systematization of hypotheses (laws) which have already been formulated and empirically controlled, making deduction of new hypotheses possible. In psychology however, only a few explicitly formulated and comparatively well-controlled hypotheses exist, and it would be impractical to delay formulating theories until such hypotheses are available, as it is much more difficult to formulate psychological hypotheses than the formulate physical hypotheses, since the phenomena and relations which are studied in psychology are so complicated. Therefore axiomatization in psychology may have the practical function of constructing suggestions for hypotheses, which then constantly must be the objects of empirical control and revision. In this way the suggested theories will have the practical effect of leading the empirical research so that haphazard collections of facts (descriptions of observations) are avoided.

Only a very few axiomatized psychological theories exist. The most wellknown are Hull's and, to some extent, Lewin's theories, and they will be discussed later.

The problem of axiomatization is connected to another problem in theoretical psychology, namely the problem of whether psychological theories should be *reductive* or *constructive*. '*Reductive theories*' are 'theories whose primary hypotheses can be deduced from the hypotheses of another more fundamental science'. Many have seen it as a goal for the future to create a *unified science* by reducing all scientific theories to physics, so that all scientific hypotheses could be deduced from a few primary physical hypotheses. For psychology this would mean that its theories would be reduced to physiology, the primary hypotheses of psychological theories being deduced from physiological hypotheses. Others have, however, maintained that it is not possible to create a unified science through the reduction of hypotheses (although it might be possible through a reductive definition of terms). Temporarily, at least, it is a necessity in sciences such as biology and psychology (as in physics, of course) to form '*constructive theories*', i. e. 'theories whose primary hypotheses cannot be deduced from the hypotheses of another science', most often because they include undefined hypothetical terms which cannot be reduced to the terms of another science. The primary hypotheses of a constructive theory can then only be explained by forming as a still more comprehensive constructive theory with new primary hypotheses from which the previous primary hypotheses can now be deduced as secondary hypotheses. Formally speaking this is the same as reducing a theory, as has especially been stressed by *H. Feigl* (25). All theories, both reductive and constructive, 'explain' by deduction from still more general hypotheses.

Symbolization of Psychological Theories

In psychology symbolically formulated theories are even rarer than axiomatized theories. *Lewin's* topological psychology is the best known example (but as it is not completely axiomatized, it cannot be called a calculus). The reason for the difficulties in symbolic presentation in psychology is evidently that only very few quantitative relations have been formulated in psychological hypotheses yet, so that mathematization is (temporarily) almost impossible. Lewin has used the non-numerical geometrical discipline, topology, but there are also other forms of symbolical presentation than mathematizing, as logical symbols may be used. *J. H. Woodger* (103) even maintains that the traditional mathematics to some degree has been developed for the purposes of physics and is consequently often useless for biological purposes. He writes (p. 3):

> 'in so far as the *direction* of the development of mathematics has been given a bias by the special requirements of the problems of physics (and of the particular mode of treating those problems which happens to have been followed), in so far it may, in some of its most fully developed branches, be unsuitable for the use of other sciences, e. g., for the biological sciences.
>
> 'It is thus necessary that we should free ourselves not only from the conventions of natural language but also from the accidental restrictions of traditional mathematics, i. e. the mathematics which has arisen to meet he needs of physics.'

Woodger recommends the use of symbolic presentation by means of *logical symbols* in biology. This may be of great value in the construction of theories, also in cases where complete symbolization in connection with axiomatization (i. e. formation of a calculus) is not possible, as symbolic presentation in all cases means an abbreviated and unambiguous presentation. What Woodger says about biology is, in my opinion, just as true about psychology.

Formalization of Psychological Theories

Actual formalization is rare in psychology. At any rate it does not—as far as I know—exist in the sense stated in Chapter 2, namely as an explicit formulation of the meta-theory of a theory. Attempts are, however, made by some psychologists as for example *Hull* and *Lewin*, who write some chapters on general philosophical (epistemological and logical) problems as an introduction to their theories. Others have only formulated the general presuppositions of their theories. An explicit formulation of a meta-theory does not exist however[1]). (It is true that Lewin often uses the word 'formalization' in a paper, but he uses it in a very broad sense in cluding both axiomatization and symbolization). Formalization is, however, not necessary to anly large degree as long as one is only dealing with of axiomatized and maybe partly symbolized theories, since it is then possible to assume implicitly the syntactical rules of everyday language and the rules for transformation of classical logic.

THE SEMANTICS OF PSYCHOLOGICAL THEORIES

Psychological Terms

As in other sciences both empirical and hypothetical terms (or 'variables' as they are often called in psychology[2]) are to be found in psychological theories. *E. C. Tolman* (93) was the first to introduce explicitly the hypothetical terms in psychology, and he termed them '*intervening variables.*' This description derives from the fact that their function was to be that of explanatory connecting links between *the empirical terms*, or *variables* of the psychological theories: on one side *the dependent variables, the behavior*, and on the other side *the independent variables*, the factors to which the behavior has a functional relation ('causal relation') and which are often experimentally controllable. This functional relation is so complicated that it is at present almost impossible to formulate hypotheses about it, and this is the reason why, according to Tolman, it is necessary to use 'intervening variables' as explanatory connecting links between the experimentally controllable variables and the behavior variables.

In a later article (94) Tolman has classified psychological theories in three classes according to the character of the qualities which are ascribed to their hypothetical (intervening) variables—apart from their purely functional relations to the empirical variables. It is, in other words, a classification of hypothetical variables according to the interpretation of their '*surplus meaning.*' Three classes of hypothetical variables can, in accordance with the presuppositions and terms of this thesis, be redefined in the following way:

---

[1]) Except in Hulls et al.: 'Matematico-Deductive Theory of Rote Learning' (1940) which is not analysed here.

[2]) 'Terms' and 'variables' will here most often be used as synonyms. In cases of doubt they may be used in such a way that 'terms' refer to the actual words, whereas 'variables' refer to the objects which are designata for the terms in question (i. e. in psychology: processes and/or dispositions in the organism).

1. *Neutral-formal* hypothetical terms are names for hypothetical processes and/or dispositions manifesting themselves *equally in both introspectively and physiologically-behavioristically* observable phenomena. They are (as a rule) thought to be localized in the organism, but otherwise they can freely be ascribed to all kinds of qualities necessary or practical in their (explanatory) function as connecting links between the independent empirical variables and the dependent behavior variables. Lewin's 'Life-space' may be mentioned as an example.

2. *Neuro-physiological* hypothetical terms are names for hypothetical processes and/or dispositions, primarily manifesting themselves in *physiologically* observable phenomena, secondarily in behavioristically—and maybe also in introspectively—observable phenomena. They are for the most part thought to be localized in the nervous system, and the qualities ascribed to them are mainly based upon physiological observations—or are, at any rate, somewhat in accordance with physiological hypotheses about the function of the nervous system. An example is Lorenz's and Tinbergen's 'innate release-mechanisms.'

3. *Phenomenological* hypothetical terms are names for hypothetical processes and/or dispositions manifesting themselves primarily in *introspectively* observable phenomena, secondarily through physiologically-behavioristically observable phenomena. They are thought to be localized in the organism, often particularly in a (hypothetical) 'mental structure,' a 'mental life,' or 'conscious life' which may be differentiated into a conscious part and an unconsious, or subconscious part. Freud's 'ego', 'superego', and 'I.D.' may be taken as examples. It must, however, be pointed out that the phenomenological hypothetical processes and/or dispositions are *not* identical with the introspectively observable *phenomena*; these are just the primary manifestations of the hypothetical variables, whereas behavior is often taken to be secondary 'symptoms', 'indications', or 'expressions' for the hypothetical variables. It must also be stressed that these introspective phenomena can only be *directly* experienced by the observer (for example the psychologist) himself, whereas they at others (for example at the persons used in the experiment) are observed more *indirectly* through their '*verbal report,*' *which is a kind of behavior*. For these reasons introspective phenomena in other individuals are always a kind of hypothetical construction. In connection with this last statement it is interesting to compare the epistemological position of introspective phenomena in human psychology and animal psychology (where they also exist, labelled 'subjective experiences', 'phenomenal world', etc.) *The similarity* is that in both cases (except for the self-observation by the psychologist) we have a kind of hypothetical construction which is of a lower 'degree of abstraction' than the hypothetical processes they are regarded to be representatives for or manifestations of. But there is *the difference* that this degree of abstraction is higher in animal psychology, because we do not have verbal behavior and the whole biological, specific character as our base. It can, moreover, be maintained that these hypothetical constructions are *superfluous* in animal psychology, as one might just as well construct the hypothetical processes directly, on the basis of the physiological and behavioristic

observations. Varied verbal behavior, which aids our comprehension of human psychology, does not exist here, and the possibility of making use of *analogies* from the private introspection of the psychologist is not present in animal psychology.

Based upon the above argumentation it may be said that it would be most practical to work with neutral-formal or neuro-physiological variables, at least in animal psychology. But of course Tolman is right when he maintains that it depends *only upon convention* what kind of hypothetical variables are used to construct a psychological theory. He himself recommends, however, the use of neutral-formal variables, as does *L. von Bertalanffy* (in 52). *D. Kreck* (52), on the other hand, and *D. O. Hebb* (52) recommend the use of neuro-physiological variables.

In addition to the classification of hypothetical variables mentioned above, Tolman gives another classification of variables formed on another basis, namely *a classification of function variables and disposition variables.* Function variables are variables which represent something *dynamic* and relatively brief, i. e. they may in qualitative hypotheses take part in processes as 'cause' or 'effect'—and in quantitative hypotheses be variables in functional relations—explaining *actual behavior* (an action). Disposition variables are variables representing something *statically-structured* and are therefore in psychology most often used to describe the permanent structure of the organism ('character-traits', 'intelligence factors', etc.) whereas they may be part of hypotheses about the actual behavior as 'co-determining variables' or as 'constants' (if the hypotheses are quantitative). In theories of motivation the function variables are the most important, so when nothing else is mentioned the variables in this book will be function variables.

In many years there have been some analyses and discussions of 'intervening variables in theoretical-psychological literature' similar to the general epistemological discussion already mentioned, to which no references, however, have been made in the psychological discussions.

Thus it has been criticised that the designations 'intervening variables' and 'hypothetical constructions' have been used synonymously in psychology. It has therefore been suggested by *K. MacCourquodale* and *P. E. Meehl* (58) that a linguistic distinction between the two designations should be agreed upon and that the following definitions should be adopted: 'Intervening variables' are terms which can be defined reductively (operationistically), whereas 'hypothetical constructions' are terms which cannot be defined reductively, for which reason empirical control of hypotheses containing hypothetical constructions is always necessary, but can never by sufficient.

It has, however, been pointed out by *Melvin H. Marx* (59a) that there is only a difference in degree between the two kinds of terminology, as it will always be difficult in practice to reduce intervening variables completely by operationistic definitions. But according to Marx it is still the goal of science gradually to replace the hypothetical constructions with intervening variables. It is therefore suggested that during the transitional period one should use an intermediate form between hypothetical constructions and 'orthodox' intervening variables, namely operationistic, intervening variables defined according to the experimental situation.

In accordance with the result of the general analysis of theoretical terms the replacement of hypothetical constructions with intervening variables cannot be considered one of the goals of psychology, because this would make *prediction* impossible. As it is also difficult to define the difference between the two kinds of terminology, the following usage will be applied here: '*Hypothetical variables*' equal '*theoretical terms (or concepts) in psychological theories*' (thus including both actual 'intervening variables' and 'hypothetical constructions'); in accordance with this the *empirical terms* (or concepts) in psychological theories will often be called '*independent and dependent variables*[3]).'

Psychological Protocol Statements

Corresponding to the general epistemological discussion on physicalistic protocol statements versus phenomenalistic protocol statements there has in psychology been a violent discussion about *behavioristic versus introspective protocol statements*, i. e. protocol statements about the behavior of an organism and the introspective report of an individual, respectively. Most often it has been formulated as a discussion about *methods*, but as the results of the methods must be formulated in protocol statements, the problem of introspective versus behavioristic methods is, epistemologically, the same as the general problems of phenomenalistic versus physicalistic protocol statements. As mentioned in Chapter 2 it is more or less agreed that *what kind of protocol statements one chooses* depends *only upon convention*. Still, it would (maybe) be easier to create a common scientific language—and easier, as a whole, to carry out intersubjective control of research results—if physicalistic (behavioristic) protocol statements were chosen. But *if* the choice has fallen upon the phenomenalistic (introspective) protocol statements it should be possible to 'translate' these into physicalistic (behavioristic) protocol statements, when it is made practical by inter-subjective empirical control.

Thus psychological theories might be classified according to the kind of protocol statements (methods) upon which they are based. But often there is a relation between the choice of protocol statements and the choice (the interpretation) of the hypothetical variables. Based upon this *psychological theories can be classified as mentalistic, behavioristic, and neutral-formal theories:* 1) Purely *behavioristic* theories include neuro-physiological variables and are exclusively controlled through behavioristic protocol statements (methods). 2) Purely *mentalistic* theories include phenomenological variables and are exclusively controlled through introspective protocol statements (methods). It must, however, be repeated here, that if the theory is not exclusively based upon the self-observations of a psy-

---

[3]) The reader is also referred to a paper by *A. Ginsberg* in *Psychol. Review* (1964, 61, 119–132).

chologist (which is probably not the case with any of the modern scientific-psychological theories), then the introspective results, or protocol statements must be communicated from the subjects to the experimenter as an introspective report, which is a kind of verbal behavior, whereby behavioristic protocol statements (and methods) aquire an epistemologically important, special position in scientific psychology. (This is only true in psychology proper and not in pure *phenomenology* —a purely descriptive basic discipline in all sciences). But in spite of this similarity between behavioristic and mentalistic theories—that they must in the end be controlled with behavioristic methods—there is the difference that they use a very different 'language' or terminology, a neuro-physiological-behavioristic and a mentalistic-introspective terminology, respectively. 3) *Neutral-formal* theories include neutral-formal variables and can be controlled by introspective and/or behavioristic protocol statements. A good part of modern 'behavioristic' theories belong to this last sub-group. Finally some mixed forms may be found.

As a consequence of the above statements the old *psycho-physical problem* must be said to be divided into the problems of the choice (interpretation) of hypothetical variables and the choice of protocol statements (methods); and at the present stage of development of science both problems must be described as *purely questions of convention*[4]).

There is another problem which, in my opinion, also has some connection with the problem of the choice of protocol statements, namely the problem of *molar versus molecular theories. E. C. Tolman* first introduced this classification in his main work in 1932 ('Purposive Behavior in Animals and Men'). In the introduction to his book he characterizes Watson's theory as a 'molecular behaviorism', because it per definition studies the relation between stimuli and movements of the muscles; contrary to this he characterizes his own kind of behaviorism as a 'molar behaviorism', because *it studies larger units,* namely the relation between the total environment and the 'behavior-act'. About this he writes (p. 70) that it is

'more than and different from the sum of its physiological parts. Behavior, as such, is an 'emergent' phenomenon that has descriptive and defining properties of its own. And we shall designate this latter as the *molar* definition of behavior.'

And late (p. 7):

'And it is these, the molar properties of behavior acts, which are of prime interest to us as psychologists. Further, these molar properties of behavior-acts cannot in the present state of our knowledge, i. e., prior to the working-out of many empirical correlations between behavior and its physiological correlates, be known even inferentially from a mere knowledge of the underlying, molecular, facts of physics and physiology.'

After thus having defined and explained his opinion about molar behaviorism,

---

[4]) To complete the picture it should be mentioned that the solution to the psychophysical problem given here is a further development of the solution given by logical empirism (which briefly states that the psycho-physical problem is only a linguistic pseudo-problem), a solution which is closer to the old 'neutral monism' than any of the other classical psycho-physical theories: (1) materialistic monism, (2) idealistic m., (3) neutral m., (4) interactionistic dualism, (5) parallelistic d., and (6) epiphenomenalistic d.

Tolman mentions others who have previously expressed a similar point of view (Holt, Weiss, Kantor, etc.) without having formulated explicitly the distinction between molar and molecular. Even Watson, he finds, was actually a molar behaviorist.

Since Tolman introduced the classification molar versus molecular, it has been used very often in psychology and often in a very uncritical way, with the result that the two terms have gradually becomes ambiguous. *Littman and Rosen* (56), for example, show that at least seven different ways of using the classification can be found, mixed with at least three different reasons for using the classification. The most frequent way of using the classification molar versus molecular is, however, an application which is analogous to the distinction in physics between *macroscopic* and *microscopic* phenomena. This has been pointed out by *Hull* (35) who furthermore maintains that the lesson to be learned from this is that the study of macroscopic (molar) phenomena may be of great scientific value, even if we do not know anything about the basic microscopic (molecular) phenomena. Hull also says that the distinction is relative rather than absolute, in other words, it is a difference in degree, which means that molar theories later may be reduced to (be deduced from) molecular theories. Hull's definition of and way of using the classification corresponds—in my opinion—to *E. Tranekjær Rasmussen's* (120) distinction between *'high-level' and 'low-level' phenomena.* The more high-level the phenomena, the more microscopic the theory, and the more low-level the phenomena, the more macroscopic the theory. The classification is, however, not centered so much about the hypothetical variables and more primary hypotheses of these theories; the classification molar versus molecular is rather centered about the secondary hypotheses and protocol-statements of the theories in question, so that *molar theories* are theories whose protocol statements describe *comparatively macroscopic phenomena*, whereas *molecular theories* are theories whose protocol statements describe *comparatively microscopic phenomena.* (The term 'comparatively' indicates that it is only a question of differences in degree.)

This classification of protocol statements is independent of the other classification of phenomenalistic versus physicalistic protocol statements. If they are used simultaneously (if they are 'mixed') the result will be a classification in molar behavioristic versus molecular behavioristic theories and molar mentalistic versus molecular mentalistic theories. (Molar mentalistic theories correspond most closely to Gestalt theories, while molecular mentalistic theories correspond to the classical introspective theories (Wundt and Titcheners).)

Psychological Hypotheses

Psychological hypotheses are, as other scientific hypotheses, more or less general statements with a large or small degree of probability. There are, however, a few whose degree of probability is so high that they are commonly accepted as psychological 'laws.'

There are, however, as maintained by *Kenneth W. Spence* in a very detailed and systematical analysis, several *different types* of psychological hypotheses. In a treatise (85) he writes that the following four types of *empirical hypotheses* may be found in psychology:

1. R = f(R)
2. R = f(S)
3. R = f(O)
4. O = f(S)

These are all hypotheses about relations between *empirical* variables. The first type includes hypotheses about the correlation between different forms of behavior, which are especially tudied through psychological tests. The second type includes hypotheses about the functional relations between the environmental stimuli and the behavior, which are expecially studied in experimental psychology. These stimuli may, by the way, exist simultaneously with the behavior (psychology of perception), or they may go before the behavior (the psychology of learning). The third and fourth type of psychological hypotheses deal with the functional relations between the behavior and the internal organic condition (or processes) and between this and the stimuli of the environment. Theoretically, these hypotheses are a differentiation of the second type. They are especially studied in physiological psychology, but because of the difficulties connected with observing the nervous processes and especially the prain processes, only a few results have been achieved in this area. As a consequence of these practical difficulties it has been necessary to introduce hypothetical variables in psychology instead of empirical variables representing observable organic processes and conditions. The result is the following *theoretical hypotheses,* which are a supplement to the empirical laws of the third and the fourth types:

5. $H = f(S_{t\text{-}n})$
6. $H = f(S_{t\text{-}o})$
7. H = f(time)
8. H = f(H)
9. R = f(H)

Common to these five types of hypotheses is that they all include at least one *hypothetical* variable. Thus the relation between the hypothetical variables and the previous stimuli (both internal and external) is formulted in the fifth type. In type, six the realtion between hypothetical variables and present stimuly is formulated and in the seventh type the dependence of the hypothetical variables upon time. In the eighth type *the interrelations* between the hypothetical variables are formulated, whereas the ninth type formulates the relations between the behavior and the hypothetical variables. According to Spence these nine types of hypotheses represent all possible forms of relations between the variables in a psychological theory.

In my opinion these nine types of hypotheses are not equally important—at least not in the following study—and therefore Spence's classification will be simplified a little. It is suggested that it should be modified in such a way that it includes three main classes of psychological hypotheses. At the same time it is suggested that the way of writing the hypotheses should be simplified so that *the time-relation* between the variables becomes clear. Thus the classification of psychological hypotheses is as follows:

1. *Purely empirical hypotheses* ($S \rightarrow R$), i.e. hypotheses exclusively dealing with relations between empirical variables. This class includes Spence's class one to four.
2. *Partly empirical hypotheses* ($S \rightarrow H$ *and* $H \rightarrow R$), i. e. hypotheses dealing with relations between hypothetical variables and independent and dependent empirical variables, respectively. This class includes Spence's fifth, sixth, and ninth classes.
3. *Purely theoretical hypotheses* ($H \rightarrow H$), i. e. hypotheses exclusively dealing with the relations between hypothetical variables.

It must, however, be stressed that each of the three main classes includes both hypotheses with *simple relations* between only two variables, and hypotheses with *complicated relations* between several variables. The last case is most conveniently symbolized by the following formula $A = f(B \times C \times D)$.

The problem of one or more variables in psychological hypotheses is—as far as I can see—connected to a problem which has been discussed frequently in Theoretical Psychology, namely the problem of *mechanistic versus field-theoretical* hypotheses and theories. The exact difference between these two classes of theories is unclear, but it seems that a field-theory, to a larger extent than a mechanistic theory, explains a phenomenon (for example behavior) on the basis of a *totality* of co-existing and inter-dependent variables. In other words, a field theory should be a theory which exclusively or mainly includes hypotheses which formulate relations between *several* interdependent variables—while a mechanistic theory mainly should include hypotheses about simple relations between two variables. But then the classification becomes practically identical with the classification of *static versus dynamic* theories, as dynamic theories are often defined as theories which explain by means of 'interaction of processes' (or by means of 'forces'), whereas static theories (just as mechanistic theories) explain on the basis of a given and established *structure* (the structure of the organism, for example).

These two types of theories have been defended and opposed by different psychologists and caused much discussion. The supporters of the field-theories (the Gestalt-psychologists, Lewin and Kaila) have maintained that they are in better agreement with the development of modern science than are the mechanistic theories. Spence, on the other hand, maintains that the difference claimed to exist does not al all correspond to the difference between mechanistic theories and field-theories in physics, and in his opinion it is a misconception to think that the field-theories are more 'correct' than the mechanistic theories. In some areas—for example electro-magnetic phenomena—field-theories are the most usable, in other areas—for example the kinetic gas theory—the mechanistic theories are the most usable. This may also be true in psychology. According to *L. von Bertalanffy* (in 52) it is, however, possible to form a synthesis of the field-theoretical and the mechanistic principles by means of *the principle of progressive mechanization.* He writes (p. 29):

'Primarily, organic processes are governed by the interplay within the entire system, by a dynamic order, and this is at the basis of regulability. Secondarily, progressive mechanization takes place, that is, the splitting of the originally unitary action into individual actions occuring in fixed structures.'

Thus the synthesis is achieved by making the mechanistic principle secondary with relation to the dynamic. Bertalanffy also points out (p. 34) that:

'we find in modern science a transition from self-actional to interactional and transactional conceptions. Classical neurophysiology and psychology are selfactional, i. e. take into account only linear causal trains. Gestalt theory is interactional, emphasizing dynamics within unified systems. The general trend of science, however, is directed towards transactional conceptions, namely, the organism in its environs.'

What is needed, then, is a classification according to the level of development of three classes: *mechanistic ('self-actional'), dynamic ('inter-actional'), and actual field-theoretical ('transactional') theories.*

Most psychological hypotheses are still *qualitative hypotheses,* i. e. general statements which only formulate a relation between variables without indicating quantitative relations or dimensions. Gradually a number of *quantitative hypotheses,* i. e. general statements formulating a mathematical functional relation between variables, have also been formulated in psychology, however. Yet, most quantitative hypotheses in psychology are *statistical hypotheses,* most often formulated as *correlations* between variables (or 'factors'). The few non-statistical, or deterministic quantitative hypotheses which can be found in psychological theories are '*average-laws,*' which are only probable to a large extent (approaching 1 or 0) when they are formulated about very large groups of individuals; but if they are applied to the single action of a single individual their degree of probability or exactness will be very small. Thus the modern point of view mentioned in Chapter 2, that all scientific hypotheses are statistical hypotheses with a high or low degree of probability, has itself a high degree of probability with regard to the quantitative hypotheses of pcychology. There is, however, in psychology as in other sciences much disagreement about the question of *deterministic versus statistical theories.* Some psychologists (for example Lewin) are of the opinion that psychological theories ought to be deterministic; others (for example *E. Brunswik*) consider it necessary that the theories are statistical.

In psychology a special kind of qualitative hypothesis, the so-called *tendency-*

hypotheses, can be found. They are in a way analogous to quantitative statistical hypotheses, being formulated thus, 'A has a tendency (or disposition) to react in this and this way'. The special nature of these hypotheses is first of all that they are rather inexact in their formulation and therefore difficult to control empirically. Secondly, they are hypotheses of 'the lowest degree,' i. e. the least general hypotheses which exist and from which only very few protocol statements can be directly deduced. Thus their explanatory value is very small, but if only this is clear and one is not led to believe that the terms included in them *explain* this tendency-hypothesis which they briefly express (as in the classical anecdote on the soporific effect of opium, explained by the soporific power of opium) they have *some* value, and it is then possible later to explain the tendency-hypotheses on the basis of hypotheses of higher degrees. *H. Feigl* (25, p. 193) writes about this:

'Wherever science can get beyond this relatively crude level of categorization in terms of substances, causes, and effects, and manages to replace them by a language of events, field conditions, and functional relations, dispositional properties are no longer indispensable. But on the way to this final stage, which is realized fully perhaps only in modern field physics, there is usually first a gradual reduction in the number of the (on the given level) basic dispositional properties.'

In psychology, as in the other biological sciences, another special kind of hypothesis, the so-called '*teleological hypotheses*' can be found. These hypotheses have usually been said to be the opposite of the '*causal hypotheses*', as the difference between them lies the fact that causal hypotheses are statements which explain a phenomenon on the basis of its relation to a *previous* or *simultaneous* phenomenon ('the cause'), while teleological hypotheses are statements which explain a phenomenon on the basis of its relation to a *future* phenomenon ('goal,' or 'purpose'). Both kinds may be said to be *deterministic* hypotheses, as the difference, according to *E. Nagel* (119), 'is one of selective attention rather than of asserted content'.

As teleological hypotheses have not been accepted as scientific hypotheses in the last century, biological sciences have attempted to explain the teleological phenomena (biologically practical processes of adjustment, purposive behavior included) on the basis of causal hypotheses. This has, according to *Braithwaite* (4), been tried in three ways: 1) Attempts have been made to explain *all* biological processes of adjustment as being determined by *consciousness of purpose*. But against this it has been said that it is inadmissible anthropomorphism, because consciousness of purpose can only be observed for certain in human behavior. 2) It has also been attempted to explain all biological processes of adjustment as being caused by *hypothetical constructions* such as 'needs', 'drives', etc. 3) Finally the attempt has been made to explain the biological processes of adjustment on the basis of *known physical-chemical laws*. This attempt has, however, not yet been successful, and therefore I believe (contrary to Braithwaite) that the explanation based upon hypothetical constructions is the most practical solution at present, and that it must be used until a less hypothetical explanation is possible. According to H. Feigl (25) this may happen in the near future. He writes (p. 208):

'The recent contributions of cybernetics and of analytical biology have shown clearly that the metaphysical quest for *teleological explanations* must—and can—be replaced by the scientific search for *explanations of teleology*. The phrase 'teleological mechanisms' is significantly and fortunately no longer a contradiction in terms. With the new cybernetic neurophysiological explanations of memory, of purposive activity and of symbolic communication, a new and higher level of explanation has at last been attained.'

Psychological Models

Many different models have been used in psychology—most often twodimensional diagrams. A model used very frequently is the following simple diagram:

$$S \rightarrow R,$$

which, however, lately has been replaced by the somewhat less simple, but more adequate diagram:

$$S \rightarrow O \rightarrow R.$$

S and R (in both diagrams) symbolize stimuli and reaction, respectively, whereas O symbolizes the organism with its known physiological processes and hypothetical variables. This model is actually the basis of the general division of psychological terms or variables into: independent variables (S), hypothetical variables (O), and dependent variables (R). But this basic diagram has been varied to a very large extent in more or less complicated diagrams as models for psychological theories.

Such complicated diagram-models are often at the same time program-suggestions for a deductive theory (cf. Chapter 2 on models). Thus such theories often fall between classifying theories and deductive theories (as is for example true of Tolman's theories).

R. A. Hinde (122) has called attention to the fact that 'the models or analogies used in the study of behaviour range between two extremes—those which resemble very closely that which they represent, and those (the 'as if' type) which are extremely remote from it' (p. 322). The first type is not as dangerously misleading, but neither is it as fruitful in thought-economy, as the other type.

In recent years three-dimensional psychological models have also been constructed. Thus *I. P. Howard* (University of Durham) has constructed a 'mechanical rat,' which can learn to run through any labyrinth without making mistakes. In the same way psychologists interested in cybernetics have often interpreted electronic 'brains' and servo-mechanisms as psychological (and neuro-physiological) models.

Definition of 'Psychology'

Seen from a *historical* point of view many different definitions of 'psychology' have been suggested in the course of time. When the original definition—'the science of the soul'—was generally rejected because of the theological meaning of the word, many different definitions based upon combinations and derivatives of the word '*consciousness*' were tried out, as for example 'the science of consciousness,' 'the science of phenomena of consciousness,' 'the science of the conscious life,' 'the science of conditions of consciousness,' etc. But since it was difficult to agree upon a definition of 'consciousness'—and partly in reaction against the barrenness of much of the older introspective psychology—'the science of the behavior of the organisms' (or synonyms for this) became the commonly accepted definition of 'psychology' in the United States at the turn of the century. McDougall was the first to formulate this definition; but it was Watson's article in Psychological Review in 1913 that led to it becoming the most common definition of psychology in America. Even opponents to Watson's original behaviorism (as for example K. Lewin) define psychology as the science of behavior.

Systematically all these different definitions of psychology which have been offerend can be classified according to whether they define 'psychology' on the basis of *empirical terms* (representing more or less directly observable phenomena, as for example 'behavior' or 'phenomena of consciousness'), or on the basis of *hypothetical terms* (representing the unobservable, constructed processes or conditions as for example 'life of the mind,' 'conscious life,' 'potential of reaction,' etc.). Besides, the definitions can be classified according to whether the terms used can be expressed by a *mentalistic-phenomenological,* or by a *physiological-behavioristic* terminology (cf. the classification of theories p. 20). These two classifications may be *combined* (mixed) whereby a classification of four classes appears, namely definitions on the basis of:

1) mentalistic-hypothetical terms, and 2) physiological-hypothetical terms; 3) phenomenological-empirical terms, and 4) behavioristic-empirical terms. Finally more complicated intermediate forms and mixed forms may be found, as a definition of psychology may be formulated in both hypothetical, empirical, phenomenological, neutral-formal, and behavioristic terms (for example Jørgen Jørgensen's definition: 'Psychology is the science of the conscious life and its appearances, whether these are of a behavioristic, physiological, or phenomenological character'—p. 171 in the revised edition of Chapter VI in 'Psykologi på biologisk Grundlag').

Summary

This chapter contains a brief survey of the philosophy of psychological theories in general—that is, *Meta-Theoretical Psychology.* An attempt has been made to deal with the scattered isolated problems which are discussed in the literature of theoretical psychology from a general, philosophy-of-science point of view.

Psychological theories may be classified according to their formal development as *classifying* theories and *deductive* theories. In psychology *axiomatization* has had the double function of systematizing hypotheses which have already been formulated, and especially of giving suggestions for new hypotheses. Psychological theories may also be classified as *reductive* (deducable from physiological theories) or *constructive* (non-reductive). *Symbolization* in the form of mathematization is still difficult in psychology, and therefore it has been attempted to make use of symbols from topology, or from general symbolical logic. *Formalization* is still rare in psychology.

Psychological *terms, or variables* can be divided into *empirical* variables (the *dependent* behavioristic variables and the *independent*, controllable 'causes' of behavior) and *hypothetical* variables (including both operationistic definable 'intervening variables' and actual hypothetical constructions). By *convention* these may be interpreted as *neuro-physiological*, as *phenomenological*, or as *neutral-formal* variables. Besides, variables may be classified as *function*-variables (which are dynamic) and *disposition* variables (which are static).

Psychological *protocol statements* may be classified as *behavioristic* and *introspective* statements. When it is practical with regard to inter-subjective empirical control, introspective protocol statements may be changed into behavioristic. Depending upon the kind of protocol statements and the way of interpreting the hypothetical variables, psychological theories may be classified as *mentalistic* theories, *behavioristic* theories, and *neutral-formal* theories. Thus the old psycho-physical problem has been divided into the problems of choice of protocol statements, and the interpretation of hypothetical variables; both problems are purely questions of convention.

The psychological theories may be classified according to the complexity of the phenomena described by the protocol statements as *molar* and *molecular* theories. The classifications molar versus molecular and behavioristic versus mental theories may be 'mixed.'

Psychological *hypotheses* may be classified as *purely empirical, partly empirical, and purely theoretical hypotheses* as to whether they include exclusively empirical variables, empirical and hypothetical variables, or exclusively hypothetical variables, respectively. Depending upon the number of variables in the hypotheses the theories may be classified as *mechanistic* (with only two variables) and *field-theoretical* hypotheses (with several interdependent variables). Psychological hypotheses may furthermore be classified as *qualitative* hypotheses (including the tendency-hypotheses) and *quantitative* hypotheses, most of which in psychology are *statistical* hypotheses (especially correlations). Finally the deterministic hypotheses may be classified as *causal* and *teleological* hypotheses, which explain a phenomenon on the basis of a past (maybe present), and a future phenomenon, respectively. Various attempts have been made to reduce teleological hypotheses to causal hypotheses.

Most *models* used in psychological theories are two-dimensional diagrams. A simple psychological model frequently used is the following:

$$S \rightarrow O \rightarrow R.$$

The many *definitions of 'psychology'* given in the course of time may be classified according to whether they use: *A:* 1) *hypothetical* terms, or 2) *empirical* terms; and *B:* 3) *mentalistic-phenomenological* terms, or 4) *physiological-behavioristic* terms. The most frequently used definition is the following: '"*Psychology*" = *the science of behavior*.'

Chapter 4

Theories of Motivation

The reason for choosing theories of motivation as the object of a meta-theoretical study is that motivation variables play a very important role in the theories of modern psychology. In order to keep the size of the study within reasonable limits, it will be limited to *the period after 1930* when many German psychologists because of the Nazi regime emigrated to America, whereby a very appropriate mutual influence between the psychological schools of that time began. Furthermore, only the theories from this period which are judged to be of most importance will be included, just as only the latest and most systematical and inclusive presentations of the theories of the psychologists in question will be treated. As this is *not* a historical psychological study, but a *meta-theoretical* psychological study, no complete and continuous historical presentation of the theoretical development of the whole period or the individual psychologist will be attempted. A very brief historical introduction to the study will, however, be given (at the end of this chapter), and an outline of the production of the psychologist in question will be given as an introduction to the individual theories.

The study is divided naturally into two parts: an *analytical* study of the individual theories resulting in a reconstruction of the theories in question, and a *comparative* study of all theories.

The method used in the analysis of the individual theories will correspond rather closely to the general presentation in Chapter 3:

OUTLINE FOR ANALYSIS

Biographical introduction.

I. *The general structure of the theory*

is analyzed and classified according to the following headings:

- a. Summary of the theory:
  - 1. Content.
  - 2. Presuppositions.
- b. Syntactical relations:
  - 3. Stage of development of the theory.

4. Constructive or reductive theory.
c. Semantic relations:
5. Mentalistic or behavioristic theory.
6. Molar or molecular theory.
7. Field-theoretical or mechanistic theory.
8. Statistical or deterministic theory.
d. The Model.

II. *Definitions and hypotheses of motivation.*
The individual definitions and hypotheses of motivation in the theory are closely examined; they will especially be classified according to the modified classifications of *Tolman* and *Spence* (cf. Chapter 3).

III. *Reconstruction.*
A critical and systematical reconstruction of the theory and especially of its most fundamental definitions and hypotheses of motivation will be made. No detailed axiomatization, symbolization, or formalization will, however, be made, only a more explicit and *systematical reformulation* still preserving the individuality of the theory (the contents of its fundamental definitions and hypotheses).

After the examination of the individual theories a *systematical comparison* of all the examined theories will be made in the last chapters, including both the theories as a whole, and their variables and hypotheses of motivation.

Before beginning the study it is, however, necessary to have *a criterion* for selecting the theories, hypotheses, and variables of motivation, in other words, it is necessary to have *a temporary definition of the term 'motivation'*. This temporary definition will be based upon a few definitions from psychological works of reference:

James Drever (A Dictionary of Psychology. Penguin Books 1952):
'Motivation: term employed generally for the phenomena involved in the operation of incentives and drives,' and further: 'Motive: an affective-conative factor which operates in determining the direction of an individual's behaviour towards an end or goal, consciously apprehended, or unconscious,' and finally: 'Motivate: to provide an incentive; to act as an incentive.'

P. T. Young (in The Encyclopedia of Psychology by Harriman, et al.): 'Definition: Motivation is the process (a) of arousing or initiating behavior, (b) of sustaining an activity in progress, and (c) of chanelling activity into a given course. Broadly considered, the analysis of motivation must take account of all factors which arouse, sustain, and direct behavior.

'The concept of motivation is thus a very broad one. It is not so broad as psychology itself, however, since psychological explanation includes consideration of both non-motivating and motivating factors.'

Ruscha Facwortbuch der Phychologie (Zürich, 1946): 'Motiv = Beweggrund, Antrieb.'

Of these definitions I prefer Young's 'Broadly considered, the analyses of motivation must take account of all factors which arouse, sustain, and direct behavior', because it seems to include the meaning of all the other definitions. Written in the terminology of this study, this temporary definition of '*motivation*' *becomes: 'Motivation' = all variables which arouse, sustain, and direct behavior.*

Before this criterion is used to select the theories of motivation which are to be examined, a very brief outline of the development of the theories of motivation up to this century will be given.

Theories of Motivation before 1900

O. H. Mowrer calls attention to the fact that the history of the theories of motivation—in spite of their great importance in modern psychology—is very sparse. It will briefly be presented here (based mainly upon (62)).

Aristotle and other philosophers of antiquity have described 'desire,' or 'drives' as one of the 'mental forces,' or 'abilities' on a par with others such as perception, imagination, and feeling. In the *Middle Ages* Thomas of Aquinas and others distinguished between 'sensual desire' and 'rational will'. For the famous philosophers of *more modern times* (Descartes, Hobbes, and Spinoza) 'drives' ('desire,' or 'striving') were still an important class of psychological variables on a par with affective and intellectual processes. *Hedonism*, a theory of motivation which was used very frequently during the 18th and 19th centuries, taught that Man always acts to achieve pleasure and avoid unpleasure. For *the English empiricists* (Locke, Berkeley, and Hume) the intellectual variables dominated other kinds of psychological variables to a high degree. *Kant* was the first to put 'Cognition,' 'emotion,' and 'will' on the same level in psychological classification, and this 'tripartition' has dominated psychology until the beginning of this century. In this classification motivational variables were divided into two groups: 'emotion' and 'will. *W. Wundt*, the real founder of experimental psychology, accepted, however, a close relationship between 'emotion' and 'will,' as 'will,' according to Wundt's theory, is a special series of emotions which ends with the feeling of determination spontaneously resulting in action. Influenced by the biological approach to psychology started by Darwin's theory of evolution, psychologists began, towards the end of the 19th century, to regard '*instincts*' as the primary motives of behavior in both Man and animals. Thus it was maintained by *W. James* that of all beings Man was the creature that had most instincts, and that these instincts were primary in relation to 'the will.' Later instincts dominated the theory of McDougall, which will be examined in a following chapter. The Danish philosopher H. Høffding regarded the will as the most fundamental psychological functions. At the turn of the century *N. Ach* made an experimental examination of some of the motivational variables, the socalled 'determining tendencies', and thereby inspired a psychological theory which will be examined in one of the following chapters, namely K. Lewin's fieldtheoretical psychology. At the same time psycho-analysis was founded by *S. Freud* who maintained that innate, primitive motives (instincts, or drives) were of fundamental importance for the behavior of the individual, especially for its development (with adjustments and maladjustments). A few of the theories analyzed here are strongly influenced by psycho-analysis.

Influenced by all these theories of psychology from the 19th century, there were in the first quarter of 20th century constructed theories of motivation, which included variables as 'instinct', 'drive' and 'need'. All this variables play a part in the theories, which will be examined in the following chapters.

Earlier Examinations of Theories of Motivation

S. Koch analyzes motivational variables in an article in Psych. Review (47), especially discussing the theories of Hull and Lewin and only these two theories. In the last chapter of his book 'Dimensions of Behavior' (Lund 1949) *Gösta Carlsson* has made a brief analysis of motivational variables. In 'Explanation of Human Behavior' (London 1951) *F. W. Smith* has made an anlysis and comparison of six important pscychological theories (McDougall, Lewin, Allport, Watson, Hull, and Tolman); it is, however, not based upon the systematic meta-theoretical presuppositions which have been used here. In an article on 'Cognition and Motivation in Psychological Theory' (51) *David Krech* has analyzed motivational and cognitive variables and their interrelations in some modern psychological theories. It may furthermore be mentioned that *K. W. Spence* in a chapter in S. S. Stevens's 'Handbook of Experimental Psychology (87) has made a similar (though more restricted examination of theories of *learning*. Finally it should be mentioned that *E. Brunswik* (15) and *C. R. Griffith* (29) have published works which are both philosophical and historical examinations of psychological theories[1]).

List of References to Part I

1. Amons, R. B. & C. H. Amons: Psychology of the scientist: I. Introduction. (Percept. & Motor skills, 1962, 15 (3), 748–50).
2. Andrews, F. M.: Creativity and the scientist. (Dissertation Abstracts, 1963, 23 (9), 3524).
3. Ayer, A. J.: Logical Positivism. (Free Press Illinois, 1959).
4. Benton, M.: Creativity in research and invention in the physical sciences. An annolated bibliography. (USN Res. Lab. Rep. 1961).
5. Bergman, G.: Philosophy of Science. (Univ. Wisconsin Press).
6. – Theoretical Psychology (in Annual Review of Psychology, 1953).
7. Bjørkman, M.: Psykologisk Forskning. (Almquist, Stockholm, 1962).
8. Bloomfield, L.: Linguistic Aspects of Science (Int. Encyclop. of Unif. Sc. vol. I, no. 4).
9. Boring, Bridgman, Feigl., Israel, Skinner and Pratt: Symposium on Operationism (Ps. Rev. 1945 vol. 52, nr. 5).
10. Boring, E. G.: A history of experimental psychology. (Appleton-Cent. Co. N.Y., 2. ed. 1950).
11. – History, Psychology and Science: Selected Papers. (Wiley, N.Y. and London 1963).
12. – Psychologist at large. (The article: Psychological factors in the scientific process).
13. Braitwaite, R. B.: Scientific Explanation (Cambridge 1953).
14. Brown and Ghiselli: Scientific Method in Psychology. (McGraw-Hill, N.Y., 1955).

---

[1]) A meta-theoretical study of '*Modern Learning Theories*' was published 1954 by Estes et al. It includes an analysis of the theories of Hull, Tolman, Skinner, Lewin and Guthrie, but they are treated as theories of *learning processes*. The analysis of the individual theories is much more thorough than it has been possible to make it here, among other things because several persons have worked together on the project. But only five theories are examined, and *no* comparison is made. It is not possible here to compare their outline of analysis with mine, but they seem to cover approximately the same points.

15. Brunswik, E.: The Conceptual Framework of psychology (Int. Encycl. Univ. Sc. vol. II, nr. 5).
16. Campel, N. R.: Foundations of Science. (Dover, N.Y., 1957).
17. Campell, David P.: The Vocational Interests of American Psychological Association Presidents. (American Psychologist 1965, 20, 636–644).
18. Carlson, G.: Dimensions of Behavior (Lund, 1949).
19. Chambers, J. A.: Relating personality and biographical factors to scientific creativity. (Psychol. Monographs, General & Applied, 1964, 78 (7), Whole No. 584. 20 pp.)
20. Clark, K. E.: America's psychologists: A survey of a growing profession. (Washington D.C. American Psychological Association, 1957).
21. Cofer and Appley: Motivation, Theory and Research.
22. Cooley, W. W.: Research Frontier: Current research on the career development of scientists. (Journal of Counseling Psychology, 1964, 11 (1), 88–93).
23. Datta, Lois-Ellin: Test instructions and the identification of creative scientific talent. (Psychol. Reports, 1963, 13 (2), 495–500).
24. Esper, E. A.: A History of Psychology as a Biological Science. (Saunders, Philadelphia, 1965).
25. Feigl, H.: Principles and Problems of Theory Construction in Psychology (in Current Trends in Psychological Theory of W. Dennis et al. (Pittsburgh, 1951).
26. Garrett, Henry E.: Great Experiments in Psychology. (Appleton, N.Y., 1941).
27. Garwood, D. S.: Personality factors related to creativity in young scientists. (Journal of Abnormal & Social Psychol. 1964, 68 (4), 413–19).
28. Golann, Stuart E.: Psychological study of creativity. (Psychol. Bull., 1963, 60 (6), 548–565).
29. Griffith, C. R.: Principles of Systematic Psychology (Illinois 1943).
30. Hays, R.: Psychology of the scientist: III. Introduction to passages from the 'idea books' of Clark L. Hull. (Percept. & motor skills, 1962, 15 (3), 803–806).
31. Hempel, C. G.: Fundamentals of Concept Formation in Empirical Science (Int. Encycl. of Unif. Sc. vol. II, no. 7).
32. – Analyse logique de la psychologie (in Revue de Syntese 1935).
33. Hilgard, E.: Motivation i Learning Theory (in S. Koch (edt.): Psychology—A study of a science. Vol. V, 1963).
35. Hull, C. L.: Principles of Behaviour (London and New York, 1943).
36. – Psychology of the scientist: IV. Passage from the 'idea books' of Clark L. Hull. (Percept. & motor skills, 1962, 15, (3) 807–882).
37. Hyman, R.: The Nature of Psychological Inquiry. (Prentice-Hall, N.Y., 1964).
38. Jørgensen, J.: Filosofiske Forelæsninger (København 1935).
39. – Psykologi på biologisk grundlag (Kbhvn. 1941).
40. – The Development of Logical Empirism (Int. Encycl. Unif. Sc. vol. no. 9, 1952).
41. – Remarks concerning the concept of mind and the problem of other people's mind (Theoria, 1949, 15, 116–27).
42. Kaila, E.: Den mänskliga Kunskapen (Stockholm 1939).
43. – Personlighetens Psykologi (Stockholm 1943).
44. – Tankens oro (Helsingors 1944).
45. – Physikalismus und Phänomenalismus (Theoria, 1942, 8, 85–125).
46. Kantor, J. R.: Interbehavioral Psychology. (Principia Press, Indiana, 1958).
47. Koch, S.: Logical Character of Motivation Concept (Psych. Review, vol. 48, 1941, p. 15–13 and p. 127–154).
48. – Theoretical Psychology, 1950: An Overview (Ps. Rev. 1951, 58, 147–54).
49. – Psychology—A study of a science. (McGraw-Hill, N.Y., Vol. I–VI, 1959–63).
50. Kriedl, P. H.: Differential interest patterns of psychologists. (Unpubl. doct. dissert. Univ. of Minnesota, 1949).
51. Krech, D.: Cognition and Motivation in Psychological Theory (in Current Trends in Psychological Theory by W. Dennes et al. Pittsburgh 1951).
52. Krech, D. and Klien, G. S. (edts.): Theoretical Models and Personality Theory (Durham 1952).
53. Lehman, H.: The creative production rates of present versus past generations of scientists. (Journal of Gerontology, 1962, 17, 4–9–417).

54. Lewin, K.: The Conceptual Representation and the Measurement of Psychological Forces (Durham, 1938).
54 a. – Principles of Topological Psychology (1936).
55. Lewis, C. J.: An Analysis of Knowledge and Valuation (Illinois 1946).
56. Littman, R. A. and Rosen, E.: Molar and Molecular (Ps. Rev. 1950, 57, 58–65).
57. Lockman, R. F.: Characteristics of APA remembers in the 1962 'National Scientific Register'. (Amer. Psychologist, 1962, 17 (10), 789–792).
58. MacCorquodale and Meehl, P. E.: On a distinction between hypothetical constructs and intervening variables (Ps. Rev. 1948, 55, 95–107).
59. Mandler, G. and Kessen: The language of psychology. (Wiley, N.Y., 1959).
59 a. Marx, M. H.: Intervening variable or hypothetical construct? (Ps. Rev. 1951, 58, 235–47).
60. Maslow, A. H.: The Psychology of Science. (Harper, N.Y. and London, 1966).
61. Morgan, D. N.: Creativity today. A constructive analytical review of certain philosophical and psychological work. (Journal of Aesthetics & Art Criticism, 1953, 12, 1–24).
62. Mowrer, O. H.: Motivation (Annual Rev. of Psych, vol. 3 1952).
63. Murphy, G.: Historical Introduction to Modern Psychology (New Yerk 1951).
64. Ness, Arne: Erkenntnis und Wissenschaftliches Verhalten. (Oslo, 1936).
65. – Science as Behavior (in 'Metapsykology, Universitetsforlaget, Oslo, 1962).
66. Neurath, O.; Bohr, N.; Dewey, I.; Russel, B.; Carnap, R.; Morris, C. W.: Encyclopodia and Unified Science (Int. Enc. Unif. Sc. vol. I, no. 1).
67. Pelz, D. C.: Freedom in research. (International Science and Technique, 1964, nr. 31. 54–66).
68. – Social fatcors in the motivation of engineers and Scientists (School Science and Mathematics, 1958, 58, 417–429).
69. Peters, R. S. (edt.): Brett's History of Psychology. (London, A & U 1953).
70. Popper, K. R.: The Logic of scientific discovery. (Hutchinson of London, 1959).
71. Postman, Leo (edt.): Psychology in the Making. (Knopf, N.Y., 1962).
72. Pratt, C. C.: The Logic of modern Psychology (1939).
73. Razran, Gregory: Russian Psychologist's Psychology and American Experimental Psychology: A Historical and a Systematic Collation and a Look into the Future. (Psychol. Bulletin, 1965, Vol. 63, 42–64).
74. Reicheback, Hans: The Rise of Scientific Philosophy. (Univ., California Press, 1951).
75. Roe, Anne: The making of a scientist. (N.Y. Dodd-Mead, 1953).
76. Rosenthal, R.: On the social psychology of the psychological experiment. (Amer. Scientist 1963, 51, 268–83).
77. Russel, B.: The Analysis of Mind (1922).
78. – Our Knowledge of the External World (London 1929).
79. – An Inquiry into Meaning and Truth (London 1940).
80. – Human Knowledge (London 1948).
81. Ryle, G.: The Concept of Mind (London 1949).
82. Scriven, M.: Views of Human Nature. (In Wann (edt.): Behaviorism and Phenomenology). (Univ. Chicago Press, 1964).
83. Smedslund, J.: Studies in Psychological Theory (Oslo 1951).
84. Smith, F. V.: Explanation of Human Behavior (London 1951).
85. Spence, K. W.: The Nature of theory construction in contemporary psychology (Ps. Rev. 1944, 51, 47–68).
86. – The methods and postulates of 'behaviorism' (Ps. Rev. 1948, 55, 67–78).
87. – Theoretical Interpretations of Learning (in Stevens et al.: Handbook of Experimental Psychology, 1951).
88. Stevens, S. S.: The operational basis of psychology (Amer. J. Psych. 1935, 47, 323–30).
89. – The operational definition of psychological concepts (Ps. Rev. 1935, 42, 517–27).
90. – Psychology and the Science of Science. (Ps. Bull. 1939, 36, 221–63).
91. Tegen, Einar: Amerikansk psykologi. (Stockholm, 1949).
92. Thomae, H. (edt.): 'Algemeine psychologie II. Motivation'. (Handbuch der Verlag für Psychologie Gøttingen, 1965).
93. Tolman, E. C.: Operational behaviorism and the current trends in psychology (to be found in Collected Papers 1951).
94. – A. Psychological Model (in Parsons et al.: Toward a general theory of action, 1951).

95. Törnebohm, H.: A logical analysis of the theory of relativity. (Almquist, Stockholm, 1962).
96. – Discourse Analysis. (Theoria, 1955, 21, 42–54).
97. – Fysik och Filosofi. (Univ. Gothenburg, 1957).
98. Toulmin, S.: The Philosophy of Science (London 1953).
99. Turner, M. B.: Philosophy and the Science of Behavior. (Appleton, N.Y., 1967).
100. Valpola, V. and Tørnudd, P.: Vetenskapeligt samarbete och inter-disciplinära problem (Nordisk Sommeruniversitet, Helsinki, 1963).
101. Watson, I. R.: The Great Psychologists: From Aristotle to Freud. (N.Y., 1963).
102. Wolman, B. B.: Contemporary Theories and Systems in Psychology. (Harper, N.Y., 1960).
103. Woodger, J. H.: The Technique of Theory Construction (Int. Encycl. Unif. Sci. vol. II, no. 5).
104. Woodworth, R. S. and Mary Sheehan: Contemporary Schools of Psychology. (N.Y. 3. ed., 1964).
105. Wright, G. H.: Den logiska Empirism (Helsingfors 1943).
106. Beck, L. W.: Constructions and Inferred Entities (Philosophy of Science, 17, 1950).
107. Bohr, N.: Atomteori og Naturbeskrivelse (Kbhvn. 1929).
108. Carnap, R.: Testability and Meaning (Phil. Science. 1936 and 1937).
109. – Formal and Factual Science. (Erkenntnis 1934).
110. – The Interpretation of Physics (Feigl and Brodbeck p. 309–18).
111. – The Two Concepts of Probability. (Feigl and Brodbeck p. 438–55).
112. Einstein, A.: Geometry and Experience (in F. and B. p. 189–94).
113. – The Fundaments of Theoretical Physics (in F. and B. p. 253–61).
114. – The Laws of Science and the Laws of Ethics (in F. and B. p. 779–80).
115. Feigl, H. and Brodbeck, M.: Readings in The Philosophy of Science (New York 1953).
116. Feigl, H.: Notes on Causaility (in F. and B. p. 408–18).
117. Jørgensen, J.: Hvad er Psykologi? (Munksgaard 1955).
118. – Sandhed, Virkelighed og Fysikkens Metode (Munksgaard 1956).
119. Nagel, E.: Teleological Explanation and Teleologica Systems (in F. and B. p. 537–58).
120. Rasmussen, E. Tranekjær: Bevidsthedsliv og Erkendelse (Kbhvn. 1956).
121. 'Årsagsproblemet' Nord. Sommer Univ. 1951 (especially the studies by M. Blegvad, Højgård, I. C. Madsen and G. Rasch).
122. Hinde, R. A.: Ethological Models and the Concept of 'Drive' (Brit. J. Phil. Sci. 1956, VI, 321–31).

Part II

ANALYSIS OF THEORIES

PART I dealt with the general meta-theoretical problems of psychology and presented the presuppositions for the following study. This consists of two natural parts, *an analytical part ('Part II') and a comparative part ('Part III').*

The analytical part contains analyses of several psychological theories of motivation. Each theory is analyzed, first with regard to its *structure*, then with regard to its *content* of motivation definitions and hypotheses, and finally *a reconstrcution* of the theory is made (cf. the outline in Chapter 4). The reader who is not especially interested in the individual theories may prefer to read only the paragraphs containing the reconstructions.

In the process of analyzing the theories many quotations will be given, as these form the basic material for this study in the same way as experts from research protocols form the basic material for experimental studies. The quotations also serve as confirmation for the statements made about the theories in question, thus making it unnecessary for the reader to have the books referred to at hand in order to evaluate them.

Chapter 5

McDougall's Theory

After broad and many-sided preparatory studies the English-American psychologist William McDougall (1871–1938) produced a series of psychological works of which the best known is '*An Introduction to Social Psychology*' which was published for the first time in 1908 and has, since then, appeared in at least thirty editions. This is his most important book, and he gives here a presentation of his theory of instinct and applies it to social-psychological problems. Earlier he had written some shorter books of which the best known is the popular '*Psychology, the Study of Behavior*' (1912) whose most remarkable feature is that psychology is defined (anticipating Watson) as the study of behavior. Later he published a text book, '*An Outline of Psychology*' (1923), and the more specialised '*An Outline of Abnormal Psychology*' (1926). Further he has written a philosophical work, '*Body and Mind: A History and Defence of Animism*' (1911). Finally, in 1932, his last comprehensive and systematic presentation of his theory, '*The Energies of Men*[1])', was published. This book will (in agreement with the principles of selection given in Chapter 4) be chosen for this study, although comparisons with his older main work, '*Social Psychology*'[2]) will also be made.

THE STRUCTURE OF THE THEORY

Summary of the Theory

The content of McDougall's theory may briefly be described as follows:

All life-processes—also 'mental life' and behavior—*are purposive*, as they express a fundamental striving to preserve the existence of the individual and the species. In Man and the higher animals this fundamental striving ('hormé') is differentiated into a series of innate, but modifiable *primary* motivation variables which are called '*instincts*,' or (later) '*propensities*.' These primary motivation variables determine and organize all mental processes and all behavior in the direction of special *goals:* The cognitive processes are made purposive (are 'guided'

---

1) From now on abbreviated to E. M.' The 8th edition from 1950 is used here.
2) From now on abbreviated to S. P.' The 12th edition from 1917 is used here.

and 'utilized'), a primary emotion particular to each instinct is experienced, and a purposive behavior is started, or at least an impulse to act in a certain way is experienced. The emotion and the impulse to act are the most primary and least modifiable links in this process (McDougall's theory is original in considering the primary emotions as part of, or aspects of instincts). Several instincts may through learning processes be centered around an object in a system called '*a sentiment*'. (McDougall has taken this concept from A. F. Shand, who in turn has taken the concept of the instinct-emotion combination from McDougall[3]). In Man these sentiments are most often the direct motivation to action, but the innate instincts, of which the sentiment 'consists', are still the fundamental drive or energy. In grownup, mature persons several sentiments may be organized in a more or less well integrated system called the '*character*'. (Cf. A. F. Schmith's summary of McDougall's theory p. 127 and 128 in his book (6))[3]).

In the preface to the second edition of E. M. (1934) (which he himself calls: 'the last word in what is likely to be my last book on psychology') McDougall gives a very explicit presentation of the presuppositions of his theory. He presupposes (p. XII–XIV): 1) 'that psychic activity is no less real than physical process and no less causally efficacious, a part of nature,' 2) 'that psychic activity is always and everywhere teleological, a forward striving towards some end or goal; and that such teleological or purposive causation is in no sense disguised from of the mechanistic causation postulated by the physical sciences.' These two presupsuppositions are special '*hormic*' *axioms*. 3) 'I assume continuity of evolution, physical and mental, from the simplest animal forms to man, and an abbreviated and distorted recapitulation of the phylogenetic process in all ontogeny.' This presupposition can be taken to be an expression of McDougall's special comparative—psychological point of view, which distinguishes him from psychologists such as A. F. Shand, whom he otherwise resembles. As an addition to the above mentioned presuppositions one must mention 4) 'that underlying and determining the main lines and limits of mental activity (i. e. purpositve intelligent strivings) of any creature, is a complex organization which we conveniently call its mental structure. The nature of this organization, as also the processes of its growth and differentiation, may be inferred from the creature's observed activities.' This and the first presupposition constitute the '*mentalistic*' *axioms*.

Level of Development of the Theory

McDougall's theory (like most other psychological theories) is *a classifying theory*, describing, classifying, and (partly) explaining the behavior of Man and animals. But the explanations are only implicit in the classifications (of instincts,

---

[3]) Cf. A. F. Shand: The Foundations of Character (1914). A comparison of the theories of Shand, Murray, and McDougall may be found in K. B. Madsen: Behov og Følelser (Needs and Emotions) (unpublished thesis 1950).

sentiments, etc.) and no explicit deduction based on an axiomatization has been made, nor has any symbolization or formalization of the theory taken place.

Constructive or Reductive Theory

It is more difficult to classify McDougall's theory as a constructive or reductive theory. It is, for the most part, based upon both physiological and (especially) comparative-biological data. Thus McDougall writes (in E. M., p. 21) that this theory,

'makes use to the fullest extent of all knowledge of the organism attained by physiology, expecially the physiology of the nervous system and of the chemistry of the body. It insists that mental activities are physiological functions of the whole organism, functions that are of the first importance in effecting its adaptions to its environment.'

But in spite of this emphasis upon the significance of physiological and comparative data in a psychological theory, McDougall's theory can not be classified as a reductive theory as he neither attempts not desires to reduce psychology to physiology. On the contrary, his 'animation' of all life-processes (his emphasizing that purposive striving is the most essential of all life-functions) points more towards a reduction of all biological sciences to psychology. Probably it is most correct to classify McDougall's theory as *a constructive biological-psychological theory*, since he stresses a fundamental difference between the physical sciences, where only *mechanical* causal processes occur and the biological sciences (including psychological and social sciences), where also *teleological* processes occur; moreover he presupposes that each of these sciences has to *construct* its own theories based upon its own set of primary presuppositions (mechanistic and teleological determinism, respectively). This can be seen from what has already been quoted in the second presupposition, and to a still higher degree from the following paragraph (E. M. p. 5):

'Nature seems, then, to present to our contemplation events of two different kinds, the physical and the psycho-physical. The former are the events of the inorganic realm, which physical science explains with ever-increasing success in terms of mechanistic causation (the principle of causation that finds the explanation of present events in terms only of the causal influence of antecedent events, without reference of any kind to possible future events). Psycho-physical events, on the other hand, cannot be completely explained in this way; for the explanation of them we have to take into account foresight of the possible future course of events and striving guided by such foresight. All such events, all foresighted strivings, seem to be instances of a second fundamental type of causation, that type which we call *purposive* or *teleological*.'

Mentalistic or Behavioristic Theory

It is even more difficult to place McDougall's theory in this classification. McDougall was the first explicitly to define psychology as 'the study of behavior' (in his 'Primer of Physiological Psychology', 1905, and later on the front page of his 'Psychology, the Study of Behavior', 1912). His whole attitude is also—as mentioned before—of a general-biological or comparative-psychological character, and therefore he criticises the totally introspective psychology time and again. In S.P. (p. 15) he writes:

'psychologists must cease to be content with the sterile and narrow conception of their science as the science of consciousness, and must boldly assert its claim to be the positive science of conduct or behavior. Psychology must not regard the inrospective description of the stream of consciousness as its whole task, but only as a preliminary part of its work. Such introspective description, such 'pure psychology' can never constitute a science, or at least can never rise to the level of an explanatory science; and it can never in itself be of any great value to the social sciences. The basis required by all of them is a comparative and physiological psychology relying largely on objective methods, the observation of the behavior of men and of animals of all varieties under all possible conditions of health and disease.'

In my opinion this quotation shows that McDougall in this respect was ahead of his time. And the following quotation from E. M. (p. 16) shows that he was still positively inclined towards a certain form of behaviorism—without being an extreme behaviorist:

Since psychology must study the organism as a whole, regarding its conscious activities as functions of the whole organism, recognizing that the organism is the seat of many events which, though not introspectively observable, are yet in many respects very similar to those we can observe; and since the observation of behaviour is in all departments of psychology important and in some (as in animal psychology) our only available method, it may be said that all psychology is, or should be, behaviouristic. *Behaviouristic psychology* (in this sence) is approved by many psychologists and philosophers who neither deny the value of introspection nor believe in the validity of purely mechanistic explanations of human and animal behaviour.'

These quotations show that McDougall's theory is based upon both introspective and behavioristic methods, or, in other words, upon both phenomenalistic and physicalistic *protocol statements;* but mainly upon physicalistic (behavioristic) methods and protocol statements.

On the other hand, McDougall's interpretation of the hypothetical variables must rather be described as *mentalistic*. This has already been shown in the fourth presupposition and is quite clear from the following quotation (E. M., p. 7), which also shows McDougall's *dualistic hypothesis* concerning the psychophysical problem, a dualism which can be described as a '*psycho-physical interactionism.*'

'We thus have abundant grounds for assuming that the events of the two kinds can and constantly do exert reciprocal influence; and we do well to follow where the facts lead us, accepting the interplay of mechanistic physical and of purposive mental events. No sufficient reason has been adduced for regarding such interplay or reciprocal influence as impossible, or the assumption of it as improper. Yet, in speaking of *psycho-physical interaction*, we must recognize that the expression may distort the truth in that it seems to separate the psychical and the physical; whereas these may be mut two partial aspects of the concrete reality, two aspects of a system of psychophysical activity which are distinguishable but inseparable.'

The last few lines, however, point towards a *neutral monism*, which says that both physical and psychical phenomena are aspects or modes of a neutral reality; a hypothesis which is called an 'obscure doctrine' by McDougall himself (E. M.,

p. 8). Nevertheless the 'obscure doctrine' appears still more clearly in the following quotation (E. M., p. 4):

'it becomes a fair working assumption that conscious activity (allied in nature to our experience of desireful foresight) and goalseeking behaviour are always but two partial aspects of one total system of activity, a psycho-physical activity.'

Consequently McDougall's theory must be classified as *a mixture of mentalistic and behavioristic theories*, as the interpretation of its hypothetical constructions is mainly mentalistic, whereas its protocol statements are mainly behavioristc. It is a theory which has much in common with the in-between form called the neutral-formal theories, but it differs from these in being less systematic in this respect.

Molar or Molecular Theory

It is quite easy to classify McDougall's theory as a *molar theory*, even though his theory (also in E. M.) was written before this distinction was made by Tolman, so that McDougall has not himself written anything explicitly about this. But it is quite evident at several points in his book that his theory deals with rather large units: the behavior of the whole organism, whole acts—not single reflex movements. Thus he writes about psychology (E. M., p. 6):

'Its task is to describe as fully as possible the observable events of the human organism and to explain them by the aid of causal hypotheses.'

The whole organism, then, in the area of study of psychology. Also in another connection (p. 16) he writes: 'Since psychology must study the organism as a whole.' And he writes about 'The Psychology expounded in this book' (E. M., p. 21):

'It insist that mental activities are physiological functions of the whole organism ... It repudiates the attempt to exhibit these functions as aggregations of elements of any kind.'

Finally, as a last example it may be mentioned that in the definition of the most fundamental variable in the theory ('instinct', or 'propensity'), which will be quoted later, the molar character of the theory is obvious, as this variable is defined so that it includes all mental processes of the organism (cognitive, affective, and conative) and its whole behavior.

McDougall's theory is thus both in principle (in its presuppositions) and in detail (in the definitions of its variables) *an extremely molar theory*.

Field-Theory or Mechanistic Theory

Regarding the next point of the analysis it is rather easy to see that McDougall's theory is *not* a mechanistic theory. It is quite evident from the quotations already given that McDougall attacks the purely mechanistic theories (outside the physical sciences) and explicitly calls his own theory a *dynamic* theory. Thus the subtitle of E. M. is: 'A Study of the Fundamentals of Dynamic Psychology.'

But even though the theory cannot be described as 'mechanistic,' it cannot be classified as a field-theory either, as the relations dealt with in its more or less explicitly formulated hypotheses, between variables are relatively simple, which can be seen from the analysis of the individual hypotheses in the following paragraphs. None of its hypotheses deal with as many variables as the hypotheses in for example the theories of Lewin and Tolman. Therefore it seems best to adopt *L. von Bertalanffy*'s classification which distinguishes between mechanistic ('self-actional'), dynamic ('inter-actional'), and field-theoretical ('transactional') theories (cf. Chapter 3) and according to which McDougall's theory must be classified as *a dynamic theory*.

McDougall distinguishes between two different forms of dynamic psychology. He writes (E. M., p.24):

'But there are two very different froms of purposive psychology ... which in principle are quite distinct. Both recognize, as fundamental facts of all our mental activity foresight of and desire for goals ...

The difference between these two theories is that the one form assumes a series of certain goals for the behavior of each species of organism, whereas the other form assumes that the actual goal of the behavior—at any rate in Man—is the feeling of pleasure which is produced when these different goals are obtained. The two forms of dynamic psychology are called *hormic psychology* and *hedonism*. McDougall's theory belongs to the first kind[4]).

Statistical or Deterministic Theory

In McDougall's theory there are no quantitative hypotheses and, consequently, no statistical hypotheses. Moreover he often points out the importance, or rather the necessity of deterministic hypotheses. Thus he writes (in E. M., p. 6):

'It has often been proposed that Science should content itself with description and should forswear all explanation in terms of causation. But the whole history of Science shows clearly that such a policy would be fatal to its progress. It is the search for causal explanation that produces fruitful hypotheses, which in turn lead to new observations and more aqewuate descriptions. In this respect psychology is no exception. Its task is to describe as fully as possible the observable events of the human organism and to explain them by the aid of causal hypotheses.'

Thus McDougall's theory must be classified as *a deterministic theory*. But it is af special kind of determinism, viz. *a teleological determinism*. From several of the above quotations it can be seen that McDougall distinguishes clearly between mechanistic and teleological explanations, but considers both of them to be causal explanations. He writes (E. M., p. 22):

'we recognize the validity of both the mechanistic and the purposive principles of explanation, each in its own sphere; admitting that neither mechanistic nor purposive causation is fully intelligible in any deep or ultimate sense.'

---

[4]) Cf. *Tolman's* comparison of his own and McDougall's theories (p. 421–423).

McDougall's theory is thus one of the rare *explicitly* teleological theories of later years. But it is, however, of the kind where the teleological phenomena (the purposive behavior) have been reduced to causal processes. It is not quite clear which of the three methods of reduction noted by Braithwaite (cf. Chapter 3) is used by McDougall. Mostly he makes use of hypothetical constructions (the second method of reduction), namely 'instincts', or 'propensities'. This method of reduction is in my opinion the most practical at the present stage of research. But there are also statements scattered in his books which correspond to Braithwaite's first method of reduction (the anthropomorphistical), namely statements about a more or less indistinct 'purpose consciousness' as a basic feature in all life processes or all living organisms. Anthropomorphistical statements of this kind appear also in the quotations already given for example in the second presupposition (cf. the summary of the theory) as well as in the following paragraph (E. M., p. 21):

'We must frankly and fully recognize this peculiarity of organic events: we must regard our own most developed froms of activity, our deliberate purposeful efforts, as the instances in which the nature of goal-seeking activity is most fully revealed to us; and we must seek to explain the lower obscurer forms of organized activity in the light of our understanding of these higher forms into whose nature we have more insight, rather than seek to explain the higher in terms of the lower and more obscure, in terms of principles of explanation taken over from the physical sciences...'

It is these more philosophical (meta-theoretical) statements in McDougall's books which cause his critics to accuse him of anthropomorphism. In his own psychological theory as before mentioned he mainly makes use of the most practical way of explaining the teleological phenomena: explanation by hypothetical constructions. Thus his theory must be classified as *a teleological deterministic theory*.

The Model

Neither in E. M., nor in S. P.[5]) has McDougall presented, or explicitly described any illustrative model of the total theory, and I have not been able to find indications that he implicitly operates with a particular (illustrative) model.

Summary

Broadly speaking McDougall's theory may be described in the following way:

McDougall's theory is a classifying, constructive, dynamic, teleological-deterministic, molar, and mixed mentalistic-behavioristic theory.

---

[5]) The diagram p. 125 in S. P. might be considered an illustrative model of the theory.

The first two thirds of E. M. contains most of McDougall's motivation theory (the rest is mainly about abnormal psychology) and will form the basis for the present analysis. It will be compared with the theory described in S. P.—especially with regard to the instinct variable.

'Instinct' in S. P. and *'propensity'* in E. M. are the most important motivation variables in McDougall's theory. In both books the variable most closely related to them is *'emotion.'* These fundamental motivation variables have (in both presentations) been organized in the variable *'sentiment.'* In addition some less important variables will be discussed.

The 'Instinct' variable in S. P.

McDougall's frequently quoted definition of 'instinct' in S. P. (p. 29) is as follows:

> 'We may then define an instinct as an inherited or innate psycho-physical disposition which determines its possessor to perceive, and to pay attention to, objects of a certain class, to experience an emotional excitement of a particular quality upon perceiving such an object, and to act in regard to it in a particular manner, or, at least, to experience an impulse to such action.'

As may be seen from this definition, 'instinct' in McDougall's theory is a *hypothetical* motivation variable, more correctly described as a *disposition* variable ('An inherited or innate psycho-physical disposition'—cf. Chapter 3), related to (determining the course of) a series of hypothetical *function* variables: a *cognitive* process ('to perceive, and to pay attention to, objects of a certain class'), an *affective* process ('to experience an emotional excitement of a particular quality'), and a *conative* process ('an impulse to such action'). The last mentioned hypothetical variable has a direct functional relation to the dependent empirical variable ('action'), whereas the first mentioned hypothetical variable, the cognitive process, has a direct functional relation to the independent empirical variable ('objects of a certain class'). McDougall interprets all hypothetical *functional* variables *mentalistically*. On the other hand, the hypothetical *disposition* variable (the psycho-physical disposition) is more a *neutral-formal* variable. Probably McDougall himself regarded the disposition variable only as a *hypothetical* variable, the functional variables were—in agreement with his dualistic hypothesis—regarded as *empirical* variables, as aspects or manifestations of the disposition.

Whether or not all variables in this whole complex of variables are *motivation* variables is of course dependent upon the definition of 'motivation,' but the usual definition (and the criterion formulated in Chapter 4: 'motivation' = all variables which arouse, sustain, and direct behavior) includes only the affective and conative processes, plus maybe the psycho-physical disposition itself, which are motivation variables. But it is characteristic of McDougall's definition of 'instinct' that it includes so many different variables. He criticises older definitions of instinct (as for example that of Spencer) because they 'takes account only of the behaviour or movements to which instincts give rise. But instincts are more than innate tendencies or dispositions to certain kinds of movement. There is every reason to believe that even the most purely instinctive action is the outcome of a distinctly mental process' (S. P., p. 26).

And he continues (p. 26).

'every instance of instinctive behaviour involves a knowing of some thing or object, a feeling in regard to it, and a striving towards or away from that object.'

McDougall's instinct definition is thus very comprehensive. It is also characteristic of his instinct theory that 'instinct' means something modifiable, not something which cannot be changed during the life of an individual. He writes (p. 31):

"all the higher animals learn in various and often considerable degrees to adopt their instinctive actions to peculiar circumstances.'

Still, not all parts of the instinctive process are equally easy to modify, only 'the afferent or receptive part and the efferent or motor part are capable of being greatly modified, independently of one another and of the central part, in the course of the life history of the individual; while the central part persists throughout life as the essential unchanging nucleus of the disposition' (p. 33); and this he formulates in the following way:

'the emotional excitement, with the accompanying nervous activities of the central part of the disposition, is the only part of the total instinctive process that retains its specific character and remains common to all individuals and all situations in which the instinct is excited.'

Thus McDougall's 'instinct' is both something very modifiable and something very comprehensive nearly too inclusive, since it thereby becomes vague and less useful. Many have criticised him because of this.

The 'Propensity' Variable in E. M.

In spite of criticism McDougall long retained his definition of instinct and still used it in 'An Outline of Psychology' (1923). Moreover, he here wrote as follows (Outline of Psychology, p. 213–214):

'We have examined and found wanting of the alternative views or theories of human action, the reflex theory and the pleasure-pain theory. We have rejected by implication another widely held theory of human action, namely, the ideo-motor theory, which proclaims that all acts are the expression of 'ideas', and that every 'idea' is by its very nature a tendency to movement; for I have rejected 'idea' as a confused and confusing term. But something more in criticism of this ideo-motor theory must be said on a later page. For the sake of completeness of review of theories of action, let me very briefly state and examine yet other alternatives.

'Some authors, while recognizing that animals are moved wholly or chiefly by instinctive impulses, are yet unwilling to admit that the same is true of man. Or, while recognizing in man some very simple instincts, such as instincts to crawl, to walk, to climb, to suck, to run, to vociferate, they ascribe his more complex modes of behavior to what they are pleased to call 'innate propensities.' These authors seldom take the trouble to attempt to define these 'propensities.' If they did so, they would, I think, find them to be identical with what we have called the instinctive tendencies. The work 'propensities' is a good one. There is no reason why we should not speak of instinctive tendencies as 'innate propensities,' and of the individually acquired tendencies that we have called sentiments as 'acquired propensities.' But the use of the word merely to obscure the fact of the essential similarity of human to animal behavior is to be deprecated. I think that those who recognize as instincts in man his various motor capacities, while ascibing his more complex behavior to 'propensities,' are misled by the false doctrine which identifies as instinct with a mere motor mechanism. We may fairly ask such persons where they will class the behavior of the higher mammals. Is it the expression of instincts or of 'propensities'? And if the latter, what is the relation of 'propensities' to instincts? . . . Clearly, this distinction is one of no value and cannot be observed. If we give the name 'innate propensity' to the relatively unspecialized instincts of the human species, and the name instinct to the more highly specialized propensities of the insects, we shall be in difficulties with the mammals and birds, whose instincts are in the main intermediate in the scale of specialization between those of the insects and those of man. The differences between the less and the more specialized instincts are perfectly gradual.

This has, as an exception, been quoted for historical-psychological reasons, because it shows how McDougall at that time still kept to his definition of instinct and was a little reserved—if not directly negative in his attitude—towards the idea of 'propensity'. Later he changed his opinion and also his theory, and in the last presentation (in E. M.) he writes (p. 77):

'and many psychologists have been content to follow them in seeing, in such stereotyped patterns of movement, the essential marks of instinctive behaviour. Accordingly, since but vague traces of such movement patterns can be observed in human behaviour, they have asserted that human behaviour is not at all instinctive and that the human species has no instincts.

'Others fixing their attention upon the general propensities towards goals common to the species (rather than upon innate abilities) and regarding these as of the essence of instinct, have maintained that the life of man is just as truly rooted in instincts as that of the animals.

'To this latter group I myself belong; and in many earlier writings I have expounded this view. Recognizing now, clearly as I believe, and only now for the first time, the crux of this difficulty and of this divergence of opinion, I propose to avoid the use of term 'instinct' in defining the constitution of man, and to content myself with the term innate or native propensity. This change of usage does not imply any radical change of view. It implies a stricter usage of the words *instinct* and *instinctive* and a recognition of the questionable propriety of applying those words in the description of human nature and activities. I recognize that, in the fullest and most universally accepted sense of the word, instinctive action is peculiar to the lower animals, and that the extension of the word to the behaviour of higher animals and of man has led to unfortunate confusion and controversy which have obscured, rather than elucidated, the true relations between higher and lower forms of action.'

From now on he mainly uses the word adjectively as a descriptive representation of innate actions. He writes (p. 31):

'In so far as the adjective served to mark an action as belonging to a peculiar class (the class of innately prescribed actions) that was a useful and well-justified usage.'

McDougall still maintains—as a solution to the old problem of the relation between 'instinct' and 'intelligence'—that the word 'instinctive' must always be used in connection with the word 'intelligence' to describe behavior, as all animal behavior is at the same time more or less instinctive and more or less intelligent. He writes (p. 32):

'We must avoid this ancient error from the outset by recognizing that all animal behavior is both instinctive and intelligent; that, while every act of any animal is to some extent prescribed by the inherited constitution, that constitution itself provides the capacity for adaption, for adaptive deviation from the pattern common to the species.'

But McDougall still uses the word 'instinct' about lower animals with the following meaning (p. 49):

'A propensity "geared" to certain abilities is, then, the innate basis of a train of instinctive activity directed to some particular goal, such as mating, feeding, or building. And where such a complex unit of organization matures in virtue of the momentum of heredity and operates effectively the first time it is brought into play, we properly call it *an instinct.*

'An instinct is that special part of the creature's organization (a functional unit) which expresses itself in a train of instinctive action.'

As may be seen, the variables 'propensity' and 'ability' are now the most important hypothetical (explanatory) variables in McDougall's theory. He writes about them (p. 64):

'A tendency is an active energy directed towards a goal. A "propensity" is the name given in these pages (in accordance with old usage) to any part of the innate constitution whose nature and function it is to generate upon occasion an active tendency. The distinction between, on the one hand, ability and, on the other, propensity and tendency is of fundamental importance. Many psychologists ignore it; and others deny it, saying that an ability is *ipso facto* a propensity or tendency, contains its own motive power, does not need activation from outside itself.'

And he writes even more clearly about the same (p. 86):

'In our study of instinctive behaviour we saw that the typically instinctive action expresses two distinguishable features of the native endowment; on the one hand, a special ability, simple or complex (as the ability of the wasp to recognize and master the prey natural to her species); on the other hand, a propensity, which, on being roused from its dormant state, generates an active tendency: and the tendency is, in some sense, an energy; and not merely energy in general or a special kind of energy, but an energy which is directed to a goal, which works towards that goal and is brought to rest only on the attainment of it; an energy which activates the ability and brings it into the service of the tendency as a means towards its end or goal.'

Finally he gives the following explicit definitions (p. 118):

'The usage here adopted, after much consideration of this problem in terminology, is as follows:

'A *propensity* is a disposition, a functional unit of the mind's total organization, and it is one which, when it is excited, generates an active *tendency*, a *striving*, an *impulse*, or *drive* towards some goal: such a tendency working consciously towards a foreseen goal is a *desire*.'

It is evident that McDougall in his terminology now explicitly distinguishes between the hypothetical *disposition* variable, 'propensity,' and the hypothetical *functional* variable, 'tendency.' Moreover, the cognitive hypothetical variable, 'ability,' has been seperated from the actual motivation variables. Instead of the very complicated variable 'instinct' he now operates with several simple variables, which appear in many different relations.

The Variable 'Emotion'

In both presentations of McDougall's theory dealt with here, the variable 'emotion' holds a very central position. Thus an 'emotional excitement" was the central, unchangeable part of the total 'instinct'-complex as it is defined in S. P. McDougall formultes this explicitly (in S. P., p. 47) thus:

'Each of the principal instincts conditions, then, some one kind of emotional excitement whose quality is specific or peculiar to it; and the emotional excitement of specific quality that is the affective aspect of the operation of any one of the principal instincts may be called a primary emotion.'

This (almost) one to one relation between primary emotions and instincts is—as mentioned before—an original feature of McDougall's theory. Later a list of the primary emotions and instincts will be given.

In E. M. the realtion between 'propensity,' 'feelings,' and 'emotions' is also strongly emphasized.

Thus feelings of pleasure and unpleasure are caused partly by 'success' and partly by the lack of success. McDougall formulates it like this (p. 138).

'All successful or prosperous striving, we found, makes for pleasant feeling; all thwarted or baffled striving, all failure, makes for unpleasant feeling;'

About the relation between 'propensity' and 'emotions' in general he writes 'that emotion is experienced only when and if action is checked" (p. 150); and about the more special relation (p. 150):

'the evocation of each propensity liberates energy which flows most naturally into some system of channels peculiar to its tendency, channels of bodily adjustment and action.'

On the same subject he also writes (p. 151):

'If the occasion is such as to evoke strongly some one of the native tendencies, while leaving the others unstirred, we have little difficulty in finding an appropriate name. On such an occasion we may be said to experience one of the primary emotions.'

It is also true about the more complex emotions that they are a function of the propensities which operate at a given moment. They are complex because *several* propensities can operate *at the same time*, either in co-operation (organized into a sentiment) or in conflict. But before these more complicated conditions are dealt with in detail, some classifications of the fundamental motivation variables will be cited.

Lists of Instincts, Propensities, and Emotions

In S. P. (Chapter III) McDougall gives the following list of 'the principal instincts and the primary emotions of man':

Instinct	*Emotion*
1. Flight	Fear
2. Repulsion	Disgust
3. Curiosity	Wonder
4. Pugnacity	Anger
5. Self-abasement	Subjection
6. Self-assertion	Elation
7. Parental I.	Tender E.
8. Reproduction I.	
9. Desire for Food	
10. Gregarious I.	8–12: no well-defined emotional tendencies.
11. Acquisition I.	
12. Construction I.	

McDougall gives us two criteria for the classification of a variable as a primary instinct and emotion: 1) the presence of the same instinct and emotion in higher animals, and 2) the presence of the instinct or emotion in Man with an unnaturally increased intensity.

'That is to say, we must look to comparative psychology and to mental pathology for confirmation of the primary character of those of our emotions that appear to be simple and unanalysable' (p. 49).

In 'An Outline of Psychology' McDougall gives the following list p. 324.

Names of Instincts (Synonyms in Parentheses)	*Names of Emotional Qualities Accompanying the Instinctive Activities*
1. Instincts of escape (of self-preservation of avoidance, danger instinct)	Fear (terror, fright, alarm, trepidation).
2. Instinct of combat (aggression, pugnacity)	Anger (rage, fury, annoyance, irritation, displeasure).
3. Repulsion (repugnance)	Disgust (nausea, loathing, repugnance).
4. Parental (protective)	Tender emotion (love, tenderness, tender feeling).
5. Appeal	Distress (feeling of helplesness).
6. Pairing (mating, reproduction, sexual)	Lust (sexual emotion or excitement, sometimes called love—an unfortunate and confusing usage).
7. Curiosity (inquiry, discovery, investigation)	Curiosity (feeling of mystery, of strangeness, of the unknown, wonder).
8. Submission (self-abasement)	Feeling of subjection (of inferiority, of devotion, of humility, of attachment, of submission, negative self-feeling).
9. Assertion (self-display)	Elation (feeling of superiority, of masterfulness, of pride, of domination, positive self-feeling).
10. Social or gregarious instincts	Feeling of loneliness, of isolation, nostalgia.
11. Food-seeking (hunting)	Appetite or craving in narrower sense (gusto).
12. Acquisition (hoarding instinct)	Feeling of ownerschip, of possession (protective feeling).
13. Construction	Feeling of creativeness, of making, of productivity.
14. Laughter	Amusement (jollity, carelessness, relaxation).

As may be seen the list has become a little longer, as two instincts, the laughter instinct and the help-appeal instinct, have been added.

In E. M. McDougall gives a list of 'innate propensities' in 'the human species.' Contrary to the two previous lists this one does not contain any names of special emotions, maybe because McDougall—as mentioned above—now maintains that the emotions depend upon the course of the behavior caused by the propensity; a simple, primary emotion can only occur in cases where one and only one innate propensity operates. In Man behavior will in most cases becaused by several propensities, and therefore complex emotions will amost always occur. Also here it is true that:

'Our comparative survey suggests the guiding principle that the innate propensities of man are those common to all the higher mammals, together with some few that are peculiar to him or are so slightly developed in other species as to be not surely recognizable.' (E. M., p. 97).

As a result of his year-long studies, McDougall 'recognizes in the human species the following innate propensities' (p. 97 and 98 E. M.):

1. To seek (and perhaps to store) food (food-seeking propensity).
2. To reject and avoid certain noxious substances (disgust propensity).
3. To court and mate (sex propensity).
4. To flee to cover in response to violent impressions that inflict or threaten pain or injury (fear propensity).

5. To explore strange places and things (curiosity propensity).
6. To feed, protect and shelter the young (protective or parental propensity).
7. To remain in company with fellows and, if isolated, to seek that company (gregarious propensity).
8. To domineer, to lead, to assert oneself over, or display oneself before, one's fellows (self-assertive propensity).
8. To domineer, to lead, to assert oneself over, or display oneself before, one's fellows (self-assertive propensity).
9. To defer, to obey, to follow, to submit in the presence of others who display superior powers (submissive propensity).
10. To resent and forcibly to break down any thwarting or resistance offered to the free exercise of any other tendency (anger propensity).
11. To cry aloud for assistance when our efforts are utterly baffled (appeal propensity).
12. To construct shelters and implements (constructive propensity).
13. To acquire, possess, and defend whatever is found useful or otherwise attractive (acquisitive propensity).
14. To laugh at the defects and failures of our fellow creatures (laughter propensity).
15. To remove, or to remove oneself from, whatever produces discomfort, as by scratching or by change of position and location (comfort propensity).
16. To lie down, rest and sleep when tired (rest or sleep propensity).
17. To wander to new scenes (migratory propensity).
18. A group of very simple propensities subserving bodily needs, such as coughing, sneezing, breathing, evacuation.

The list has again become longer, as the four last propensities have been added to the previous list. McDougall points out himself that *the list is hypothetical*, a tentative suggestion, which must be revised by future research.

Sentiments

As mentioned before McDougall has taken the idea of 'sentiment' from A. F. Shand. Shand's 'sentiment' means an organized system of emotions; whereas McDougall describes it in S. P. as a system of instincts (with corresponding emotions), and in E. M. it means a system of propensities. Thus he writes (in E. M., p. 221):

'The theory of the sentiments is the theory of the progressive organization of the propensities in systems which become the main sources of all our activities; systems which give consistency, continuity and order to our life of stricing and emotion; systems which in turn become organized in larger systems, and which, when harmoniously organized in one comprehensive system, constitute what we properly call *character*.'

In everyday psychological usage the ideas of 'emotion' and 'sentiment' are very often confused. McDougall writes about the distinction (p. 222):

'Emotion is a fleeting experience; sentiment is an acquired disposition, one gradually built up through many emotional experiences and activities;'

'Sentiment' is thus a *disposition* variable contrary to 'emotion' which is a *functional* variable. Further it appears from the above quotation that 'sentiment' indicates an *acquired* disposition—contrary to propensity which is an *innate* disposition. In this McDougall does not agree with Shand who assumes an innate disposition for certain sentiments. But already in S. P. McDougall writes (p. 59):

'We have seen that a sentiment is an organized system of emotional dispositions centered about the idea of some object. The organization of the sentiments in the developing mind is determined by the course of experience; that is to say, the sentiment is a growth in the structure of the mind that is not natively given in the inherited constitution.'

Further he criticizes directly Shand's theory in this respect (in a footnote p. 159, S. P.):

'Mr. Shand has suggested that the sentiment of love is innately organized. I cannot see any sufficient grounds for accepting this suggestion, and I believe that any such assumption will raise more difficulties than it solves.'

While McDougall in S. P. uses the word 'idea' about that around which the sentiment is centered, he formulates it in E. M. in the following way (p. 223):

'The essential nature of a sentiment, the scheme or plan of it, is, then, a mental system in which a cognitive ability (in the older terminology, an 'idea') has become, through the individual's experience, functionally linked with one or more native propensities, linked in such a way that, when the ability comes into play (i. e. when the corresponding object is perceived or otherwise thought of) the propensity also is brought into action and engenders, its peculiar emotional tendency directed upon the object.'

From Shand McDougall has also taken the classification of sentiments as 'love' and 'hate'. He writes about this in E. M. (p. 227):

'every sentiment within which the protective or parental propensity is organized may properly be called a sentiment of love; and that all sentiments in which the propensities of fear and anger are incorporated may with equal propriety by called sentiments of hate ... Each sentiment is a unique formation, a structural and functional unit of the total organization of the mind. Its uniqueness corresponds to the uniqueness of its object;'

Besides the classification in hate and love, sentiments may also be classified in another way according to the nature of their objects (collective objects, abstract objects, etc.).

While McDougall in S. P. rather closely follows Shand's theory of sentiments (with the above mentoned reservation) he elaborates the theory further in E. M. as he distinguishes between '*tastes*' and '*sentiments*.' He writes about this distinction (p. 239):

'Broadly, we may say that sentiments are likings and dislikings for objects, while tastes are likings and dislikings for particular modes of activity. Broadly speaking again, we may say that, while our sentiments determine the major goals towards which we strive, our tastes determine our choice of means, the kinds of activities and instruments we use, the roads we prefer to follow, in pursuing those goals.'

In McDougall's theory the organization goes beyond the forming of sentiments in mature human beings with the forming of '*character*,' which is a system of sentiments. ('Such a system of sentiments is character,' E. M., p. 188). The '*raw material*' of character is:

1) *disposition:* 'A man's disposition is, then, the sum total of his propensities' (p. 171).
2) *temper:* The variation in the way in which the innate propensities work towards their goals.
3) *temperament:* 'The personal qualities that are determined by the chemical influences of the bodily metabolism exerted upon the general working of the brain of nervous system' (p. 177).

'Temper' and 'temperament' are thus innate conditions under which the innate propensities are organized into sentiments and character and cause the behavior of the individual.

Hypotheses in McDougall's Theory

Besides the hypotheses implicitly included in the above quotations, a few explicitly formulated hypotheses ('laws') can be found here and there in E. M.

Thus '*a very fundamental law of striving*' is (p. 119):

'a tendency once set in action towards a goal has a certain persistence and power of assertin itself over against all distractions, until its goal is reached. We see this law of striving clearly manifested in animal behavior.'

A few pages further on he writes about '*Law of Satisfaction and Dissatisfaction*' (p. 122):

'Any tendency towards a goal having been aroused, the striving process reaches is natural termination when, and only when, that goal is attained. Such attainment is accompanied by a feeling of satisfaction ... On the other hand, so long as we are making no progress, we have an unpleasant feeling, one of unease, of strain, of dissatisfaction or displeasure; a feeling that grows stronger when we encounter some special difficulty checking our progress, and waxes to a maximum if we are finally checked and have to desist from our unfinished task, owning our inability to accomplish it.'

And McDougall writes about *concentration* (p. 130):

'It may be stated as a general law that the more intense is any particular striving, the more does it dominate the whole organism to the exclusion of all other forms of activity.'

Later (p. 142) there is a hypothesis of *co-operation between tendencies:*

'Tendencies springing from different propensities, if they set towards and find their satisfaction in a common goal, merge into one striving or conation which derives its energy from these several sources; such striving is proportionately intense and sustained.'

About the propensity '*anger*' he has the following hypothesis:

'It seems to be the universal law of this propensity (both in men and animals) that it is called into play by thwarting or obstruction of any other active tendency.'

In a rather long paragraph (p. 150) a very important hypothesis about *the origin of emotions* is hidden:

'If, on any occasion when some propensity is strongly excited within you, the situation is a is a familiar one with which you can deal by some well-directed activity, your energy flows out in such activity, you vigorously act or plan to act. Such overt outwardly directed activity, involving welldefined cognition and well-directed striving, seems to drain off into these channels the greater part of the energy released; and, in consequence, the emotional disturbances of the internal organs and their reflex effects on consciousness are proportionately slight. On the other hand, if there is no obvious line of effective action, nothing to be done about it, the liberated energy of the impulse finds its way more freely into the internal organs, producing greater disturbance of their functioning; hence, under such conditions, the emotional quality of the experience is more prominent. This is the element of truth in the statement, made by many authors, that emotion is experienced only when and if action is checked.'

One explicitly formulted hypothesis is called '*the law of depth of feeling*' (p. 161):

'feeling is deep or profound in proportion to the extent of the system within which it plays its role.'

And finally three explicitly formulated hypotheses about '*the organization of the affective life*' can be found in E. M. (p. 209):

'first: *the energy of a propensity becomes concentrated upon some one member (or special group of members) of that class of objects to which the propensity responds instinctively* ...'

'Secondly, a propensity becomes responsive to an object of a new kind, an object to which it was natively inaccessible...' (p. 210).

'a third principle, namely, *an object resembling in certain respects the instinctive or natively given object of the propensity may, under favourable conditions, evoke that propensity and become its habitual object.*' (p. 210).

As may be more clearly seen from the reformulation of the above mentioned hypotheses in the following, almost all of these are of the type which, in the modified classification of *Spence*, exclusively deals with the inter-relations between *hypothetical* variables. Relations to *empirical* variables are only seldom and vaguely formulated. The relations to the *independent* empirical variables are almost never specified.

RECONSTRUCTION OF THE THEORY

As can be seen from the analysis of McDougall's theory in the previous passage it is *a very unsystematic theory*, and therefore it is very important to make a systematic reconstruction. The reconstruction will be made on the basis of the definitions and hypotheses quoted in two sections on the presuppositions and on the theory of motivation.

The Presuppositions

Even though McDougall's theory is far from being a fully developed deductive theory, and even though no actual meta-theory has been formulated, McDougall has formulated explicitly the presuppositons of the theory (especially in the preface to the second edition of E. M.), so that it would be most correct also to deal with them in the reconstruction. However, the presuppositions cannot in this case be taken as statements which—as in a real meta-theory—deal with the theory without being part of the theory as such. The four presuppositions quoted in the summary of the theory will be reformulated in the following way:

1. *The principle of hormism:* Psychic activity is a purposive teleological-deterministic process (which differs from a mechanistic-deterministic process).

2. *The principle of interacting dualism:* Teleological, psychic processes and mechanistic, physical processes *interact*. The psychic activity of the individual (the purposive, intelligent striving) is determined by a complex '*mental structure*' which is a hypothetical construction.

3. *The principle of evolution:* A continuity can be found in the biological development from the simplest animal forms to Man, and the phylogenetic development is recapitulated in ontogeny.

McDougall's first and second presupposition have thus been combined in '*the principle of hormism*', while his third presupposition has been named '*the principle of evolution*'. McDougall's fourth presupposition and his (previously quoted) psycho-physical presupposition (from Chapter 1) are both combined in '*the principle of interacting dualism*'.

McDougall's Theory of Motivation

The definitions and hypotheses quoted in the section on the theory of motivation have been reformulated and systematized in the following way:

Hypothesis 1: The behavior of Man and animals is mainly caused by 'propensities,' 'emotions,' and 'abilities'; in Man also by 'sentiments,' 'tastes,' and 'character.'

Definition 1: '*Propensities*' are innate dispositions which, together with a stimulus from the environment, cause a *tendency* (striving, impulse, drive) towards a goal.

Definition 2: '*Abilities*' are innate dispositions which determine certain achievements (problem-solving and learning-processes) when they are activated by a tendency.

Definition 3: '*Instincts*' are innate combinations, typical of the species, of a 'propensity' and an 'ability.' They appear only to a very small degree in Man.

Definition 4: '*Emotions*' are conditions where a flow of energy goes to the internal organs, produced when external behavior caused by a tendency is blocked.

Definition 5: '*Sentiments*' are systems of propensities which, through the experience (learning processes) of the individual, become functionally related to a 'cognitive ability' so that tendencies are activated when the ability is activated by the perception of a certain object (or class of objects). '*Tastes*' are sentiments whose 'objects' are forms of activity.

Definition 6: '*Character*' is an individual's system of sentiments which is organized and functions under the influence of the innate *temperament* of the individual (i. e. the way in which the innate propensities function—probably determined by hormones)[6]).

Besides the first very general hypothesis with the subsequent six definitions of the variables in question, the following more specific hypotheses are proposed for the reconstruction of theory. They are reformulations of the hypotheses quoted at the end of the previous section.

Hypothesis 2: When a propensity is activated its tendency is active until the goal has been reached (or the organism exhausted).

Hypothesis 3: The more intense a tendency is, the more it will dominate the behavior of the organism (exluding the behavior caused by other tendencies).

Hypothesis 4: If tendencies can be satisfied by a common goal, they cause only one single common action whose intensity and duration is determined by the number and the strength of the individual tendencies.

Hypothesis 5: On the origin of emotions: A. The more frustrated (checked or blocked) an action becomes, the more the energy of the tendency will flow to the internal organs, and the more emotionally dominated, therefore, the state of the organism will become. *B.* The easier the action is carried through, the less emotionally dominated the state of the organism will become. *C.* The emotion roused by the frustration appears subjectively as dislike or dissatisfaction with a specific quality depending upon the kind of the frustrated tendency.

Hypothesis 6: When a partly frustrated action is carried through until the goal is reached, the satisfaction achieved is stronger than usual, and the change in the emotional state of the organism caused by this will subjectively appear as a feeling pleasure with a special quality depending upon the kind of the satisfied tendency.

Hypothesis 7: The specific propensity 'aggression', which has a tendency to remove or destroy the frustrating object, is activated by the frustration of a tendency.

Hypothesis 8: The more inclusive a system of tendencies which is being frustrated or satisfied, the more intense the emotional state (and the experienced emotion) of the organism.

---

[6]) As is seen here, 'temperament' and 'temper' are combined, since 'the personal qualities' (by which McDougall's 'temperament' was defined) are regarded as being equal to 'temper' (the different ways in which innate propensities can function).

Hypothesis 9 includes 3 hypotheses about the learning processes which determine the organization of propensities into systems (sentiments and character): *A*. The tendencies of a propensity are, because of the learning processes, gradually being concentrated around one single member (or a special group of members) of that class of objects to which the propensity originally reacted. *B*. Through a learning process ('conditioning') a propensity can be brought to react to a quite new class of objects. *C*. A propensity may, through learning processes, be brought to react to an object which in certain respects is similar to the constitutionally activating object.

Conclusion

In conclusion, therefore it seems that McDougall's theory is not a very highly developed one, but even as a classifying theory it is very *unsystematical*. Its hypothetical variables are rarely reductively (operationistically) defined, and they lack exactly formulated relations to the empirical variables. Its hypotheses are only qualitative, and often they are not explicitly formulated. It is therefore very *difficult to control empirically*.

But in spite of these logical and epistemological disadvantages, McDougall's theory has been of great importance to psychology. First of all he is one of the first to stress how important it is to make psychology *an objective science* which can be of value to other sciences and in practical life. Next, he has put great emphasis upon *the importance of comparative studies* for the psychology of Man; and last, but not least: McDougall is one of the psychologists who has most forcefully *stressed the importance of motivation*.

McDougall was at the same time too versatile and too original to join or to establish a 'school', but maybe this is why he has achieved a great and lasting influence upon the development of psychology.

References

1. William McDougall: An Introduction to Social Psychology (1908).
2. — Psychology, the Study of Behavior (1912).
3. – An Outline of Psychology (1923).
4. – An Outline of Abnormal Psychology (1926).
5. – The Energies of Men (1932).
6. F. V. Smith: The System of William McDougall (in The Explanation of Human Behaviour 1951).

Chapter 6

Tolman's Theory

The American psychologist *Edward Chase Tolman* (1886–1961) became known in psychology due to his often quoted work '*Purposive Behavior in Animals and Men*' (1932), which was the result of several years of experimental and theoretical work and in many ways was both an integration of contemporary schools in psychology and something new in theoretical psychology. This work was followed by a series of papers of which the most well known are 'Operational Behaviorism and Current Trends in Psychology' (1936), 'Determiners of Behavior at a Choice Point' (1938), and 'Cognitive Maps in Rats and Men' (1948). These together with a series of papers from both before and after 1932 were published in 1951 with the heading: '*Collected Papers in Psychology.*' The latest theoretical-systematical work is his papers, '*A Psychological Model,*' published in Parson, Shils et al, 'Towards a General Theory of Action' (1951, p. 279–365). But as this latest work is not his most conprehensive one, this chapter will deal with the following the works: 'Purposive Behavior in Animals and Men'[1]) and 'A Psychological Model'[2]), with most emphasis upon the first one.

THE STRUCTURE OF THE THEORY

Summary of the Theory

Tolman gives a summary of *the content* of this theory in P. B. p. 406–409 in connection with a diagram (figure 72).

The system consists of: 1) independent variables ('the initiating (independent) causes of behavior'), 2) 'intervening variables' (or 'behavior-determinants' as they are often called in P. B.), and 3) behavior as such.

1. *The independent variables* or causes of behavior are stimuli (S), heritage (H), previous training (T), and 'the initiating physiological state' (P). The two variables, heritage (H) and training (T), influence the existence (the strength) and course of the other variables in some rather undefined way. The initiating physiological

---

[1]) In future abbreviated to P. B.
[2]) In future abbreviated to P. M.

state (P) determines which stimuli the organism reacts upon, so that these two independent variables together cause a series of 'intervening variables.'

2. *The 'intervening variables'* or 'behavior-determinants' consist of three factors, namely: a) 'capacities,' b) 'immanent determinants,' and c) 'behavior-adjustments.'

a. '*Capacities*' are 'intervening variables' directly caused by the two independent variables, heritage (H) and training (T). They influence the other 'intervening variables,' or rather, they are factors in the equations which represent the functional relations between the different variables.

b. '*Immanent determinants*' include two kinds of intervening variables, namely 'purposes', or 'demands', and 'cognitions', which also include two kinds: 'means-end-readiness' and 'expections' ('perception', 'mnemonization', and 'inference').

c. '*Behavior-adjustment*' which is defined as 'the non-overtly observable surrogate for an actual running-back-and-forth.' 'It constitutes ideation in contrast to simple awareness.'

3. *Behavior* as such is indirectly caused by the independent variables S, P, T, and H through the intervening variables, whose complicated co-operation can be seen in Tolman's diagram (figure 72 in P. B.). The individual variables and their functional relations will be more closely analyzed in the following section.

The content of *Tolman's theory in P. M.* is mainly the same, but the different variables have been given other names. *The independent variables* are for the most part the same, only training is *not* counted as an independent variable.

Also *the intervening variables* are mainly the same, namely: 'Capacities and Temperamental Traits' (corresponding to 'capacities' in P. B.), 'Needsystem' (corresponding to 'demands'), 'Belief-Value-Matrix' (corresponding to 'means-end-readiness'), and 'Immediate Behavior Space' (corresponding to 'behavior-adjustment'), plus 'Restructured Behavior-Space' which is a result of 'locomotion, learning,' and 'psychodynamic mechanisms' (this variable does not correspond directly to anything in P. B.).

The behavior as such is caused directly by an intervening variable called 'locomotion,' which again is directly caused by the other above mentioned intervening variables. The complicated co-operation of the different variables can be seen from Tolman's diagrams (figure 1 and figure 2 in P. M.).

Tolman analyzes the presuppositions of his theory himself in P. B. by indicating its relation to other systems (p. 417–423). He calls his theory a 'Purposive Behaviorism,' by which he indicates that it is dependent upon both Behaviorism and 'Purposivism'; furthermore it is dependent upon Gestalt psychology.

'A Purposive Behaviorism agrees with a strict behaviorism in asserting that organisms, their behavior and the environmental and organic conditions which induce the latter, are all that there is to be studied. It differs from a strict behaviorism such as that of Watson, Weiss, or of Mayer —in that for a purposive behaviorism behavior qua molar has characteristic descriptive properties all its own ...' (p. 418): 'For a Purposive Behaviorism, behavior, as we have seen, is purposive, cognitive, and molar, i. e., "gestalted." Purposive Behaviorism is a molar, not a molecular, behaviorism, but it is none the less a behaviorism. Stimuli and responses and the behavior-determinants of responses are all that it finds to study.'

The relation to *Gestalt psychology* is described in the following way (p. 419):

'Next, it may be asked in how far the present system, asserting as it does that behavior has meaning, is molar, and does not break up into atomistically defined reflex units, is a Gestalt Psychology'.

But Tolman stresses the following differences between his Purposive Behaviorism and orthodox Gestalt theory: Gestalt theory is a mentalistic or introspective psychology, whereas his is behavioristic. He emphasises *the analysis* of the variables of the theory more than do the Gestalt psychologists, and finally the variables of his theory are purposive and not only cognitive.

The relation to '*Purposivism*', especially to that of McDougall, is seen from the fact that Tolman owes the name 'Purposive Behaviorism' to McDougall (used in 'Psychologies of 1925'). Moreover Tolman maintains (p. 422):

'That McDougall's 'instincts' are in many ways similar to what we have called the appetites and aversions'.

But there is an important difference:

'whereas, for McDougall the hormic drives... seem to be in the last analysis, mentalistic, introspectively defined affairs for us, they are... but functionally defined entities—quite objective variables...' (p. 422); and he continues: 'Our purposivism is, in short, not a fundamental or metaphysical purposivism', but 'In a word, the fact of purpose, as we conceive it, is an objective fact. It is the fact that behavior is docile relative to objectively determinable ends. Our psychology is a purposivism; but it is an objective, behavioristic purposivism, not a mentalistic one' (p. 423).

In the last chapter of P. B. Tolman gives a presentation of the general philosophical background of his theory which must be called '*pragmatism*,' as he takes all scientific knowledge as a map of existence, the purpose of which is satisfaction of human needs. He writes (p. 430):

'That "map" knowledge is "true" which "works", given the particular behavior-needs and the particular behavior-capacities of the type of organism gathering such knowledge. Physics and purposive behaviorism are both, therefore, but humanly conditioned, "behavioral" maps... In conclusion, it seems—we ask the philosopher—that we are asserting, are we not, a pragmatism? For we are asserting that all human knowledge, including physics, purposive behaviorism and our own present remarks, are but a resultant of, and limited by, human behavioral needs and human behavioral capacities. Outside reality is for us human beings that which our limited biological needs and our limited biological capacities find it to be ... But what outside reality may be, in and for itself, abstracted from all human behavioral needs and all human behavioral capacities, we do not, cannot, and need not know.'

Later Tolman's general philosophical outlook changed, under the influence of Bridgeman and Stevens, into a more positivistic-operationistic direction. Thus he writes in 'Operational Behaviorism' (p. 115 in 'Collected Papers'):

'I am going to present a brief statement of my own brand of psychology. I shall call it Operational Behaviorism ... the term 'operational' has been chosen with two different meanings in mind. In the first place, I have chosen it to indicate a certain general positivistic attitude now being taken by many modern physicists and philosophers.'

In this thesis he gives, moreover, the first detailed presentation of the concept of 'intervening variable', which later has been used extensively in psychological theory.

While Gestalt psychology was just one among many parts of the total background of Tolman's theory in P. B., Lewin's field-theory, derived from Gestalt psychology, is a very important part of the background of Tolman's theorie in P. M. But it will be dealt with more thoroughly in the following analysis where Tolman's theory is placed in the different classifications of psychological theories.

Level of Development of the Theory

It is rather difficult to classify Tolman's theory with regard to the level of development. But it is probably most correct to classify it as *a classifying theory on the point of changing into a deductive theory. The* system includes a lot of practical classifications which make it possible to formulate laws, but these laws are only formulated as a program and not in such a way that they allow the exact deduction of phenomena, even under the most standardized laboratory situations (as does for example Hull's theory). Tolman describes, defines, and classifies the different variables rather precisely, but he only hints at their inter-functional relations with arrows in diagrams and with a few vaguely formulated qualitative functional relations. Even in his latest systematical presentation, 'A Psychological Model', he writes (p. 284): 'All I shall do is to develop my own model and to *indicate* the sorts of interconnecting causal functions assumed in it'. Tolman has, however, in one article in Psychological Review (1939), 'Prediction of Vicarious Trial and Error by Means of the Schematic Sow-bug' tried to formulate a detailed theory of a rather special form of behavior which should be rather exact under standardized laboratory conditions (but still without any quantitative formulations). It can thus be seen that the level of development of Tolman's theory is deductive-programmatic (between classifying and actual deductive systems).

Constructive or Reductive Theory

Regarding the classification of psychological theories as *reductive* and *constructive* theories, Tolman's theory can be classified as *a typical constructive theory*. The pioneering element in his theory was that it explicitly opposed the reductive principles, which had till then been dominating in behavioristic psychology, and preferred to formulate a constructive theory. This is correlated closely with the molar character of Tolman's theory. Tolman writes in P. B. (p. 8):

'Behavior as such cannot, at any rate at present, be deduced from a mere enumeration of the muscle twitches, the mere motions *qua* motions, which make it up. It must as yet be studied first hand and for its own sake,' and further (p. 416): 'Our task, *as psychologists* is the collecting and ordering of the *molar behavior* facts per se. And this task can, in large part, be performed in relative ignorance of both physiology and neurology.'

Tolman has also written a whole article in Psych. Review (1938) on this subject alone (can be found in 'Collected Papers'). He writes here (p. 179):

'I would define physiology as a study of the laws determining the *activities* of muscles and glands; I would define psychology as a study of the laws determining the *behavior* of whole organisms; and I would define sociology as the study of the laws determining the *conduct* of groups of organisms.

Accepting these definitions, one's first reaction concerning the interrelations of the three sciences would be to think of physiology as the most basic, psychology as the next most basic, and sociology as the least basic—or, in other words, to conceive the facts and laws of psychology as dependent upon those of physiology and the facts and laws of sociology as dependent upon those of psychology. But the thesis that I am actually going to try to uphold here is the reverse and, at first sight, seemingly absurd one, to wit: that the facts and laws of psychology are, rather, in some part dependent upon those of sociology and that the facts and laws of physiology are similarly in some part dependent upon those of psychology.'

It can thus be seen that Tolman's theory is a typical constructive theory, and as such it was an important pioneer work in theoretical psychology (in connection with introduction of the concept of 'intervening variable', which is a hypothetical or symbolic *construction*).

Mentalistic or Behavioristic Theory

Since Tolman characterizes his theory as 'behaviorism' (but with varying adjectives: 'Purposive', 'molar', and 'operational'), it would seem very easy to classify it as a behavioristic theory. It is, however, not really so simple, first of all Tolman does not (completely) refuse to use introspective protocol statements (and methods). He writes about this (P. B., p. 244):

'In short, the dicata of "introspection" present to the listener nothing which, theoretically at least, cannot be conveyed by other more gross forms of behavior.'

Besides, his hypothetical variables are of the neutral-formal type which are *not* to be interpreted as neuro-physiological variables (as the theory in that case would be reductive). Neither are they to be interpreted as phenomenological variables, although his use of mentalistic terminology has made many 'pure behaviorists' do so. He writes about this (p. 3, P. B.):
Thus Tolman's theory must—according to both its hypothetical variables and its protocol statements—be classified as a neutral-formal theory (in spite of his own description, 'behaviorism').

'"Mental processes" are for the behaviorists, naught but inferred determinants of behavior, which ultimately are deducible from behavior and these inferred determinants are both objectively defined types of entity."

Molecular or Molar Theory

It is almost obvious that Tolman's theory must be classified as *a molar theory*, since it, as mentioned, was Tolman who introduced this classification in theoretical psychology in order to be able to separate the purely physiological-psychological (molecular) theories and experiments. The difference between the two classes of theories consists (according to Tolman, cf. Chapter 3) in the difference between *the descriptive units*, which can be either microscopic (processes in the sense organs, the nervous system, and the muscles), or macroscopic (the total behavior of the total organism in relation to the environment). But even though there is only a difference in degree between these classes, it is not difficult to classify Tolman's theory as a molar theory. And even though this classification, as mentioned in Chapter 3, has later been misused in psychology, the classification must be considered one of Tolman's most important contributions to theoretical psychology.

Field-Theory or Mechanistic Theory

With regard to this classification it is rather easy to classify Tolman's theory as *a field-theory*, explaining behavior as caused by a totality of independent and hypothetical variables with rather complicated interactional relations. In his theory Tolman explicitly discribes certain functional relations as field-relations. Thus he writes in P. B. (p. 177, Chapter XI) 'Inference—The Means-end field'):

Further experiments undoubtedly would discover many other such general *field-relations* to be added to such a list[3]), even in the case of rats. Means-end-relations are, fundamentally, field-relations ... The means-end-set-up is not a single linear set-up but a field set-up.'

Besides, Tolman compares his own theory with Lewin's, and after the comparison he writes (p. 179):

'The similarity of this doctrine of *Topologie* and *Feldkräfte* to the present one of the means-end-field, is obvious. The two doctrines really support and reinforce one another.' And even more directly he writes (p. 37): 'In general, it is to be said that a great deal of the doctrine to be outlined in the present treatise seems to bear a close relationship to the doctrine of Lewin, as the latter is to be gleaned from his writings and from those of his students.'

In P. M. the similarity with Lewin's theory is even greater. He writes here (p. 283):

'The theory to be presented here will then be quite frankly one which develops (by various analogies drawn from simple physics and mechanics, from Lewin's 'topological and vector' psychology, and from common experience) a sui generis model.'

In P. M. he frequently uses diagrams which resemble Lewin's but apparently he sees them as having only purely pedagogical and illustrative functions (and not geometrical deductive functions as Lewin does). But even if Tolman's theory might also be described as a topological psychology, it may certainly be *classified as a field-theory.*

Deterministic or Statistical Theory

With regard to the classification deterministic versus statistic, it is rather easy to classify Tolman's theory as *a deterministic theory*, as it is an attempt to depict the functional relations (and not only the statistical correlations) between the different variables, necessary to explain the behavior. But Tolman writes very little explicitly about the problem apart from the following passage in P. B. (p. 422):

'And, even should it finally turn out, on a basis of further experiments, that there is for the behavior of organisms, just as for the behavior of electrons, some principle of ultimate indeterminateness (i. e., a kind of Heisenberg's uncertainty principle), this need not lead us to assume or suppose any metaphysically "other" as "butting in" to the course of organic nature. The finding of such an uncertainty principle would, to be sure, mean important and exciting things. It would mean that we must talk in terms of probabilities, of statistical averages, rather than in terms of unique individual cases. It would not mean, or at any rate would not need to mean, however, any metaphysical bifurcation or dualism—any breakdown in the possibility of final deterministic, descriptions per se."

---

[3]) The list in question contains: 'distance, direction hierarchicalness, common final pathness; multiple tracks, mutual opposition between alternative paths, the identity of the same detour when encountered from opposite ends, and the closing or fitting together of the successive parts of one total path.'

Even if Tolman's statement is not quite clear, his idea seems to be that for some time to come it is necessary to try to construct deterministic theories in psychology.

The Model

The model which gives a comprehensive presentation of Tolman's theory (see figure 72 in P. B. and figure 1 and 2 in P. M.) is rather complicated with a system of interacting variables (as in Lewin's model). But nevertheless it is a step forward from the simple S—O—R model, as is seen from the classification in independent variables, intervening variables, and dependent variables (in which respect, though, it differs from Lewin's model).

Summary

This analysis of Tolman's theory may be summarized as follows: *Tolman's theory is a classifying theory in the process of changing into a deductive theory; it is constructive, neutral-formal, molar, field-theoretical, and deterministic.*

MOTIVATION DEFINITION AND HYPOTHESES

Motivation Variables in P. B.

Of the independent, empirical variables in 'Purposive Behavior' only one can be described as a motivation variable, namely P. In the glossary (p. 447) it is defined in the following way: '*Initiating physiological state.* The releasing physiological cause of an appetite or an aversion.'

In the same place it is also pointed out that 'this initiating state is a metabolically aroused condition' when included in an appetite, but when we are talking about an aversion 'this initiating state results from: a) a specific environmental presence plus b) an innate, or acquired, means-end-readiness (sign-gestalt-readiness).'

It can clearly be seen from the quotation that P is an *empirical* variable and a *functional* variable. This last is maybe only true of appetite, as P with regard to aversion should rather be classified as a *disposition* variable. Thus, under 'Resumé of Doctrine' (p. 275), the three 'constitutive phases' of aversion are said to be: '1) an initiating physiological state, which however is relative enduring and of constant strength for any given organism...'

Another motivation variable is '*demand*' (D), or 'purpose' as it is also called. It is defined in the following way:

'*Demand.* An innate or acquired urge to get to or from some given instance or type of environmental presence or of physiological quiesence or disturbance. Demands (i. e. purposes) and cognitions together constitute the two fundamental types of immanent determinat. A demand, or purpose, is objectively defined, and testified to, whenever an organism persists through trial and error to or from a given type or instance of goal-object or situation and shows a capacity for docility in thus persisting to or from.'

In the above definition it is quite clear that 'demand' is a *hypothetical* variable, or 'behavior-determinant' as Tolman calls them in P. B.—only later does he introduce the well-known description 'intervening variables.' It is also quite clear that demand is a *functional* variable, for even though it is classified as 'innate or acquired' in the beginning of the definition—something which might indicate that it was a disposition variable—it can be seen from the operationistc part of the definition that it must be a functional variable.

If this definition is compared to the previous definition of 'physiological state' it becomes clear that 'demands' are classified as '*appetites*' and '*aversions*' determining *positive* purposive behavior and *negative* avoidance behavior respectively.

According to Tolman's own classification of 'immanent determinants' (e. g. p. 446), which groups them into '(a) purposes (demands) and (b) cognitions', there should not be any other actual motivation variables in his system. But the mentioned variables are very closely related to one variable which Tolman himself classifies under 'cognitions', namely '*sign-gestalt-readiness*' and '*sign-gestalt-expectation*'. *They will therefore be analyzed further.*

Tolman uses the descriptions 'means-end-readiness' and 'sign-gestalt-readiness' as synonyms. He prefers the last one because it emphasizes the totality quality. These terms are, however, defined with little difference in choice of words. Thus '*means-end-readiness*' is defined as:

'a selective condition which an organism, due to innate endowment or past training, brings with him to specific concrete stimulus situations. It is set in action by virtue of a demand ... It causes the organism to be responsive to stimuli ...' (p. 456).

In the definition of 'sign-gestalt-readiness' (p. 454) it is described as 'a generalized "universal" propensity.'

In my opinion the classification of this variable is somewhat ambiguous. There is, however, no doubt that sign-gestalt-readiness is a *hypothetical* variable, since Tolman explicitly writes (p. 456) that 'it is one of the most important kinds of immanent determinant.' It can also be seen quite clearly from the quotation that 'sign-gestalt-readiness' is a *disposition variable.* Moreover, Tolman has the parallel terms 'sign-gestalt-*expectation*' and 'means-end-*expectation*' to indicate the corresponding functional variable, as this is defined as 'the specific and particular embodiment of a means-end-readiness' (p. 449). Maybe it is a little difficult to distinguish between the disposition variable and the variable 'means-end-capacity'. The latter is only a general disposition variable, however, that determines which readiness-variables can be formed in an individual. It is most difficult to decide whether sign-gestalt-readiness is a motivation variable or cognitive variable. Tolman himself gives the following classification (p. 446):

'Immanent determinants subdivide into two fundamental kinds: (a) purposes (demands) and (b) cognitions. The cognitions, in their turn, still further subdivide into (i) means-end-readiness and (ii) expectations.'

Thus Tolman explicitly classifies 'readiness' as a cognitive variable. But at the same time this variable is so intimately connected to motivation variables that it is difficult to separate them from each other. This has already been shown in the above and becomes even clearer in the definition of '*drive*'.

This term is a generic term which includes several variables. Thus Tolman writes (p. 275) in 'Resumé of Doctrine':

'The fundamental drives or motivations underlying all behaviour are to be conceived as certain, innately provided, general physiological demands plus certain more or less vague sign-gestalt-readiness as how to satisfy these demands.'

He adds that these fundamental drives can be classified as 'appetites' and 'aversions,' each of which have 'three constitutive phases,' namely 1) 'an initiating physiological state,' 2) 'the demand,' and 3) 'the sign-gestalt-readiness.'

As can be seen from the above, sign-gestalt-readiness forms a 'constitutive phase' in 'drive,' elsewhere (p. 443) described as 'the general term used to designate a motivation.' But in the above quoted definition of 'immanent determinant' he classified sign-gestalt-readiness under 'cognitions' which were explicitly distinguished from purposes. Tolman's theory is, in other words, not systematic or it does not clearly distinguish between motivation variables and cognitive variables.

It has already been mentioned several times that Tolman classifies drives as 'appetites' and 'aversions'. These two classes include, according to 'a tentative list' (p. 288):

Appetites:	*Aversions:*
Food-hunger	Fright (injury-avoidance)
Sex-hunger	Pugnacity (interference-avoidance)
Excretion-hungers	
Specific contact-hungers	
Rest-hunger	
Sensory-motor-hungers	
(i. e. the esthetic and play hunger)	

Besides this classification Tolman has another classification of drives as '*first-order drives*' (the above mentioned appetites and aversions) and '*second-order drives*.' The 'second-order drives' are defined in the following way:

'*Drives (second-order)*. The term second-order drives is used to designate certain secondary demands and sign-gestalt-readiness (e. g. gregariousness, curiosity, imitation, self-assertion, self-abasement, etc.). Such second-order drives to be ancillary in their effects to the ends of the first-order drives.

'A second-order drive, in so far as it is innate, is to be designated as an aversion going off innately in response to a relatively general type of environmental situation ...'

As can be seen from the quotation, these second-order drives can, according to

Tolman, be *innate*. They are, however, referred to as second-order drives, because they are subordinated (are means-end-related to) the first-order drives. It can also be seen from the quotation that Tolman does not count 'initiating physiological state' as a second-order drive in the definition, because he considers it doubtful whether it is necessary or practical to do so or not.

Motivation Hypotheses in P. B.

Apart from the definitions quoted and the 'Resumé of Doctrine' (p. 275) there are no explicitly formulated hypotheses in P. B. The relations between all variables in the theory are presented in the diagram figure 72 page 407. According to this the functional relations may be roughly described in the following way:

An 'Initiating Physiological State' (P) determines a 'Demand' (D), which again determines a 'Sign-Gestalt-Expectation' (Exp.). This sign-gestalt-expectation is, however, also determined by a stimulus (S) and several cognitive functions, but it would lead too far to deal with these here. The existence of these *functional* variables is also determined by different forms of 'readiness' plus other general *disposition* variables ('capacities').

Motivation Variables in P. M.

In 'A Psychological Model' the independent, *empirical* motivation variable is referred to as '*drive*,' or more elaborately: 'conditions of drive arousal or satiation.' It is clearly pointed out (p. 280) that it is 'organ and tissue states which ultimately define 'drives' as they are discussed here.'

The quotation indicates clearly that 'drive' in P. M. is an *empirical* motivation variable, while drive in P. B. was a generic term for the hypothetical variables 'demand' and 'sign-gestalt-readiness' plus also in some cases the empirical variable 'initiating physiological state.'

'Need' is the other important motivation variable in P. M. Tolman writes about this variable and its relation to drive (p. 288):

> 'let us consider first the concept of "need" itself. It is to be distinguished from the concept of "physiological drive", which is to be conceived as an independent variable. In most previous psychological literature the tendency has been to use the two terms interchangeably and the two concepts have not been clearly distinguished. I propose, however, to differentiate between them and to use the term "drive" for an initiating physiological condition only and to use the term "need" for a postulated resultant, intervening, behavioral process to be defined in the last analysis as a readiness to get to and to manipulate in consummatory fashion (or get from) certain other types of object.'

This statement is quoted in full because it among other things explicitly shows that 'need' is a *hypothetical* variable of the *neutral-formal* type (as are all Tolman's hypothetical variables in both P. B. and P. M.), The quotation also contains an interesting suggestion for the more exact use of the terms 'need' and 'drive'.

Unfortunately Tolman has not succeeded in getting others to follow his suggestion. Although many psychologists do now distinguish between the empirical and the hypothetical motivation variables, they often use quite different terms, in many cases even the *same* terms but with reversed meaning ('need' for the empirical and 'drive' for the hypothetical variable). In some ways Tolman has contributed to this terminological confusion himself with his many and constantly changing terminological suggestions.

It remains to be said that need must be classified as a *functional* variable. Thus in the operationistic definition of 'need' (p. 335) Tolman says:

'a need is to be defined as a readiness or tendency to persist toward and to perform a consumatory response ...

'Once the consummatory response to the standard goal object has been achieved, the given tendency ... *ceases*.'

Especially the last (italicized) word in the quotation shows that 'need' is a functional variable.

In P. M. Tolman classifies 'needs' in *three* classes (p. 321 and 335):

1. '*Primary needs*,' as for example hunger, thirst, etc.
2. '*Secondary* or socio-relational needs,' as for example 'affiliation,' 'dominance,' etc. They are assumed to be *innate*.
3. '*Tertiary* needs' 'which must definitely be assumed to be the product of learning, which are fairly universal in any given population. The tertiary needs will consist in wants to get to and from ... certain relatively universal types of cultural provided goals,' as for example 'wealth, academic success, etc.' (p. 321 and 322).

As can be seen from the above quotation, Tolman's classification is more differentiated than the usual ones (including primary and secondary needs). He does not give a complete list, but only mentions examples.

It must be pointed out that a novel feature in S. M. is that all 'needs' form a '*Need System*'. This includes—apart from the three classes already mentioned—a special need which is described with a term taken from Freud, namely 'libido'. By this term Tolman indicates 'some physiological energy' which 'vary in average magnitude from individual to individual.' It is also pointed out (p. 289) that 'this libido-need has no specific goals of its own,' but determines the amount of energy available for the other needs.

The other variables will only be mentioned briefly.

The *empirical* variables include—besides drive—'stimulus situation' and 'heredity, age, sex, drugs, endocrines, etc.' These latter determine directly the only actual *hypothetical disposition* variables in the system, namely 'Capacity and Temperamental Traits' which again determine the existence of *the hypothetical functional* variables. These include, besides Need System, 'Belief-Value-Matrix'. This variable—or rather this system of variables—corresponds according to Tolman himself to his 'means-end-readiness', it is simply more divided. It is thus a *cognitive* variable, but as in P. B. the difference is not clear. The variable 'value' in 'Belief-Value-Matrix' especially is very directly functionally related to needs. A third system of hypothetical functional variables is 'Immediate Behavior Space', which corresponds to 'Behavior Adjustment' in P. M. or more or less to Lewin's 'Lifespace'. It is a neutral-formal variable which is a substitute for the mentalistic variable 'consciousness'. In this variable system three variables, namely 'need-push', 'valence', and 'field-force', are directly functionally related to 'value' (and thus indirectly to needs). As is indicated by the name 'immediate behavior space' this variable system is the one which most distinctly consists of present *functional* variables, while 'Need System' and 'Belief-Value-Matrix' are conditions which may be said to stand between the actual disposition variables ('capacity and temperamental traits') and the real functional variables ('behavior space' and 'locomotion').

Finally it should be mentioned that 'immediate behavior space' determines behavior through a hypothetical variable called '*locomotion*'.

When this system is compared with *Lewin's, a noticeable similarity* is found. The most essential *difference* is that Tolman includes 'capacities and temperamental traits' which represent individual differences. Also Tolman's theory has the 'Belief-Value-Matrix' which does not correspond directly to anything in Lewin's theory (not to the same degree as 'behavior space' and 'need system').

Motivation Hypotheses in P. M.

In P. M. Tolman has some *explicitly* formulated hypotheses, which all deal with the inter-functional relations between needs (especially between 'libido' and other needs). They are all formulated on page 319 and will be quoted in the following reconstruction of Tolman's theory.

For the sake of completeness it should finally be pointed out that quite a few *implicit* hypotheses can be found, depicted by arrows in Tolman's diagrams.

RECONSTRUCTION OF THE THEORY

This last section of the chapter will present a reconstruction of the theory. As the theory in 'A Psychological Model' may be considered Tolman's *own* reconstruction of his theory in 'Purposive Behavior', only a reconstruction of the theory in 'A Psychological Model' will be given here.

Tolman's theory is one of the most comprehensive and many-sided psychological theories, but it contains very few explicit definitions and hypotheses (partly because of its short and programmatic character). Therefore the reconstruction will be made with particular aim at this shortcoming and only with details when the motivation variables are dealt with.

Tolman's use of hypothetical or 'intervening' variables is one of the most characteristic things in his theory, and this will therefore be explicitly formulated in a primary hypothesis.

Hypothesis 1: Behavior is a function of a totality of inter-dependent hypothtical variables, which again is a function of independent, empirical variables.

Next it will be practical to make an explicit classification of the independent, empirical variables:

Definition 1: The independent empirical variables in a psychological theory are:

1) the stimulus situation.
2) 'conditions of drive arousal or satiation.'
3) 'individual-difference-producing variables: heredity, age, sex, drugs, endocrines, etc.'

Of these independent variables 'drive' is of especial interest in a theory of motivation, and it will therefore be explicitly defined in the following:

Definition 2: 'Drives' are conditions in the organs or tissues of the organism which differ from the biological optimum conditions of these systems.

It will now be practical to classify explicitly the hypothetical variables in the following way:

Hypothesis 2: The hypothetical variables of the theory consist of the following systems of variables:

1) Need System, 2) Belief-Value-Matrix, 3) Immediate Behavior Space, 4) Locomotion, 5) Restructured Behavior Space. These variable systems are functionally interrelated and related to the independent empirical variables and to the behavior.

First of all the most general of these functional relations will be formulated explicitly:

Hypothesis 3: 'Need System' is a system of hypothetical motivation variables which is a function of all present drives and the stimulus situation, and consists of several specific needs and a diffuse libido-need.

Hypothesis 4: 'Belief-Value-Matrix' is a system of hypothetical variables which is a function of a 'Need System' and the stimulus situation. In this system the variable 'value' is a direct function of a specific need.

Hypothesis 5: 'Immediate Behavior Space' is a system of hypothetical variables which is a function of the 'Belief-Value Matrix' and the stimulus situation. In this system the variables 'need-push' and 'valence' especially are direct functions of 'value.' 'Immediate Behavior Space' can be reconstructed as the result of locomotion, learning-processes, and psychodynamic mechanisms.

Hypothesis 6: 'Locomotion' is a hypothetical variable which is a function of 'Immediate Behavior Space' and of which behavior is a direct function.

The special motivation hypotheses are formulated below:

Hypothesis 7: 'Libido-need' is a hypothetical motivation variable which is a function of all present drives and the general physiological condition of the total organism and is reciprocally interrelated with the specific needs.

Hypothesis 8: A 'specific need' is a hypothetical motivation variable which is a direct function of a specific drive and also of the other present drives and the stimulus situation. The specific need, with other hypothetical variables as connecting links, is functionally releated to a specific form of behavior ('a consummatory response'), which can be used to measure that particular need.

Definition 3: The specific needs can be classified in three classes:

1) 'primary needs' including viscerogenic needs (hunger, thirst, sex, temperature, oxygen, rest, sleep, etc.) plus fear, aggression, and orientation.

2) 'secondary or socio-relational needs' including 'need gregariousness,' 'need love,' 'need approval,' 'need dominance,' 'need submission,' etc.

3) 'tertiary (acquired) needs' for 'culturally provided goals.'

At last can be added the explicitly formulated hypotheses (p. 319 in P. M.) which can be quoted here without any reformulation:

Hypothesis 9: 'Any independent physiological drive condition or stimulus which arouses a need will be assumed to do so by first increasing the total amount of charges in the libido compartment. (This compartment, it will be remembered, is conceived to be in contact with each of the specific need compartments).'

Hypothesis 10: 'The arousal of a specific need will also be assumed to involve an increased permeability of the membrane dividing such a specific-need compartment from the libido compartment so that there will be an increased flow of charges from the libido into the specific need.'

Hypothesis 11: 'It will be assumed, further, that the arousal of a specific need may also cause an increase in the permeability of the membranes dividing this specific-need compartment from certain other specific-need compartments.'

Hypothesis 12: 'Still further, such increased permeabilities of the membranes between pairs of specific compartments must be assumed to be either bidirectional or unidirectional.'

Conclusion

Even though the theory must be classified as an insufficiently developed deductive theory (a programmatic, mainly classifying system with insufficient explicit formulation of laws and definitions), Tolman is one of the psychologists who have had the greatest influence upon the development of theoretical psychology, as he has formulated a number of important meta-theoretical concepts (as for example 'intervening variable', 'molar behaviorism', etc.). Thus Tolman cannot be said to be systematical, but *he is an inspiring pioneer in theoretical psychology.*

Later developments

Before he died (1961) Tolman wrote a rather concentrated and thorough exposition of his theory, entitled 'Principles of Purposive Behavior' in *S. Koch*'s 'Psychology—A Study of a Science' (vol. 2, 1959; p. 92–157). This paper is—as are many of the contributions to Koch's work—very interesting from a meta-scientific point of view. We therefore shall make a brief analysis of it in the following pages:

The Structure of the Theory. The formal development of Tolman's last theory is like the earlier ones, a rather programmatic sketch of a deductive system. He himself expresses it thusly (p. 97):

'Apparently, I have no scientific supergo which urges me to be mathematical, deductive and axiomatic.'

And later he adds (p. 150):

'To attempt to build psychology on the analogy of *a* closed mathematical or logical system seems to me a "bad error".'

But as with Tolman's other expositions of his theory he presents here also a rather precise reformulation of his theory in big complicated diagrams (fig. 1, p. 99).

Tolman's theory remains a *constructive* theory and he expresses the belief that psychologists will have to wait 'a good long time' before 'our biochemical and neurophysiological friends' can 'catch up and help us.' (footnote 27, p. 114).

Tolman still considers himself as a 'behaviorist', a 'purposive' one. But he admits (p. 147), that:

'Køhler's designation of me as a cryptophenomenologist was probably correct.'

And later he exhibits considerable self-criticism (p. 148):

'There is, however, I would admit probably one greater defect in my cryptophenomenological position. My intervening variables seem to be less communicable to others and probably colored by special peculiarities of my own phenomenology.'

I think that what Tolman says here about his 'cryptophenomenological' theory could as well be said about every phenomenological theory.

In spite of these slightly self-ironical descriptions, I think it is most correct to classify Tolman's theory as a *neutral-formal* theory.

In the last exposition of Tolman's theory it remains *molar*.

As it readily can be seen from the diagrams Tolman's theory is a *field-theory* including rather complicated interaction among variables.

Tolman is explicit about determinism in his last theory (p. 96):

'. . . if we knew enough all responses (performances), great or small, could be predicted . . .
What I actually do as a rat psychologist is to try to predict merely the average responses of a specifically defined group of rats under a specific set of conditions. This would mean that I could expect to predict the response of the individual rat only with a certain degree of probability.'

Thus Tolman has grown to be more of a '*probability-determinist*'.

The Content of the Theory. Tolman still classifies the variables into 'independent', 'intervening' and 'dependent variables.' It is highly interesting to read Tolman's reaction to Meehl's and MacCorquodale's distinction between 'intervening variables' and hypothetical constructs':

'And intervening variables, as I conceive them, will have in part the properties of *hypothetical constructs* and not merely be intervening mathematical quantities.' (Footnote, p. 98).

I think that this quotation shows that Tolman would agree with the conclusions drawn in *this* book (Chapter 3), where it is suggested that 'intervening variables' *could* be conceived as (almost) identical to 'hypothetical constructs' with a neutral surplus meaning. We are thus in accord with Tolman in combining 'intervening variable' with 'hypothetical construct' and designating the result as 'hypothetical variable'.

If we look at Tolman's diagram (fig. 1) which describes 'approach-learning', we note that he divides 'independent variables' into 'present' and 'past'. Among these is a motivational variable symbolized as 'D_H', which stands for 'hunger drive' or rather 'hunger drive-*stimulation*' as Tolman now prefers to call it. 'Drive-stimulation' is an independent variable which can be discriminated ('even by rats'), has energizing properties and 'value-giving properties' (which means that drive-stimulation sets up both positive and negative goals).

Besides the hunger-drive-stimulation Tolman also assumes, that even in a simple case of approach-learning a 'pure curiosity drive-stimulation' and a 'drive against effort' are always at work. In this connection it is worth noting that it is the *satisfaction* of the almost always present 'curiosity drive', which is the ultimate 'effect' in Tolman's acceptance of the 'law of effect'.

The drive-stimulations are both present and past.

The other independent variables consist of the present stimuli and the sum of the past stimuli. These past stimuli are partly determined by the organism's own reactions and form a 'pattern of feedback stimuli'.

This 'pattern of feedback stimuli' has resulted in the creation of shaping of 'acquired cognitive dispositions', which are designated '*beliefs*' or 'means-end readinesses'.

These *disposition* variables combine with the present stimuli (S) and drive-stimulations (D_H) to determine some *function* variables called 'expectations, perceptions, representations, valences'. Among these are the representation of 'the actual discriminated and effective (or, if you will permit me, "perceived") drive-stimulation on that occasion'.

All these intervening variables determine in combination the dependent variable (R).

We can present a very short reconstruction of Tolman's last theory in this way:

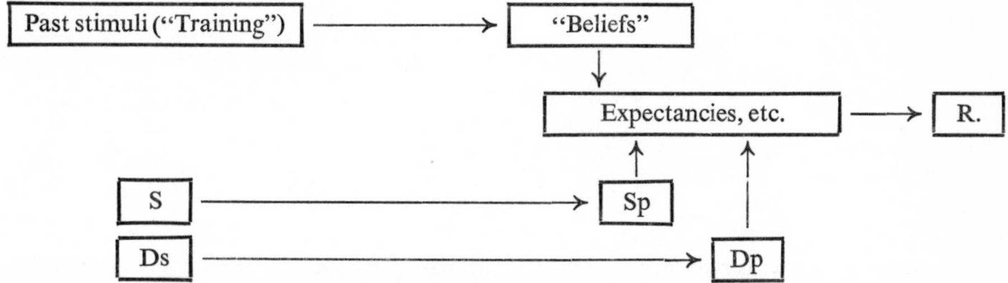

We shall not embark on a more thorough analysis of the variables[4]) but we should emphasize some of the main trends in Tolman's theory. It can easily be seen by inspecting the diagram that Tolman has preserved his original classifications into 'independent, intervening and dependent variables', and also his classification into disposition and function variables (here designated as 'means-end readinesses' contra 'expectations, perceptions, representations, valences'). These two classifications are the inventions of Tolman himself, and besides these he has introduced a clear distinction between 'present' and 'past' among the independent variables. By the invention and use of all these meta-theoretical classifications, Tolman retains his position as one of the most original and sophisticated meta-theoretical thinkers in psychology.

References

1. Smith, F. V.: The Explanation of Human Behaviour p. 239–256 (1951).
2. Murphy, G.: Historical Introduction to Modern Psychology p. 267, 272, 281–282 (1951).
3. Tolman, E. C.: Purposive Behavior in Animals and Men (1932).
4. – The Nature and Functioning of Wants (Ps. Rev. vil. 56, 1949).
5. – Collected Papers in Psychology (1951).
6. – A Psychological Model (in Parsons and Shils et al.: Toward a General Theory of Action (1951).
7. – Principles of Purposive Behavior (in S. Koch (edt.): 'Psychology—A Study of a Science' (vol. 2, 1959)).
8. Woodworth, R. S.: Contemporary Schools of Psychology, p. 103–108 (1949).

---

[4]) The interested reader is referred to Tolman's own paper in S. Koch's book.

Chapter 7

Young's Theory

The American psychologist *Paul Thomas Young* has become known through a series of experiments on food-choice which he described in a number of articles (outlined in Ps. Bull. 1941 and 1948 and in Ps. Rev. 1949 by himself). He has also written two books: 'Motivation of Behavior' (1936)[1]), which will form the main basis of this chapter, and 'Emotion in Man and Animal' (1943)[2]), of which will be studied the passages dealing with the psychology of motivation and the passages with which it differs from 'Motivation'.

Young's 'Motivation' is the only book studied in this thesis that exclusively deals with general motivation, for which reason the passages on motivation definitions and motivation hypotheses will be longer than usual.

THE STRUCTURE OF THE THEORY

Summary of the Theory

Most of chapters in 'Motivation' are about methods and empirical data. Young himself writes about his book in the preface: 'The book is factual in its approach' (p. VII). The theoretical formulations appear mainly in the concluding paragraphs of the chapters and in the last chapter.

On the basis of these paragraphs, *the content* of Young's theory may be formulated briefly thus: 'Motivation' includes *the energy-release* and *the energy-regulation* of behavior. The energy-release is caused by internal or external stimuli and is a release of chemical energy in the organism. When the release is determined by stimuli from internal organs, the energy-release (the 'motivation') produced is called a primary drive. The release of energy can also be caused by external stimuli, which then most often have an acquired connection to internal stimuli. Most often the internal stimuli are caused by processes determined by disturbance in the homeostasis of the organism and its different organs. Such a state of disturbance

---

[1]) In future abbreviated to 'Motivation'. The references to page-numbers refer, when nothing else is mentioned, to this book (7th edition, December 1950).

[2]) In future abbreviated to 'Emotion' (4th edition, July 1950).

in the organism or in one of its organs is called a need or an appetite. Often the individual experiences this as a demand, a want, a desire, or a wish. The energy-regulation is determined by *neural-mental* structures, which can partly be innate partly acquired. Especially in Man the acquired, and particularly the socially determined, energy-regulating and behavior regulating structures are of great importance. When motives are blocked or if a conflict arises between motives, a disorganization of the condition and behavior of the individual, called 'emotion', results.

In the preface to the book and in its first and its last chapter, Young has formulated *the presuppositions* of his theory. It is of great importance that he presupposes a comprehensive attitude to the psychological problems, which Young calls '*the attitudinal approach*'. He gives his reasons for this in the introductory chapter where he writes (p. 36): 'Scientific development implies a constant interaction of observing and reflecting.' And both observation and reflection is dependent upon *the attitude* of the individual, which gives the observation structure and meaning and which is formulated as logical constructions when reflecting. The changing 'isms' and schools of science—especially in the history of psychology—show the importance of the different changing attitudes of the scientists. Therefore Young finds that no single attitude or point of view should be emphasized at the expense of the others, but all possible attitudes (points of view) should be combined into one synthesis. Thus Young writes (p. 531):

'One aim which we recognize as fundamental is to formulate psychological principles so that their validity does not depend upon any particular point of view.'

With regard to psychology, two different attitudes, or points of view, have been especially important, namely the objective and the subjective attitude. Young points out that it is a question of a difference in the attitude, or point of view, on the basis of which the organism is studied, *not* a question of a difference in 'basic reality'. This assumption will be analyzed more carefully in a following passage.

This comprehensive attitude—or 'multiple-aspect hypothesis' as Young also calls it—is, with special reference to the psychology of motivation, formulated in the following way (p. 37):

'The writer assumes that there is only one kind of motivating structure within the organism and that this structure is fully adequate to explain all the pertinent facts of psychology. We aim to formulate the principles of motivation so that they will be valid regardless of point of view.'

There are, however, still two points of view, or attitudes, which are both very important and therefore must be combined. Young formulates it in the following way (p. 43):

'There are two interrelated views, however, which make a strong appeal. One of these limits the scope of motivational psychology to the description and explanation of purposive behavior. The other, broader in outlook, defines the field in terms of biomechanics or the energetics of activity including the problem of the regulation of behavior. The writer has attempted to show the interrelation of these two formulations and to demonstrate that both must necessarily be supplemented by a genetic account of the development of motives.'

As can be seen from these quotations, Young's presuppositions are very comprehensive, and this characterizes his book, although the objective, biological view might be said to be predominant.

Level of Development of the Theory

Young writes in the preface to 'Motivation' (p. VIII):

'The book is factual in its approach ... Speculation and theory have been strictly subordinated to the presentation of laboratory findings,'

And this is true to such a degree that Young's presentation can only be described as a 'theory' if the word is used in its broadest sense, including also every descriptive system of symbols. The book contains—as mentioned above—mainly descriptions of experimental methods and results; but in between—especially in the last passages of the chapters—some motivation definitions, motivation classifications, and more or less general hypotheses can be found. These hypotheses are not systematized, however, and thus the theory *cannot* be described as a deductive system, but rather as *a classifying theory.*

Young himself writes explicitly about 'the nature of explanation in scientific psychology' (p. 41):

'Scientific explanation may be defined as a fairly complete description of some object, event, or relation, in which the facts to be explained are brought into relation with other facts, and in which functional relationships and correlations are discovered.'

After this more general description of the scientific explanation, Young classifies scientific explanations in three groups: conditional, genetic, and hypothetic, which explain from present, past, and future factors, respectively. Thus this classification is less specific than Spence's classification of psychological hypotheses (cf. Chapter 3).

Constructive or Reductive Theory

It is a little difficult to place Young's theory in this classification, as his comprehensive presuppositions might lead one to expect a constructive theory. Especially his neutral ('biological') monism, which will be analyzed in a later section fits into such a theory. But quite a number of passages in the book indicate that it would be most correct to classify Young's theory as *a reductive theory,* since in spite of his neutral and comprehensive presuppositions he, nevertheless stresses that physiological processes are the most fundamental variables in motivation. He writes (p. 43):

'The scientific study of motivation falls within mechanics, or more narrowly, within biomechanics.' And in connection with Lashley's criticism of psycho-analytical theory he writes (p. 67–68): 'An adequate picture of motivation must emphasize the basic energy transformations going on within the organism; but these are physical energy transformations, not mental. The older notion of vital spirits moving through neural tubes vanished when a more exact neurology came on the scene. And so will the conceptions of vital and mental forces vanish with the continued development of physiological psychology.'

Later he gives a reason for the reduction to physiology, as he writes in his discussion of the concept of 'drive' (p. 136):

'Although the original conception of drives, and their classification, are based upon observations of behavior, not until they come to be differentiated in terms of inner bodily mechanisms will law and order be discovered in this rapidly developing field of psychology.'

The above quotations thus show that it is correct to classify Young's theory as a reductive theory.

Mentalistic or Behavioristic Theory

As the psycho-physical problem is dealt with very thoroughly in Young's book, and as his solution in my opinion is one of the most rational formulations of the problem, it will here be made the subject of a detailed analysis.

Young's psycho-physical theory, his 'biological monism' (as it is called in 'Emotion') is included in his fundamental presupposition, 'the attitudinal approach,' or 'the multiple-aspect hypothesis.' Briefly, it says that the psychical and the physical are merely different data or aspects, which appear due to different observation-attitudes or points of view, and which are various founded upon the same neutral and fundamental reality.

The consequences of this theory are given in different statements concerning the detail-problems of motivation psychology dealt with in different chapters of the book, and the theory is formulated genetically in the last chapter.

Thus Young starts the theoretical discussion of the motivation problem by declaring (p. 36) 'that there are both physical and psychological approaches to the study of human conduct.' What Young here calls 'psychological' is identical with 'introspection-psychological,' and 'physical' includes both 'physiological-psychological.'

About these different approaches Young writes (p. 37):

'There is no real incompatibility between physical and mental views of motivation. The real mechanism of behavior can be regarded either as a brain or a mind, as both, or neither, depending upon one's viewpoint.'

This was the first general formulation of his psycho-physical hypothesis. Later he applies this hypothesis to different motivation-psychological problems and concepts. He writes about the concept of 'inclination' (p. 156):

'These and similar inclinations can be examined from various points of view. To the behavioral psychologist an inclination is an incipient movement or a preparatory set for some specific movement. To the physiologist an inclination is an internal bodily process or state which incites the organism. To the experimental psychologist an inclination is a conscious demand, a craving or aversion. Despite these differences of viewpoint, it is here assumed that there is a single process going on in the organism. The term 'inclination' refers to this process regardless of the viewpoint from which it may be observed.'

In the passage quoted above the physical point of view has been divided into the physiological and the behavioristic approaches.

In a similar passage about affective conditions, Young points out (p. 60) that 'the aim of psychology is to formulate principles which are independent of any limited interest or viewpoint.'

Later Young discusses hypothetical constructions, both mentalistic and behavioristic, and writes about these and their inter-relations (p. 185):

'To assume a *mental* determinant on the basis of individual conscious experience is just as valid as to assume an inner neural determination on the basis of objectively observed behavior. In reality the mental and bodily determinants of behavior are identical, both being assumed to explain certain facts of experience. There are not two complete outfits of motivating machinery within the personality, but only one.'

On the same subject he writes later (p. 237–238):

'Mental organization is assumed to be identical, in reality, with part of an individual's neural organization. The psychologist of today is concerned with a single living organism, not with a body plus a mind. To be sure, this organism is being analyzed from diverse points of view.'

Apart from the more general formulations, quoted here, Young's 'biological monism' has been applied to more special definitions of concepts as for example reactions (p. 351–352) and emotions (p. 458 and 461).

Finally, Young presents his hypothesis of 'the physical mind' in the last chapter. As a introduction to this he writes (p. 529):

'To think clearly in psychology it is necessary to distinguish between the purely physical organism and the psychophysical individual. They are not distinct real beings, but they are distinct logical conceptions.'

After this clear and logical formulation the hypothesis is presented as follows (p. 532):

'Point for point, the properties of the mind turn out to be identical with known properties of the brain. We hold to the theory that the mind and the brain are one and the same reality. All the facts about motivation, as we have reviewed then in this book, fit this identity hypothesis'. 'The main difference between the conceptions of mind and brain is that the former is assumed from an *individual* point of view, and the latter from an *objective*. The single basic reality we designate as a *physical mind*. The words 'individual' and 'personality' can also be used in this sence, without departing very far from current usage.'

As can be seen clearly from the quotations, Young's psycho-physical theory must be a neutral monism in agreement with the theories of many logical-empiristic philosophers. Therefore his theory can neither be classified as a purely mentalistic, nor as a purely behavioristic theory, but must be called *a typical neutral-formal theory* (although sympathetic towards behaviorism).

Molar or Molecular Theory

It is difficult to place Young's theory in this classification because he makes very few formulations concerning this subject—and no explicit statements at all (although Tolman had introduced the distinction some years before). The few relevant statements which appear in the book are all consequences of his 'multiple-aspect hypothesis.' He writes (p. 52):

'Although, as noted above, behavior can be analyzed into the segments which make it up, it can also be regarded and studied as an unanalyzed whole.'

This quotation shows that Young considers the molecular (analyzing) and the molar (non-analyzing) study as two supplementing research possibilities.

Later he identifies these different viewpoints with regard to both the physiological and the behavioristic attitude. He writes (p. 459):

'As distinct from a restricted physiological view, the behavioral aspect takes into the picture the dynamic relations between organism and environment.'

The quotations given above are the most direct statements concerning the subject, and on the basis of these and the study of the book as a whole I believe that Young's theory *cannot* be classified as *either* a molar, *or* a molecular theory, but must be called *both a molar and a molecular theory.*

Field Theory or Mechanistic Theory

Young's book was published before Lewin's topological psychology brought up the question of distinguishing between mechanistic and field-theoretical psychology. But at several points Young emphasizes explicitly the inter-relation of the motivating factors, and his theory must therefore be classified as *mainly a field theory.*

Thus Young writes about the internal and the external factors (p. 139):

'The environmental and the organic factors in motivated behavior are constantly interrelated.' Young points out the inter-relations of the motivating factors still more clearly in the following (p. 146):

'It is best to consider any bit of behavior as dependent upon the total organic and environmental state. Internal bodily conditions are so delicately balanced and interdependent that it is almost impossible to find wholly unrelated variables.'

But contrary to Lewin, who apparently completely neglects the static structure of the organism and its influence upon behavior, Young points out that the structure of the organism is a limiting condition for its functions; he writes (p. 233):

'Structure is a condition of function; structure limits behavior, but *qua* structure it is inert.' At the same time, however, he points out that (p. 232): 'Bodily structure is not static; it is constantly developing, both with maturation and as a result of activity.'

Young's comprehensive attitude appears also here, but nevertheless his theory must be characterized as being mainly field-theoretical or, as it is called in Chapter 3, *a dynamic theory.*

Statistical or Deterministic Theory

It is rather difficult to place Young's theory in this classification. The immediate impression is that it is a typical deterministic theory. He writes already on the first page that 'all behavior is motivated' and 'everyday activities are all causally determined.' And later he writes (p. 42) that 'motivational psychology is identical with explanatory psychology.' After this there should be no doubt that for Young motivational psychology is identical with explanatory psychology. Moreover, he writes about the indeterministic concept 'spontaneous activity' (p. 48) that

'"spontaneous activity" is not "spontaneous" at all, in the strict sense of the word. With further knowledge it would be placed in the class of causally determined behavior.'

But anti-theoretical statements can be found in a few places in the book and these disagree with the quotations given above and the general impression of the book as a whole. The clearest example, but at the same time one which most disagrees with the main content of the book, is the following (final) statement (p. 534–535):

'If causation be ruled out of motivational psychology, the whole study becomes one which deals with interrelationships among observed natural processes. All the facts and problems discussed in this book can be handled in a non-causal, matter-of-fact way. The elimination of causation from the study of motivation leaves a purely descriptive science, coextensive with psychology itself, which operates in terms of events and their conditions.'

Maybe the explanation of this apparent self-contradiction is that Young only means to mention *a possibility*, and not a possibility he wants to explore or has explored in his book. If this is correct, Young's theory must absolutely be classified as *a deterministic theory*.

The Model

Young has two especially illustrative presentations of the presuppositions of his theory. One of these (figure 84, p. 528) symbolizes his psycho-physical presupposition, as it shows 'the experiencing relationship,' or, in other words:

'the fact that every experienced phenomenon, just as it is given, depends for its existence upon bodily processes within the observer.'

The other illustration (figure 85, p. 530) symbolizes 'the multiple-aspect hypothesis,' as it shows the organism in its environment with arrows symbolizing the different attitudes or viewpoints from which the organism can be studied. At the same time everything is related to a time-axis.

Besides these presentations of the most important presuppositions of the theory, a large table can be found (p. 150–151) giving an outline of different motivation variables, their determining factors, and their effects upon behavior.

Summary

This analysis of the theory as a whole can be summarized in the following description: *Young's theory is a classifying, reductive, neutral-formal, molecular-molar, dynamic, and determinstic psychological theory.*

Young's Definition of Motivation

Young has given one of the clearest definitions of the concept of 'motivation'; it was therefore his definition[3]) was preferred as a criterion for the selection of motivation variables, hypotheses, etc., in Chapter 4. Contrary to most other psychologists, Young distinguishes in his definition between *energy-release* and *energy-regulation,* treating them as two fundamental aspects of motivation. Young writes in the final statement in his introductory analysis of the concept of motivation (p. 45):

'*Final Definition of Motivational Psychology.* Motivational psychology may be defined as the study of all conditions which arouse and regulate the behavior of organisms. The *arousal* of behavior necessarily implies a release of physical energy from the tissues. The *regulation* of behavior includes the control of activity through purposive determinations, as well as the restriction of activity by organic structure.'

In spite of Young's 'multiple-aspect view' it is the objective (and especially the physical-physiological) aspect which is emphasized in the definition of 'motivation.' This can be seen even more clearly in the following paragraph (p. 69):

'Viewed physically, motivation is the process by which movement is produced and regulated. The basic questions in a study of motivation are concerned with the release of potential energy, and with the direction and regulation of energy expenditures so as to produce purposive activity.'

And it is mentioned explicitly in the following (p. 77):

'In the last analysis the energy with which we are concerned throughout this book is *physical,* and the conditions called *motivating* are those which release this physical energy and regulate the direction of its expenditure.'

Young writes even more precisely about the motivating energy (p. 10):

'the immediate energy source of behavior and of all muscular work is certain chemical substances stored in the body.'

Even though Young thus emphasizes the objective (physical-physiological) aspect of motivation in his definition, his definition is in other respects comprehensive, as it includes *all* variables—both the empirical and the hypothetical—which enter into the process of motivation.

Young's 'Drive'

'Drive' is the most important motivation variable in Young's theory, and many pages are used to describe it.

First of all Young analyzes the different definitions of 'drive'. He mainly finds six different main types of definitions (p. 75):

1. 'Drive' is energy.
2. 'Drive' is that stimulus which releases the energy.
3. 'Drive' is general activity.
4. 'Drive' is any tendency to behavior.

---

[3]) Harriman (ed.): 'Encyclopedia of Psychology.'

5. 'Drive' is a specific, goal-directed activity.
6. 'Drive' is a motivating factor in the personality.

He writes about these (p. 78):

'If the meanings of drive listed on page 75 be carefully considered, it will be discovered that some of these describe behavior and others stress the conditions which cause or determine behavior.'

The matter is complicated even more because 'drives' and 'incentives' are often confused. Young writes about this (p. 45):

'To distinguish organic from environmental motivating factors, it has been suggested that the former be called *motives* and the later *incentives*. Thus, desires, intentions, and goal sets are *motives*. Praise, reproof, reward, punishment, money, food, mate, etc., are *incentives*. Incentives can be subdivided into two groups as *social* and *nonsocial*.'

And about the drawbacks of the different definitions Young writes (p. 74):

'The above meanings of the term "drive" are so divergent that confused thinking will inevitably result unless the concept be defined precisely.'

Attempting to explain the reasons for the confusion he writes (p. 79):

'Confusion about the definition of drive arises, not from any intrinsic disorder within the facts of drive, but only because there are diverse viewpoints. The sane solution is to recognize that differences of interpretation exist, and then to be clear about one's own position.'

He mentions as possible different viewpoints (p. 84):

'In the physical sense, drive is the energy which makes the machine go. In the behavioral sense, drive is goal-oriented behavior, or else the general level of activity whether purposive or not. In the physiological sense, drive is a tissue condition which gives rise to persistent stimulation, or else drive is the persistent stimulus (drive stimulus) itself. In the strictly psychological sense, drive is a motivating factor of personality—such as a wish, purpose, ideal—which regulates and directs one's conduct.'

And he formulates his own definition in the following way (p. 153–154):

'The above analysis leads to a precise definition of drive. In the strictly physical sense, drive is energy which is released by complex bodily and environmental stimulations. This released energy is shown internally in bodily changes (physiological drive) and out-wardly in behavior (behavioral drive). There are different views of a single motivational process, which might be called the mechanical, physiological, and behavioral aspects of drive. The definition of drive as energy must, of course, be broadened so as to take account of regulating and directing factors.'

As can be seen from the above quotations and the definition of 'drive,' Young's theory is also in this respect characterized by his biological monism in that he emphasizes the objective aspect of drive. Young's 'multiple-aspect view' also characterizes his definition of 'drive'; but while it might be said to be practical to have a rather broad definition of 'motivation', it is in my opinion not practical to have a broad definition of 'drive'. Thus Young's definition includes both hypothetical and empirical variables. The dependent behavior variable is described as 'behavioral drive'. It is, however, not clear whether both 'physical drive' and 'physiological drive' indicate different aspects of a hypothetical motivation variable, or whether they also include some empirical, independent variables. The lack of clarity can also be seen with regard to another motivation variable, 'need', which will be analyzed later.

Young classifies 'drive' as 'primary and secondary drives'. He writes about this classification—with reference to Tolman—most explicitly and most clearly (p. 154):

'Reference to the physiological state of an organism is a sound basis for differentiation between primary and secondary drives.'

And in accordance with this he defines 'primary drive' in the following way (p. 155):

'A drive, in our sense, is primary when the physiological basis for the purposive behavior has been clearly demonstrated, and when it has been differentiated from the organic bases of other drives.'

'Secondary drive' is defined negatively in relation to 'primary drive' thus (p. 155):

'All other drives will tentatively be called secondary until a specific organic basis can be clearly demonstrated.'

Young lists the following 'primary drives' (e. g. p. 150–151):

1) 'Hunger' 2) 'nausea' 3) 'thirst' 4) 'sex' 5) 'nursing' 6) 'urinating' 7) 'defecating' 8) 'avoiding heat' 9) 'avoiding cold' 10) 'avoiding pain' 11) 'air hunger' 12) 'fear and anger' 13) 'fatigue' 14) 'sleep' 15) 'curiosity, observation, manipulation' 16) 'tickle.'

In this list 'social instinct' is also mentioned, but since Young cannot give any physiological basis for it; 'social instinct' can, according to his own definition, not be counted as a 'primary drive'.

Young includes 'fear and anger' in a group of primary drives which he calls 'the emergency reactions'. As a group they differ physiologically from the other primary drives (production of adrenalin), but taken one by one they can only be identified through purely behavioral criteria. He summarizes this in the following way (p. 140):

To summarize, the total group can be differentiated from other basic drives on a bodily basis; but, within the group, distinctions can be made only on a behavioral basis.'

It is rather uncertain whether 'curiosity, observation, manipulation' ('the exploration drive') is to be counted as a primary or a secondary drive. In the table in question (p. 150–151) under 'bodily structures chiefly involved' in the drives he has written 'receptors' above 'curiosity, etc.'. Thus there *are* organic functions which can be taken to be a physiological basis for 'drive'; but then Young writes (p. 155) that:

'some secondary drives depend upon persisting environmental conditions such as novelty.'

And he writes further about this (p. 142):

'The exploratory drive is an excellent example of behavior which depends upon persisting environmental conditions (novelty) rather than upon a physiological state.'

As Young has not given any list of 'secondary drives' it is rather difficult to reach a conclusion.

Young's 'Need'

'Need' is another motivation variable, which is not, however, as important as 'drive.' The interrelations between these motivation variables are, as can be seen from the following, somewhat unclear in Young's theory.

About the definition of 'need' he says for example (p. 80):

'The concept of bodily need can be defined objectively in terms of survival. The organism *needs* these substances and energies the withholding of which will lead to its death.'

About another possible definition he writes (p. 81):

'Another possible way of defining bodily need objectively is in terms of the *optimal* conditions for survival, including growth, reproduction, health, etc.'

The definitions have in common that 'need' is defined physiologically. The advantage of this is, according to Young, that (p. 81):

'The definition of bodily need in terms of tissue requirements allows a distinction between objective need and the manifestations of need in behavior.'

'Need' is closely related to the principle of 'homeostasis.' Having quoted the principle of homeostasis stated by Claude Bernard and Cannon, Young writes (p. 82):

'The principle of homeostasis is important in relation to bodily need ... Thus, in the last analysis the maintaining of homeostasis is a process of meeting bodily needs.'

Besides the relation between 'need' and 'homeostasis' Young also explicitly discusses the relation between 'need' and 'desire,' and he writes (p. 81) that 'Need objectively considered, is not the same as conscious desire.'

But he does not write anything explicitly about the relation between 'need' and 'drive', something which is a quite important lack. Most physiologists use these concepts in a very unclear and confusing way, and in Young's theory it is especially difficult to separate 'need' and 'drive' (particular 'physiological drive'). The most direct statement Young gives in the summary of Chapter 2 (p. 84):

'It is a basic physiological principle that organisms tend to maintain approximately constant physical and chemical bodily states, and that they must succeed in doing so if the individual organism and the species are to have optimal conditions for survival. From this it follows that protoplasm *needs* certain substances and energies from the environment. The evolutionary process has gradually developed bodily mechanisms well adapted to the satisfying of these needs. In maintaining homeostasis, drive plays a definite rôle.'

According to this Young's conception of 'drive' should be 'a bodily mechanism' which satisfies 'needs.' If this is compared to a later detailed description of 'drive,' the problem can be solved completely. Young writes (p. 137):

'All fundamental drives have certain common characteristics, namely: (a) a persistent condition in the tissues; which gives rise to (b) a sustained stimulation of afferent nerves; from the latter (c) a release of energy in nerves, muscles, and other tissues, which raises the activity level; and (d) in developed organisms, goal-directed behavior; with (e) a goal object or a consummatory reaction which is capable of removing the persistent tissue condition mentioned in (a), thus restoring homeostatis.'

As Young often briefly defines 'drive' as 'Drive is energy' (e. g. p. 78), it might be most correct to interpret (and reconstruct) Young's theory in such a way that 'drive' is identical with that part of the process described above which is called '(c) a release of energy ...', and 'need' identical with the first part of the same process ('a persistent condition in the tissues ...').

If this interpretation (or reconstruction) of Young's theory is correct (practical), then the above mentioned problem of classifying 'drive' is solved, since '*drive*' *must then be classified as a physiologically interpreted, hypothetical motivation variable.*

Energy-Regulating Variables

While 'need' and 'drive' almost exclusively must be described as energy-producing or energy-releasing variables, there are motivation variables in Young's theory which must be described as energy-determining or energy-*regulating*. It is typical that they have many different names, as Young takes over the terms from everyday language and other psychologists without any attempt to redefine them. But the most important variables in this group are '*set*,' '*attitude*,' *and* '*purpose*.'

About these Young writes (p. 186):

'Regardless of the standpoint from which motivation is studied, one finds it necessary to assume the existence of regulating and directing determinants of human conduct. A purpose which persists and a neural, or neuromuscular, set are one and the same thing.'

In the above quotation 'set' and 'purpose' are defined as the objective (physiological) and the subjective aspect of a regulating or directing variable, respectively. Later 'sets' are described more precisely (p. 216):

'These *sets* are in the nature of very general preparations, readiness, or diffuse arousals of the neural mechanisms.'

Further Young places 'sets' in the class of 'preparatory adjustment' (p. 217):

'Between the most specific and the most general of preparatory adjustments there are all gradations; no hard and fast line of distinction can be drawn. The most specific determination is a *set* for a definite, limited, precisely defined action. The most general determination is in the nature of an ill-defined mood or readiness for some type of activity . . .'

The frequently used term 'attitude' is later defined in the following way (p. 242):

'The main characteristic of an attitude is that it predisposes the individual to react positively or negatively, to accept or reject, a given proposition.'

Still, he finds it practical to limit 'attitude' to verbal variables for these reasons (p. 242):

'It is necessary, if attitudes are to be measured, to accept a somewhat limited definition of an attitude, describing it as that *mental organization which predisposes an individual towards or away from a verbal statement*.'

As can be seen from these definitions, Young classifies the energy regulating motivation variables in several ways:

1) general ('readiness') and specific ('sets' whose subjective aspect is called 'purpose').

2) verbal ('attitude') and non-verbal.

But besides these he also introduces a classification of energy regulating variables as:

3) later or *passively* regulating and dynamic or *actively* regulating variables. In the first class the anatomy of the organism with its limitation of possibilities for activity is included, and so are 'habits' and previous experience. To the other group belong 'sets' and 'readiness.'

Young writes about this classification (p. 261):

'A distinction must be drawn between *latent organization* and *dynamic determination*, and this distinction is valid whether the problems of motivation be approached through a study of behavior and its physiological basis, or through an analysis of conscious experience and its conditions.'

Later he adds, however, that it is only a difference in degree, and he writes (p. 533–534):

'It is still problematical whether a sharp line of distinction can be drawn between passive and active forms of organization. There are all gradations of activity from zero to maximum. At one extreme are the purposive determinations, postural adjustments, goal sets (whether induced by verbal suggestion or by non-verbal conditions) which *actively* determine behavior. At the other extreme are the patterns of latent neural organization which make up our idle habit systems, which comprise our sleeping attitudes, and which form the basis for the whole world of past experience so far as any trace of it is retained. Between these extremes are the general preparatory adjustments, the vague expectations of some kind of event, the recent or vivid experiences which perseverate for a while just as if they were expending intrinsic energy of releasing mental tension.'

As can be seen from the above quotation, the class of energy-regulating motivation variables is very large, and it is thus difficult to keep motivational psychology separated from the psychology of learning for example. It is especially difficult if one maintains that the latent or passively regulating variables are also motivation variables, whereas it is easier to keep the dynamic or actively regulating variables and especially the energy-producing variables apart as motivation variables.

Finally it should be pointed out that Young's classification of energy-regulating variables as latent (passively determining) and dynamical (actively determining) variables corresponds closely to the classification of variables as functional variables and disposition variables which was given in Chapter 3. According to this classification Young's energy-producing and the dynamic energy regulating variables are *functional* variables, while the latent energy-regulating variables are *disposition* variables.

Affective and Emotional Processes

Young discusses several theories of affective processes, and he uses his 'multiple-aspect-hypothesis' to form a synthesis which he formulates in the following way (p. 351–352):

'The phrase "affective reaction", as stated above, designates the organic processes upon which the reports of liking and disliking are based. Our conception is that the affective reaction is a unitary process in nature. It may be observed from various angles. Feelings of pleasantness and unpleasantness are the *subjective* aspect of the ultimate affective reactions. The *behavioral* aspect of the processes appears as the dynamic activity of accepting or avoiding, plus a lot of other expressive reactions ... Another aspect of affective reaction is the *physiological* ... This process may be some sort of blocking or inhibition for unpleasantness, and a release of blocking or facilitation for pleasantness.'

Thus affective processes are *not* real motivation variables, but accompanying processes which appear when the motivational process is blocked (or when blocks are removed). Later he writes in connection with a criticism of hedonism (p. 383):

'We can admit that in general unpleasantness is associated with avoidance and pleasantness with pursuit *as a fact* without accepting psychological hedonism as a motivational *theory*. This factual, empirical envisagement of hedonism we will call *factual hedonism*. Factual hedonism implies no theory as to the determination of conduct, but is only the assertion of the demonstrable fact that unpleasantness is associated with avoidance whereas pleasantness is associated with the attainment of a goal.

On the side of interpretation we regard pleasantness and unpleasantness as individual experiences which reflect the dynamic interplay of motivating processes.'

Young's comprehensive and synthesis-forming attitude can also be seen in his analysis and theory of emotion. Through his historical analysis he reaches the result that two main theories have been formed about emotions. One defines emotions as disorganization of behavior, the other defines emotions as purposive, energy-mobilizing reactions. Young writes about these two, apparently contradictory theories (p. 448):

'Now we do not have to choose between the two main interpreations of emotional excitement. Both appear to be correct. Consequently our task is to bring them into true relation with each other."

Young avoids the contradiction by choosing one of the definitions and by excluding the other form of reaction per definition. He writes (p. 457):

'The foregoing discussion leads us to define emotion as a disruption of disorganization of behavior."

About the other theory he writes (p. 471):

'The work of Cannon extends the Darwinian principle of utility from the outer responses of emotion to the glandular and visceral changes of emotional reaction. According to our view the sympathetic-adrenal reaction is an energizing, motivating response, but not necessarily an emotional one. It is emotional only when there is disruption of behavior."

Thus Young achieves harmony by exluding escape, fighting, and other strong energy-mobilizing reactions from the class of emotional reactions, which solely includes disorganized behavior. He writes even more clearly about this in the concluding statement of the chapter (p. 478):

'These highly motivated, goal-directed activities should be distinguished from the organic state of emotional disruption. The latter is not a direct factor in motivation but rather an outer symptom of the blocking or thwarting of motives, or perhaps of an overexcited, overmotivated state of the organism. When emotion occurs there is an imbalance of motives.'

As is stated explicitly in the above quotation, Young does not consider emotions to be real motivation variables (they are 'not a direct factor in motivation'), but he takes them to be symptoms of blocked motives. Consequently 'unpleasant' affective reactions must be some kind of emotion, whereas 'pleasant' affective reactions are symptoms indicating that the blocks opposing the motivational process which have caused the emotions have been removed. For the sake of completion it should be said further that emotions and affective reactions are *hypothetical* variables, interpreted physiologically ('the organic state of emotional disruption') or maybe rather neutral-formal variables which can function both subjectively ('feelings') and objectively (disorganized behavior and physiological processes).

As a consequence of his definition of emotions he writes about the classification of emotions (p. 458):

'If this analysis is correct, the task of classifying emotions is really that of classifying the conditions under which disruption occurs, along with the objectively distinguishable kinds of disruption ... To classify emotions one must turn to the motives which are obstructed, as well as to the bodily processes which are manifest.'

Briefly: Emotions must be classified in accordance with the motives that are blocked.

Many informal, implicit hypotheses of motivation are also to be found; but it would lead much too far to analyze them here. The most important of them will be reformulated in the reconstruction of the theory in the last section.

Young's Theory in 'Emotion'

In his book 'Emotions in Man and Animal' Young has elaborated the theory of emotions which he outlined in the chapter on emotions in 'Motivation'.

In the preface to 'Emotion' Young briefly formulates his presuppositions: 'The attitudinal approach' and 'the biological monism,' which are both known from 'Motivation.' In the first chapter he elaborates the analysis of emotions which has already been quoted from 'Motivation'. In 'Emotion' he formulates his definition of emotions in the following way (p. 51):

'An emotion is an acute disturbance or upset of the individual which is revealed in behavior and in conscious experience, as well as through widespread changes in the functioning of viscera (smooth muscles, glands, heart and lungs), and which is initiated by factors within a psychological situation.'

In Chapter 2 he presents his theory of 'Attitudes and Motives, Determinants of Emotion.' He begins by stating that attitudes and motives 'are the basis of our affective life,' because attitudes predispose for certain emotions, which then can change the attitudes of the individual. Emotions are caused by conflicts, frustrations, and the satisfaction of motives.

He defines attitude (p. 65) thus:

'An attitude can be described best as a neural readiness or predisposition within the individual to respond in a particular way toward some object or external situation. Characteristically, this response is either positive or negative.'

As can be seen, his definition is almost the same as the one given in 'Motivation.' Also his definition of motive resembles very much the one given before. He formulates it in this way (p. 66):

'Motives, in contrast to attitudes, are factors which initiate activity, sustain the activity in progress or change the course of behavior.'

About the relation between motives and attitudes he writes (p. 66):

'Attitudes are latent neural organizations except when they are called into action (activated) by stimulating situations (motives). When attitudes are latent they are wholly inert (non-motivating); but if activated, they become motivating. At such times they regulate or direct the course of behaviour. This is their essential characteristic. They may be regarded as motivators of behavior, not in the sense of initiating activity (as motives do), but by guiding activity into certain specific channels ...'

As can be seen from this rather detailed formulation, 'attitude' is still an energy-regulating and energy-directing (disposition) variable, whereas 'motive' as compared with the definition in 'Motivation' has been limited to the energy-producing and energy-releasing (functional) variables only.

The rest of Chapter 2 deals chiefly with 'social attitudes.'

In Chapter 3 he presents his theory of 'Needs and Appetites, the Basis of the Affective Life.' In this chapter he defines 'needs,' 'appetites,' 'drives,' and 'desires.'

He writes about 'needs' (p. 149):

'Needs fall into at least three categories: biological, social, and personality needs.

'Biological need is a conception which can be defined objectively by reference to certain criteria such as survival, growth, reproduction. The basic biological needs of an organism are simply the conditions required for survival, for maintaining a state of health, for growth and for reproduction ...'

The social and personal 'needs' are not further defined, but a list of examples is given. He writes about 'appetites' (p. 150):

The concept of appetite is more strictly psychological than that of need. Appetites are persistent physicochemical states of the organism which lead to a rise or fall in the level of activity. The changed activity persists until a particular consummatory or goal response is made. The goal response restores homeostasis or internal equilibrium.'

As can be seen from the above quotations the definitions of 'needs. and (especially) of 'appetites', which in 'Motivation' were only presented parenthetically and mainly in connection with descriptions of the theories of other psychologists, is very detailed here.

About the relation between 'needs' and 'appetites' Young writes (p. 153):

'A *need* is not a motivating factor. The word simply designates an objective maintenance relationship between the organism and its environment, which can be treated quantitatively. *Appetites,* in contrast, are typically motivating states of the organism. The appetites for air, foodstuffs, water, mate, sleep, rest, and elimination are physicochemical states of the organism. These bodily states liberate energy and excite the nervous system, thus initiating behavior.'

In my opinion Young's formulation is somewhat unclear. His remark that 'need is not a motivating factor' seems particularly self-contradictory, and it is difficult to see the difference between 'need' (at any rate as it is usually used) and 'appetite'. But apparently Young means that 'need' is just a term indicating a lack in an organism of something or other as compared to an optimal standard or norm; while 'appetites' are *the physiological conditions* in the organism caused by this lack by which energy is released and behavior caused.

Young writes about 'drives' that so many different meanings are attached to this term at present in psychology, that it is rather confusing. He mentions that 'drive' has at least five meanings (p. 151):

1) 'a persisting stimulus which liberates energy and arouses bodily movement,'
2) 'a physicochemical state which changes the exitability of nerve cells,'
3) 'purposive behavior,'
4) 'a change in the level of general activity,'
5) 'a determination to act, a set of the individual toward a specific goal.'

He writes further about this (p. 152):

'The above definitions of drive are interrelated and overlap somewhat. The most useful definition of drive is probably a physiological one, combining numbers 1 and 2 above, which interprets the bodily state as a motivational source or explanation of behavior. In this sense appetites and aversions, as defined above, are drives.'

As can be seen from the above quotation Young has changed his definition of 'drive' a little in 'Emotion'; 'drive' has become less extensive and is more or less replaced by 'appetites' (and 'aversions'). But in my opinion Young's formulations have not become clearer (more unambiguous) through this revision.

Finally, the definition of 'desires' is formulated in the following way (p. 152):

'A desire is a conscious experience. It is the subjective aspect of a motive and is always goal oriented. In so far as desires rest upon the physicochemical state of the organism, they are the conscious aspect of appetites; but the concept of desire is broader than this. The anticipated goal of a desire may refer to any object or activity under the sun.'

According to the above quotation 'desire' has the same meaning in 'Emotion' as in 'Motivation' where it was used together with some synonyms ('wants', 'wish', 'cravings', and 'purpose'); but in the latter book it has nearly taken the place which 'purpose' had in the first book, describing the subjective aspect of all motives.

The remaining chapters of the book deal with: emotional development, physiological changes during emotions, patterns of emotional reactions, emotions as conscious processes, direct determinants of emotions (namely intense motivation, frustration, conflict, release of tension, and the total psychological situation), predisposing conditions (previous experience and organic factors), and 'attitudes and motive in relation to emotion.' But there is nothing novel concerning motivational psychology.

RECONSTRUCTION OF THE THEORY

The analysis of Young's theory shows that it is a theory with some definitions and many hypotheses, but also with some contradictions and some ambiguities, and therefore a reconstruction is necessary. As Young himself gives much attention to the presuppositions of the theory these will be reformulated in the first part of the reconstruction, and after this the most important definitions and hypotheses of motivation will be reformulated.

Presuppositions of the Theory

The 'multiple-aspect-hypothesis,' which is a formulation of his 'attitudinal approach' is the most important presupposition of Young's theory. Young introduces and explains the background of this hypothesis in Chapter 1 and elaborates it further in the last chapter[4]). But since no brief and clear formulation can be found, the following formulation is suggested:

'*The Multiple-Aspect-Hypothesis*': All cognition (observation and reflection) is determined by the attitude of the individual in question. Any subject can be understood on the basis of many different attitudes. Scientific understanding must therefore be formulated as a combination of the results reached on the bacis of all possible attitudes.

Subordinated to this presupposition—mostly as a special psychological application of it—is the presupposition of biological monism which Young formulates most

[4]) Cf. the quotations in the passage on the presuppositions of the theory.

briefly and clearly in the chapter on 'The hypothesis of a physical mind' (p. 531–532)[5]). On the basis of this the following reformulation is suggested:

'The Hypothesis of Biological Monism': 'Brain' and 'mind' represent different concepts of the same reality (which may be called 'a physical mind'); the concepts have been developed on the basis of a subjective and an objective attitude, respectively. Any process or condition in 'the physical mind' can have a 'subjective and objective aspect'.

These are the two most important presuppositions in Young's theory.

Motivation Definitions and Hypotheses

As shown in the preceding analysis of Young's theory his book contains many defintions and especially many hypotheses of motivation. A great deal of these need to be reformulated and put into a more systematic order.

The following reformulation of Young's basic definitions of motivation is suggested.

Definition 1: 'Motivation.' All behavior is 'motivated,' i. e. determined by (in functional relation to) *energy-release and energy-regulation.* In the total process of motivation several variables take part in the following relations: The behavior is determined by 'drives' and maybe by simultaneously operating 'attitudes' or 'sets.' 'Drives' are determined by external or internal stimuli; the internal stimuli are determined by 'appetites' which again are determined by 'needs.'

The following reformulations of Young's definitions of motivation variables are suggested, his own revisions in 'Emotion' being taken into consideration:

Definition 2: 'Need.' 'Need' is the term for lacks in the organism or deviations from biological standards or norms (homeostasis).

As can be seen this reformulation follows Young's revised definition in 'Emotions', rather closely as 'need' is here defined as an empirical, bio-physio-chemical variable.

Definition 3: 'Appetite.' 'Appetite' is the term for organical conditions determined by needs and determining an energy-release (in the nervous system).

This reformulation has also been based on the definition in 'Emotions,' according to which 'appetites' are empirical, independent motivation variables.

Definition 4: 'Drive.' 'Drive' is the term for conditions of energy-release in the mind, determined by afferent nervous impulses from external or internal stimuli (appetites) and determining behavior.

In this case the reformulation agrees with the original definition from 'Motivation,' according to which 'drive' is a hypothetical functional variable.

---

[5]) Cf. the quotations in the passage on *mentalistic or behavioristic theory.*

Definition 5: 'Attitude.' 'Attitude' is a term for latent dispositions, which, when activated (by drives), have an energy-regulating and behavior-determining function.

This reformulation approximates the definition in 'Emotions' where attitude is a hypothetical disposition variable.

Definition 6: 'Set.' 'Set' is the term for an energy-regulating and behavior determining condition in the mind, determined by drives and determining purposive behavior.

This formulation follows to some degree the definition in 'Motivation' where 'sets' are hypothetical functional variables.

Definition 7: 'Emotion'. 'Emotion' is a term for conditions of disorganization in the organism, caused by over-stimulation, frustration, or conflict.

Apart from these reformulations of the fundamental motivation definitions, the following reformulations of the most important motivation hypotheses in Young's 'Motivation' are suggested.

First a reformulation of the rather general hypothesis about the relation between behavior and all motivation variables (p. 24):

Hypothesis 1: If the motivation is changed, a change in the *kind* of behavior, or in the *degree* of activity, or both may result.

Later in the book (p. 102) another general hypothesis about the relation between the termination of motivation and the behavior can be found. This can be-formulated in the following way:

Hypothesis 2: If an organism approaches satisfaction, the degree of activity is gradually lowered.

While the previous hypotheses dealt with the relation between the dependent behavior variable and all independent and hypothetical motivation variables, the following hypothesis deals with the relation between an empirical and a hypothetical motivation variable[6]), which can be reformulated thus (p. 119):

Hypothesis 3: The intensity of the 'drive' of an organism does not correlate to any high degree with (is not directly proportional to) the intensity of the determining 'need'.

The following reformulations of hypotheses concerning different primary motivation processes are suggested. First a hypothesis concerning *food*-motivation (p. 107):

---

[6]) Cf. Spence's modified classification of psychological hypotheses quoted in Ch. 3.

Hypothesis 4: If a 'need' for a special food arises, it may determine the arousal of a corresponding 'appetite,' and determined by this a 'drive' may result which again determines an adequate food-choice behavior.

A hypothesis about *thirst* can also be formulated (p. 121):

Hypothesis 5: If an organism has a 'need' for water, this will determine an 'appetite' consisting of a dry mouth and throat which determines nervous impulses to the brain, determining a 'drive' (the subjective aspect of which is the experience of thirst).

And a hypothesis about *sex* motivation can be formulated in the following way (p. 125):

Hypothesis 6: The sex 'appetite' is a production of the sex hormones, which together with external stimuli determine the sex 'drive.'

The hypotheses about the interrelation between different motivation variables are reformulated below. First a general hypothesis (based upon p. 152 and 494):

Hypothesis 7: If two or more different motivation variables appear simultaneously they influence (reinforce or reduce) each other. No constant hierchy between different motivation variables exists.

Some special hypotheses will be formulated on the basis of experiments concerning different primary drives (based upon p. 146–147):

Hypothesis 8: If a need for water and a thirst-drive determined by this is strengthened, a simultaneous hunger-drive will be reduced.

Hypothesis 9: If a strong hunger-drive arises it will block and reduce a simultaneous sex-drive.

Hypothesis 10: If a strong hunger-drive arises it will strengthen an 'exploratory-drive.'

A hypothesis about the prestige motive or the self-assertion drive can be formulated in the following way (based upon p. 389–390 and 95):

Hypothesis 11: In most individuals (in our culture) a social self-assertion drive exists, determined by primary drives and learning processes.

The above hypotheses about the interrelation between motivation variables are all of the H→H type (cf. Spence's modified classification in Chapter 3).

The hypotheses about incentives, punishment and reward, are reformulated below. First a general hypothesis about the combination of incentives (p. 24):

Hypothesis 12: If two or more incentives operate simultaneously, the effect upon the motivation is stronger than when only one incentive operates.

A number of hypotheses of punishment and reward may be formulated. First about their effect as compared to the mere success or failure (p. 32):

Hypothesis 13: If incentives such as reward, punishment, praise, and reproof are used, the effect upon the motivation is stronger than that caused by success and failure alone.

Next about the combination of punishment and reward (p. 307):

Hypothesis 14: If punishment and reward are combined the effect is stronger than if they are used individually.

The hypothesis about the punishment optimum can be formulated in the following way (p. 287):

Hypothesis 15: There is an optimum value for the strength of the punishment used as an incentive in the process of learning any kind of behavior. This punishment optimum varies with the difficulty of the task, with the individual in question, and with the intensity of the pain incentive.

About the effect of the social forms of punishment and reward, namely praise and reproof, the following hypothesis can be formulated (p. 416):

Hypothesis 16: The effectiveness of praise and reproof varies with the self-esteem of the individual. When the self-esteem of the individual is fairly high, a little reproof will be more effective than praise. When the self-esteem of the individual is relatively low, praise is more effective than reproof.

Finally some hypotheses about the relation between motivation variables and other variables (habit-forming and perception) can be formulated.

First a hypothesis about the importance of the process of learning to motivation variables such as 'attitudes' and 'sets' ('purpose') (p. 169 and 171):

Hypothesis 17: The presence of energy-regulating and behavior-directing motivation variables (as 'attitudes' and 'sets') is—at any rate in Man and other mammals—mainly determined by learning processes.

Next a fundamental hypothesis about the importance of motivation for the habit-formation (the learning process) (p. 228):

Hypothesis 18: If a habit is to be formed, the individual must be motivated to carry out learning behavior.

Also a hypothesis of the importance of motivation for the continued existence of the habit can be formulated (p. 301):

Hypothesis 19: A learnt habit depends for its continued existence as a latent disposition upon a motivation variable which activates it every now and then.

Finally a hypothesis of the relation between motivation and perception can be formulated (p. 204):

Hypothesis 20: The structure of the perception of an individual is among other things dependent upon its motivation variables, both the present 'drives' and 'sets' and the permanent 'attitudes.'

Together with the seven definitions these twenty hypotheses in my opinion form an explicit and systematic reconstruction of the most important elements in Young's theory.

Conclusion

It only remains to be pointed out that even though the theory is not very exactly and systematically formulated, Young's work distinguishes itself by a comprehensiveness in outlook and a variety of experimental and other, empirical descriptions.

Later Developments

P. Th. Young has integrated the two books analyzed in this chapter into one volume published in 1961 with the title: '*Motivation and Emotion*—A survey of the determinants of human and animal activity.' With its more than six hundred pages it is the biggest book about motivation written by a single author. It is at the same time one of the most comprehensive and well-balanced expositions of motivational psychology. We therefore shall analyze it in the following pages[7]).

The structure of the theory. There are no important changes in the structure of the theory. It can still be described as 'a classifying, reductive, neutral-formal, molecular-molar, dynamic and deterministic psychological theory'. Young still argues for his 'multiple-aspect-approach' or 'relativistic point-of-view' (as he calls it in his new book). He thinks that it is 'an alternative to eclecticism' as well as to the dogmatic 'fixed point-of view'.

The present author thinks that Young's book contains more of a *descriptive frame-of-reference* than of an explanatory theory, but it is a very fruitful descriptive system both for research and for educational purposes. And in his most recent book Young's *hedonic* theory plays a more important role than it did in his earlier books. We shall comment on it in connection with the analysis of the content of Young's theory.

The content of the theory. Young retains his all-inclusive definition of motivation as 'the process of arousing action, sustaining the activity in progress, and regulating the pattern of activity' (p. 24). This definition is so all-inclusive that 'motivation' almost equals 'the determinants of activity' (cf. sub-heading on the title-page in Young's book).

---

[7]) It should also be mentioned that Young has written several papers dealing with his food-preference-experiments. A good survey is presented in his paper 'Hedonic, organization and regulation of behavior'. (Psych. Review. 1966, Vol. 73, no. 1, 59–86).

After an analysis of the several concepts of *drive* Young writes (p. 107):

'The concept of *drive* is useful when a general explanation is required in terms of organic conditions.'

After an analysis of the concept of '*need*' Young writes (p. 143):

'The student of motivation should be warned that the concept of *need* is commonly used in a dynamic as well as a non-dynamic sense.'

But he nevertheless concludes that: 'It is possible objectively to define the needs of an organism by reference to homeostatis as well as by other criteria such as growth, reproduction and health.'

Another motivational concept presented in Young's latest book is '*motive*', which he compares with '*habit*' in this way (p. 138):

'The acquired neural organization that directs an animal towards his goal has been called *habit* and *motive*. The term *habit* emphasizes the fact that a bit of neural organization has been learned. The term *motive* emphasizes the fact that acquired neural organization orients and organism to a goal, regulates and directs his behavior as he approaches a goal, and is activated in some way by excitations from the environment and from a state of organic need.'

As the reader will observe from this quotation, there is only a slight difference (if any) between 'habit' and 'motive' in Young's use of the terms.

When comparing the motivational variables 'need', 'drive' and 'motive', we find that 'need' is an *empirical* variable, an organic state objectivity defined in terms of homeostasis or other criteria, while '*drive*' is an *hypothetical* variable which is determined by a need or an external stimulation. 'Need' and 'drive' are both *function*-variables. '*Motive*', on the other hand, is both a function- and (acquired) disposition-variable. It is a *hypothetical* variable like 'drive'. 'Motive' signifies both an energy-*releasing* and an energy-*regulating* function (unlike 'drive', which is limited to an energy-*releasing* function).

In his most recent book Young continues to employ the terms, 'purpose', 'set', and 'attitude' for purely energy-*regulating* variables, as in his earlier books. Therefore, it is not necessary to comment upon them at this time.

We can conclude this analysis of Young's motivational variables by stating that Young's motivational terminology is one of the most well-differentiated in modern motivational psychology. There is only one term which is a little inexact and confusing, i. e., 'motive'.

Among Young's hypotheses we shall only concern ourselves with those which constitute his 'hedonic theory'.

Young reviews his own extensive research in food-preference and correlates it with the modern physiology of activation (reticular activation system) and punishment and reward (the septal region). He then summarizes his 'hedonic theory' in the following '*statement of principles*' (p. 198–201):

'1. Stimulation has affective as well as sensory consequences.
2. An affective arousal orients the organism toward or against the stimulus-object.
3. Affective processes lead to the development of motives.

4. The strength of a recently acquired motive is correlated with the intensity, duration, frequency and recency of previous affective arousals.
5. The growth of motives is dependent upon learning as well as upon affective arousals.
6. The laws of conditioning apply to affective processes.
7. Affective processes regulate behavior by influencing choise.
8. Neuro-behavioral patterns are organized according to the hedonic principle of maximizing the positive and minimizing the negative affective arousal.'

Concluding statements. The present author thinks that Young's 'hedonic theory' can be said to be empirically well-demonstrated, and that it is integrated in his descriptive frame-of-reference in a well-proportioned manner, so that it now appears as one of the most original and valuable contributions to modern motivational psychology.

References

P. T. Young: Motivation of Behavior. N. Y. and London 1936.
- Emotions in Man and Animals. N. Y. and London 1943.
- The experimental analysis of appetite. (Ps. Bull. 1941, *38*, 129–164).
- Appetite, palatability and feeding habit: a critical review. (Ps. Bull. 1948, *45*, 289–320).
- Food-seeking Drive, Affective Process, and Learning (Ps. Review, 1949, *56*).
- Emotion as disorganized response (Ps. Rev. 1949, *56*, 184–191).
- Motivation and Emotion. (N. Y. and London 1961).
- Hedonic Organization and Regulation of Behavior (Psychol. Review, 1966, vol. 73, No. 1, 59–86).

Chapter 8

Allport's Theory

The American psychologist *Gordon W. Allport* (born 1897) has made an important contribution to the psychology of personality with his book, '*Personality—A psychological interpretation*' (1937)[1]). He has also written about different personality-psychological and social-psychological problems. Thus he has published together with Vernon: '*Studies in Expressive Movements*' in 1933, '*The Psychology of Radio*', in 1936 together with H. Cantril and '*The Psychology of Rumor*' in 1947 together with L. Postman. Besides this he has written some articles which have later been published under the heading, '*The Nature of Personality: Selected Papers*' (1950). The reason for dealing with Allport's work here is that he has made an important contribution to the psychology of motivation with *the hypothesis of functional autonomy*. The analysis of Allport's theory of motivation will be based upon his main work, 'Pers.' from 1937.

THE STRUCTURE OF THE THEORY

Summary of the Theory

Briefly the content of Allport's theory can be summarized thus (according to his diagram, p. 466):

Human behavior has two aspects, the *adaptive* and the *expressive* aspect, which, however, always appear simultaneously as aspects of concrete units of behavior, actions. Each aspect of behavior is determined by its own set of '*central determinants*' which together form a more or less co-operative system known as the 'personality' of the individual. This very important term is defined by Allport in a definition which is a synthesis of forty-nine other different definitions and which reads as follows (p. 48):

'Personality is the dynamic organization within the individual of those psychophysical systems that determine his unique adjustments to his environment.'

---

[1]) In future abbreviated to 'Pers.' The English reprint (Constabl, London, 1951) has been used. When nothing else is said, page numbers refer to 'Pers.'

All central determinants are activated by stimuli from the environment or from internal organs, where especially the internal stimuli (biological 'needs' or 'drives') are of great importance for the behavior. It is, however, only in the young, immature individual that these are the dominating, motivation variables, as different *aquired motives* develop in connection with these biological motives and gradually begin to function independently of the innate, biological motives, thus becoming the dominating motives in the grown, mature individual.

The presuppositions of Allport's theory are summarized by himself at the end of the book. Of these one must first mention that *the subject of his theory is the human personality* as it is known from everyday life. Connected with this is the presupposition that the *general* laws of psychology must be able to explain and predict the development and behavior of *a concrete individual chosen at random* (they must be 'idiographic'). The psychology of personality must therefore be relatively *molar*, and study rather comprehensive and complex units (which, in Allport's opinion, personality traits are). Finally one of his methodical presuppositions: '*the empirical-intuitive theory of understanding*', should be mentioned. Briefly it says that, 'Existentially considered, personality is a many-sided structure. It is also *perceived* as such' (p. 562). Thus Allport tries to give an explanation of the everyday intuitive understanding of Man in his theory. Moreover it must be pointed out that Allport's work both theoretically and methodically is characterized by a thorough *eclecticism*.

Level of Development of the Theory

As most psychological theories Allport's is *a classifying theory*, containing descriptions, classifications, and some scattered explanations of the behavior and personality of Man. But no axiomatization of the different hypotheses can be found. The most systematical formulation of his theory appears under the heading, 'Resumé of the Doctrine of Traits' (p. 339–342). No symbolization can be found, either, on the contrary Allport is against the use of symbols. He thus writes in connection with the problem of terminology (p. 310):

> 'As inadequate as common speech may be in representing the complex structure of personality, it is several grades more adequate than the mathematical symbols and neologisms that psychologists sometimes employ.'

As no actual formalization of the theory can be found, either, Allport's theory must be classified as a classifying theory.

Constructive or Reductive Theory

Allport's theory must be classified as *a constructive theory*, even though no explicit formulations concerning the problem in his work are to be found, as some statements which may be interpreted as constructive theses appear. The sub-title of the book may be interpreted in this way, as 'A psychological interpretation' can be used to separate this theory from both physiological and sociological theories of personality. Also his previously quoted definition of personality can be interpreted as being constructive, as the expression 'psychophysical system' may be interpreted as a term for hypothetical constructions to be used in explanations *without* reduction to physiological variables or hypotheses. Allport also writes about the relation between psychology and physiology in a footnote (p. 141), where he quotes J. S. Mill:

'Indeed, for that matter, the study of all the aspects of the development of personality may be said to be more advanced on the psychological level than on the physiological. "To reject the resource of psychological analysis and construct the theory of the mind solely on such data as physiology at present affords, seems to me a great error in principle, and an even more serious one in practice. Imperfect as is the science of mind, I do not scruple to affirm that it is in a considerably more advanced state than that portion of physiology which corresponds to it; and to discard the former for the latter appears to me an infringement of the true canons of inductive philosophy..." J. S. Mill, *System of Logic*, Bk. VI, chap. IV, Sec. 2. This judgment made one hundred years ago is as appropriate today as when it was first written.'

As can be seen from the quotation, Allport is directly opposed to a reduction of psychology to physiology, and his theory must therefore be described as a constructive theory.

Mentalistic or Behavioristic Theory

It is a little difficult to classify Allport's theory as purely mentalistic or purely behavioristic. In the often quoted definition of personality the expression 'psychophysical systems' is used, and in the comments on the definition he says (p. 48):

Psychophysical Systems. Habits, specific and general attitudes, sentiments, and dispositions of other orders are all psychophysical systems. In later chapters these dispositions will be ordered within a theory of *traits*. The term 'system' refers to traits or groups of traits in a latent or active condition. The term 'psychophysical' reminds us that personality is neither exclusively mental nor exclusively neural. The organization entails the operation of both body and mind, inextricably fused into a personal unity.'

This quotation indicates an inspecific *dualistic* theory, and the theory must therefore with regard to the interpretation of the hypothetical variables be described as a mentalistic theory.

Concerning the method (and thereby also the kind of protocol statements) Allport is, as already mentioned, very eclectic. He often points out that any method which can be used must be used in order to achieve as comprehensive and thorough a description of personality as possible. He writes, however, that (p. 313):

'One precaution is the constant return to *the observable stream of behavior*, the only basic datum with which the psychology of personality has to work.'

Apparently he believes that in cases of doubt inter-subjective, empirical control must be obtained through the use of behavioristic protocol statements (and methods). Therefore the theory may be classified as a *mainly mentalistic theory* (with a mentalistic interpretation of hypothetical variables and with optional use of protocol statements and methods).

Molecular or Molar Theory

It is very easy to classify Allport's theory as *a molar theory*. He writes explicitly about this himself (p. 457):

'the first and most important rule for experimental analysis may be phrased as follows: *The study of narrow ("molecular") aspects of conduct, though often exact, yields results that are of little value in understanding human personality. Far more significant is research at complex ("molar") levels where the structured forms of personal organization are freely manifested.*'

Field-Theory or Mechanistic Theory

It is difficult to classify Allport's theory with regard to the classification mechanistic theory versus field-theory. He writes about this problem (p. 192):

'If the psychology of personality is to be more than a matter of coefficients of correlation it *must* be a dynamic psychology, and seek first and foremost a sound and adequate theory of the nature of human dispositions.'

Even though he wants to describe his theory as a dynamic theory, he is rather critical in his attitude towards the general dynamic theories, which is shown by the following quotation (p. 192):

'Unfortunately the type of dynamic psychology almost universally held, however sufficient it may seem from the point of view of the *abstract* motives of *abstract* personalities, fails to provide a foundation sound enough of flexible enough to bear the weight of any *single* full-bodied personality. The reason is that all prevailing dynamic doctrines refer every mature motive of personality to underlying original instincts, wishes, or needs, shared *by all men*.'

Thus Allport's criticism is directed towards the much too abstract and general character of the motivation variables of the usual dynamic psychology, and he believes that he has improved dynamic psychology with his hypothesis of the functional autonomy of motives, which in his opinion gives a more satisfying explanation of the concrete, individual human motives. (The theory of motivation will be analyzed in the next passage).

Also a criticism of field theory can be found (p. 364):

'But in practice, the field theory inclines to put too great emphasis upon the momentary determination of conduct without giving due credit to the enduring systems of personality, often quite unaffected by changes in surrounding conditions.'

But in spite of these different critical remarks about dynamic and field-theoretical psychology, Allport is more positive in his attitude towards these forms of theory than towards the purely mechanistic theories. Moreover Allport's theory often deals with 'interactional processes' or the inter-functional relation between variables. Thus the previously quoted, very important definition of personality contains the expression: 'Personality is the dynamic organization', and in his comments on the definition he writes (p. 48):

'*Dynamic Organization.* To escape from the sterile enumerations of the omnibus definitions it is necessary to stress active organization. The crucial problem of psychology has always been mental organization (association). It is likewise the outstanding problem dealt with in this volume. Hence "organization" must appear in the definition. Yet this organization must be regarded as constantly evolving and changing, as motivational and as self-regulating; hence the qualification "dynamic". Organization must also imply at times the correlative process of *dis-organization*, especially in those personalities that we are wont to regard as "abnormal".'

As a result Allport's theory must be classified as *a dynamic theory*—an intermediate form of the pure mechanistic theories and the pure field-theories.

Statistical or Deterministic Theory

It is comparatively easy to place Allport's theory as *a deterministic theory.* First of all the expression: 'those psychophysical systems that *determine* his enique adjustment..." can be found in his important definition of personality, and in the comments to the definition he writes (p. 48):

'*Determine.* This term is a natural consequence of the biophysical view. Personality *is* something and *does* something. It is not synonymous with behavior or activity; least of all is it merely the impression that this activity makes on others. It is what lies *behind* specific acts and *within* the individual. The systems that constitute personality are in every sense *determining tendencies,* and when aroused by suitable stimuli provoke those adjustive and expressive acts by which the personality comes to be known.'

This shows that Allport's theory is not statistical. Several times he criticizes purely statistical psychology. But he also criticizes deterministic psychology the hypotheses of which are nothing but general laws which ignore of which cannot be used upon the unique personality development and structure of the individual, a so-called *nomothetic* theory; the psychology of personality must be *idiographic,* i. e. it must be able to describe and explain the single individual's development and special personality structure. Allport says, however about this distinction that 'the dichotomy, however, is to sharp: it requires a psychology divided against itself ... It is more helpful to regard the two methods as overlapping and as contributing to one another' (p. 22). This combination Allport thinks may be attained by the principle that '*a general law may be a law that tells how uniqueness comes about*' (p. 194 and 558). The individual characteristics must not be inexplicable exceptions, on the contrary, the general laws should be formulated in such a way that it is possible, by combining them, to explain and predict any persons's individual development and unique personality structure.

On the basis of this, Allport's theory may be described as *an idiographic-deterministic theory,* i. e. as a theory not only formulating 'average' laws, but deterministic laws which are valid for the individual, concrete person.

The Model

Allport uses different diagrams to illustrate his theory. Maybe the most important of these is the diagram, figure 17, page 246, where the lower part symbolizes his 'trait' theory as opposed to a factor theory in the upper part of figure 17. He also gives a diagram (figure 15, p. 141) which symbolizes the process of integration by which variables from different levels (conditioned reflexes, habits, traits, and 'selves') are integrated into a total personality. Finally he has a diagram (figure 29, p. 466) which gives a schematic presentation of the functional relations between the different variables of his theory.

Summary

This analysis of the theory as a whole can be summarized in the following description. *Allport's theory is a classifying, constructive, mentalistic, molar, dynamic, and idiographic-deterministic theory.*

MOTIVATION DEFINITIONS (AND HYPOTHESES)

Allport's theory of motivation is presented partly in one single chapter (Chapter VII) and partly in smaller paragraphs scattered in other chapters—often in connection with a criticism of other theories of motivation.

In my opinion it is therefore most practical *first* to give a summary (with quotations) of the paragraphs on motivation as they appear in 'Pers.', and *then* to make an analysis of the most important motivation variables and hypotheses, in accordance with the modified classifications of Tolman and Spence (and then finally to make a reconstruction of the theory in the last section of the chapter).

Summary of the Theory of Motivation

As already mentioned the words: '... psychophysical systems that determine ...' can be found in Allport's definition of personality, and in the comments on this definition (p. 48) he says: 'Habits, specific and general attitudes, sentiments, and dispositions of other orders are all psycho-physical systems. In later chapters these dispositions will be ordered within a theory of *traits* ...' As can be seen there are, among the variables called 'psycho-physical systems' or 'traits,' variables which are not usually considered to be motivation variables ('habits'), and others are dubious—but more about this later.

In the paragraph on 'Motivation' (Chapter IV, p. 112–114) Allport criticizes the theory of instinct (especially McDougall's formulation) and then he writes (p. 113):

'Rejecting the instinct hypothesis it becomes necessary to provide an alternative. A beginning, but only a beginning, may be made in the theory of Drive ... The doctrine of drive is a rather crude biological conception often employed as a factotum by psychologists with a simple mechanistic outlook. The hypothesis herewith offered is that the doctrine, while inadequate to account for *adult* motivation, does none the less offer a suitable portrayal of the motives of *young infants*, and for that reason serves very well as the *starting point* for a theory of motivation.'

Later he writes about the biological drive-theory (p. 119):

'To make the criticism more specific, there is first of all a tendency to keep the list of primary organic cravings too limited.'

This is the reason why his theory only deals with animals and infants and must be supplemented with the hypothesis about motives that are functionally independent of the biological 'drives'.

He writes about this hypothesis in Chapter VIII: 'The Transformation of Motives,' which has the following introduction (p. 190):

'Somehow in the process of maturing the manifold potentialities and dispositions of childhood coalesce into sharper, more distinctive motivational systems. *Pari passu* with their emergence these systems take upon themselves effective driving power, operating as mature, autonomous motives quite different in aim and in character from the motivational systems of juvenile years, and very different indeed from the crude organic tensions of infancy.'

Later he writes (p. 191):

'To understand the dynamics of the normal mature personality a new and somewhat radical principle of growth must be introduced to supplement the more traditional genetic concepts thus far considered. For convenience of discussion this new principle may be christened the *functional autonomy of motives*.'

Then he again summarizes different theories of motivation and reaches the following conclusion (p. 193).

'But *the common factor in all these explanations is the reduction of every motive, however elaborate and individual, to a limited number of basic interests, shared by all men, and presumably innate.*'

The criticism of these theories is summarized in the following statement (p. 193):

'The very fact that the lists are so different in their composition suggests—what to a naive observer is plain enough—that motives are almost infinitely varied among men, not only in form but in substance.'

And he continues the criticism (p. 194):

'It is manifest error to assume that a general principle of motivation must involve the postulation of abstract or general motives. The principle of functional autonomy, here described, is general enough to meet the needs of science, but particularized enough in its operation to account for the uniqueness of personal conduct.'

This 'principle of functional autonomy' is most thoroughly and explicitly formulated thus (p. 194):

'The dynamic psychology proposed here regards adult motives as infinitely varied, and a self-sustaining, *contemporary* systems, growing out of antecedent systems, but functionally independent of them.'

And he adds (p. 194):

'Theoretically all adult purposes can be traced back to these seed-forms in infancy. But as the individual matures the bond is broken. The tie is historical, not functional.'

Allport has developed this hypothesis of 'functional autonomy' of motivation from *Woodworth's* hypothesis of 'transformation of "mechanisms" into "drives".' Allport has corrected this hypothesis on one point, however as he maintains (p. 204) that:

'it seems to be neither the perfected talent nor the automatic habit that has driving power, but the imperfect talent and the habit-in-the-making ... Motives are always a kind of striving for some form of completion; they are unresolved tension, and demand a "closure" to activity under way.'

The chapter also includes a presentation of empirical observations which verify the hypothesis of functional autonomy, and arguments against different criticisms of the hypothesis, as well as a list of all the conditions which are explained by the hypothesis.

In a later chapter Allport analyzes the central variable in his theory, 'trait,' and its relation to other variables. He writes among other things about 'Traits and Determining Tendencies' (p. 290):

'The phrase "determining tendency" has both a narrow and a broad connotation. In its narrower sense it refers specifically to a mental set that facilitates the solution of a special problem or the execution of a certain act. In its broader sense, it is *any* directive tendency or condition of readiness for response. The doctrine of traits may be ordered to this broader conception. All traits are directive tendencies, but conversely all directive tendencies are not traits. Some directive tendencies are far too narrow and specific in their reference, and too fleeting in time to satisfy the criteria of a trait.'

The paragraph ends with the following definition of 'trait' (p. 295).

'We are left with a concept of trait as *a generalized and focalized neuropsychic system (peculiar to the individual), with the capacity to render many stimuli functionally equivalent, and to initiate and guide consistent (equivalent) forms of adaptive and expressive behavior.*'

In the next chapter the analysis of 'trait' is continued. Here a few hypotheses about the function of 'trait' can be found (p. 313):

'No single trait—nor all traits together—determine behavior all by themselves. The conditions of the moment are also decisive.'

'Only one maximally integrated activity takes place at any one time, and this activity is the product of a final convergent path wherein all available energy, though not all potential energy, is channelized to meet the present demand. From moment, to moment there is redistribution of this available energy, with the result that consummatory acts are ever changing and are the product of the interaction of all manner of determining factors, of which traits are only one.'

In a later paragraph Allport tries to answer the question: 'Do Traits Drive or Merely Direct?' He writes here as an introduction (p. 319):

'Characteristic of the nervous machinery, says neurophysiology, is its arrangement in *levels*, the more complex higher levels standing in the dual role of driver and restrainer to the lower simpler levels. Therefore, since traits, on the physiological side, are undoubtedly neural dispositions of complex order, they may be expected to show motivational, inhibitory, and selective effects upon specific courses of conduct. Brief as this statement is, it is the sum and substance of the present aid from neurophysiology. So far as it goes it suggests that the operation of a trait is dynamic, both in governing the reception of the stimulus and in directing the response.'

Later on he formulates the question (p. 321):

'But is the personalized trait dynamic in the sense of being selfactive? does it in and of itself *initiate* behavior? Strictly speaking, no; any disposition must be *aroused* before it is dynamically active ... Not every motivational system is at all times in a kinetic phase ... Either external stimuli or segmental tensions of an organic order may arouse them; but such antecedent stimulation in itself is not the motive.'

The analysis leads Allport to introduce a distinction between 'traits' (p. 329):

'Nor is it correct to think of all traits as motives—often they seem to have a defining or directive influence upon conduct, without true motivational significance. Some traits have less to do with *stress* than with *style* ... Some traits seem to have *motivational* (directional) significance, and some mere *instrumental* significance.'

Later he adds, however (p. 323):

'This distinction is a useful one. But it must not be overworked. There is no sharp line between motivational traits and stylistic traits between *direction* and *manner of expression*[2]).'

---

[2]) At this point Allport's terminology is inconsequent, as he calls 'motivational traits' 'directional' in one of the above quotations (from p. 323), whereas he elsewhere (p. 324) calls them 'driving' or 'dynamic' traits as contrasted to 'directive' traits. Thus the word 'directive' is used indiscriminately about both 'motivational' and 'instrumental' traits. The inconsequence can also

Apart from these sections motivation is only dealt with in 'Resumé of the Doctrine of Traits' (p. 339–342) and in the summary at the end of the book (p. 558–563).

As can be seen from the above, Allport's theory is rather unsystematic, for which reason the theory will be reconstructed in the last section when the analysis of the motivation variables and hypotheses has been finished.

Motivation Variables

In Allport's theory most of the motivation variables are referred to as 'psychophysical systems' or 'traits.' They are *hypothetical* variables in the sense that (p. 340):

'Traits are not directly observable; they are inferred (as any kind of determining tendency is inferred).'

'Traits' may further be classified as *phenomenological* variables, since the designation 'psychophysical systems', which has been used about them in this definition of personality and the comments on the definition, may be interpreted to mean that Allport himself understands or interprets them in a mentalistic way. Still, not all 'traits' are called introspectively perceivable, as some of them are considered to be 'involuntary' and—assumingly—relatively unconscious *disposition* variables (especially the mainly stylistic-expressive traits determined by temperament and convention). It might therefore be more correct to classify them as *neutral-formal* variables. It is difficult to reach a conclusion, though, since Allport's theory in this respect is very unclear (cf. also the passage on 'Mentalistic or Behavioristic Theory'). It is, however, quite certain that Allport's hypothetical variables should not be classified as neuro-physiological variables.

Allport does not divide 'motivational traits' into sub-classes. He merely mentions (p. 341) that:

'Some traits are clearly motivational, especially those sub-classes ordinarily known as interests, ambitions, complexes, and sentiments.'

Whether motivational variables *other* than 'motivational traits' can be found in Allport's theory at all is rather difficult to say. In the beginning of the book he maintains that 'drive' is a term which can be used when dealing with the motives of infants (cf. the quotation given from p. 113); but later he writes (p. 320):

'If biological drive plays a part (thirst, hunger, sex), it does so, not as *the* motive, but merely as an irritable state of bodily tissues set within an intricate and personalized psychophysical system.'

---

be seen in his diagram (page 466) where he classifies *all* 'personal traits' (motivational and stylistic) among the 'central determinants' which chiefly determine the 'expressive aspect' of the behavior. In my opinion 'motivational traits' should be placed among those determinants which chiefly determine the 'adaptive aspect' of the behavior (where some determinants which in my opinion must be motivational, namely 'task attitude' and 'specific intentions' have been mentioned).

This problem of the classification of 'traits' can be solved by introducing a new classification of variables in dynamogenic and directive variables (cf. Chapter 18).

And in a previously given quotation (p. 321) he writes about 'determining tendencies (including traits)' that:

'Either external stimuli or segmental tensions of an organic order may arouse them; but such antecedent stimulation in itself is not the motive.'

The above quotations indicate that 'drive' in Allport's theory, when it concerns *mature* persons, is only important as an *empirical* variable, which is functionally related to (stimulates) the hypothetical motivation variable 'motivational trait' according to the hypothesis of functional autonomy, which will be dealt with in the following.

Motivation Hypotheses

The most significant motivation hypothesis in Allport's theory is his hypothesis of *the functional autonomy of motives*, which—in spite of its central position in the theory—is only very loosely formulated. The most explicit and concise formulation is the one which has been quoted previously (from p. 194):

'The dynamic psychology proposed here regards adult motives as infinitely varied, and as self-sustaining, *contemporary* systems, growing out of antecedent systems, but functionally independent of them.'

This hypothesis is supplemented by another hypothesis already quoted:

'Only skills in the process of perfecting (mechanisms-on-the make) serve as drive.'

When combined these two hypotheses explain *the ontogenesis of motives* in Man, as for example 'attitudes,' interests, and sentiments. Allport also points out (p. 206–207) that they explain 'the force of delusions, shell shock, phobias, and all manner of complusive and maladaptive behavior.' They also explain how social altruistic motives arise in the originally egoistic individual and the motivating function of ideals and 'talents' (the intellectual aptitude).

Besides these *genetic* hypotheses of motivation, some hypotheses about the *functional* relation between motivation variables can be found in different places in Allport's presentation, especially the ones previously quoted (p. 313):

'No single trait—nor all traits together—determine behavior all by themselves. The conditions of the moment are also decisive';

'Only one maximally integrated activity takes place at any one time, and this activity is the product of a final convergent path wherein all available energy, though not all potential energy, is channelized to meet the present demand.'

The last hypothesis deals with the co-operation of motives, whereas the first one deals with the dependence of motives upon other (empirical) variables.

RECONSTRUCTION OF THE THEORY

The most significant part of Allport's theory is his definition of personality which is also the part which least needs to be reformulated as it is a synthesis of forty-nine other definitions. The only thing I should like to alter is his dualistic expression: 'psychophysical systems', which I suggest should be changed to the more neutral: 'psychological variables'. Therefore the reformulated definition would be:

Definition 1: Personality is the dynamic organization within the individual of those psychological variables that determine his unique adjustments to his environment.

The variable 'trait' is the second most important part of Allport's theory, and it is suggested that this should be defined and classified in the following way:

Definition 2: The determining psychological variables can be classified as 'motivating' and 'instrumental' traits of personality. The 'motivating traits' are dynamic variables, i. e. variables which arouse and sustain behavior (influenced by internal and external stimuli). The 'instrumental traits' are directive variables, i. e. variables which co-determine the direction and form of the action.

The following reformulations of the most important motivation hypotheses of the theory are suggested:

Genetic Hypothesis 1: The motivating traits of the personality of the grown individual have developed through maturation and learning processes in relation to the innate biological needs, of which, however, they may be functionally independent.

Genetic Hypothesis 2: Only developing, instrumental variables ('mechanisms of behavior') can function as motivating variables. When the development has ended with complete automatization of the function of the variable, it ceases to be motivating and becomes an instrumental variable.

Function Hypothesis 1: The function of the determining (motivating and instrumental) variables is determined by (is functionally related to) the present external (and maybe also internal) stimuli.

Function Hypothesis 2: At any given moment only one integrated action appears in an individual, and this is determined by a co-operation of all psychological variables functioning at that moment.

Conclusion

The most important contribution to general psychology in Allport's work is, as I have tried to point out, his definition of personality and his hypothesis on the functional autonomy of motives in adult individuals. At least it is these two things which have been of the greatest importance in the development of the psychology of motivation—in addition to his importance for the psychology of personality and social psychology.

Later Developments

Introduction. Since the first edition of this book appeared *G. W. Allport* has written, among other things, a new edition of his book entitled '*Pattern and Growth in Personality*' *(1961)*. In the preface Allport writes (p. IX):

'Although in one sense this volume is a revision of my book, *Personality: a Psychological Interpretation (1937)*, in another sense it is wholly new.'

And after mentioning his other books he writes (p. XII):

'In the present text I have tried to restate in simplified fashion the gist of all these writings, in the light of contemporary psychological research and theory.'

In accordance with this we think that the new volume deserves some supplementary comments.

The Structure of the Theory. Allport writes (p. IX) that 'The outlook, scope and emphasis are not greatly changed. At the same time the present volume is distinctly changed. At the same time the present volume is distinctly different.'

This apparently contradictory statement may be interpreted in this way: The *structure* of the theory is not changed very much, but the *content* of the theory is changed to some extent.

The *structure* of Allport's theory may still be described as 'a classifying, constructive, mentalistic, molar and idiographic-deterministic theory.' (cf. p. 120 in *this* book).

Allport's theory is still based on the same presuppositions which have been characterized by him as a kind of *systematic eclecticism*.'[3]) Allport's eclecticism is perhaps the broadest eclecticism found in contemporary psychology. He tries to combine trends not only from American behaviorism and psychoanalysis, but also from German 'personalistic psychology' and—as a new trend (in this volume) —'existentialistic psychology'. This last named philosophical and psychological movement has much in common with Allport's *idiographic and humanistic orientation* to psychology, and it also converges with Allport's interest for the psychology of religion. The present author thinks that it is perhaps fairest to characterize Allport's, systematic electicism' as more in harmony with *humanistic* trends ('personalistic' and 'existentialistic psychology') than with the *natural-scientific* trends (behavioristic and psychoanalytic psychology). On the other hand it must be admitted that Allport is not a onesided 'existentialist', and perhaps his very broad all-embracing eclecticism can be a bridge between these two opposite trends in modern psychology. The present author would like at this point to express disagreement with Allport about *the connection between philosophy and psychology*. Allport writes (p. 567) 'The philosophy of the person is inseperable from the psychology of the person', and he argues for the thesis that every theory of personality *has* a concept or '*philosofy of Man*'—*explicit or implicit*, and that this 'philosophy of Man' is among the presuppositions, axioms or *meta-principles* of the theory. The present author does not think that it is *necessary* to have a 'conception of man' before starting on psychological research; a 'conception of man'

---

[3]) In this evening-lecture at the XVII International Congress of Psychology at Washington, D.C., in 1963, where he very convincingly argued for this point-of-view.

could—or perhaps rather ought to be—the result of psychological research. But we must admit that we all have a philosophy of *science* before we begin our research, and this philosophy of science can of course be more or less narrow and restrict possibilities for research. Therefore, a philosophy of *science* can imply a 'philosophy of *Man*', and we must admit that Allport was among the first psychologists who drew our attention to the problem. It might be wise when analyzing theories—at least theories of personality—to always be aware of the consequences for a 'philosophy of Man' which are implied in the meta-principles of the theory.

The Content of the Theory. As already stated the *content* of Allport's theory is changed more than the *structure* of the theory. This is, among other things, a result of Allport's keeping abreast of *empirical research* in the psychology of personality and also of his own continued *theoretical thinking* about personality. In this connection we shall now turn to three revisions of the content of Allport's theory which are of interest from the point-of-view of *this* book:

1. The definition of 'personality'.
2. The definition of 'trait'.
3. The theory of 'functional autonomy'.

1. *The definition of 'personality'*. Allport's definition of the term 'personality' is only slightly changed. He now writen (p. 28):

'Personality is the dynamic organization within the individual of those psychophysical systems that determine his *characteristic behavior and thought*' (italics added).

The careful reader may note that it is only the last four italicized words which differ from the original definition. From Allport's comments on the definition we learn (p. 29), that:

'it would be unwise to define personality only in terms of adjustment.'

The reasons for Allport's changing from defining personality in terms of 'his unique adjustment to his environment' to defining it in terms of 'his characteristic behavior and thought', are to be found in his commentary. The present author thinks that this slight revision of the definition reflects a significant change (or development) in Allport's theory of personality—or perhaps his 'philosophy of Man'—from the prevailing American 'philosophy of adjustment' to the new 'philosophy of growth' which is strongly influenced by existentialist philosophy, especially in the person af *A. H. Maslow*.

2. *The definition of 'trait'*. The main variable in Allport's theory is still '*trait*' which he regards as a variable on the adequate descriptive level (not too molecular) for the purpose of personality theory. But Allport has introduced a new terminological distinction. Instead of '*common* trait' and '*individual* (or personal) trait', he now writes about '*common trait*' and '*personal dispositions*'. The difference is, that:

'*Common traits* designate organized complexities regarded as common (or comparable) in a population of persons.'

'*Personal dispositions* are units of the same order of complexity but are regarded as "nature's own cleavages". That is to say, they are the neuropsychic units we actually find in individual persons' (p. 374).

The present author thinks that this is a valuable contribution to the terminology of personality.

But there is no change in Allport's own conception of 'traits' and 'personal dispositions'. They are still regarded as intervening variables or hypothetical constructs; perhaps there is a little more emphasis placed on the possibility of a *physiological* interpretation of these H-variables. Thus Allport refers at several points to *Hebb*'s 'cell-assemblies' as the 'possible neurophysiological patterns underlying traits' (p. 337, footnote 8).

'Trait' and 'personal dispositions' are both and at the same time disposition *and* function variables (in spite of the name).

Allport continues to regard them as more or less 'dynamic':

'Some traits and dispositions are clearly motivational, especially those ordinarily known as interests, ambitions, sentiments, complexes, values. Others are less dynamic, having an ability to steer (to stylize) behavior rather than to initiate it' (p. 375).

Thus Allport makes no clear distinction between dynamic and directive variables; they are more or less dynamic or directive, or perhaps both at the same time.[4])

3. *The theory of 'functional autonomy'*. The greatest revision of Allport's theory is in his theory of '*functional autonomy*'. He still regards this concept as central to his theory of personality, but he now introduces a distinction between 'two levels of autonomy':

'I am now inclined to believe that the phenomena should be inspected on two levels. We shall do well to speak of (1) *perseverative* functional autonomy and (2) *propriate* functional autonomy. The former level skirts close to what are (or may be assumed to be) simple neurological principles. The latter level, however, frankly depends upon certain philosophical assumptions regarding the nature of human personality—' (p. 230).

As examples of *perseverative* functional autonomy Allport mentions (1) animal evidence of perseveration, (2) addictions, (3) circular mechanisms, (4) task perseveration, and (5) routine. As examples of *propriate* functional autonomy are mentioned: ability turning into interests, self-image and life-style.

In *explaining* these two different levels of functional autonomy Allport uses, *first*, what he calls '*quasi-mechanical considerations* (which include neuro-psychological and learning principles such as 'self-maintaining circuits' ('feed-back') and 'partial reinforcement'); and *secondly*, what he calls '*propriate considerations*' (which among other things include 'principles of mastery and competence' and

---

[4]) They perhaps should be classified as 'vector-variables' in accordance with the classification introduced in Chapter 18 of this book.

'propriate patterning'). Allport summarizes these propriate principles in this way (p. 252):

'From this point of view functional autonomy is merely a way of stating that men's motives change and grow in the course of life, because it is the nature of man that they should do so. Only theorists wedded to a reactive, homeostatic, quasi-closed model of man find difficulty in agreeing.'

Conclude remarks. While we criticized Allport's original theory of functional autonomy for its lack of explanation, we now must admit that there is a marked improvement in the new theory. But as the reader may have noted, Allport *explains functional autonomy* both by referring to well-known and accepted *psychological laws or principles* ('quasi-mechanical' in Allport's terminology) and by referring to *philosophical assumptions of the nature of man.*

The present author thinks that the acceptance of this sort of explanation is dependent on one's favorite *philosophy of science*, perhaps and ultimately upon the *personality of the psychologist* himself. Allport certainly has to be acknowledged for his *explicit* formulations of *his* philosophy of science and of Man.

References

1. G. W. Allport: Personality: A psychological interpretation (1937).
2. – The Use of Personal Documents in Psychological Science (1942).
3. – The Individual and his Religion (1950).
4. – The Nature of Personality: Selected Papers (1950).
5. – The Nature of Prejudice (1954).
6. – Becoming: Basic Considerations for a Psychology of Personality (1955).
7. – Personality and Social Encouter (1960).
8. – Pattern and Growth in Personality (1961).

Chapter 9

Lewin's Theory

During World War I the German-born psychologist *Kurt Lewin* (1890–1947) started some association-experiments based on N. Ach's theories about determining tendences. Gradually he became more and more interested in the problems of motivation and published a number of articles in *Psychologische Forschung* which were mainly theoretical in character and dealt with motivation-variables, as for example 'Wille, Vorsatz und Bedürfnisse.' At the same time he and his assistants started a series of experiments the results of which were published in *Psychologische Forschung* under the heading, 'Untersuchungen zur Handlungs- und Affekt Psychologie'. When Lewin emigrated to the United States in 1932 some of his earlier papers were translated and published in a book entitled, 'A Dynamic Theory of Personality' (1935). He then published a broad and systematic presentation of his theory in two volumes: '*Principles of Topological Psychology*' (1936)[1]) and 'The Conceptual Representation and the Measurement of *Psychological Forces*' (1938)[2]). He has later published several theoretical papers especially about Social Psychology, the field in which he became most interested. These were collected and published after his death in 'Field Theory in Social Science' (1952). Lewin carried out many fruitful, pioneering experiments on problems in Social Psychology in cooperation with his assistants. After his death a number of his papers on problems of a more practical character were collected in 'Resolving Social Conflicts' (1948). Lewin's latest systematic presentation of his theory was published as a chapter in Carmichael's *Manual of Child Psychology* under the heading, *Behavior and Development as a Function of the Total Situation* (1946), but since this is a brief and popular presentation which does not contain anything new, the following analysis will be based upon T. P. and P. F. if nothing else is mentioned.

THE STRUCTURE OF THE THEORY

Summary of the Theory

The content of Lewin's theory (according to 'Behavior and Development as a

[1]) In future abbreviated to T. P.
[2]) In future abbreviated to P. F.

Function of the Total Situation') can shortly be summarized in this way:

The behavior (B) of an individual will always be a function (F) of the total situation, the life space (Lsp.), consisting of both the condition of the individual (P) and the environment (E), factors which are closely interdependent. This can be formulated:

$$B = F\ (Lsp) = F\ (P, E).$$

In order to explain or predict the behavior of an individual it is necessary, then, to know the life space at the given moment and the hypotheses which formulate the functional relationship between the life space and the behavior.

The individual is a system consisting of an internal central region and an external peripheric (perceptual and motor) region. These regions can be differentiated into a number of regions (the number depending upon the stage of development), and their boundaries can be more or less clearly defined. A state of tension in an internal region corresponds to a need in the organism.

The environment is characterized by its cognitive structure, the position of the individual, and the distribution of the forces in the life space. *The cognitive structure* is partly differentiated into psychological past, present, and future, partly into two or more levels of reality (for example the activity-level and the day-dreaming-level). Orientation, learning, and insight can be described as changes in the cognitive structure of the life space. *The position of the individual* in the life space is very important; it is especially important to find its position in relation to goal-regions (including social groups), because this together with other things determines the direction of the behavior. A goal region has a positive valence and determines a *force field* which influences the individual and produces behavior directed towards the goal-region. The negative valences are regions influencing a force field which produce behavior directed away from the region. The strength of the force is dependent among other things upon the distance between the individual and the valence. Besides the driving forces, determined by the valences, there are repulsive forces which are dependent upon barriers and induced forces, which again are dependent upon other individuals. Conflict-situations are situations where opposite forces of almost equal strength act upon the individual. The conflict will arise mainly between two positive or two negative valences, or in cases where the positive and the negative valence are placed in the same region. Conflict-situations are very important for certain forms of behavior as for example choice, punishment, and reward, emotional tension, restlessness, etc.

While the cognitive structure and valences of the environment (E) determine the forces which cause the behavior of the individual, these valences and the cognitive structure are themselves dependent upon the condition of the individual (P), especially upon the tensions in the central regions corresponding to the needs of the organism. The need and the tension dependent upon it determine in part the valences, which again determine the force-field causing the behavior of the individual. The needs can be 'real' (biologically determined) or they can be quasi-needs (determined by decisions or other sets). The needs can be satisfied by consummation of the original goal or by substitution (in daydreaming for example). Needs can be changed by external restraining forces, by satisfaction and over-satisfaction, by resolutions, by changes into other needs, and by inducement of new needs by the social environment.

As seen from this brief summary of the content of Lewin's theory, behavior is a function of a very complicated interaction of external and internal factors. This fact characterizes, according to Lewin, the theory as a fieldtheory and makes it practical to use new special mathematical concepts in the theory. The meta-theoretical background and the formal characteristics of the theory will be analyzed in the following.

Lewin is not directly influenced by Logical Empiricism or any other modern epistemological school (but maybe to some degree by the philosopher Ernst Cassirer). More likely he is influenced by his own studies of the theoretical development in other sciences, especially in physics. (As this development, however, is in agreement with the principles of Logical Empiricism generally speaking, there is no noticeable difference between these principles and Lewin's meta-theoretical presuppositions.) These meta-theoretical studies have convinced Lewin that *theory is necessary in psychology*. He writes in his last systematical presentation from 1946 (9):

> 'Without theories it is impossible in psychology, as in any other science, to proceed beyong the mere collection and description of facts which have no predictive value' (p. 241), and: 'Psychology has never avoided nor can it avoid theory, but it can try to eliminate speculative theories which are frequently introduced without clear intent or in a hidden way, and try instead to make use of openly stated empirical theories' (p. 242), and finally: 'One of the main functions of theories and constructs is to bind together all the various fields of psychology which otherwise would tend to fall apart into a number of unconnected disciplines' (p. 243).

Through these studies Lewin has found *three developmental epochs in the history of science:* 1) a *speculative* epoch where interest in speculative theories dominates and attempts are made to build up general systems on the basis of a single concept or a few dichotomic concepts, and where one attempts to discover 'the essence of things'. 2) A *descriptive* epoch where all theories are met with hostility and where one's only purpose is to collect and describe 'facts'. 3) A *constructive* epoch where interest in empirical theories dominates and where attempts are made to form constructive systems based upon a group of inter-related concepts which make it possible to link up opposites. These theories do not deal with 'things' and their 'essence' but with 'processes' and their functional relations. In physics this last epoch began with Gallilei and in psychology in the thirties with Tolman and Hull (and Lewin himself) who have stimulated psychologists to take an interest in theories and 'intervening constructs or concepts'.

It is very characteristic of the scientific development of theories in the constructive period that an attempt is made *to use mathematics in the construction of theories.* Lewin's theory is one of the psychological theories which makes most use of mathematics. Lewin differs from other psychologists who—as for example Hull—have also tried to express their theories mathematically in that he uses only one special kind of mathematical theory namely the geometrical theory called *topology*, further developed by Lewin in his *hodological geometry*. Topology is used to symbolize the structure of the life space, the organization of the individual as well as its position in the environment. Hodology is used to symbolize psychological forces. Thus Lewin is able to give a mathematical presentation of the life space of which behavior is a function. A more detailed analysis must be postponed until Lewin's theory has been analyzed and classified according to the outline from Chapter 4.

Level of Development of the Theory

It is comparatively easy to classify Lewin's theory with regard to the first step of the analysis, the level of development of the theory, as it is one of the few *deductive* theories in psychology. He has not carried out any actual *axiomatization* in T. P. and P. F., first in a later thesis (8). But he has symbolized (mathematized his theory), using the geometrical discipline, topology, to a much greater extent than is the case in any other psychological theory. Lewin has, however, been much criticized for his use of topology (among others by I. D. London (12)); it has been pointed out that he has made a rather random selection among the principles of topology, so it is impossible to make any actual calculations. *Formalization* a defined in Chapter 2 has not been carried out. Still, Lewin's theory seems to be more formalized than any other psychological theory, since he gives a detailed presentation of the meta-theoretical presuppositions of the theory and of the mathematical concepts and principles used in the first chapters of T. P. and P. F. It therefore seems best to describe Lewin's theory as *an incomplete deductive theory*, or in other words as being a partly axiomatized, partly symbolized, and partly formalized theory. (Finally it should be said here that Lewin in his above mentioned paper (8) makes use of the word 'formalizing', but in a different sense than that used here. He uses 'formalizing' as a generic term for axiomatizing and symbolizing).

Constructive or Reductive Theory

With regard to the classification: constructive or reductive, it is comparatively easy to characterize Lewin's theory as *a constructive theory*. He himself describes the third developmental epoch of science as the constructive epoch, and even though he uses the word in a broad and loosely defined way it is quite evident that his whole theory is constructed as an application of a mathematical theory, and in T. P. (a footnote p. 19 og 20):

'We do not presuppose, as New Positivism generally does, the reducibility of Psychobiology to Physics,' and (p. 21): 'The point of view according to which all psychological explanations must finally rest on physics is based essentially on the philosophical Utopia of a single universal science.—A thoroughly worked out dynamic representation of person and environment will have the character of a construction and it must have this 'conceptual' character if it is to serve as a means of deriving actual behavior.' Still more clearly it is pointed out in P. F. p. 86: 'The operational definition of psychological force coordinates this construct to psychological processes. It should be definitely recognized, therefore, that a psychological force is a psychological construct independent from any construct of physics.'

Thus it is quite evident that in Lewin's opinion psychology can not be reduced to physics, while his opinion about physiological reduction is somewhat less clear. He writes in P. F. (p. 87):

'In case one should prefer to speak of "physiological" forces rather than psychological ones we would not mind such terminology, although it might be misleading. The reality of the psychological forces is the same as that of the "biological forces governing the brain".' And (p. 101): 'We do not at all object to interpreting the inner-personal systems as representing certain brain regions.'

But in spite of this lack of precision it is seemingly correct to characterize Lewin's theory as a constructive theory consisting of neutral-formal variables. According to Lewin the theory may be interpreted physiologically, but never physically.

Mentalistic or Behavioristic Theory

It is more difficult to classify Lewin's theory as a mentalistic or behavioristic theory. Lewin himself was originally a Gestalt-psychologist and in strong opposition to behaviorism. But in his American books he sympathizes with Tolman and Hull in their attempts to construct a deductive psychological theory. He even writes (10) p. 61:

'Field theory as any scientific approach to psychology is "behavioristic" if this means the tendency to provide "operational definitions" (testable symptoms) for the concept used.'

Lewin's theory in T. P. and P. F. is based upon (can be tested by) both introspective and behavioristic protocol statements, and its hypothetical variables are so extremely neutral-formal that Lewin's theory must be classified *as a neutral-formal theory.*

Molar or Molecular Theory

It is extremely difficult to classify Lewin's theory as molar or molecular. Lewin finds it possible and advisable in principle to treat all stages of description from the most molecular to the most molar in the same theory. He writes about this (10) (p. 243 and 244):

'A problem where prejudices have greatly hampered progress of research is the treatment of units of different sizes ...'

'it is necessary to investigate units of action of widely different sizes and situations of widely different scope such as the "immediate situation" and the "situation at large".'

'It is possible to obtain objective and reliable observations in regard to units of any size if one uses methods fitted to the various types. The attempt to determine reliably large macroscopic units by observing microscopie units, however, is bound to fail in psychology as in other sciences. It is technically impossible to describe the movement of the sun by describing the movement of every ion contained in it.'

Thus one might expect that Lewin's theory included all units from the most molar to the most molecular ones; but it deals mainly with rather molar subjects such as conflict-situations and social-psychological problems. Therefore the theory may best be characterized as *mainly a molar theory.*

Field-Theory or Mechanistic Theory

It is quite easy to classify Lewin's theory in this respect as it is *the prototype of field-theories in psychology.* It would therefore be of some interest to see how Lewin himself characterized a field-theory, but he began to characterize his topological psychology and vector psychology with the one word: field-theory only in later years, and no explicit and detailed definitions of this word are to be found in his two most important books (T. P. and P. F.). But in some of his later papers, collected in 'Field Theory in Social Science' he often makes use of and defines the word field-theory. He writes (in (10) p. 25):

'The basic statements of a field theory are that (a) behavior has to be derived from a totality of coexisting facts, (b) these coexisting facts have the character of a "dynamic field" in so far as the state of any part of this field depends on every other part of the field.'

This definition is in rather close agreement with other more or less vague statements about the same subject (see Chapter 3). In a later paper in the same collection he writes (p. 45):

'Field theory, therefore, can hardly be called correct or incorrect in the same way as a theory in the usual sense of the term. *Field theory is probably best characterized as a method:* namely, a method *of analyzing causal relations and of building scientific constructs.*'

Evidently Lewin does *not* use the word field theory here to characterize a psychological theory, but a philosophical method, assumption, or attitude, most likely his own (and partly that of the Gestalt-psychologists). But in spite of this Lewin's theory must be characterized as being the most field-theoretical psychological theory.

Deterministic or Statistical Theory

It is quite easy to classify Lewin's theory as an *extremely deterministic theory.* Lewin emphasises strongly the theoretical and practical value of deterministic theories as compared to that of the purely statistical ones. He devotes a whole chapter (Chapter V) in T. P. to the analysis of causality in psychology.

First of all Lewin points out that *the single case*, the single concrete action of a given individual in a given situation, *is also determined; laws are not only valid statistically.* But in order to explain and predict a concrete action it is necessary not only to know the general psychological laws, but also the condition of the given individual and its immediate position in the present structure of the environment, in short: It is necessary to know all the individual factors which are to be inserted as parameters in the general hypotheses. For the 'cause' of something (for example of an action) is not a single 'thing', but a totality of cooperating variables.

Then Lewin points out that it is of great importance in psychology to make a distinction between *two types of causations: historical and systematic causation.*

1) *Historical* causation is used to explain a *development,* as for example the development of an individual.

2) *Systematic* causation is used to explain *a single event,* as for example the present behavior of an individual in a given situation.

Both types of causation are of importance in psychology, and they supplement each other; but according to Lewin it is still *very important to keep them apart in* psychological explanations. If the present behavior of an individual is explained as a result of experiences from early childhood or other forms of experience or training one confuses them. Systematic explanations of behavior treat it as the result of the individual's present personality and conditions (plus the present external situation). However, the present personality and conditions can be historically explained as a result of a developmental process which among other things is determined by the previous experiences and training of the individual. It is included in the systematic explanation that only concrete and co-existing factors can be the cause of action (behavior); this means that neither future nor past, but only present events can cause behavior (i. e. only the present existing results of previous learning processes and only the present existing attitudes toward future goals). Lewin finds that until now psychological theories have been inexact and unsystematic with regard to causation (as for example association-psychology and psychoanalysis).

The Model

Lewin's theory cannot be represented clearly by using the usual S—O—R model. Lewin's model is rather complicated and it is difficult to separate it from the symbolic representation of the theory, which consists of geometrical (topological) symbols more illustrative than the usual mathematical and logical models. It might be said, however that the model consists of the diagrams, while the symbolic representation consists of the formula that the diagrams clarify. The model can, moreover, be regarded as a further development of a spatial field-model as used in physics.

Summary

Lewin's theory can now, summarising what has been said about the theory as a whole, be described briefly as *a partly deductive, constructive, neutral-formal, mainly molar, field-theoretical, and deterministic theory.*

MOTIVATION DEFINITION AND HYPOTHESES

Lewin's actual theory of motivation is to be found in P. F., as T. P. only contains the general presuppositions of the theory with a topological representation of the 'life space'. The first three chapters of P. F. are also about general topics and deal with the mathematical theory of 'direction' (the vector theory). Lewin's theory of motivation appears in Chapters IV and V (p. 71–210).

Because of the field-theoretical character of the theory it is rather difficult to make it the subject of a detailed analysis. Instead a list of the most important variables will be given first, followed by a brief summary, and then a final analysis (which will mainly be based upon Lewin's 'Glossary' p. 215–218).

Force

According to Lewin's field-theory, behavior is a function of the total field—the life space—and therefore 'the basic formula of a field theory' (25) Be = F (Lsp) = F (P, E) (p. 96 and 219), which states that behavior is a function of the total life space consisting of two inter-dependent systems of variables, namely the individual (P) and the environment (E).

Of the many inter-dependent variables *force* is the most direct cause of behavior (especially locomotion). Behavior cannot be treated as a function of a single force, however, but only as a function of the resultant of all forces acting upon the individual in a given position at a given time. This is expressed in the following 'co-ordinating' definition[3]) (p. 85):

'*Definition:* If the resultant of psychological forces acting on a region is greater than zero, there will be a locomotion in the direction of the resultant force, or the structure of the situation will change so that the change is equivalent to such a locomotion.

'In formulas:

'(19) Definition: If

$$\Sigma f_{A,X} = f^{X}_{A,B} \text{ and}$$
$$|f^{X}_{A,B}| > 0, \text{ then } v_{A,B} > 0\text{'}$$

These definitions of 'force' show that it is a *hypothetical functional variable.* And as all Lewin's hypothetical variables it is a neutral-formal variable. Logically the variable is characterized by three proporties: direction, strength, and point of application. Therefore, force can be symbolized mathematically by a vector (and represented graphically by an arrow).

Valence

Force is most directly related to the variable '*valence*' which is defined as follows (p. 88):

'Definition: A region G which has a valence (Va(G)) is defined as a region within the life space of an individual P which attracts or repulses this individual. In other words:

'(20) Definition of positive valence: If

---

[3]) By co-ordinating definition Lewin means both 'co-ordinating' as it is defined in Chapter 3 and 'operational'. Lewin should have used the latter term in this connection.

$$Va(G) > 0, \text{ then } | f_{P,G} | > 0.\text{'}$$

and
'(20a) Definition of negative valence: If

$$Va(G) < 0, \text{ then } | f_{P,-G} | > 0.\text{'}$$

Valences are represented by plus or minus signs. Their logical property is strength (but not direction), and they can be symbolized mathematically by scalars (and not by vectors). Valence must be classified as a *hypothetical* variable, even though it is closely related to the independent empirical variables (the stimuli from the goal-objects).

In these definitions valence and force are functionally related to each other; but force is not only a function of the valence, but also of the distance (e) between the individual and the valence. This can be formulated in the following way (p. 89)[4]:

'(21) $$|f_{P,G}| = F\left(\frac{Va(G)}{e_{P,G}}\right).\text{''}$$

Force-field

Even though each force is a function of one valence, the relation between valence and force is not a simpel one, since each valence determines more than one force, namely one force in each region of the life space. Thus the variable 'force-field' is defined in the following way (p. 90):

'(22) Definition: A force field correlates to every region of a field the strength and direction of the force which would act on the individual if the individual were in that region.'

The positive or negative value of the valence determines a positive or negative 'central field,' which can be formulated thus (p. 90):

'(23) Definition: A positive central field is a field in which for every region X a force towards the same region G exists ($f_{X,Y}=f_{X,G}$).'

and (p. 91):

'(24) Definition: A negative central field is a field in which for every region X a force away from the same region G exists ($f_{X,Y}=f_{X,-G}$).'

Tension

Valence, however, is a function of two variables, namely 'the perceived nature of the object or activity G' (which again has a functional relation, not precisely defined, to independent (stimuli) variables) and of 'certain tensions of the inner-personal regions of the person' (t). This is expressed in the following formula (p. 107):

'(31) $Va(G) = F(t,G)$.'

In this formula 't' is a symbol for the variable '*tension*,' which possesses the following logical properties (p. 98):

'*The Concept of Tension.* Every dynamical construct in psychology needs a definition of its

---

[4]) Cf. Hull's 'Goal gradient hypothesis.'

conceptual properties and a co-ordinating definition.

'The concept of tension as used here refers to a *state* of a system of an individual. Tension has, besides others, the following properties:

'(a) It is a state of a system S which tries to change itself in such a way that it becomes equal to the state of its surrounding systems $S^1, S^2, \ldots, S^8$.

'(b) It involves forces at the boundary of the system S in tension.'

And the co-ordinating definition of the variable 'tension' (p. 99):

'As the *co-ordinating* definition of tension one can use the following statement:

'(29) Hypothesis: Whenever a psychological need exists, a system in a state of tension exists within the individual.

'This hypothesis includes also "quasi-needs" (Lewin 1935) resulting from intensions.'

'The empirical facts to which this statement refers, are those acts or behavior which generally are recognized as a syndrome indicating a need; it refers, furthermore, to the after-effect of an intention.'

In other words, this co-ordinating definition defines 'tension' as a *hypothetical* variable, which is a function of the independent, empirical variable 'need' (this functional relationship has not been elaborated). Lewin says about the variable 'need' (p. 99):

'I am speaking about the syndrome indicating a need because the term need itself can hardly be recognized as a concept in the strict sense. It is a term of the same type, as, for instance, learning, which probably will have to be eliminated in time. In other words, in formula (29) the term "need" will have to be replaced by more precise behavioral symptoms for tension.'

The inter-relationship between force, valence, and tension is expressed in the following formula (p. 107):

$$\text{'(32)} \quad f_{P,G} = F\left(\frac{t}{e_{P,G}}, G\right).\text{'}$$

Summary

Lewin's theory presents the relations between behavior and the different motivation-variables by some rather complicated functions, because, as he himself briefly formultes it (p. 108):

'*Instead of linking the need directly to the motoric, the need is linked with certain properties of the environment. The environment then determines the motoric.*'

Lewin points out that the advantage of this theory as compared to simpler and more usual theories ('linking the need directly to the motoric') is that it explains the directive tendency of the behavior (which is, however, in other theories explained as the result of a learning process), and it explains how 'a change in the cognitive structure of the environment' is 'equivalent to locomotion.'

Final Analysis

A simplified and systematized presentation of the most important motivation variables and motivation hypotheses in Lewin's theory has been given in the previous sections. This section will contain a more detailed analysis of these variables and hypotheses according to the theoretical presuppositons mentioned in the introductory chapters.

First of all it must be emphasized that the *total 'life space'* (with its cognitive structure, its valences and force field, and with the structure and tension-systems of the individual) *is a complicated system of hypothetical variables*. And, as mentioned above, all the hypothetical variables can be classified as neutral-formal; it is also important that *all* variables in Lewin's theory are *functional* variables. The only *empirical* variables included in Lewin's theory are the dependent variable '*locomotion*' (behavior) and the independent variables '*need*' and '*goal*', or rather: 'the perceived nature of the object or activity G', which again is dependent upon 'certain non-psychological 'alien' factors' (p. 107).

As a result of this almost all hypotheses (definitions and formulas) in Lewin's theory should be considered as purely theoretical hypotheses. (Cf. Spence's modified classification in Chapter 3). Only one of the above mentioned hypotheses is of the H→R type and indicates the relationship between an empirical behavior variable (locomotion) and the hypothetical variables, namely to co-ordinating definition of force (formula 19 and 19a). Nevertheless, Lewin deals very thoroughly with the measurement of psychological forces, and in the chapter about this subject (Chapter V in P. F.) several formulas of the H→R type are presented, by which force is measured by means of different behavior characteristics; but Lewin himself only considers these formulas as examples. Only a very few hypotheses are of the S→H type, which indicate the relation between hypothetical variables and independent empirical variables, namely the co-ordinating defintion of tension (def. no. 29, cf. the previous section) and the formula (no. 31) which attempts to express the functional relation between goal and valence (and tension). And all the hypotheses that formulate the functional relation between the hypothetical variables and the empirical variables (on both sides) are only formulated qualitatively. Lewin's theory is essentially different in this respect from Hull's very systematic and mathematized theory.

RECONSTRUCTION OF THE THEORY

Even though Lewin's theory is one of the most exact and systematical psychological theories, it is not flawless. But it is difficult to make a reconstruction because of its field-theoretical character; it would be almost impossible to change any variable or hypothesis without having to change all the other variables and hypotheses, too. However, a reconstruction will be attempted when some objections to the theory have been examined.

Criticism of Lewin's Theory

Ivan D. London criticizes in (12) Lewin's theory as follows:

1. 'Force' is 'a construct, which is fundamentally antropometric' and so should not be used in any science. (Nevertheless it is used in physics.)

2. Lewin's aversion towards statistics is unfortunate since statistics play an important role in modern physics.

3. Lewin's hodological space lacks the necessary mathematical basis.

4. 'To attempt a reduction of all phenomena to field formulation as Lewin attempts, is to make a big assumption, for there is no *a priori* guarantee that it can be done. Certainly, physics lends no encouragement to the belief in this possibility.' Moreover London finds that Lewin's field-theoretical presentation 'seems sterile, they have no real deductive capacity.'

5. Lewin's aversion towards analysis is in conflict with all other scientific methods, which have always been analytical. (In my opinion Lewin is not actually against analysis, though; he even blames the Gestalt psychologists for having been so).

6. 'The concepts of law and probability, the latter a statistical conception defined as *a frequency obtaining in a given class of events*, are not the contradictory and mutually exclusive concepts that Lewin would indicate. As a matter of fact, the dichotomy which Lewin sets up between 'Aristotelian' and 'Galilean' concepts falsifies the whole picture of theoretical science and gives an erroneous idea of what is going on in present-day physics.'

7. 'Lewin in reality does not utilize *one single theorem* of topology'—'Lewin's topology is not the topology of mathematics' 'a mathematically unifield theory for all of psychology along Lewin's pattern is without significant value and furthermore, in view of the sharply divergent stand of modern physics generally impossible.'

This criticism of Lewin's theory is thus extremely severe. But also others have been severe in their criticism.

S. Koch, who has in general evaluated Lewin's theory positively makes the following negative critical remarks in his article (11).

1) Lewin does not distinguish between primary and secondary principles in T. P. and P. F. He makes this distinction, however, in (8), but here he does not make any distinction between postulates and explicit definitions.

2) Lewin does not make an explicit formulation of the topological postulates which he interprets.

3) Lewin presupposes a 'logic of dynamics,' which does not exist.

4) Lewin does not distinguish between co-ordinating and operational definitions, but calls all definitions co-ordinating definitions (and defines them as such). Nevertheless he uses this label as a generic term for everything which is called co-ordinating and operational definitions in Chapter 3.

Still S. Koch is, as mentioned above, for the most part positive in his attitude towards Lewin's theory.

F. V. Smith gives the following criticism of Lewin's theory (14):

1) 'The fundamental problems of instigation are to a great extent passed over.'

2) 'The attempts to develop a terminology are not carried far enough to reveal anything novel.'

3) Lewin's system 'presents a form of integration which is essentially the integration of elementary physics imposed upon what is frequently an oversimplification of psychological conditions.'

4) 'The predictive value of any of Lewin's devices is no greater than a common sense appraisal of a situation would indicate.'

Thus, the negative criticism of Lewin's theory is abundant, but still Lewin has many 'followers,' and he has been very important, especially, for the development of modern social-psychology. Of course this is no guarantee that his theory is correct or fruitful, since it might be a result of Lewin's personal inspiration and many fruitful ideas in both experimental and theoretical work.

There are, however, a few points where the above mentioned critics (and others) agree:

1) The mathematical foundation of Lewin's theory is incomplete, as he does *not* apply the usual geometrical topology, but an incomplete system constructed by himself.

2) Lewin's theory is not formally deductive since what seem to be formally deductions are only results of common-sence reasoning.

The last statement is in agreement with what is pointed out by many behavioristic psychologists who say that Lewin's theory is exclusively 'response-inferred' as a connection between stimuli and hypothetical variables is lacking. In other words, Lewin's theory consists mainly of hypotheses of the H→H type plus some of the H→R type, but only a very few of the S→H type, and these are very inexact. Therefore, the reconstruction of Lewin's theory must take this fact into due consideration[5]).

Suggestions for a Reconstruction

As the first definition in the reconstruction of Lewin's theory the following definition of the independent empirical variable 'need' is suggested:

Definition 1: 'Need' = any condition which deviates from the optimal life-conditions of the organism (cf. homeostasis).

Thus, this definition includes only the 'real' needs, not the so-called 'quasi-needs', which cannot (yet) be defined as empirical variables (at any rate not as inter-subjective empirical variables); on the other hand, one must define hypothetical variables corresponding to what Lewin calls 'quasi-need' or '*intention*', which includes all phenomena labelled 'decisions', 'problem acceptance', and 'sets' of all kinds. These phenomena or processes are dependent upon the ('real') needs of the organism, as the intentions of the individual are directed towards phenomena which are related to its needs. This can be formulated as the first primary hypothesis in the reconstruction of Lewin's theory.

Hypothesis 1: 'Intention' (I) is a hypothetical variable which is a function of the needs of the organism.

'Tension' is the next motivation variable in Lewin's theory, and it is related to 'need' in formula no. 29 (cf. p. 129), which cannot be used in the reconstruction without being revised because Lewin does not distinguish between the empirical variable 'need' and the hypothetical variable 'quasi-need'. One may suggest the following reformulation:

---

[5]) The reader will find a very thorough, critical analysis by W. K. Estes of Lewin's theory in *W. K. Estes et al.: Modern Learning Theory (Appleton, N.Y. 1954).*

Hypothesis 2: 'Tension' (t) is a hypothetical variable which is a function of the need of the organism, or of an intention.

The previous reconstructions are all formal, but a reconstruction of content will also be suggested. As mentioned in the analysis of the theory there is a curious indirect relation between tension and the variable 'force', because valence is defined so that behavior is directly determined by the valence-dependant force and only indirectly by the need-dependant tension. This hypothesis, however, can only explain instinctive behavior (where 'valence' stands for 'signal of release' in the theory of Lorenz and Tinbergen) or an already learned habitual behavior; at any rate the hypothesis cannot explain non-learned and non-inherited behavior of the trial-and-error type where the individual has a need which is not satisfied, a tension dependent upon the need, and a force dependent upon the tension, which result in an exploratory behavior which more or less at random brings the individual into contact wity a goal-object; and only when this goal-object has satisfied the need does it have the meaning of 'valence' to the individual. In my opinion it would be practical for empirical reasons to reconstruct Lewin's theory in such a way that the hypothetical variable 'force' becomes a direct function of 'tension'; at the same time, of course, it can also be a function of the valence (and of the organism's distance from it). It is this complicated co-operation of factors that gives Lewin's theory (as well as other theories) its field-theoretical character. Thus 'force' is also dependent upon the variable 'valence', which is again dependent upon the non-psychological (physical-chemical or social) properties of the goal-object is—as is the need—an independent empirical variable which can be defined in the following way:

Definition 2: Goal-object = any complex of phenomena (an object or a situation), the presence or absence of which is necessary for the maintenance of the optimal life conditions (i. e. the satisfaction of the needs of the organism).

The hypothetical variable which Lewin calls 'valence' is dependent upon this independent, empirical variable, and this can be formulated as follows:

Hypothesis 3: 'Valence (Va) is a hypothetical variable directly related to the goal-object (G) and inversely related to the distance (e) between the goal-object and the individual (P):

$$Va = f\left(\frac{G}{e_{P,G}}\right).$$

It is now possible to introduce and implicitly define the variable psychological 'force' in the following terms:

Hypothesis 4: 'Force ($F_{P,G}$) is a hypothetical variable which is a function of both tension and valence:

$$F_{F,G} = f(t \times Va).'$$

Finally we have the last of the variables: the dependent, empirical variable, behavior, a function of 'force,' which can be formulated in the following way:

Hypothesis 5: The behavior of the organism (Be) is a function of the hypothetical variable 'force' ($F_{P,G}$):

$$Be = f(F_{F,G}).$$

Conclusion

In spite of the very severe criticism of Lewin's theory, quoted in the previous sections it is only just to finish this chapter on Lewin's theory on a more positive note. E. C. Tolman writes in his obituary (15) that Lewin was probably the greatest and most productive person in the history of psychology apart from Freud. But Lewin differed from Freud in that he was equally interested in both theoretical analysis and experimental research. And Darwin Cartwright writes in the introduction to (10):

> 'When the intellectual history of the twentieth century is written, Kurt Lewin will surely be counted as one of those few men whose work changed fundamentally the course of social science in its most critical period of development. During his professional life of only about thirty years, the social sciences grew from the stage of speculative system building, through a period of excessive empiricism in which facts were gathered simply for their intrinsic interest, to a more mature development in which empirical data are sought for the significance they can have for systematic theories. Although the social sciences are only barely into this third stage of development, Lewin's work as accelerated greatly the rate of development. Though he was primarily a psychologist and made his major contributions in that field, the influence of his work has extended well beyond the bounds of traditional psychology.'

In my opinion Lewin's works are very valuable and might be favorably compared with both those of Hull and Tolman.

References

1. K. Lewin: Die psychische Tätigkeit bei der Hemmung von Willensvorgängen. Zeitschr. f. Psych. b. 77 (1917), 212–48.
2. – Das Problem der Willensmessung (Psych. Forsch., 1921–22, vol. 1 and 2, p. 191–302 and 65–140).
3. – Vorbemerkungen über die seelischen Kräfte (Psych. Forsch. 1928, v. 7, p. 294–329).
4. – Vorsatz, Wille und Bedürfnis (Psych. Forsch. 1928, v. 7, p. 330–85).
5. – A Dynamic Theory of Personality (1935).
6. – Principles of Topological Psychology (1936).
7. – The Conceptual Representation and the Measurement of Psychological Forces (1938).
8. – Formalization and Progress in Psychology (1940; reproduced in (10)).
9. – Behavior and Development as a Function of the Total Situation (1946), reproduced in (10).
10. – Field Theory in Social Science (edited by D. Cartwright 1952).
11. S. Koch: The Logical Character of the Motivation Concept (Ps. Review, v. 48, 1941, 15–38 and 127–54).
12. I. D. London: Psychologists' Misuse of the Auxiliary Concepts of Physics and Mathematics (Ps. Review; 1944, 51, 266–91).
13. Murphy, G.: Historical Introduction to Modern Psychology, chap. 21 (1951).

14. Smith, F. V.: The Explanation of Human Behavior (1951).
15. Tolman, E. C.: Kurt Lewin, 1890–1947 (Ps. Review v. 55, 1948).
16. Woodworth, R. S.: Contemporary Schools of Psychology, p. 151–155, 1949.
17. Estes et al.: Modern Learning Theories (1954).
18. D. Cartwright: Lewinian Theory as a Contemporary Systematic Framework (in S. Koch (edt.): Psychology—A Study of a Science). (McGraw-Hill, N.Y., vol. II, 1959).

Chapter 10

Murray's Theory

In the large work, '*Explorations in Personality*' (1938)[1]), the American psychologist *Henry A. Murray* (born 1893) has presented a very interesting and fruitful theory of motivation. The book was written by twenty-eight psychologists and psychiatrists who studied the personality of fifty young men, using many different clinical and experimental methods, under the leadership of Murray. Even though the book is primarily an examination of the psychology of personality ('personology' as it is called by Murray), the theoretical part is of great general-psychological interest, especially for the present analysis of theories of motivation, because motivation variables play a much greater role in this theory than is the case in other theories of personality (as for example Allport's). Most of the book (including the theoretical part) has been written by Murray himself. He has written a few articles earlier, and after having published his main work he has (together with Kluckhohn) written an outline of the psychology of personality (as an introductory chapter to the symposium, 'Personality in Nature Society and Culture, edited by Kluckhohn and Murray[2]). He has, moreover, written a chapter on the classification of need in Parsons and Shills: 'Toward a General Theory of Action' (1951). In these two chapters Murray revises his theory a little, but, in agreement with the criterion of selection which has been used in this study of theories of motivation, only the formulation of the theory as it appears in 'Explorations in Personality' will be analyzed and reconstructed.

THE STRUCTURE OF THE THEORY

Summary of the Theory

Chapter 1, 'Introduction,' and Chapter 2, 'Proposals for a theory of Personality', are the most important theoretical parts of E. P. The other chapters of the book are either mainly methodological, or they deal with subjects which are of less interest for a theory of motivation (for example Chapter 5 on 'Childhood Events').

---

1) In future abbreviated to E. P. All pages mentioned refer to this work.

2) First edition, 1948.

On the basis of Chapter 2 the content of the theory can briefly be summarized as follows:

Personology studies individual personalities. A personality is a lifelong series of *episodes;* every episode is a more or less complicated *action* which most often is the reaction of the organism to its (physical and social) environment. Every action is determined by integrating, or '*regnant*' *brain-processes*, which can be both conscious and unconscious. These determining, regnant processes are the results of many cooperating factors as can be seen from the following quotation (p. 141):

'Thus, as we see it, regnancies are the resultants of external press, of freshly aroused emotional needs (Id), of conscious intentions (Ego), of accepted cultural standards (Superego) and of customary modes of behaviour (habit system) in varying proportions. The relative strength of these influences determines what tendencies will be objectified.'

The most important of the above mentioned factors in Murray's theory are '*need*' and '*press*.' They are so important that every episode in the development of a personality can be described as a combination of a 'press' and a 'need,' a '*theme*.' The concept of need is the most important of all concepts in Murray's theory; and his theory, maybe more than any other, has given this concept a central position in modern psychological theories. Murray summarizes his own definition and hypotheses of 'need' in an exellent way:

'A need is a construct (a convenient fiction or hypothetical concept) which stands for a force (the physico-chemical nature of which is unknown) in the brain region, a force which organizes perception, apperception, intellection, conation and action in such a way as to transform in a certain direction an existing, unsatisfying situation. A need is sometimes provoked directly by internal processes of a certain kind (viscerogenic, endocrinogenic, thalamicogenic) arising in the course of vital sequences, but, more frequently (when in a state of readiness) by the occurrence of one of a few commonly effective press (or by anticipatory images of such press). Thus, it manifests itself by leading the organism to search for or to avoid encountering or, when encountered, to attend and respond to certain kinds of press. It may even engender illusory perceptions and delusory apperceptions (projections of its imaged press into unsuitable objects). Each need is characteristically accompanied by a particular feeling or emotion and tends to use certain modes (sub-needs and actones) to further its trend. It may be weak or intense, momentary or enduring. But usually it persists and gives rise to a certain course of overt behaviour (or fantasy), which (if the organism is competent and external opposition not insurmountable) changes the initiating circumstance in such a way as to bring about an end situation which stills (appeases or satisfies) the organism.'

The many classifications of need and their inter-relations will be analyzed later.

Each episode or theme in an individual's life is—as mentioned—characterized by the existence of a need, most often in relation to a certain '*press*,' i. e. a stimulus-situation which has a (potential) influence upon the life of the organism. Whether the action caused by the need leads to success or to disappointment often has a determining influence upon the further development of the personality, as each episode leaves lasting '*traces*' in the brain and determines the actions of the individual in new episodes. This is the reason why the study of the ontogenetic development of the individual (and especially the development of the infant) is so important in personology. In his respect—as in many other respects—Murray's personology is strongly influenced by *psycho-analysis.*

Murray deals explicitly with the *presuppositions* of his theory in Chapter 1. Here he maintains that 'personalities constitute the subject matter of psychology' (p. 3). But the part of psychology which directly studies personality as a whole—and not only the individual functions or processes as do the other disciplines—he calls '*personology.*' Murray maintains that personality psychologists can be divided into two groups: 'the peripheralists' and 'the centralists.' The attitude of the peripheralists is objective, positivistic, mechanistic, elementaristic (or atomistic), and sensationistic, whereas the attitude of the centralists is subjective, rationalistic, totalistic (or holistic), and dynamistic. Murray gives the following summary of the difference between the two groups (p. 10):

'In summary, it may be said that the peripheralists are apt to emphasize the physical patterns of overt behaviour, the combination of simple reflexes to form complex configurations, the influence of the tangible environment, sensations and their compounds, intellections, social attitudes, traits, and vocational pursuits. The centralists, on the other hand stress the directions or ends of behaviour, underlying instinctual forces, inherited dispositions, maturation and inner transformations, distortions of preception by wish and fantasy, emotion, irrational or semiconscious mental processes, repressed sentiments and the objects of erotic interest.'

Murray points out, however, that these two groups are *not* homogeneous, as a a psychologist can in some respects be a centralist and in other respects a peripheralist. He and his assistants did not quite agree on all points, either, but their work was an attempt to unite conflicting ideas; about the possibility and value of such a unified psychology Murray writes (p. 11):

'It might even be possible, by slight modifications here and there, to construct a scheme which would fit together most of the prevailing theories. For a common theory and a common language is for psychology an urgent requisite.'

But in spite of this neutral, integrating tendency Murray admits that in many ways he and his assistants are centralists, because it was necessary as a counterweight to the dominating peripheralistic tendency in American psychology (in the thirties). He thus writes explicitly that they favored the dynamic viewpoints (p. 36), and that they were less anti-theoretical than the peripheralists. He writes about this (p. 21):

'Now, at every stage in the growth of a science there is, it seems, an appropriate balance between broad speculation and detailed measurement. For instance, in the infancy of a very complex science—and surely psychology is young and complicated—a few mastering generalizations can be more effective in advancing knowledge than a mass of carefully compiled data.'

And further on the same subject (p. 22):

'Our conclusion is that for the present the destiny of personology is best served by giving scope to speculation, perhaps not so much as psycho-analysts allow themselves, but plenty.'

As can be seen Murray does not fear theories, and considers them not only necessary, but also very valuable at the present stage of the development of psychology. It is therefore of particular interest to analyze the level of development of his theory as well as its other main features.

Level of Development of the Theory

Murray gives chapter 2 the title 'Proposals for a Theory of Personality', and his work has to a high degree the character of a *program* for a theory. But it is a very fruitful program, as he and his assistants have already shown by collecting a rather extensive mass of observations. This theory is only insufficient in formal respects, and it must be described as *a classifying theory.*

Twenty-five 'primary propositions' are given (p. 38–49), but these propositions differ greatly in kind when seen from a meta-theoretical point of view; some of the statements actually belong in the meta-theory of the theory, for example:

'This is a statement of the *organismal* theory.'
'This proposition belongs to the organismal theory of reality.'

The same is true of the first twenty-one paragraphs of 'primary propositions', as this deals with choice of terminology, etc.

The remaining 'primary propositions'—which belong to the theory as such—deal with terms on very different levels of abstraction. Thus there are definitions of purely empirical variables or descriptive terms—as for example 'actone' (paragraph 8, p. 41); and there are also definitions of and postulates about very hypothetical variables such as 'need' and 'regnancy'. All these different 'propositions' are only listed without any attempt to systematize them, and therefore the theory *cannot* be described as a deductive theory, not even if the rest of the chapter in question is regarded as statements of 'secondary propositions'. The very logical system or organization characteristic of a deductive system is lacking. Murray's theory is only a common continuous presentation, but in spite of this shortcoming, it is so full of exact definitions and general hypotheses that it is also one of the most interesting psychological theories when seen from a purely formal (logical, syntactical) point of view.

Constructive or Reductive Theory

It is rather difficult to place Murray's theory in this classification. On the one hand the theory has much in common with a reductive theory, as Murray strongly emphasizes the importance of the brain-process. He writes (p. 45):

'... the unity of the organism's development and behaviour can be explained only by referring to organizations occurring in this region. It is brain processes, rather than those in the rest of the body, which are of special interest to the psychologist.'

And he goes on, giving the following reasons (p. 73):

'*An activity in the brain has been conceptualized because it is the regnant processes in this region which we, as psychologists, must ultimately attempt to formulate. If we do not, we shall never bring together into one conceptual scheme the facts of behaviour, the facts of brain physiology and pathology and the facts of consciousness.*'

But on the other hand Murray's theory has also much in common with constructive theories. He often uses rather mentalistic or introspective terminology; for example, he gives the following argument (p. 47):

'It seems that it is more convenient at present in formulating regnant processes to use a terminology derived from subjective experience. None of the available physico-chemical concepts are adequate. It should be understood, however, that every psychological term refers to some hypothetical, though hardly imaginable, physical variable, or to some combination of such variables. Perhaps some day the physiologists will discover the physical nature of regnant processes and the proper way to conceptualize them.'

A closer analysis shows that the brain-processes—'regnancies'—referred to in Murray's theory are *purely hypothetical constructions* built exclusively upon introspective and behavioristic observations—and neuro-physiological data are not used. Actually they have only their *localization* in the brain in common with neuro-physiological constructions, otherwise they are rather mentalistic or neutral-formal constructions. It must therefore, based upon the above, be most correct to classify Murray's theory as *a mainly constructive theory.*

Mentalistic or Behavioristic Theory

It is also rather difficult to place Murray's theory in this classification, even though he writes fairly explicitly on this subject. Thus many rather behavioristic, meta-theoretical statements can be found in Murray's theory. Already in 'Preface' (p. IX) he writes:

'our primary aim was to discover some of the principles that governed human behaviour.'

Later he writes (p. 54) that:

'it is easier to agree about objective facts than about subjective facts,' for which reason:

'it is best to start with behaviour.'

On the other hand mentalistic statements can also be found. Murray writes thus (p. 47):

'It is not only more convenient and fruitful at present to use subjective terminology,' but, he continues further down the page:

'The need to describe and explain varieties of inner experience decided the original, and, I predict, will establish the final orientation of psychology.'

This apparent contradiction between behavioristic and mentalistic features of the theory disappears through an integration by means of the principle of 'regnancies.' Murray writes about this (p. 51–52):

'Thus, to explain a conscious event, as well as to explain a behavioural event, all the major variables of a regnancy must be known. According to this conception, then, the goal of the introspectionists and the goal of the behaviourists become the same: to determine the constitution of significant regnancies.'

As can be seen from the quotation, integration results when both behavioristic and introspective data are related to—as manifestations or results of—*'regnant' brain-processes.* These must be described as hypothetical constructions or variables, even though Murray does not explicitly describe them in this way, since it is an implicit consequence of the following statement (from p. 45): 'A need or drive is just one of these hypothetical processes.'

Murray formulates the relation between the regnant processes and the subjective data in his version of the psycho-physical dualism, a version which must be described as an epiphenomenalistic hypothesis[3]), as follows (p. 46):

'According to one version of the double aspect theory—seemingly the most fruitful working hypothesis for a psychologist—the constituents of regnancies in man are capable of achieving consciousness (self-consciousness) though not all of them at once.'

Another formulation of the same hypothesis can be found later (p. 49):

'We have adopted the version of the double-aspect hypothesis which states that every conscious process is the subjective aspect of some regnant brain process, but that not every regnant process has a conscious correlate.'

Murray also gives a very clear and simple 'operational definition of the concept of 'consciousness' (p. 113–114):

'By consciousness we mean introspective or, more accurately, immediately-retrospective awareness. Whatever a subject can report upon is considered conscious; everything else which, by inference, was operating in the regnancy is considered unconscious. According to this convenient pragmatic criterion, consciousness depends upon verbalization.'

The result of this analysis must be that Murray's theory can neither be described as behavioristic nor as mentalistic, but must be classified as *a neutral-formal theory*, because its hypothetical variables are interpreted as neutral constructions (although maybe with a physiological tendency, as they are placed in the brain), and because it is controlled through both behavioristic and introspective protocol-statements (although maybe mainly through introspective).

Molar or Molecular Theory

It is comparatively easy to place Murray's theory in this classification as it must be described as *an extremely molar theory*. At several points Murray writes explicitly about this. He writes, for example, while listing the characteristics of a dynamic theory, as follows (p. 71):

'Finally, dynamism is distinguished by its gross or *molar* descriptions of behaviour, some of which merely record the difference between the beginning and the end situation.'

Murray emphasizes the molar character of his theory in the following statement even more clearly (p. 115):

'It has been maintained that personology conceptualizes the reactions of individuals on a molar (gross) level. Though it is not limited to the construction of such formulations, this is its distinctive task. The concepts of need, trend and effect, for example, are molar concepts. They describe the general course of behavior.'

As Murray himself points out the most important variables in his theory are extremely molar in character, just as the subjects dealt with in its protocol statements are very comprehensive (total life spans and episodes (themes in the life span)).

Field-Theory or Mechanistic Theory

It is relatively easy to classify Murray's theory as *a mainly field-theoretical theory*. Murray explicitly describes his theory as a *dynamic theory*, but according to the

[3]) Cf. Chapter 3.

terminology defined in Chapter 3 of this book, 'dynamic' is synonymous with 'intermediate between the most mechanistic and the most field-theoretical theories'.

Already in the introduction to his 'primary propositions' Murray writes (p. 36) about his theory that it 'is the outcome of a prejudice in favour of the dynamical, organismal viewpoint.' And he gives the following reason for this (p. 36):

'Since psychology deals only with motion—processes occurring in time—none of its proper formulations can be static. They all must be dynamic in the larger meaning of this term.'

The field-theoretical character of the theory appears even in his 'primary propositions.' Thus he writes in paragraph 18 (p. 46):

'Regnant processes are, without doubt, mutually dependent. A change in one function changes all the others and these, in turn, modify the first. Hence, events must be interpreted in terms of the many interacting forces and their relations, not ascribed to single causes.'

Later Murray writes about *the concept of force* (p. 59):

'it will be indispensable (i. e. a convenient fiction) to the psychologist for a long time to come.' and further (p. 59):

'We need such a term for it is impossible to construct a dynamical theory without it.'

Murray is, however, not extremely field-theoretical in his attitude. He attempts here—as elsewhere—to unite the two contradictory viewpoints, as can be seen from the following quotation (p. 69):

'My own position is that in some events it is mechanism and in others it is dynamism that prevails ... In most behavioural events both principles seem to be operating (in different proportions).'

He formulates his conclusion of the discussion on this subject in the following way (p. 72):

'... the conclusion should be that mechanism and dynamism represent two complementary aspects of organic life. Certainly there is no dynamism without mechanism. Furthermore, there are, it seems, gradations between actions which are predominantly dynamic and those that are predominantly mechanical.'

It seems to be correct to describe Murray's theory as a dynamic theory in that it is an intermediate form between the mechanistic and field-theoretical theories (although closer to the field-theoretical).

Statistical or Deterministic Theory

It is a little more difficult to place Murray's theory in this classification, among other things because he very seldom writes anything explicitly about this himself. Yet, he writes about his and his assistants' work (p. 33):

'... the entire organized procedure may be regarded as an experiment to test the ability of the constructed theory to classify and causally relate the facts.'

One of his 'primary propositions' (paragraph 12, p. 43) also touches upon this subject. It says, among other things:

'Life is an irreversible sequence of non-identical events. Some of these changes, however, occur in a predictable lawful manner.'

This means that Murray on the one hand *tries* to give a deterministic (causal) explanation, but that he, on the other hand, maintains that only *some* of the life-phenomena appear in a predictable and lawful way. In other words, the theory presupposes *a limited determinism*. Besides the statements already mentioned, many statements are given in the book which show this, for example the following (p. 39):

'at every moment, an organism is within an environment which *largely* determines its behaviour' (the italics are mine).

In spite of this limited determinism, the theory cannot be described as statistical. Although some statistical correlations between variables have been formulated they are rather temporary in character, and the theory is full of more or less explicitly formulated (qualitative) deterministic hypotheses about the development and behavior of the individual, just as the words 'explain', 'determine', and 'predict' are used very often. As a whole Murray's theory must be described as *a mainly deterministic theory*.

The Model

Apart from his tables of classes Murray does not work explicitly with illustrative models of any kind, and I have not been able to find signs of implicitly presupposed models.

Summary

This analysis of the theory as a whole can be summarized in the following description of *Murray's theory: it is mainly classifying, constructive, neutral-formal, molar, dynamic, and mainly deterministic.*

MOTIVATION DEFINITIONS AND HYPOTHESES

Murray's theory is a personological theory; but as mentioned before the motivation variables and the motivation hypotheses play a very important role. The most important motivation variables in the theory are '*need*', '*press*' and '*cathexis,*' and '*emotions*' and '*affections.*'

'Need' in Murray's theory

More than anybody else Murray holds the responsibility for introducing the concept 'need' and giving it such a central position in modern psychology. Contrary to many other psychologists (for example Hull and Tolman) Murray uses *'need' as a synonym for 'drive'*. Thus it says in the index (p. 753): 'Drive, see Need'. But he almost exclusively uses 'need', while 'drive' only appears now and then in parenthesis after 'need' in order to point out that they are synonyms.

In Murray's theory need is exclusively *a hypothetical variable*. Murray stresses this explicitly time and again. Already in his 'primary propositions' (paragraph 9, p. 42) he writes:

'A behavioural trend may be attributed to a hypothetical force (a drive, need or propensity within the organism. The proper way of conceptualizing this force is a matter of debate. It seems that it is a force which (if uninhibited) promotes activity which (if competent) brings about a situation that is opposite (as regards its relevant properties) to the one that aroused it.'

Later he points out that 'need' is not only a hypothetical concept, but also an '*intervening*' variable in Tolman's sense of the word. He writes (p. 60):

'Between what we can directly observe—the stimulus and the resulting action—a need is an invisible link, which may be imagined to have the properties that an understanding of the observed phenomena demand. "Need" is, therefore, a hypothetical concept.'

Murray also points out directly that 'need' does not stand for an empirical variable (e. g. hormones) as is often the case in the theories of other psychologists (for example Hull). He writes about this (p. 63):

'A hormone may be the generator of a drive, but it cannot be the drive itself. A chemical substance, is one thing, the excitation which it sets up in the brain is another.'

But while is quite evident that 'need' in Murray's theory is exclusively a *hypothetical* variable, it is less clear how Murray's 'need' can be placed in Tolman's classification. Is it a neuro-physiological, a phenomenological, or a neutral-formal variable? Many statements could be quoted which indicate that it is a *neuro-physiological* variable. Thus it is stated in 'primary propositions' (p. 45) in connection with a discussion on regnant brain-processes:

'A need or drive is just one of these hypothetical processes. Since, by definition, it is a process which follows a stimulus and precedes the actonal response, it must be located in the brain.'

And the neuro-physiological character of 'need' stands out even more clearly in the following (p. 62):

'... the need process must be placed in the brain, for this is the only area to and from which all nerves lead. It is even conceivable that some day there may be instruments for measuring need tension directly.'

But many statements which indicate that 'need' is a *neutral-formal* variables could also be quoted. For example (p. 54):

'A Need is a hypothetical process the occurrence of which is imagined in order to account for certain objective and subjective facts.'

The neutral character of 'need' can be seen even more clearly in the following quotation (p. 125):

'Since, according to our conception, a need manifests itself in a variety of ways, it is not possible to confine oneself to a single operational definition. It seems that the best objective basis is the behavioural attainment of an apparently satisfying effect, an effect which brings the activity to a halt (usually by facilitating a vital process). The best subjective criterion is the occurrence of a wish or resolution to do a certain thing (to bring about a certain effect).'

On the basis of this analysis I believe that Murray's '*need*' must be described as *a neutral-formal* variable which is localized in the brain (therefore possessing a certain neuro-physiological character).

'If an attempt is made to analyze where 'need' should be placed in the classification function versus disposition, one discovers that the word is *used with two meanings*. In most definitions and other statements in the theory were 'need' is used it has the character of a functional variable. Murray writes about this (p. 60):

'Strictly speaking, a need is the immediate outcome of certain internal and external occurences. It comes into being, endures for a moment and perishes. It is not a static entity. It is a resultant of forces.'

And even more explicitly it is stated (p. 61):

'a need is by definition, the force within the organism which determines a certain trend or major effect.'

But in the personological application of the theory 'need' is very often used as a *disposition* variable, as a term for the more lasting personality-traits which determine the constant recurrence of a 'need.' Murray writes about this meaning of the word and about its dual use (p. 61):

'Thus, we may loosely use the term "need" to refer to an organic potentiality or readiness to respond in a certain way under given conditions. In this sense a need is a latent attribute of an organism. More strictly, it is a noun which stands for the fact that a certain trend is apt to recur. We have not found that any confusion arises when we use "need" at one time to refer to a temporary happening and at another to refer to a more or less consistent trait of personality.'

Murray could have avoided misunderstandings and misinterpretations by using 'need' as a generic term for function variables and disposition variables, 'drive' as a term for function variables exclusively, and 'attitude,' which he occasionally uses in his lists in a parenthesis after 'need,' as a term for disposition variables.

Classification of 'Needs'

Murray classifies 'needs' in several ways from different points of view. First of all he divides 'needs' into '*viscerogenic*' and '*psychogenic*' needs[4]). He writes about this (p. 76):

'Needs may be conveniently divided into: 1, primary (viscerogenic) needs, and 2, secondary (psychogenic) needs. The former are engendered and stilled by characteristic periodic bodily events, whereas the latter have no subjectively localizable bodilyorigins; hence the term "psychogenic."

Then there is the classification: *positive* and *negative* needs. Murray says about this classification (p. 79) that the first group is called 'positive' or 'adient' needs because they force the organism in a positive way towards other objects,' and the second group is called 'negative' or 'abient' needs because they force the organism to separate itself from objects.'

Finally there is the third classification which only includes the viscerogenic needs. Murray writes about this (p. 80):

'The division of needs into lacks with intakes, distensions with outputs, and harms with retractions may also be useful.'

By combining these three classifications the following table of viscerogenic need is obtained (p. 79):

---

[4]) The two terms 'viscerogenic' and 'psychogenic' are not well chosen. The first one is too narrow, because it among other things also includes needs which are determined by processes in the receptors in the skin. The other one is almost too broad, as the viscerogenic needs in a certain phase (the inducible phase) can also be psychogenic (determined by external stimuli which have an aquired connection to the internal stimuli).

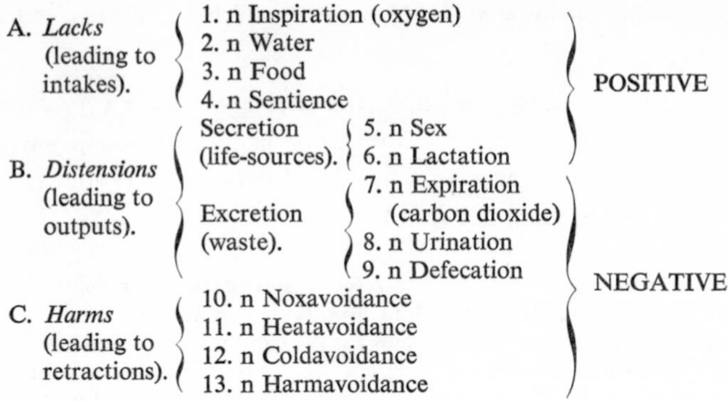

Besides the classifications already mentioned Murray uses two other classifications. First there is the classification: *manifest* and *latent* needs. He writes about this classification (p. 112):

'... we have found it necessary to distinguis between needs that are overt (manifest) and those that are not. In our study the latter (semi-objectified and subjectified forms of activity) were classed together as 'latent' needs (1n).'

And he continues his description of these groups in the following statements (p. 111 and 112):

'A. *An objectified (overt or manifest) need.* This includes all action that is 'real' (seriously and responsibly directed towards actual objects), whether or not it is preceded by a conscious intention or wish.

'2. *A semi-objectified need.* Here we class overt activity that is playfully and imaginatively (irresponsibly) directed towards real objects, or that is seriously directed towards imagined objects.

'3. *A subjectified need.* This covers all need activity that finds no overt expression.'

In addition to this classification there is the classification: *conscious* and *unconscious* needs, where Murray, as already mentioned, by 'conscious' means 'whatever a subject can report upon'. This classification can be combined with the above so that:

'A conscious as well as an unconscious need (un) may be either subjectified or objectified' (p. 114).

Murray and his assistants used the following list of psychogenic needs in their study:

Alphabetical list of manifest needs

1. n Aba = n Abasement (Abasive attitude).
2. n Ach = n Achievement (Achievant attitude).
3. n Aff = n Affiliation (Affiliative attitude).
4. n Agg = n Aggression (Aggressive attitude).
5. n Auto = n Autonomy (Autonomous attitude).
6. n Cnt = n Counteraction (Counteractive attitude).
7. n Def = n Deference (Deferent attitude).
8. n Dfd = n Defendance (Defendant attitude).
9. n Dom = n Dominance (Dominative attitude).
10. n Exh = n Exhibition (Exhibitionistic attitude).
11. n Harm = n Harmavoidance (Fearful attitude).

12. n Inf = n Infavoidance (Infavoidant attitude).
    n Inv = n Inviolacy (Inviolate attitude). This need is considered to be a composite of Infavoidance, Defendance and Counteraction.
13. n Nur = n Nurturance (Nurturant attitude).
14. n Ord = n Order (Orderly attitude).
15. n Play = n Play (Playful attitude).
16. n Rej = n Rejection (Rejective attitude).
    n Sec = Seclusion (Seclusive attitude). This need has been taken as the opposite of Exhibition, not as a separate variable.
17. n Sen = n Sentience (Sentient attitude).
18. n Sex = n Sex (Erotic attitude).
19. nn Suc = n Succorance (Succorant attitude).
    n Sup = n Superiority (Ambitious attitude). This need is considered to be a composite of Achievement and Recognition (see below).
20. n Und = n Understanding (Intellectual attitude).

The following needs are occasionally referred to but were not systematically used in the present study:

n Acq = n Acquisition (Acquisitive attitude).
n Blam = n Blamavoidance (Blamavoidant attitude).
n Cog = n Cognizance (Inquiring attitude).
n Cons = Construction (Constructive attitude).
n Exp = n Exposition (Informing attitude).
n Rec = n Recognition (Self-forwarding attitude). This was included under Exhibition.
n Ret = n Retention (Retentiv attitude).

'Press' and *'Cathexis'*

These two terms are very closely interrelated in Murray's theory and are also related to 'need,' for which reason they will be analyzed here.

'Press' is a term which denotes the effect of the stimulus-situation upon the well-being of the organism (biological and social conditions of existence). Murray's best definition is given in his 'Glossary' (p. 748):

'p = press: kind of effect an object or situation is exerting or could exert upon the S. It is a temporal gestalt of stimuli which usually appears in the guise of a *threat of harm* or *promise of benefit* to the organism.'

Murray points out that it is difficult to describe and classify press without being involved in a tautology without meaning, and he says (p. 117):

'The question is, how shall we classify situations *in their own right* (i. e., irrespective of the *response* that they evoke in the organism)?'

He believes, however, that the problem can be solved by using the concept 'press', which is a term for the effect—or potential effect—of the stimuli-situation upon the organism. It is, however, not the effect of the situation as it is seen in the reaction of the individual (for then we would have the tautology), but its changes in the biological or social conditions of existence of the organism which determine the reaction (behavior) of the individual.

Murray classifies 'press' in different ways. The most important classification is: *alpha press and beta press*. About this he writes (p. 122):

---

[5]) Murray deals with the classification-problem in his thesis in Parsons and Shills: 'Toward a General Theory of Action' (1951).

'In identifying press we have found it convenient to distinguish between 1, the *alpha* press, which is the press that actually exists, as far as scientific inquiry can determine it; and 2, the *beta* press, which is the subject's own interpretation of the phenomena that he perceives.'

It must be pointed out here, that 'alpha press' according to the terminology of this study is an *empirical* variable which is functionally related to (determines) the hypothetical variable 'need' (maybe through a beta press), whereas '*beta press*' is a hypothetical variable which on the one hand is functionally related to (is determined by) a corresponding alpha press and on the other hand is functionally related to (determines) a need.

Besides this classification Murray also gives two other classifications of press: *positive* and *negative* press (p. 120), and *mobile and immobile* press. These classifications can be further differentiated and combined.

The concept of 'cathexis,' which Murray has taken from Freud, is in certain ways similar to 'press,' as it is defined in the following way (p. 744):

'Cathexis, the power of an object to arouse a response of a certain kind in the subject.'

But Murray briefly indicates the difference between the two terms thus (p. 121):

'The *press* of an object is what it can *do to the subject* or *for the subject*—the power that it has to affect the well-being of the subject in one way or another. The cathexis of an object, on the other hand, is what it can *make the subject do.*'

Finally, Murray summarizes his definitions and classifications concerning 'cathexis' in the the following words (p. 105–106):

'An object, (0) that evokes a need is said to "have cathexis" (c) or to "be cathected" (by the subject or by the need). This is one of Freud's many valuable concepts. If the object evokes a positive adient need (indicating that the S likes the 0) it is said to have a positive cathexis (value); if it evokes a positive contrient or a negative abient need (indicating that the S dislikes the 0) it is said to have a negative cathexis. Such cathexes may be temporary or enduring. Sometimes one object is endowed with both positive and negative cathexis (ambivalence). Cathexes be further classified according to the need which the 0 evokes in the S.'

'Cathexis' must, in the terminology of this study, be called an *empirical* variable—even though there might be said to be certain hypothetical features in the concept as it is very closely related to the hypothetical variable 'need.'

'*Emotions*' *and* '*Affections*'

The variable 'emotion' is in Murrays theory very closely related to the motivation variable 'need.' Murray gives the following definition of emotion (p. 89):

'..."emotion" is a *hypothetical concept* that stands for an excitatory process in the brain—most probably in the interbrain (thalamic region)—that may manifest itself subjectively or objectively or both. Thus an emotion may occur without the subject's being aware of it (unconscious emotion). Usually it is felt, the subjective manifestation being that quality of an experience which is generally designated by the word "emotional" ("excited"). The objective manifestation is a compound of autonomic disturbances ("autonome"), affective actones, and the intensification or disorganization of effective behavior (motor and verbal).'

As can be seen from this definition 'emotion' is very similar to 'need.' Both are *hypothetical* variables; but the following *differences* can be mentioned: 1) 'emotions' are localized in the interbrain, 'needs' in the brain (as a whole, or maybe only in the cerebrum); 2) the subjective manifestation of 'emotions' is more diffuse than is that of 'needs'; 3) the objective manifestation of 'needs' is a purposive and organized behavior, whereas the objective manifestation of 'emotions' is an excited and disorganized behavior. It is therefore doubtful whether 'emotions' can be described as motivation variables. There is, however, as mentioned, a very close relation between 'emotions' and 'needs' in Murray's theory, as he here mainly follows McDougall's theory. Murray writes, (p. 90):

'We do not find, however, that all emotions have drives or all drives have emotions, but the more important emotions (ex: 1, fear, anger, disgust, pity, shame, lust and 2, elation, dejection) are associated either 1 with a certain drive, or 2, with the fortune—facilitation (success) or obstruction (failure)—of a drive.'

On the basis of the above quotations, 'emotions' in Murray's theory may briefly be described as *'accompanying conditions of needs'*.

The variable 'affection' is so similar to 'emotion' that it is difficult to distinguish between them, as can be seen from Murray's definition (p. 90):

'Affection is considered to be a hypothetical concept which stands for some process in the brain —probably in the interbrain—that manifests itself subjectively as feelings of pleasure or unpleasure (which vary in intensity), and objectively (with much less clearness) as compound of affective actones.'

Thus the first part of the definition is identical with the definition of 'emotion' (both are hypothetical variables localized in the interbrain). The two variables differ only a little, mainly in their subjective manifestations, as 'affections' manifest themselves as 'feelings of pleasure or unpleasure'. Affections are also accompanying conditions of needs, as (p. 91):

'Every need arises out of a disequilibrium (lack, distension, harm or threat) which considered by itself is *unpleasurable*.'

Conversely, 'pleasure' is an accompanying condition of 'the satisfaction of need tension.' This is not only true about 'effect pleasure,' but also the two other 'sorts of pleasure' which Murray includes, 'activity pleasure' and 'achievement pleasure,' can be taken as accompanying conditions ('effect pleasure') of particular needs (activity and achievement).

Murray does not mention the relation between 'emotions' and 'affections.' But based upon the quoted definitions the relation can be formulated in the following way: *Both 'emotions' and 'affections' are accompanying conditions of needs.* Affections include '*unpleasure*' which accompanies all unsatisfied needs, and '*pleasure*' which accompanies the satisfaction of a need. '*Emotions*' are special terms for those affections which accompany certain (primary) 'needs'.—In this formulation only the six first emotions mentioned in the quotations are included (p. 90), namely: 'fear', 'anger', 'disgust', 'pity', 'shame', and 'lust', whereas 'elation' and 'dejection', which—according to the same quotation—should accompany 'the faciliation or obstruction' of any need, *cannot* be differentiated from 'pleasure' and 'unpleasure' respectively. If this analysis is correct, *'emotions' can be characterized as a special class of 'affections'* in Murray's theory.

Motivation Hypotheses

As Murray's theory is a classifying—and not a deductive—theory, no system of explicitly formulated hypotheses can be found, but scattered around in the book are some more or less implicitly formulated motivation hypotheses.

Thus the following hypothesis on the connection between motivation ('need') and learning processes appears (p. 63):

'It seems highly probable that many of the s-r connections which are considered stable by experimenters are stable only under the conditions of their experiments, that is, when the same need —usually hunger—is active in the organism.'

And on the same page a more general hypothesis on the relation between motivation and behavior can be found (p. 63):

'When a need becomes active a characteristic trend of behaviour will usually ensue even in the absence of the customary stimuli.'

Later a hypothesis of the importance of motivation variables as personality variables is given (p. 78–79):

'The viscerogenic needs are of unequal importance as variables of personality. The personological significance of a need seems to depend upon whether there are marked differences between individuals in the frequency, intensity and duration of its activity, and upon whether the strength of any psychogenic needs are functions of such differences. A need, furthermore, does not usually become a dominant element of personality if there is no obstruction to its satisfaction.'

The following page contains a rather vaguely formulated hypothesis on the very important relation between primary and secondary needs. Unfortunately this is, as far as I know all that Murray has written about this important subject. It says (p. 80):

'The secondary or psychogenic needs, which are presumably dependent upon and derived from the primary needs, may be briefly listed. They stand for common reaction systems and wishes. It is not supposed that they are fundamental, biological drives, though some may be innate.'

In another paragraph Murray deals with periodical variations in 'needs', summarized in the following (implicitly formulated) hypotheses (p. 85):

'Many of the viscerogenic needs are characterized by rather regular rhythms of activity and rest, rhythms which seem to be determined by an orderly succession of physiological events.'

'Among psychogenic needs we also find some evidence of periodicity, particularly in the alternations of contrasting needs.'

He also introduces a division of a 'need cycle' into different periods, as can be seen in the following (p. 85–86):

'For convenience, a single need cycle may be divided into: 1, a *refractory* period, during which no incentive will arouse it; 2, an *inducible* or *ready* period, during which the need is inactive but susceptible to excitation by appropriate stimuli; and 3, an *active* period, during which the need is determining the behaviour of the total organism.'

In his discussion of 'affections' Murray mentions the hedonistic theory which he reformulates in the following way (p. 93):

'Instead of saying that all behaviour is a search for pleasure, it seems better to say that all behaviour is the riddance (or avoidance) of painful tension, encouraged perhaps by pleasure-evoking images of expected goals.'

In a later paragraph he discusses the relation between 'needs' and 'actones.' Here he says something which reminds one very much of Allport's principle of functional autonomy (p. 99).

'... the actones thus established by repetition may in a constant environment become as determining as the needs.'

Besides this, he gives a very important hypothesis about the relation between behavior and 'needs' (p. 100):

'... only under rare or abnormal conditions do we find behavior patterns that exist for long without satisfying underlying needs.'

Finally in the same paragraph he gives a hypothesis on the connection between 'abilities' and 'needs' (p. 105):

'... early abilities determine in large measure what needs develop and become dominant.'

In one of the last paragraphs of the theoretical chapter Murray asks the question (p. 128):

'What factors determine the establishment of a need as a ready reaction system of personality?'

He answers the question in a paragraph (p. 128–129) from which the following quotations are taken:

'... the relative strength of needs at birth (or shortly after birth) is different in different children.'

'Later, the strength of some needs may be attributed to intense or frequent gratifications (reinforcements), some of which rest on specific abilities.'

'Indeed, some needs may emerge out of latency because of gratuities or the change attainment of end situations through random movements.'

'Some needs may become established because of their success in furthering other more elementary needs.'

'Certain innate or acquired abilities will favour the objectification of some needs and not of others.'

'A need may also become established by repetition, due to the frequent occurrence of specific press.'

'Emulation (n Similance S n Superiority) is a potent factor in accentuating certain needs...'

'Certain cultures and sub-cultures to which an individual is exposed may be characterized by a predominance of certain needs.'

These statements are in my opinion the most important (implicit) hypotheses of motivation in Murray's theory.

RECONSTRUCTION OF THE THEORY

Murray's motivation theory contains, as can be seen from the above analysis, many explicit and exact definitions and classifications of motivation variables together with some more implicit motivation hypotheses. Therefore, a reconstruction of Murray's theory must especially consist of an explicit reformulation of the implicitly formulated hypotheses, and a *systematization* of the theory as a whole. The following reconstruction will therefore be made on the basis of the above analysis.

The hypothetical variable 'regnant brain processes,' which determines both the behavior and the subjective data, is a very characteristic and fundamental feature of Murray's theory. Therefore these regnant processes will be dealt with in the first hypotheses and definitions in this reconstruction of the theory.

Hypothesis 1: All behavior and all subjective psychological data are manifestations of 'regnant processes.' But not all regnant processes have subjective manifestations.

Definition 1: 'Regnant processes' are (hypothetical) brain processes which are post-sensoric and pre-motoric and form a dynamically-temporally organized field whose function is to integrate and regulate the activity of the whole organism.

Among these regnant processes is Murray's most important motivation variable, 'need':

Definition 2: 'Needs' are regnant processes which subjectively manifest themselves as wishes and decisions and objectively as behavior which changes an unsatisfying starting-situation into a satisfying end-situation.

Definition 3: Needs can be classified as:

1) 'viscerogenic' and 'psychogenic' needs (depending upon whether they are determined by organic processes or not).

2) 'positive' and 'negative' needs (depending upon whether they cause striving towards or away from an object).

3) 'manifest' and 'latent' needs (depending upon whether they manifest themselves as realistic behavior or as imaginative behavior).

4) 'conscious' and 'unconscious' needs (depending upon whether the individual can give an introspective report about them or not).

It is not necessary to reconstruct or repeat the schemes of classification which can be made by combinations of these classifications. Neither is it necessary to repeat Murray's list of definitions of the different 'needs.' It must, however, be pointed out that the list in my opinion is almost too long when evaluated on the basis of the epistemological principle of parsimony which demands that a scientific theory has as few presuppositions (primary statements and basic concepts) as possible. This criticism is, however, only directed towards the list of psychogenic needs, as psychologists as a whole agree about the number of viscerogenic needs, while Murray's list of psychogenic needs is much longer than other psychologists' lists of secondary motivation variables. But it must be admitted that Murray's list is based upon rather thorough empirical studies.

The following hypotheses and definitions in the reconstructed theory deal with Murray's second basic concept, 'press', and its relation to 'needs'.

Hypothesis 2: All psychogenic needs and viscerogenic needs in their inducible phase are functionally related to (are determined by) 'press.'

Definition 4: 'Press' is a term for the effect—or potential effect—of the stimulus-situation upon the optimal, bio-social conditions of existence of the organism.

Definition 5: 'Press' can be classified as 'alpha' and 'beta' press. 'Alpha press' is the term for an empirical variable, namely the objectively establishable qualities of the stimulus-situation (cf. Definition 4). 'Beta press' is the term for a hypothetical variable, namely the subjectively experienced qualities of the stimulus-situation (cf. Definition 4).

Hypothesis 3: A functional relation exists between 'alpha press' and 'beta press,' and between 'beta pres' and 'needs.'

'Cathexis' is another important motivation variable in Murray's theory. It is closely related to 'needs' and has a certain similarity to 'press', therefore the following definition in the reconstruction will deal with this variable.

Definition 6: 'Cathexis' is the term for that quality of an object which (co-)determines the existence of a need in an individual. Cathexes can be classified in accordance with the needs which they (co-)determine.

Finally the reconstructed theory of motivation must also contain definitions and hypotheses concerning 'affections' and 'emotions,' as these are accompanying conditions of 'needs.' Based upon the analysis in the previous paragraph they can be formulated in the following way:

Definition 7: 'Affections' is a term for accompanying conditions of needs manifesting themselves subjectively by experiences of 'pleasure' and 'unpleasure' and objectively by changes in the autonomous processes and the changes in behavior determined thereby. They can be classified as pleasure and unpleasure in accordance with their subjective manifestations.

Hypothesis 4: 'Unpleasure' always appears together with (is functionally related to) the starting condition of each need. 'Pleasure' always appears together with the final condition (the satisfaction) of each need.

Definition 8: 'Emotions' is a term for the affections which accompany primary needs.

Besides the more primary hypotheses and definitions which have now been reformulated, some of the more or less secondary hypotheses, quoted in the passage about hypotheses of motivation in the analytical section, must also be included in the reconstruction of the theory. They will here be systematized according to universality and subject matter beginning with Murray's hypothesis on hedonism (p. 93):

Hypothesis 5: All behavior is a release from—or avoidance of—unpleasant tensions.

Next the hypothesis of 'inquiring behavior' (p. 63):

Hypothesis 6: When a need becomes active, a characteristic direction of behavior will result, even in the absence of the usual external stimuli.

A third rather important hypothesis (from p. 100) deals with the importance of 'reinforcement' (even though this term is not directly mentioned):

Hypothesis 7: When actions are repeated it is nearly always because they satisfy a need.

The following hypothesis is a supplement to the seventh, as it deals with the cases where the seventh hypothesis is *not* valid, namely when actions are repeated after having aquired functional autonomy (p. 99):

Hypothesis 8: Often repeated actions may in a constant environment produce variables (habits), which without needs determine behavior.

The reconstruction must also include a hypothesis about the periodicity of needs as a reformulation of the statements quoted from p. 85–86. It can be formulated in the following way:

Hypothesis 9: There is a certain degree of periodicity in the appearance of nearly all needs. Most viscerogenic needs are characterized by a rhythm of activity determined physiologically. Among psychogenic needs there is often a periodic alternation of contrasting needs. A need-period or cycle can be divided into: 1) a refractory phase during which the need cannot be activated at all, 2) an inducible phase during which the need can be activated by appropriate (external) stimuli, 3) an active phase during which the need is active and determines the behavior of the total organism.

The following formulation for a hypothesis dealing with the inter-relations between needs is suggested:

Hypothesis 10: Needs can have the following inter-relations:

a. Fusion.
b. Subsidiation.
c. Ambitendency and contrafaction (simultaneous or successive appearance of opposite needs which do not block each other).
d. Conflict (simultaneous appearance of opposite needs which block each other).

A reconstruction of Murray's theory of motivation should also contain some hypotheses about the reasons why a need is more intense and appears more often in some individuals than in others (even though these hypotheses deal with topics bordering on personology). Based upon the statements quoted from p. 87–79, 105, and 128–129, the hypotheses can be formulated in the following way.

Hypothesis 11: There are individual differences with regard to frequency, intensity and duration of the different needs. The factors determining these individual differences are among other things:

a. innate factors, which directly determine the difference;
b. innate differences in 'abilities,' which also determine differences in 'needs';
c. differences in the ease and the frequency with which a need is satisfied by the environment in the earliest years;
d. differences in the frequency of the appearance of special press;
e. differences in the subsidiary relation of the need to fundamental needs;
f. differences in cultural factors which further or repress the appearance of special needs.

Conclusion

Even though Murray's theory has been critized above for being somewhat unsystematical, it is still—as compared to many other psychological theories—a relatively exactly and systematic formulated theory; especially it contains many exact and practical definitions and classifications. But it is not so much its formal logical qualities as its *empirical* qualities that make it so excellent. Few psychological theories are based upon such a comprehensive collection of observations. Murray and his assistants were among the first to examine the hypotheses of psychoanalysis experimentally, and this alone is of great importance.

Later Developments

Introduction. Murray has continued to contribute to the literature of the psychology of personality with several papers in journals and chapters in textbooks[6]). The most systematic exposition of his theory in recent years is to be found in his chapter in *S. Koch*'s 'Psychology', which we shall take up in the following pages.

The Structure of the Theory. Murray has concentrated principally upon answering questions posed by Koch about the historical and biographical origins of Murray's theory, and he has done it in such a way that it could be a norm or ideal for an 'intellectual autobiography'. As *this* book, however, does not deal with the history or biographical study of psychology, we shall only mention this part of Murray's chapter very briefly.

It is obvious from this chapter that Murray's education as a medical doctor and especially his experiences connected with his research in embryology have helped to shape his whole intellectual position and attitude toward science. It is also understandable that when turning his interest toward psychology, he was most attracted by the psychoanalytic theory, and especially by the works of *Freud* and *Jung*. Although he is also critical concerning some features in Freud's theory, he regards it as 'the greatest since the works of Aristotle' (p. 37), and he admits that his own theory can be conceived of as a modern form of a psychoanalytic theory of personality, which in addition is strongly influenced by other psychologists. Among these he acknowledges especially his indebtedness to *W. McDougall* and *K. Lewin*. Among philosophers he singles out the influences of *Whitehead* and *Bergson*, and from the field of biology mentions his debt to *Darwin* and *L. J. Henderson*.

Influences from all these sources have helped to shape Murray's theory, so that in his own words it can be characterized in this way:

'Though imperceptible to us and therefore inferential, covert mental processes and products, some with and some without the property of consciousness, happen to be intrinsically attractive to a cogitator of my persuasion, and I see no insuperable barrier to their being incorporated in a unified body of scientific facts and propositions' (p. 11).

And more about *methods:*

'From medical practice I derived the "multiform method" of assessment ... Also derived from medicine were consequential convictions respecting ... the ultimate scientific value of systematic

---

[6]) See the reference at the end of this chapter.

thorough, and detailed case histories; and (3) the necessity of an adequate classification of the entities and processes within the domain of one's elected discipline' (p. 11).

From his research in embryology Murray learned much as we can see from this quotation:

'In short, I take "life"—say, the ceaseless processes of metabolism—as *given*, just as Newton took motion as given, and do not look for something antecedent to it, except in an evolutionary sense.' (p. 15).

From Darwin, Bergson and other 'philosophers of evolution' Murray has learned that:

'creativity—is a centrally determining capacity of nature, more especially of human nature.' (p. 38).

In accordance with this Murray criticizes Freud's inventory of drives, and adds:

'Construction ... is more fundamental, in my view, than any of these instincts as operationally defined by psychoanalysts ...' (p. 39).

And finally Murray writes about 'the tolerance of uncertainty':

'In my philosophy there are no absolute or inevitable laws, no enduring certainties: every observation, every inference, every explanation, and every prediction is a matter of less or greater probability. To this most psychologists, I trust, would be ready to assent.' (p. 50).

I hope that these few quotations have given the reader an understanding of the main lines in the structure of Murray's theory and meta-theory, and perhaps at the same time, a fair impression of his provocative style. We shall conclude this paragraph about the structur of Murray's theory by restating that it remains 'a mainly classifying, constructive, neutral-formal, molar, dynamic, and mainly deterministic theory'.

The Content of the Theory. While there is no change in the structure of Murray's theory, there are some changes to be noted in the content of the theory. Perhaps we have the key to these changes in Murray's description of 'the influence of social evolutionists' on this thinking where he writes (p. 45):

'I have been influenced by Darwin, specifically, by the theory that the group more than the individual has been the evolutionary unit. Being of this persuasion, I have come to think that no theoretical system constructed on the psychological level will be adequate until it has been embraced by and intermeshed with a cultural-sociological system.'

Whatever the explanation for the changes, it is obvious that Murray's interests have developed in the direction of the border-line between social psychology and personology. Thus he and some of his co-workers[7]) have concentrated upon the study of the smallest social unit: *the dyadic system:*

'The notion came and stuck that a dyadic (two-person) relationship, whether transcient or enduring, should be formulated as a single system, equal analytic attention being devoted to each participant.' (p. 30).

---

[7]) Among them the Danish psychologist, *Gerhard Nielsen:* 'Studies in Self-Confrontation' (1964).

Among other changes in the content of Murray's theory to which he himself draws attention is the new interpretation of the concept '*cathexis*':

'From Freud I gratefully accepted the concept of cathexis (value, valence) as a useful variable in formulating personalities as well as single interaction of personalities.' (p. 29).

'My present notion of cathexis is not far from the elaborate definitions of it that were published in *The Clinical Study of Sentiments*[8]), except now the more favored term is "value" and the concept has been incorporated in a larger system. The term "sentiment", "attitude" or "established evaluation" points to dispositional property of a personality which corresponds to the cathexis of an entity.' (p. 30).

It is clear from this quotation that the changed concept is a hypothetical variable of the dispositional kind rather than an *empirical* variable.

In connection with the introduction of the 'dyadic system' into this theory, Murray also redefines his term '*thema*' in this way (p. 31):

'The idea matured that the basic pattern of a single dyadic interaction might be most simply represented by *i*, a symbol denoting the immediate direction, the need-generated orientation (goal), of the proactivity emanating from the first interactor, followed by *ii*, a symbol denoting the emotional response of the second interactor, and when indicated, a symbol denoting the need-generated orientation (goal) of his reactivity.'

'The simplest formula then would be either an N-P (if the subject initiated the interaction) or P-N (if the alter acted first).' (p. 31).

From the above quotation it is clear that 'thema' has changed from a term denoting Need-Press combination in a single individual to a term denoting a Need-Press (N-P) or Press-Need (P-N) combination in the interaction between two individuals.

In addition the main variable '*need*' is changed to the variable '*thematic dispositions*':

'It has become more and more apparent to me that the energetic components of personality can be better defined as thematic dispositions than as general actional dispositions' (p. 34).

This change means that instead of speaking of a person having a 'need for aggression' one should 'specify the nature of the pertinent press (stimulus)' to which the person with 'supersensitive dispositions'.

This new hypothetical variable 'thematic dispositions' is—as indicated in the term—a *dispositional* variable. Thus Murray has avoided the confusion implied in his old term 'need', which was sometimes a dispositional and sometimes a functional variable.

Another term which refers to a completely new concept is '*serials*':

'It is a term for "a number of interrupted successions of proceedings ... each temporal segment of which is progressively related to the last ... though separated by an interval of time ...' (p. 34).

---

[8]) Murray and Morgan: 'A Clinical Study of Sentiments'. (Genet. Psychol. Monogr. 1945. No. 32).

Thus 'serials' is an *empirical* variable describing behavior like Murray's many other fruitful descriptive terms ('actone', 'dyadic system', etc.).

Finally we shall look at some new terms which Murray introduces designating hypothetical variables of the *functional* category:

'*Ordination*' is a term for 'processes concerned with the selection and integration of plans of action.' (p. 35).

Murray describes this further as:

'thinking, one might say, on the efferent, rather than on the afferent, side of the cortical arc, and some psychologists might, therefore, be disposed to subsume his mental processes ... under conation, on the grounds that their function is to orient and coordinate action. But against this is the fact that they are often very "intellectual" (higher mental processes in the strictest sense)....' (p. 35).

Intimately related to the variable 'ordination' are two other hypothetical functional variables:

'The selection from numerous alternatives of a concrete and specific goal, purpose, or aim to appease one or more needful dispositions, I am calling *orientation*. It is the subsequent phase—the selection and temporal articulation of ways-means, strategies, or tactics (represented by images and words)—that I am calling *ordination*.' (p. 36).

'The preliminary processes of imagination—fantasies and trial experiments in the mind—I am calling *prospections*.' (p. 35).

The present author thinks that it is a very valuable distinction, which Murray has introduced with his term 'ordination', the distinction between the '*afferent* intellectual processes' (or cognitive processes in the more usual sense) and the '*efferent* intellectual processes' (planning or 'ordination').

Concluding remarks. We hope that the reader has got the impression that Murray's 'preparations for (a) scaffold of *a* comprehensive system—his many original and valuable concepts—are so scientifically fruitful that they may well be preparations for the scaffold of *any* comprehensive system which will appear in the psychology of personality in the future.

References

1. H. A. Murray *et al.*: Explorations in Personality (Oxford Univ. Press, N.Y. 1938).
2. H. A. Murray and Kluckhohn, C.: Outline of a conception of personality (in Murray and Kluckhohn (eds.)): 'Personality in Nature, Society and Culture'. (Knopf, N.Y. 1948, 2. ed., 1953).
3. H. A. Murray: Toward a classification of interaction, (in T. Parsons and E. A. Shils (eds.)): Toward a General Theory of Action. (Harvard University Press, Cambridge, Mass. 1951).
4. – Drive, time, strategy, measurement (in G. Lindzey (edt.): Assessment of Human Motives (Grove Press, N.Y. 1958)).
5. – Preparations for the scaffold of a comprehensive system (in S. Koch (edt.): 'Psychology—A Study of a Science, Vol. 3). (McGraw-Hill, N.Y., 1959).
6. Bibliography of Henry A. Murray (in R. W. White (edt.)): 'The Study of Lives' (Prentice-Hall, N.Y. 1963).

Chapter 11

Hull's Theory

In the thirties the American psychologist *Clark L. Hull* (1884–1952), who had previously dealt with other aspects of psychology, began to publish a series of theoretical studies in *Psychological Review* (1, 2, 3, 4, 5, 6) dealing with a systematization of theories of 'learning.' These articles presented some 'miniature systems,' as he called them, i. e. theories dealing with limited areas of the psychology of the learning process. In 1940 he published he largest of these 'miniature systems,' produced in co-operation with a number of assistants; this system—'A Mathematico-deductive Theory of Rote Learning'—is so far the most mathematized theory published in psychology. Still, only a relatively small part of the psychology of learning was studied. Hull, then decided to construct a theory including the whole of psychology, both 'individual' psychology and social psychology. He did not, however, start on his work on social psychology before his death; but the 'individual'—or general—psychology is dealt with in his two main works: 'Principles of Behavior' (1943)[1]) and 'A Behavior System' (1952)[2]). As these two books together form his latest, most inclusive, and most systematical work, only they will be dealt with in this chapter.

THE STRUCTURE OF THE THEORY

Summary of the Theory

The content of Hull's theory may briefly be summarized as follows (according to Hull's own summary, page 347 in B. S.):

The organism is regarded as 'a completely automatic entity' without any 'entelechy, no disembodied mind, soul, or spirit which in some way tells the various parts of the body how to co-operate behaviorally, to attain successful adaptation, i. e., how to achieve survival.' This biological adaptation is achieved partly through eight 'adaptive automatic behavior mechanisms.'

The 'unlearned stimulus-response connections or reflexes' or *'inborn response tendencies,'* determined by the phylogenetic development, which makes possible the adaptation of the organism to different types of 'emergency' situations, are the first automatic behavior mechanisms.

---

[1]) In the following abbreviated to P. B.

[2]) In the following abbreviated to B. S.

The second automatic behavior mechanism is '*the primitive capacity to learn; to profit by past experience*,' the simplest form of which is the conditioned reflex, which adapts the organism to situations where the innate forms of behavior are not adaptation effective.

'*The antedating defense reaction*' is the third behavior mechanism. It is produced by a combination of 'the learning law' and 'the stimulus-generalization law,' and it makes the organism able to avoid painful, injurious, or dangerous stimuli.

The fourth automatic behavior mechanism is '*negative response learning*' which protects the organism against carrying out useless actions be repressing or bloking the innate (or previously acquired) actions, which are not effective by other more effective actions.

Trial-and-error-learning or 'combined occurrence of negative and positive response learning in the same process' is the fifth automatic behavior mechanism.

The sixth automatic behavior mechanism 'is properly described as *positive-negative* stimulus trial learning. It is usually known as *discrimination learning*.'

The seventh automatic behavior mechanism is 'a second type of *antedating defense reaction*' consisting of a reaction '*determined*' by or positively associated with a 'stimulus trace' which may last for seconds after the physical stimulus has come to an end. In this way a stimulus trace following a signal stimulus (a 'danger signal') can continue to exist when the dangerous, injurious, or painful situation and the thereby determined flight-behavior begins. The flight behavior may by a few repetitions become associated with the signal stimulus (through its stimulus trace) so that flight behavior later can be started by the signal stimulus alone, before the occurrence of the dangerous situation.

The eighth automatic behavior mechanism is:

'*the fractional antedating goal reaction* together with its proprieceptive stimulus correlate. r_G—s_G. The r_G is a pure-stimulus act which tends to antedate all goals established by a given organism. It follows that the proprioceptive goal stimulus (s_G) will automatically precede each such goal, as well, of course, as the acts by which the goal has already been attained. Thus each s_G is a stimulus leading to the realization if its particular goal. Clearly the automatic (stimulus) guidance of organismic behavior to goals is adaptive in the highest degree. Further study of this major automatic device presumably will lead to the detailed behavioral understanding of thought and reasoning, which constitute the highest attainment of organic evolution. Indeed the r_G—s_G mechanism leads in a strictly logical manner into what was formally regarded as the very heart of the psychic: interest, planning, foresight, foreknowledge, expectancy, purpose, and so on.'

The different forms of behavior which are started by these automatic behavior mechanisms are dealt with in Hull's last book: trial-and-error-learning, discrimination-learning, behavior chains, behavior related to objects in space (conflict-behavior and detour-problems included), maze-learning and intelligent behavior (combination of previously acquired behavior chains), and estimating behavior. Still lacking in his theory is a special study of the traditional problems of perception, emotions, and abstract thinking (but Hull's pupils are working on these problems).

These were the main aspects of *the content* of Hull's theory; but such a summary does not give any impression of *the formal characteristics* of the theory: its exactness and its systematical structure; this can only be attained through a thorough study of his main works.

Hull's theoretical *presuppositions* are presented in the introduction to P. B. It is in close accordance with the basic epistemological principles defended by most logical empirists (briefly summarized in the first chapters of this book). Hull summarizes it with the statement that the methods of science can be characterized as being *hypothetical-deductive*, since hypotheses (or postulates as he prefers to call them) are formulated on the basis of empirical research and to as large an extent as possible are expressed in mathematical formula (thereof the name: *matematico-deductive* method). From these hypotheses (postulates or axioms) statements or theorems which describe empirical (maybe experimental) data are deduced.

Hull has followed this program very closely. He has in P. B. formulated a series of postulates on the basis of his own and (mainly) *other psychologists*' empirical research results. The different postulates and theorems are not equally probable. Many of them ar well verified, others are still not very probable, and a few have not yet been tested in any experiment and must thus be regarded as *predictions* of future research results. In many cases, moreover, postulates are formulated as mathematical functions based on curves corresponding to empirical data, most often obtained from maze experiments with rats or experiments on conditioned reflexes with other animal species. Later on these postulates have been revised a few times (published in Psych, Review 1950 and in 'Essentials of Behavior' (1951), which is only a revised summary of P. B.).

The last revision of the postulate system was published in B. S. (1952). In this work Hull's theory has been further developed, 17 corollaries and 133 theorems having been deduced from the 17 postulates, so that the complete system should include the whole of general psychology—or at any rate 'mammalian behavior'—from the simplest trial-and-error-behavior to the most complicated problem-solving-behavior.

Level of Development of the Theory

It is comparatively easy to classify Hull's theory with regard to its level of development, as the theory is one of the few *deductive* theories which are to be found in psychology. In this case the deductive system consists of 17 axioms (postulates) and some secondary hypotheses, namely 17 corollaries and 133 theorems. The secondary hypotheses are, however, not deduced in a strictly formal way from the primary axioms or postulates, only more informal generalizations or conclusions on the basis of the empirical data have been made in the 133 theorems, whose most important terms (or variables) are more closely (implicitly) defined in the postulates. Only in the miniature systems has Hull made a strictly formal deduction (as a mathematical logical 'proof').

In addition to the axiomatization, a partly symbolic presentation of the theory has also been made, among other things in the form of a mathematization of several hypotheses which are formulated as mathematical equations (often representing curves) on the basis of the empirically established functional relations. Besides this mathematization a symbolization of the theory has also been made by having many of the variables in the hypotheses represented by artificial signs (or symbols in a more narrow sense of the word). But a real calculus has not been constructed.

Neither has a strict formalization in the sense: an explicit formulation of a meta-theory, been made. But a very detailed presentation of the general meta-theoretical presuppositions is, as already mentioned, given (especially in P. B.). As a whole Hull's theory may be characterized as *an axiomatized and partly symbolized deductive theory*.

Reductive or Constructive Theory

In this classification Hull's theory belongs to *the constructive theories* as it attempts to explain behavior on the basis of hypotheses with hypothetical constructions (variables) of a neutral-formal character. There are a few who have misunderstood this and regarded the theory as a reductive theory. But a closer study of the theory will show that variables and hypotheses are formulated exclusively on the basis of and as explanations of *behavior* data; there is no deduction on the basis of physiological data and hypotheses.

Mentalistic or Behavioristic Theory

Seemingly it would be quite obvious to classify Hull's theory as a behavioristic theory because he is regarded to be one of the modern behaviorists, the so-called 'neo-behaviorists.' According to the classification made in Chapter 3 his theory is, however, not purely behavioristic, but belongs to *the neutral-formal theories*, as the hypothetical variables of the theory are not to be interpreted as neuro-physiological, but as neutral-formal variables. On the other hand, the protocol statements of the theory—or, in other words: the method through which the theory is controlled empirically—are purely behavioristic. Hull writes about this in B. S. (p. 344):

'From the present point of view the subjective states such as pain and pleasure are characteristic internal conditions and are observable by means of internal receptors. These receptors discharge into the nervous system quite as do the external receptors, (such as the retina and the cochlea) and so in different combinations are able to evoke responses of various kinds, including those of verbal symbolism which constitute introspective reports and valuative judgments.'

And he reaches the following conclusion (p. 345):

'Consequently, intospective reports concerning internal conditions are useful for rough qualitative purposes; nevertheless they become inadequate wherever primary quantitative laws are in the process of systematic formulation or precise validation. Fortunately, as we have tried to show above, in the formulation of natural law it is not necessary to depend on such unsatisfactory evidence. We can utilize symbolic constructs.'

As these quotations and Hull's other works show, Hull is not a fanatical, one-sided, or naive behaviorist, but a very all-round oriented and realistic theorist.

Molar or Molecular Theory

It is easy to apply this classification to Hull's theory, as he has repeatedly explicitly characterized his theory as 'a molar behavior theory'. But, as mentioned in Chapter 3, he considers this distinction a matter of *difference of degree* and believes that a molecular and molar theories of the same subject area later may be systematized into one theory with the molecular hypotheses as the primary and the molar hypotheses as the secondary hypotheses.

Although Hull's theory, according to his own explicit formulations, must be described as a molar theory, a closer analysis of the descriptive units it deals with—especially the so-called micro-molar analysis of behavior in Chapter VII in B. S.—leads us to the result that the word 'mainly' must be added to the description of the theory, and this must then be classified as *a mainly molar theory.*

Mechanistic Theory of Field-Theory

It is a little difficult to place Hull's theory in this classification. Gestalt psychologists and other opponents to behaviorism most often characterize behavioristic theories as mechanistic. But the way in which they use the word is most often vague and negative. If we, however, use the terminology defined in Chapter 3, mechanistic theories are theories with simple hypotheses dealing with two variables, whereas field-theoretical hypotheses are more complicated and deal with several variables. An analysis of Hull's theory will show that several hypotheses have several co-operating variables, in other words, hypotheses which state that a variable is a function of a totality of mutually dependent variables. Thus a very important variable, the 'reaction potential' (${}_SE_R$), is defined by the following formula:

$${}_SE_R = f(D \times V \times K \times {}_SH_R).$$

As a consequence of this Hull's theory cannot be classified as a mechanistic theory. As it is not a typical field-theory either (as for example those of Lewin and Tolman) it must be classified as an intermediate form and be described as *a dynamic theory.*

Statistical or Deterministic Theory

It is also somewhat difficult to place Hull's theory in this classification. It seems most correct, however, to describe it as a *deterministic* theory, as the quantitative formulation of the hypotheses is presented as mathematical functional relations and not as statistical correlations. Furthermore, Hull has recommended choosing deterministic hypotheses in an article (3), where he writes:

'that it is not unreasonable to hope for the isolation of both primary and secondary behavioral laws which will hold within a narrow margin of error for averages secured from carefully controlled empirical conditions.'

Still Hull has also made allowance for the variation in the behavior as such (not only for the distrubition of measurements), as he ascribes to the organism—or rather to the nervous system—a hypothetical variable which is called 'behavioral oscillation' and which is presented as Postulate XII (p. 11 in B. S.):

'Postulate XII. Behavioral Oscillation (${}_SO_R$).

A. A. reaction potential (${}_SE_R$) oscillates from moment to moment, the distribution of behavioral oscillation (${}_SO_R$) deviating slightly from the Gaussian probability form in being leptokurtic with β_2 at about 4.0; i. e., the distribution is represented by the equation

$$y = y_0 \frac{1}{\left(1+\frac{x^2}{a^2}\right)^m}.\text{''}$$

Hull has also made allowance for the variation which is determined by individual *differences*, as he maintains that these take part as certain 'constants' in the functional relations (cf. the classification in disposition and function variables, Chapter 3). This is formulated as the last of his postulates (p. 13 in B. S.):

'Postulate XVII. Individual Differences (2, p. 115).

The 'constant' numerical values appearing in equations representing primary molar behavioral laws vary from species to species, from individual to individual, and from some physiological states to others in the same individual at different times, all quite apart from the factor of behavioral oscillation ($_{S}O_{R}$).'

And as a summary of what he has said about the variations in behavior Hull states (p. 333 in B. S.):

'This in no sense implies a breakdown of primary natural-science dynamic laws. It is true that the natural laws involved are not the laws of Newtonian mechanics. It is also true that behavior laws, owing to the principle or law of the oscillation of reaction potential ($_{S}O_{R}$), are molar in the sense that they hold strictly only for central tendencies calculated from numerous samples of carefully measured data.'

This quotation shows—as do the ones given above—that Hull's theory must be characterized as deterministic, but it is a determinism which only possesses a certain probability approaching 1.0 when the number of cases is large; maybe it should be called a '*probability-determinism*'.

The Model

The model which gives an illustrative presentation of Hull's theory can be found in a diagram in P. B. (p. 383). In reality this is a further development of the simple, but frequently used model:

$$S \rightarrow O \rightarrow R.$$

Summary

This analysis of *the structure* of Hull's theory may be summarized as follows:

Hull's theory is a deductive (axiomatized and partly symbolized) constructive, neutral-formal, mainly molar, dynamic, and mainly deterministic theory.

MOTIVATION DEFINITIONS AND HYPOTHESES

In this section an analysis will be made of *the content* of Hull's theory and especially of its content of definitions and hypotheses of motivation. It is true that Hull's theory is not a typical theory of motivation, it is rather a general theory of psychology, most detailed when it deals with the psychology of the learning process. But some of its postulates, corollaries, and theorems when the theory is analyzed, are found to be *hypotheses of motivation*, and these will be further discussed later in this section. It is more difficult to make a reasonable, systematic analysis of *the definitions* of motivation variables in the theory, because these definitions are mainly implicit, and are included in the postulates. There are, more over, some more informal definitions in the Glossary of Symbols,' which can be found at the end of both main works.

The most simple table of variables in Hull's theory is given in his previously mentioned diagram in P. B., p. 383. Unfortunately he has not made a corresponding diagram in B. S. where a few other variables have been added. The analysis of the motivation variables will therefore follow the diagram p. 383 in P. B., but I have found it most practical to start from the end and go backwards.

The Reaction Potential

The empirical *behavior variables* are: 'probability of reaction, latency of reaction, numbers of unreinforced reactions to produce experimental extinction; and amplitude of reaction.' According to Postulates XIV, XV, and XVI (p. 13 in B. S.) these behavior variables are *directly* dependent upon the socalled '*reaction potential*,' symbolized as $_SE_R$ (because it was originally called 'excitatory potential' in Hull's miniature systems). This important variable is defined implicitly in the following postulate (B. S., p. 7)[3]):

'Postulate VIII. The Constitution of Reaction Potential ($_SE_R$).
The reaction potential ($_SE_R$) of a bit of learned behavior at any given stage of learning, where conditions are constant through-out learning and response-evocation, is determined (1) by the drive (D) operating during the learning process multiplied (2) by the dynamism of the signaling stimulus trace (V), (3) by the incentive reinforcement (K), and (4) by the habit strength ($_SH_R$), i. e.,

$$_SE_R = D \times V \times K \times {_SH_R}.\text{'}$$

'Reaction potential' is, as can be seen from this postulate, a very complex variable. Whether or not it is a motivation variable will depend upon the final definition of 'motivation,' but according to the temporary definition (motivation = arousing, sustaining, and directive variables) it will be difficult to exlude $_SE_R$.
Furthermore, this variable must—as already mentioned—be classified as a *hypothetical* variable, more exactly as belonging to the *neutral-formal* subgroup, as Hull several times stresses (especially in P. B.) that these are 'logical,' 'symbolic,' or 'theoretical *constructions*' corresponding to Tolman's 'intervening variables' (explicitly mentioned by Hull as his model).

As $_SE_R$ is exclusively defined by the *hypothetical* variables, it can be characterized as *a hypothetical variable of the second order*. But the empirical basis is firm, as this variable, as mentioned, is directly related to empirical behavior variables. In the classification of psychological variables as function and disposition variables $_SE_R$ must be placed as *a function variable*, as it definitely takes part directly in the process which determines behavior; and furthermore it appears as a 'real' variable

---

[3]) When nothing else is said the following references are to the postulates in B. S. p. 5 to 14.

in formula expressing the hypotheses (contrary to amore constant disposition variable).

Finally it should be mentioned that reaction potential, when influenced by '*inhibitory potential*' (I_R) and '*behavioral oscillation*' ($_SO_R$), is modified to 'effective reaction potential' and 'momentary effective reaction potential,' respectively (according to Postulates IX and XII in B. S.; cf. also the diagram p. 383 in P. B.).

Only two of the hypothetical variables which are included in the constitutional formula of $_SE_R$ (according to Postulate VIII quoted above) are motivation variables, and these will be analyzed in detail in the following while the two others, which are not motivation variables, will only be briefly discussed. These are '*the stimulus-intensity component (V)*,' which, according to Postulate VI, is a '*monotonic increasing logarithmic function of S*,' and '*habit*' ($_SH_R$), which, according to Postulate IV, is a 'positive growth function of the number of trials' with 'reinforcements.'

'*Drive*' and '*Need*'.

'*Drive*' (D) is the most important motivation variable in Postulate VIII. It is introduced and defined implicitly in Postulate V, which will therefore be quoted here (from B. S., p. 6):

'Postulate V. Primary Motivation or Drive (D).

A. Primary motivation (D), at least that resulting from food privation, consists of two multiplicative components: (1) the drive proper (D') which is an increasing monotonic sigmoid function of h, the number of hours af food privation; and (2) a negative or inanition component (ε) which is a positively accelerated monotonic function of h decreasing from 1.0 to zero, i. e.,

$$D = D' \times \varepsilon.$$

where

$$D' = 37{,}824 \times 10^{-27{,}496\frac{1}{h}} + 4{,}001,$$

and

$$\varepsilon = 1 - .00001045h^{2.496}.\text{'}$$

This postulate gives a good impression of the exactness ot Hull's theory, but also of its limitations (which will be discussed later). It shows, moreover, that 'drive' is a *hypothetical* variable of the *neutral-formal* type (as are all Hull's hypothetical variables). This is explicitly pointed out with regard to D in P. B. p. 57. It is also a *function* variable, as it takes part direct in the process from stimuli to behavior as a 'real' variable (contrary to a more constant disposition variable). Hull writes about *the number* of primary drives (in P. B. p. 59):

'The major primary needs or drives are so ubiquitous that they require little more than to be mentioned. They include the need for foods of various sorts (hunger), the need for water (thirst), the need for air, the need to avoid tissue injury (pain), the need to maintain an optimal temperature, the need to defecate, the need to micturate, the need for rest (after protracted exertion), the need for sleep (after protracted wakefulness), and the need for activity (after protracted inaction). The drives concerned with the maintenance of the species are those which lead to sexual intercourse and the need represented by nest building and care of the young.'

Postulate V formulates D's functional relation to the independent *empirical* variable '*drive condition*' (C_D). This variable is not defined explicitly in this postulate, but an example of 'drive condition' is given in Paragraph B, namely 'food privation'. But in 'Glossary of Symbols' in B. S. (p. 357) the variable is explicitly defined in the following way:

'C_D = condition producing a drive.'

And in 'Glossary' in P. B. (p. 403) it is defined in more detail:

'C_D = conditions which produce the drive (D), the objective conditions from which D may be calculated.'

The last half of the last definition shows clearly that C_D is an independent *empirical* variable; and as it takes part directly in the process it must further be classified as a *function* variable.

In Postulate V, Paragraph C, another motivation variable is implicitly defined, he '*drive stimulus*' (S_D). As D, according to the postulate, is a function of S_D, and as '*drive stimulus*' also is a function of C_D, the functional relation must, in my opinion, be of such a kind that S_D is a connecting link between C_D and D. This can be symbolized as follows:

$$C_D \rightarrow S_D \rightarrow D.$$

Logically there is also the possibility that S_D and D are *parallel*, but I consider the formulation given above to be the most probable.[3a]) Yet the big draw-back of Hull's theory is that it cannot directly be seen clearly from postulates and other statements how the functional relation between S_D and D is. As a consequence of this lack it is also difficult to decide whether S_D is an empirical or a hypothetical variable; but if it is considered as being in accordance with the above formula it must be classified as an *empirical* variable, namely as the afferent nervous impulse determined by some drive condition and transmited to the brain where it determines the hypothetical variable D. In practice it may be more difficult to observe S_D than C_D, but in principle they must be called empirical variables, while D is temporarily a hypothetical variable. Contrary to this difficult classification it is rather easy to classify 'drive stimulus' as a *function* variable.

Apart from the above mentioned lack of an unambiguous formulation of the relation between C_D, S_D, and D and direct ambiguity exists in the way Hull uses the word '*need*'. This term is defined neither implicitly in postulates, nor explicitly in the 'Glossary', but is used indiscriminately as synonymous with both 'drive condition' and 'drive'. This is specially the case with the definitions in 'Glossary' in B. S. where it is said in p. 357:

'D = drive; primary motivation; need; emotion; effective or gross drive; $D = d' \times \varepsilon$.'

And in the same list p. 359:

'S_D = drive stimulus; need; drive intensity.'

[3a]) The present author has subsequently been convinced by reading many other interpretations of Hull's theory that the *parallel* interpretation *is* the most correct. Thus S_D is another *hypothetical function variable* which has a more specific *directive* function than the more general *dynamic* function which characterizes D.

'Need' is, as can be seen from the above quotations, explicitly defined as being synonymous with both 'drive' and 'drive stimulus,' but it is *not* explicitly mentioned in the definition of 'drive condition.' In my opinion, however, the only unambiguous way to use 'need' in Hull's theory is to define 'need' as a synonym to 'drive condition'[4]). It is peculiar to see this inconsistency in an otherwise very systematic theory, and it is especially strange that it is most obvious in his last work. Maybe it would have been corrected if Hull had had an opportunity to proof-read B. S. before his death.

Other Motivation Variables

Another motivation variable besides D is included in the constitutional formula of 'reaction potential'; namely '*the incentive component*' (K), which is defined implicitly in the following postulate (from B. S., p. 7):

'Postulate VII. Incentive Motivation (K).

The incentive component (K) of reaction potential ($_SE_R$) is a negatively accelerated increasing monotonic function of the weight (w) of food or quantity of other incentive (K') given as reinforcement, i. e.,

$$K = 1 - 10^{-a\sqrt{w}}$$

K is, as can be seen from the above, a *hypothetical* (neutral-formal) variable, which is directly functionally related to an independent *empirical* variable called 'the physical incentive' (K'), for example food. It should be added that K is also a *function* variable.

'*Inhibitory potential*' (I_R) is another motivation variable, defined implicitly in Postulate IX, Paragraph A (B. S., p. 9):

'Postulate IX. Inhibitory Potential.

A. Whenever a reaction (R) is evoked from an organism there is left an increment of primary negative drive (I_R) which inhibits to a degree according to its magnitude the reaction potential ($_SE_R$) to that response.'

'Inhibitory potential' is, as can be seen from the quotation, defined as a 'primary negative drive'. This variable must therefore, like D, be classified as *a neutral-formal hypothetical function variable.* It plays a rather big part in Hull's theory, as can be seen, for example, from the fact that Postulate IX besides the already quoted paragraphs includes four paragraphs about I_R's functional relations to different empirical variables. There are also 13 corollaries concerning I_R.

Finally there is a variable in Hull's theory which maybe can be characterized as a motivation variable, namely the so-called '*fractional antedating goal reaction*' (r_G).

This variable cannot be found in P. B., but we find it in the older miniature-

---

[4]) This is also the way in which it has been interpreted in the last edition of Woodworth: '*Experimental Psychology*,' where Hull's theory plays a rather important part.

systems, and in B. S. a whole chapter (Chapter V) is exclusively devoted to it while a corollary (XV) about its functions in the learning-process has been added (this will be dealt with later). No implicit definition in a postulate is given, however. The 'Glossary' only says (p. 359): 'r_G = fractional antedating goal reaction; a concrete pure-stimulus act'. One must therefore look for a definition of this variable in the informal text.

Hull writes in Chapter V, p. 124, that when a situation and a form of behavior is repeated there will be *a tendency* for S_D to determine R_G (the consummatory response) even in the beginning, because S_D is the only stimulus in the situation which is constantly present. But R_G will conflict with the necessary instrumental movements which must be carried out before R_G can appear, and the instrumental movements $_SE_R$ will dominate the $_SE_R$ of R_G. But they will allow 'the nonconflicting or fractional portion (of R_G) to persist in a covert form. We shall represent this nonconflicting part of R_G by r_G. For this reason such assumed persistence (r_G) is called the *fractional* antedating goal reaction'. As this determines the proprioceptive stimuli, called '*fractional antedating goal stimuli* (s_G),' it will act as a secondary reinforcement (which will be discussed later). Hull maintains moreover that r_G will be able to explain 'latent learning' and other problems better than Tolman's 'cognition', to which it should correspond rather closely (just as S_G should correspond to Tolman's 'expectancy'). As a whole Hull believes that he by means of r_G is able to explain phenomena such as 'foresight', 'foreknowledge', and 'purpose'.

It is clearly seen from the above that 'the fractional antedating goal reaction' is *a neutral-formal, hypothetical function variable*. But it is doubtful whether it can be described as a *motivation* variable, as it has only one of the functions mentioned in the temporary definition (namely purposefulness while it does not include the two others (the arousing and sustaining functions). The solution of this problem must wait the final definition of 'motivation' in the last chapters.

Hypotheses about Motivation

The variables already analyzed appear in many different functional relations about which Hull has formulated many hypotheses (postulates, corollaries, and theorems). The most important of these will now be analyzed more closely according to their rank in the system. The first postulate (in B. S., p. 5) is the first hypothesis in which a motivation variable is included:

'Postulate I. Unlearned Stimulus-response Connections ($_SU_R$).

Organisms at birth possess receptor-effector connections ($_SU_R$) which under combined stimulation (S) and (D) have the potentiality of evoking a hierarchy of responses that either individually or in combination are more likely to terminate a need than would be a random selection from the reactions resulting from other stimulus and drive combinations.'

This postulate shows that, according to Hull, not even the most simple innate (reflexive, instinctive) reactions can exist without motivation, which thus is a necessary condition for the appearance of behavior. This postulate alone shows that Hull's theory is not a rough S→R theory. This can also be seen from the fact that it is difficult to place the postulate in Spence's modified classification of hypotheses (cf. Chapter 3), because this postulate is rather complex and deals with functional relations between both independent empirical variables, hypothetical variables, and behavior variables. In other words, the following hypotheses are included in this postulate:

$$\begin{array}{ccc} S \rightarrow {}_{S}U_{R} \rightarrow & R \\ & \uparrow \\ C_D \rightarrow & D \end{array}$$

The same is true of most of Hull's postulates: the difficulties connected with classifying most of the following postulates are due to their being complicated, compound (field-theoretical) hypotheses. Besides some of Hull's hypotheses cannot be placed in the modified classification because it lacks that of Spence's classes which formulates a relation between a variable and time (i. e. $H = f(t)$). Therefore the classification of the following hypotheses will not be discussed further.

Postulate I is the only postulate which deals with *non-acquired* (innate) behavior. All the other postulates in Hull's theory deal explicitly or implicitly with *acquired* behavior—or with the learning of new behavior.

This is true of Postulate III (B. S., p. 5):

'Postulate III. Primary Reinforcement.

Whenever an effector activity (R) is closely associated with a stimulus afferent impulse or trace (s) and the conjunction is closely associated with the rapid diminution in the motivational stimulus S_D or sG), there will result an increment (Δ) to a tendency for that stimulus to evoke that response.'

Together with Postulate IV this postulate is the most important with regard to the learning process. It is quoted here because it formulates *the function of motivation in the learning process*, while Postulate V deals with the importance of *repetition* in the learning process. In other words, it is Postulate III which characterizes especially Hull's theory of the learning process as a '*reinforcement-theory*' (as opposed the pure 'contiguity-theories' such as that of Guthries, or the 'cognitive' theories such as that of Tolman's).

A very important hypothesis of motivation dealing with *the forming of secondary motives* is formulated in the following way (B. S., p. 6):

'Corollary i. Secondary Motivation.

When neutral stimuli are repeatedly and consistently associated with the evocation of a primary or secondary drive and this drive stimulus undergoes an abrupt diminution, the hitherto neutral stimuli acquire the capacity to bring about the drive stimuli (S_D), which thereby become the condition (C_D) of a secondary drive or motivation.'

This hypothesis increases the number of motives in Hull's theory towards infinity, as it is possible through the learning process mentioned in the first corollary to form an infinite number of secondary 'drives' on the basis of relatively few primary 'drives.'

In the same way the importance of motivation in the learning process is extended by *secondary reinforcement*, formulated in the following hypothesis (B. S., p. 6):

'Corollary II. Secondary Reinforcement.
A neutral receptor impulse which occurs repeatedly and consistently in close conjunction with a reinforcing state of affairs, whether primary or secondary, will itself acquire the power of acting as a reinforcing agent.'

Association is, as can be seen from the quoted postulates and corollaries, an important factor in Hull's theory of the learning process. It may even be said that the learning process forms more or less complicated associations, but, as already mentioned, *repetition* of simultaneousness or succession is not a sufficient condition for forming associations or habits, *motivation* must necessarily also be present, and therefore Hull's theory of the learning process is a reinforcement-theory and not a pure contiguity-theory.

Thus Postulates IV and VI are not hypotheses of motivation, but deal with the importance of repetition in the forming of habits and 'Stimulus-intensity Dynamism,' respectively.

Postulates V, VII, and VIII are quoted and analyzed in the previous section because they contain definitions of D, K, and ${}_SE_R$, respectively.

Corollaries iii to viii are hypotheses dealing especially with the learning process.

Postulate IX, A, has also been quoted and analyzed previously, because it contains a definition of I_R. The other paragraphs of the postulate contain more special hypotheses about I_R. Paragraph B deals with the decrease of I_R with time, and Paragraphs C and D deal with the growth of I_R with the number of 'unreinforced' reactions and experimental extinction. The last paragraph, E, deals with the dependence of I_R upon the quantity of activity in a reaction. The same is true about Corollaries x and xi, whereas Corollary ix deals with 'conditioned inhibition.' A closer analysis of all these hypotheses will, however, not be made as they are only of peripheral interest for a theory of motivation.

Postulate X and corollary XII deal with 'Stimulus Generalization', whereas Postulate XI deals with 'Afferent Stimulus Interaction' which in Hull's theory is equivalent to the Gestalt-principles of the Gestalt psychologists. Postulate XII delas with 'Behavioral Oscillation' and has been quoted in the first section of this chapter in the analysis of the structure of the theory. Corollary xiii is related to this, as it deals with 'Response Generalization'. Postulate XIII deals with 'Reaction Threshold' (${}_SL_R$).

Corollary xiv is of importance to motivation psychology and will therfore be quoted here (B. S., p. 12):

'Corollary xiv. The Competition of Incompatible Reaction Potentials (${}_S\bar{E}_R$).
When the net reaction potentials (${}_S\bar{E}_R$) to two or more incompatible reactions (R) occur

in an organism at the same instant, each in a magnitude greater than $_SL_R$, only that reaction whose momentary reaction potential ($_S\bar{E}_R$) is greatest will be evoked.'

As can be seen, this corollary deals with a fundamental aspect of *conflict-situations* which are of great importance in motivation psychology and its special applications (in neurosis-theory, etc.). Hull deals with conflict-situations in detail in several theorems, which will be mentioned later.

Postulates XIV, XV, and XVI deal with different quantitative behavior variables which are functions of $_SE_R$.

Postulate XVII deals with 'Individual Differences' which, as previously mentioned, appear in hypotheses as different numerical values of the invariables.

And finally there is Corollary xv which, like several other hypotheses, deal with 'reinforcement' and therefore will be quoted here (B. B., p. 14):

'Corollary xv. Secondary Reinforcement by Fractional Antedating Goal Reaction ($r_G \rightarrow s_G$).
When a stimulus (S) or a stimulus trace (S) acts at the same time that a hitherto unrelated response (R) occurs and this coincidence is accompanied by an antedating goal reaction (r_G), the secondary reinforcing powers of the stimulus evoked by the latter (s_G) will reinforce S to R, giving rise to a new S→R dynamic connection.'

As mentioned in the analysis of r_G, this corollary makes it possible to explain 'latent learning' and other difficult problems on the basis of a 'reinforcement' theory. Motivation can, with r_G as a connecting link, have rather distant and lasting influence upon relations between stimuli and reactions.

Corollary xvi (p. 23 in B. S.) deals with '*simple trial-and-error learning*' as do Theorems 1 to 10 (all in Chapter II). Theorems 10 to 17 deal with '*discrimination learning*' (all in Chapter III). None of these theorems are of particular importance in motivation psychology apart from the fact that 'reinforcement' is necessary for both forms of the learning process. The same is true about theorems 18 to 26 in Chapter IV which deal with '*the molar stimulus trace*'. Chapter V deals with '*fractional antedating goal reactions*'. Corollary xvii is formulated in connection with this, and deals with the effect of a stop in the 'reinforcement'. Theorem 29 is a motivation hypothesis and will therefore be quoted here (B. S., p. 139):

'THEOREM 29. If an organism has two drives operating and is repeatedly in a situation where one of the other drive stimulus may be reinforced by a distinct series of movements, it will later, when only one of the drives is operating, at once tend to perform the movements which formerly led to the reduction of the S_D in question.'

As can clearly be seen, the above theorem gives an explanation of the so-called 'double-driving-learning' problem.

The next theorem is also a motivation hypothesis' dealing with the effects of changes in incentives. It is formulated in the following way (B. S., p. 145):

'THEOREM 30. Other things constant, an abrupt shift in the incentive used during a maze-learning process will be followed first by a major shift in reaction potential and then by two or more progressively smaller shifts on successive trials, the series constituting a rapid learning process of the exponential variety, culminating in the course that the $_SE_R$ would have followed had the new incentive been operating continuously from the beginning of the learning.'

Theorem 31' which deals with 'latent learning' is not a motivation hypothesis. Neither are Theorems 32 to 40 in Chapter VI which deal with 'simple behavior chains.' Chapter VII about 'The Individual Behavior Link' contains quite a few relatively molecular theorems, 41 to 52, which are exclusively hypotheses about the learning process.

But Chapter VIII about 'Behavior in Relation to Objects in Space' includes a total of *50 theorems* (53 to 102) of which *the majority are motivation hypotheses* as they deal with *conflict situations*, *detour-situations*, *etc.* It would take up too much space to quote and comment on all the fifty theorems here, for which reason only a representative selection will be given.

'THEOREM 57. Both adient reaction potential and abient reaction potential in free space constitute plane fields of reaction potentialities.'

As can already be seen from the above theorem, Hull's theory is in this respect a field-theory the usually meaning of the word[5]). This will also clearly appear from the following. Theorem 58 is an important hypothesis about *conflict-situation* (B. S., p. 224):

'THEOREM 58. With sophisticated organisms operating in open space, the gradient of abient reaction potential to static objects at its point of maximum slope will be steeper than that of adient reaction potential at its point of maximum slope.'

The following hypothesis also deals with a simple conflict-situation (B. S., p. 229):

'THEOREM 63. Other things equal, in a competing adient-abient situation in which the organism is placed midway between two duplicate focal objects with clear distance reception for each, the organism will be as likely to take a path leading to one object as to the other, but if placed nearer one object it will be more likely to choose that object.'

The opposite situation is mentioned in the following hypothesis (B. S., p. 243):

'THEOREM 81. Other things equal, a naive organism placed midway between two duplicate abient objects in free space will tend to move in a direction at right angles to the line connecting the two objects.'

Hull points out that this hypothesis has already been formulated by *K. Lewin*, but, contrary to Lewin, Hull will *not* generalize this or other hypotheses of bc-havior in space into non-spatial, analogous situations.

Finally there are two hypotheses about a third kind of conflict-situation (p. 249 to 250, B. S.):

'THEOREM 86. Other things equal, with moderately sophisticated subjects, when an adient object and an abient object occupy nearly the same point in space and the maximum abient reaction potential is greater than the maximum adient potential, there will be a point of stable equilibrium at a j. n. d. distance from the adient-abient object amounting to

$$d = \frac{\log \frac{sE'_R}{sE'_R}.}{j'-j},$$

'THEOREM 87. Other things equal, when an adient-abient object occupies the same point in space and the maximum abient reaction potential is greater than the maximum adient, the oscillatory movements from the point of zero difference away from the object will be greater on the average than those toward the object, and those in a lateral direction will be greater on the average than either, the latter being generally in a circular course and the double object being the center with a radius equal to the distance from the point of zero difference.'

---

[5]) In Hull's theory 'adient' means 'behavior toward' while 'abient' means 'behavior away from.'

The rest of the theorems in Chapter VIII mainly deal with behavior in connection with blocks, i. e., the solving of simple *detour-problems*. Two of the hypotheses, however, concern motivation (B. S., p. 267):

'THEOREM 101. Other things constant, the stronger the drive to a given goal object behind a U-shaped barrier, the more the time and work which will be required by a naive organism before the occurrence of sufficient extinction to yield the execution of a succesful detour.'

The corresponding hypothesis, Theorem 102, about 'incentives' is formulated exactly the same words as those used in Theorem 101.

The hypotheses quoted should be enough to give a satisfactory impression of the fact that Hull's 'behavioristic' theory can deal with just as complicated 'field-problems' as Lewin's 'topological' theory—and even without the construction of a special kind of geometry (hodology).

Theorems 103 to 122 can be found in Chapter IX. They all deal with '*Maze-learning*' and are without particular motivation psychological importance.

Chapter X deals with 'The Problem Solving Assembly of Behavior Segments' and contains Theorems 123 to 132 which explain both *the detour-problems* of *Maier's* type and *tool-problems* of *Köhler's* type.

In Chapter XI Hull discusses 'Value, Valuation, and Behavior Theory' on the basis of the postulates of his theory, defining 'value' in the following way (p. 329):

'In short, value represents *the potentiality* of action. But action potentiality in this system is represented by $_{S}E_{R}$.'

Based upon this definition Hull analyzes different value-problems (for example social values, ethics, truth value, etc.). His last theorem deals with social co-operation (B. S., p. 337):

'THEOREM 133. Every voluntary social interaction, in order to be repeated consistently, must result in a substantial reinforcement to the activity of each party to the transaction.'

This theorem is the only one in Hull's theory which deals with social behavior. But as mentioned in the introduction he planned to extend the theory with another volume to include also social behavior. Unfortunately he died before he managed to make an outline of such a theory.

The last chapter is a summary of the content of the whole theory dealing with the eight 'adaptive automatic behavior mechanisms' already summarized in the introduction to this chapter.

RECONSTRUCTION OF THE THEORY

Hull's theory hardly needs to be reconstructed systematically[6]). But as the theory has not been formulated as a special theory of motivation the general psychological hypotheses and the motivation hypotheses will be co-ordinated in a theory of motivation.

---

[6]) The analyzed edition of Hull's theory in B. S. is Hull's own third (or fourth) reconstruction of the original system of postulates in P. B. It would be an interesting *historical* task to study *the development* in Hull's theory from the first miniaturesystems in Ps. Rev. in the thirties to B. S. in 1952. But of course this can not be included in the present meta-theoretical study.

Postulate I is suggested as the first primary hypothesis in the reconstructed theory of motivation:

Hypothesis 1: About innate behavior. 'Organisms at birth possess receptor-effector connections ($_SU_R$) which under combined stimulation (S) and drive (D) have the potentiality of evoking a hierarchy of responses that either individually or in combination are more likely to terminate a need (C_D) than would be a random selection from the reactions resulting from other stimulus and drive combinations.'

Only one change has been made, namley that 'need' is regarded to be equivalent to 'drive condition' (C_D) in accordance with the analysis in previous sections.

Postulate VIII is suggested as the second primary hypothesis:

Hypothesis 2: About the 'reaction potential' ($_SE_R$) of acquired behavior: The reaction potential ($_SE_R$) of a unit of learned behavior at any given stage of learning, where conditions are constant throughout learning and response-evocation, is determined by the following functional relation:

$$_SE_R = D \times V \times K \times {_SH_R}.$$

The variables involved are: 1) D = drive (will be defined in a following hypothesis), 2) V = the stimulus-intensity-component (defined in Hull's Postulate VI as a logarithmic function of stimulus), 3) K = the incentive component (will be defined in a following hypothesis), and 4) $_SH_R$ the habit strength (defined in Hull's Postulate IV as a function of the number of reinforcements).

After this hypothesis some hypotheses about the motivation variables involved (D and K) will be formulated, and besides some hypotheses about behavior variables dependent upon $_SE_R$, will be formulated. These hypotheses establish connections between the important hypothetical variabel, $_SE_R$, and empirical variables (both independent and dependent variables).

Hypothesis 3: About primary motivation or drive (D). Primary motivation or 'drive' (D) is a function of a 'drive-stimulus (S_D), which is determined by a 'drive-condition' (C_D) in the organism.

As can be seen, the above hypothesis is a reformulation of Hull's Postulate V, Paragraph C, in accordance with the analysis in previous sections. Paragraphs A, B and D of Postulate V will be reformulated later.

A similar general reformulation of Postulate VII is suggested:

Hypothesis 4: About incentive motivation. The incentive component of $_SE_R$ is a function of the quantity of the goal-object or the incitement.

The following summarizing reformulation of Postulates XIV and XVI is suggested:

Hypothesis 5: About measuring $_SE_R$. The reaction potential can be measured by the following dependent behavior variables: 1) reaction latence ($_St_R$), 2) reaction amplitude (A), and 3) experimental extinction (n), the following functions being valid:

1. $_SE_R = 2{,}845\ (_St_R)^{-0{,}48}$
2. $_SE_R = 0{,}2492\ A$

3a.[7]) $_SE_R = 4{,}0\ (1 - 10^{3-0{,}0110\ n}) + 0{,}46$
3b.[7]) $_SE_R = 0{,}1225 + 10^{0{,}0647\ n} + 2{,}114$

Hull's important Corollary i on the forming of secondary motivation is quoted as hypotheses 6:

Hypothesis 6: About secondary motivation. 'When neutral stimuli are repeatedly and consistently associated with the *evocation*[7a]) of a primary or secondary drive and this drive stimulus undergoes an abrupt diminution, the hitherto neutral stimuli acquire the capacity to bring about the drive stimuli (S_D), which thereby become the condition (C_D) of a secondary drive or motivation.'

A primary hypothesis about I_R must also be included in a reconstructed theory of motivation based upon Hull's theory, and the following reformulation of Postulate IX is therefore suggested:

Hypothesis 7: About 'The Inhibitory Potential.' Whenever an organism performes an action, this will determine the increase of a primary negative drive, called 'the inhibitory potential' (I_R), which inhibits the reaction potential of the action in question in proportion to the magnitude of I_R.

This inhibitory potential decreases spontaneously as a simple decreasing function of time (t), thus:

$$I_R' = I_R \times 10^{0{,}018t}.$$

As can be seen, the above hypothesis is a summary of Paragraphs A and B of Postulate IX. The other paragraphs (C to E) and Corollaries ix and xi are special hypotheses about learning.

Corollary xiv is, however, so important a motivation hypothesis that it will be included in this reconstruction:

Hypothesis 8: About conflict between $_SE_R$. 'When the net reaction potentials ($_SE_R$) to two or more incompatible reactions (R) occur in an organism at the same instant' each in a magnitude greater than $_SL_R$[8]), only that reaction whose momentary reaction potential ($_SE_R$) is greatest will be evoked.'

Finally a few primary hypotheses about the function of motivation in learning must also be included:

Hypothesis 9: About 'reinforcement.' Whenever a reaction (R) occurs simultaneously with a stimulus (S) (or stimulus trace), and a rapid *decrease* occurs at the same time or immediately after in the motivation stimulus (S_D or S_G), or in

---

[7]) 3a is valid for $_SE_R$ acquired through 'massed reinforcements' and 3b is valid for $_SE_R$ acquired through quasi-distributed reinforcements.

[7a]) Italics mine. Cf. Hilgard's reformulations p. 129–30 in 2. ed. of 'Theories of Learning' (1956).

[8]) Defined in Hull's Postulate XII.

a stimulus which has been associated with a motivating stimulus, then the result will be an increased probability for R being determined by S.

As can be seen, the above hypothesis is a summary of Hull's Postulate III and Corollary ii (which was only one postulate in P. B.). The word 'tendency' has been changed to the more exact 'probability'. And as the last primary hypothesis a reformulation of Paragraph D in Postulate V is suggested:

Hypothesis 10: About the motivation of 'habits'. Habits ($_{S}H_{R}$) can be activated by other drive conditions (C_D) than the one which operated during the forming of the habit.

In addition to the ten primary hypotheses formulated above it is suggested that the reconstructed theory of motivation should include the following secondary hypotheses, which it is unnecessary, however, to quote and reformulate here:

Secondary Hypothesis 1: About 'food-drive.' (This hypothesis corresponds to Paragraph A of Postulate V.)

Secondary Hypothesis 2: About 'food-drive.' (Corresponds to Paragraph B of Postulate V.)

Secondary Hypothesis 3: About 'food-incentive.' (Postulate VII.)

Secondary Hypothesis 4: About double-motivation. (Theorem 29.)

Secondary Hypothesis 5: About changes in incentives. (Theorem 30.)

Secondary Hypotheses 6 to 43: About conflict behavior. (Theorems 53 to 89.)

Secondary Hypotheses 44 and 45: About motivation in detour problems. (Theorems 101 and 102.)

Secondary Hypothesis 46: About social co-operation. (Theorem 133.)

Conclusion

It is probably quite clear from the above, that even though Hull's theory is not perfect I consider it the *most systematical and exact theory in psychology.* That I am not the only one who holds this opinion can be seen from the obituary notice where *Hovland* says (12): Today Hull is *the most frequently mentioned psychologist* in American psychological magazines and manuals. A study of some books and articles showed that more than 40% of all references were to the works of Hull. If the study was limited to books, chapters, or articles about the psychology of learning, the result was that over 90% of all references were to works of Hull[9]).

References

1. Hull C. L.: Knowledge and purpose as habit mechanisms (Ps. Rev. 1930, 37, 511–528).
2. – Goal attraction and directing ideas conceived as habit phenomena (Ps. Rev. 1931 38, 487–506).

---

[9]) Later I have seen in a review in Psych. Bull. by Woodworth: 'Experimental Psychology' (last edition), that Hull also in Woodworth's book is the most frequently mentioned psychologist.

3. – The goal gradient hypothesis and maze learning (Ps. Rev. 1932, 39, 25–43).
4. – Conflicting psychologies of learning – a way out (Ps. Rev. 1935, 42, 493–516).
5. – Mind, mechanism and adaptive behavior, Ps. Rev. 1937, 44, 1–32).
6. – Stimulus equivalence in behavior theory (Ps. Rev. 1939, 46, 9–30).
7. – Hovland, Ross, Hall, Perkins and Fitch: Matematico-deductive theory of rote learning (New Haven, 1940).
8. – The problem of intervening variables in molar behavior theory. (Ps. Rev. 1943, 50, 273–291).
9. – Principles of Behavior (N. Y. 1943).
10. – Essentials of Behavior (New Haven, 1951).
11. – A Behavior System (New Haven, 1952).
12. Hovland, C. I.: Clark Leonard Hull 1884–1952 (Ps. Rev. 1952, 59, 347–80).
13. Koch, S.: The Logical character of the Motivation Concept (Ps. Rev. 1941, 48, 15–38 og 127–154).
14. Murphy, G.: Historical Introduction to Modern Psychology. P. 272–74 (1951).
15. Smith, F. V.: The Explanation of Human Behavior, chap. X (London 1951).
16. Woodworth, R. S.: Contemporary Schools of Psychology, p. 108–112 (1949).

Later addition (after the chapter has been finished):

17. Hilgard, E. R.: Hull's: A Behavior System. Ps. Bull. 1954, 51, 91–94.
18. Smith, F. V.: Critical notice and appreciation of the work of the late Professor Clark L. Hull. Brit. J. Psych. 1954–65, May.
19. Fitch and Barry: Towards a Formalization of Hull's Behavior Theory. Philos. of Science 17, 1950, 260–65.
20. S. Koch: Clark L. Hull (in Estes m. fl. Modern Learning Theories N. Y. 1954)*).
21. Logan, F. A.: The Hull-Spence Approach, (in S. Koch (edt.)): 'Psychology: A Study of a Science' (vol. 2, McGraw-Hill, N. Y. 1959).

*) I believe that S. Koch's severe criticism of Hull's *mathematical* formulations is valid, but I think that Hull's *verbal* formulations of his theory may be retained

Chapter 12

Hebb's Theory

The Canadian psychologist *D. O. Hebb* has written a long series of experimental psychological articles and in 1949 his book: '*The Organization of Behavior—A Neuropsychological Theory*''[1]) was published. As indicated by the sub-title it is an attempt to construct a synthesis of neuro-physiology and psychology, and the theory might be regarded as a representative of the most modern physiologically oriented psychology. It will therefore be discussed in this book even though it is not directly a theory of motivation.

THE STRUCTURE OF THE THEORY

Summary of the Theory

Hebb has given an excellent summary of his theory and its basis which will be quoted here (from p. XIX):

'Any frequently repeated, particular stimulation will lead to the slow development of a "cell-assembly", a diffuse structure comprising cells in the cortex and diencephalon (and also, perhaps, in the basal ganglia of the cerebrum), capable of acting briefly as a closed system, delivering facilitation to other such systems and usually having a specific motor facilitation. A series of such events constitutes a "phase sequence"—the thought process. Each assembly action may be aroused by a preceding assembly, by a sensory event, or—normally—by both. The central facilitation from one of these activities on the next is the prototype of "attention". The theory proposes that in this central facilitation, and its varied relationship to sensory processes, lies the answer to an issue that is made inescapable by Humphrey's (1940) penetrating review of the problem of the direction of thought.

The kind of cortical organization discussed in the preceding paragraph is what is regarded as essential to adult waking behavior. It is proposed also that there is an alternate, "intrinsic" organization there may be disorganization. It is assumed that the assembly depends completely on a very delicate timing which might be disturbed by metabolic changes as well as by sensory events that do not accord with the pre-existent central process. When this is transient, it is called emotional disturbance; when chronic, neurosis or psychosis.

The theory is evidently a form of connectionism, one of the switchboard variety, though it does not deal in direct connections between afferent and efferent pathways: not an "S–R" psychology, if R means a *muscular* response. The connections serve rather to establish autonomous central activities, which then are the basis of further learning. In accordance with modern physiological

---

[1]) All references made in this chapter are to this book.

ideas, the theory also utilizes local field processes and gradients, following the lead particularly of Marshall and Talbot (1942). It does not, further, make any single nerve cell or pathway essential to any habit or perception. Modern physiology has presented psychology with new opportunities for the synthesis of divergent theories and previously unrelated data, and it is my intent to take such advantage of these opportunities as I can.'

Level of Development of the Theory

As most psychological theories Hebb's theory is a *classifying* theory. It includes, however, many explanatory hypotheses, but since these are not axiomatized the theory *cannot* be described as a deductive theory.

Constructive or Reductive Theory

Already in the sub-title of the book it is indicated that the theory is a *reductive* theory, a theory which especially attempts to deduce secondary psychological hypotheses from primary neurophysiological hypotheses. Hebb states as follows (p. 1):

'This book presents a theory of behavior that is based as far as possible on the physiology of the nervous system, and makes a sedulous attempt to find some community of neurological and psychological conceptions.'

He gives the following reason for forming a reductive physiologically oriented psychological theory (p. XII):

'Psychology has an intimate relation with the other biological sciences, and may also look for help there. There is a considerable overlap between the problems of psychology and those of neurophysiology, hence the possibility (or necessity) of reciprocal assistance.'

He also formulates it in the following way (p. XIV):

'The problem of understanding behavior is the problem of understanding the total action of the nervous system, and *vice versa*.'

'The method then calls for learning as much as one can about what the parts of the brain do (primarily the physiologist's field), and relating behavior as far as possible to this knowledge (primarily for the psychologist);'

Hebb writes about the strong attacks directed against 'physiologizing' psychology that they have their origin in the attempts made years ago to reduce psychology to a much too simple and incomplete neuro-physiology. With the great progress of neuro-physiological research during the recent decades conditions have changed completely. Furthermore, theories are necessary, according to Hebb, and the thing to do is to make one's theoretical background as explicit as possible, because only in this way can it be made the subject of continuous critical revisions. Hebb has elaborated this in a article: '*The Role of Neurological Ideas in Psychology*' (in 'Theoretical Models and Personality Theory' 1952).

Even though Hebb's theory, as shown by the above quotations, must be classified as a reductive theory, he several times points out the *constructive* (hypothetical or 'speculative') aspect of the theory. He writes (p. XVIII):

'In the chapters that follow this introduction I have tried to lay a foundation for such a theory. It is, on the one hand and from the physiologist's point of view, quite speculative. On the other hand, it achieves some synthesis of psychological knowledge, and it attempts to hold as strictly as possible to the psychological evidence in those long stretches where the guidance of anatomy and physiology is lacking.'

It seems therefore most correct to describe the theory as *a mainly reductive theory.*

Mentalistic or Behavioristic Theory

It is just as easy to classify Hebb's theory with regard to the classification mentalistic versus behavioristic theory. Already in the first lines of the introductory chapter he writes directly (p. XI): 'the task of the psychologist, [is] the task of understanding behavior.' Later he writes directly against mentalism (p. XIII):

'Modern psychology takes completely for granted that behavior and neural function are perfectly correlated, that one is completely caused by the other. There is no separate soul or lifeforce to stick a finger into the brain now and then and make neural cells do what they would not otherwise.'

'All one can know about another's feelings and awarenesses is an inference from what he *does* —from his muscular contractions and glandular secretions. These observable events are determined by electrical and chemical events in nerve cells.'

He also gives the following behavioristic definition (p. XIV):

'"Mind" can only be regarded, for scientific purposes, as the activity of the brain.'

In his discussion of 'insight' he also describes his attitude towards mentalism (p. 158):

'Mainly, the trouble has been to make transition from an earlier subjective psychology (resorting freely to the notion of 'mind' or conscious awareness as an *agent* in behavior) to an objective theory of neural action, without oversimplifying the facts.'

And in connection with the subject of 'motivation' he closes with the words (p. 234):

'By some such approach as the one suggested, it may become possible to understand the directedness and order in behavior, and the variability of motivation, as produced by neural function alone.'

Finally he writes about emotion (p. 238):

'It is important to be clear that in this discussion "emotion" is a reference to the hypothetical neural processes that produce emotional behavior; explicitly, it refers neither to an immaterial state of consciousness nor to the observable pattern of emotional behavior.'

As in quite evident now, Hebb's theory must be classified as a *purely behavioristic theory,* since its protocol statements (methods) are behavioristic and its hypothetical variables are physiologically interpreted.

Molar or Molecular Theory

It is also comparatively easy to place Hebb's theory with regard to this classification, as he often uses the term 'molar' himself. Already in the introductory chapter he writes (in a paragraph from p. XIX already quoted):

'The problem of understanding behavior is the problem of understanding the total action of the nervous system, and *vice versa.*'

Later he writes more explicitly about the distinction between molar and molecular (p. 11):

'The problem for psychology then is to find conceptions for dealing with such complexities of central neural action: conceptions that will be valid physiologically and at the same time "molar" enough to be useful in the analysis of behavior. (4) Psychology is still profoundly influenced by the very "molecular" conception of linear transmission through a sequence of single cells. The conception is no longer valid physiologically, just as it has long been without psychological usefulness. The attack on neural connections as an explanation of behavior was really an attack on this particular conception of the way connections operate; modern neuroanatomy and electrophysiology have changed the question completely, and the significance of synaptic connections must be examined all over again.'

'Our problem then, is to find valid "molar" conceptions of neural action (conceptions, *i. e.*, that can be applied to large-scale cortical organizations). Bishop (1946, p. 370) has made the point, in another context, that this is an essential problem for neurophysiology also. But psychologists can hardly sit around with hands folded, waiting for the physiologist to solve it. In its essence the problem is psychological and requires a knowledge of the psychological as well as the physiological evidence for its solution.'

As can be seen from the above Hebb's theory must be classified as a *mainly molar psychological theory.*

Field-Theory or Mechanistic Theory

Hebb writes about this classification of psychological theories (p. XVII):

'Psychology has had to find, in hypthesis, a way of bridging this gap in its physiological foundation. In general the bridge can be described as some comparatively simple formula of cortical transmission. The particular formula chosen mainly determines the nature of the psychological theory that results, and the need of choosing is the major source of theoretical schism.'

'Two kinds of formula have been used, leading at two extremes to (1) switchboard theory, and sensori-motor connections; and (2) field theory.'

And he characterizes his own theory in the following way (in the paragraph already quoted, p. XIX):

'The theory is evidently a form of connectionism, one of the switchboard variety, though it does not deal in direct connections between afferent and efferent pathways: not an "S–R" psychology, if R means a *muscular* response. The connections serve rather to establish autonomous central activities, which then are the basis of further learning.'

According to this Hebb's theory must be classified as *a mainly mechanistic theory.*

Statistical or Deterministic Theory

Hebb's theory must be said to be *a typical deterministic theory.* He writes about the unclear dualistic theories (p. XIII):

'One cannot logically be a determinist in physics and chemistry and biology, and a mystic in psychology.'

Later he writes against modern indeterministic theories (p. 9):

'Spontaneity of firing by central neural cells is not philosophic indeterminacy, as some writers have thought; the "spontaneity" means only that synaptic stimulation is not the sole cause of firing.'

Thus it is quite evident that in every respect Hebb's theory must be described as a deterministic theory

The Model

As illustrative models of the theory Hebb especially makes use of some diagrams (figure 10, 14 15, and 16) which outline the organization and function of more or less complicated systems of nerve cells.

Summary

The analysis of the theory as a whole can be summarized in the following description: *Hebb's theory is a classifying, reductive, behavioristic, molar, mainly mechanistic, and deterministic theory.*

MOTIVATION DEFINITIONS AND HYPOTHESES

The Concept of Motivation

As mentioned in the introduction, Hebb's theory is more or less a *general* psychological theory; but it includes (especially in chapters 8, 9, and 10) a peculiar definition and theory of motivation, which has exercised some influence (cf. the following chapter on McClelland). It is therefore interesting to analyze the definitions and hypotheses of motivation in the theory, but since it is presented in a rather unclear and unsystematic way[2]) Hebb's own presentation will not be followed directly.

Hebb's theory of motivation deviates from the previous ones especially in the treatment of the following two problems 1) *the activating function of motivation*, and 2) *the relations of motivation variables to other variables.*

Hebb writes about the first problem that 'motivation' includes two problems: 'why is an animal active at all' and 'why does the activity take a particular form' (p. 171). The first problem—the problem of activation—has until now been the more important one in psychology; but 'now however it is known that the central nervous system is continuously active' (p. 172), and therefore 'the chief problem the psychologist is concerned with, when he speaks of motivation, is not an arousal of activity but is patterning and direction' (p. 172). In other words, Hebb finds that the most important problem is the organization and direction[3]) of behavior. Therefore we can temporarily state that *motivation variables in Hebb's theory are not activating, but organizing and directing variables.*

The other problem, which in Hebb's theory is solved in a rather unusual way, is the problem of the relation of motivation variables to other variables. In most other theories this problem is solved by several hypotheses about more or less complicated functional inter-relationships. But Hebb solves it simply by *identifying motivation variables with cognitive variables*, which is possible because 'motivation'

---

[2]) It may be only the exceptional character of the theory which makes it rather difficult to understand.

[3]) Cf. the title of the book and the last word of the last quotation, respectively.

in Hebb's theory has an organizing and directing function, in other theories usually ascribed to cognitive variables.

This is summarized in Hebb's most thorough and exact definition of 'motivation' (p. 181):

'The term motivation then refers (1) to the existence of an organized phase sequence, (2) to its direction or content, and (3) to its persistence in a given direction, or stability of content.
'This definition means that "motivation" is not a distinctive process, but a reference in another context to the same processes to which "insight" refers; it also means that the waking, normal adult animal always has some motivation.'

As can be seen from this definition, Hebb's fundamental variable is '*phase sequence*,' a *hypothetical variable* which *neurophysiologically* is interpreted as a *functional variable*, a process which takes place in '*assemblies of cerebral cells*.' The definition indicates also—though not explicitly—the relation of the variable to the behavior, namely its organizing and directing effect. The definitions says, on the other hand, nothing about what relation the variable ('phase sequence') has to empirical variables, in other words, what it is that determines this *compound* '*cognitive motivation variable*'. But this can be seen in the following section.

Pain

'Pain' is one of the empirical variables which determine—or at any rate influence—the hypothetical variable, and it is defined as 'a disruptive somesthetic event.' Thus it is an *internal* empirical variable, in Hebb's theory included in the class of will be quoted here (p. 182):

'Disruptive processes are a general classification that includes more than pain. In most sensory modes there is an intensity limit at which avoidance appears. Below this point, the stimulation may be sought out—that is, it is "pleasant"; above it, the same kind of stimulation produces avoidance is unsuccessful, behavioral disturbance. With different kinds of stimulation, the avoidance limit falls in a different part of the intensity range.'

In other words, peripheral sensory stimulation *below* a certain intensity influences the 'phase sequence,' which, when we are awake, is always functioning, resulting in approaching behavior; if, on the other hand, the same sensory stimulation gets *above* the intensity in question an 'avoidance behavior' will result, maybe through a 'phase sequence.'

Hebb's special theory of motivation stands out even more clearly in the relation of motivation to 'hunger.' This point will, therefore, be especially thoroughly discussed.

Hunger

This variable is defined in the following way (p. 190): 'Hunger is defined here as the tendency to eat,' and the following rather unusual definition is added: 'Both stomach contractions and blood sugar are related to hunger but in no simple way.'

In other words, in Hebb's theory 'hunger' is a *central*, hypothetical, neuro-physiological function variable—and is *not* identical with the *peripheral*, empirical variable: lack of food. While this peripheral condition takes part in determining the hunger motive it is neither the only, nor the most important variable determining the hunger motive. In the beginning lack of food only determines random, unorganized behavior which is *not*, according to Hebb' theory, motivated; an 'organized phase sequence' which organizes and directs behavior (i. e. 'motives' in Hebb's sense of the word) comes into existence only after a learning process has taken place. Hebb summarizes this in the following way (p. 195):

'lack of food tends to disrupt behavior, producing restlessness, discomfort, irritability, and, in the extreme degree, emotional apathy. Secondly, a learning process seems to be involved in transforming this primitive disturbance into hunger as we know it in the adult animal or human being.'

As can quite clearly be seen the motivation variable ('the phase sequence') is, even in a biological motive such as 'hunger', an *acquired* and not an innate variable. This is also something characteristic of Hebb's theory.

Other Motivation Variables

Another biological motive, the *sex-motive*, is dealt with in the same way. Thus Hebb writes (p. 207):

'A third motivation, biologically primitive, is that of sex. The sex drive is also tied to a definite physiological condition, the presence of certain hormones in the blood stream. But it would once more be an oversimplification to make this the only factor: like eating, sex behavior is not reducible to any simple formula, and it serves especially to make clear a further complexity of the problem of motivation. This concerns the time relations in the organism's responsiveness to a particular class of stimulation. In sex behavior, the problem appears in the comparatively slow build-up of *interest* (that is, responsiveness to or seeking out of genital stimulation) and its requently abrupt decline, following orgasm: humoral conditions presumably remaining constant.'

Thus the sex-motive is also an *acquired*, central 'organized phase sequence,' which among other things is determined by the sex hormones in the blood.

The relation between motivation and *sleep* is formulated as follows (p. 223):

'In view of the definition of motivation proposed in the preceding chapter, that it consists of the directedness and persistence of the phase sequence, we must consider sleep to be the extreme case of a loss of motivation.'

Emotions

In Hebb's theory these variables are very closely related to motivation variables as they are the most inclusive class of motivating conditions (along with organic conditions as for example lack of food, sex hormones, etc.). A summary of definitions and hypotheses of 'pain' has already been given (p. 183), and 'pain' might be considered as belonging to the class of emotions. The quotation (p. 183) also included Hebb's fundamental hypothesis on emotional processes: Stimulation *below* a certain intensity determines 'pleasure' and 'approach behavior', stimulation *above* this intensity determines 'unpleasure' (and 'pain') and 'avoidance behavior'. Later Hebb gives a more detailed formulation (p. 232):

'The theory that has been developed implies that pleasure is not the activity of particular structures in the nervous system, and not even a particular kind or pattern of cerebral organization, but fundamentally a directed *growth* or *development in cerebral organization.* It is thus necessarily a transient state of affairs in which a conflict is being reduced, an incipient disorganization being dissipated, or a new synthesis in assembly action being achieved.'

'Those sensory conditions are called pleasant, then, which contribute to the current development in the cerebrum, or which consist of the decline of a sensory process that interferes with development.'

'Emotional disturbance' is defined as a contrast to 'pleasure' (p. 235):

'Emotional disturbance' here is used to refer to the violent and unpleasant emotions, roughly, and to the transient irritablilities and anxieties of ordinary persons as well as to neurotic or psychotic disorder.'

Later Hebb maintains that 'emotional disturbance' is not identical with 'the motor pattern' or 'a state of consciousness,' but that 'emotion is a reference to the hypothetical neural processes that produce emotional behavior' (p. 238):

Thus it is evident that 'emotion' is a *neuro-physiological hypothetical function variable.*

This hypothetical variable determines *motivated behavior* as attack and flight, but only after a *learning process* has formed an 'organized phase sequence.' Hebb formulates it in the following way (p. 250):

'a mechanism of learning might transform emotional disturbance, as a breakdown of adaptation, into the adaptive responses of attack, flight, and so on.'

This shows that '*emotion*'—as well as lack of food and sex hormones—only *determines motivated behavior* (i. e. organized and directed behavior) after a *learning process* has formed an 'organized phase sequence.'

Hebb's theory includes also a few implicit hypotheses about what determines emotions. He classes the independent variables in three groups: 1) 'metabolic changes', 2) 'conflicts', and 3) 'perceptual deficits' (including all perceptions of unusual, unexpected phenomena). And these are further combined in one hypothesis which is given in the following statements (p. 254):

'the one assumption that seems to provide a common ground for such varied sources of disturbance (including not only the metabolic changes in Class III but also the perceptual conflicts and perceptual deficits of Classes I and II) is the assumption that emotional disturbance is in the first place a disruption of the timing of neuronal activity in the cerebrum.'

But apart from the statements presented here no explicit hypotheses can be found in Hebb's theory.

RECONSTRUCTION OF THE THEORY

The analysis of Hebb's theory shows that it is an interesting and original theory, but that it has formal shortcomings: the presentation is often unclear and unsystematical. It will therefore be practical to make a systematical reconstruction of the definitions and hypotheses of motivation in the theory.

The hypothesis of 'spontaneous' continuous activity of the central nervous system must be the most fundamental hypothesis in the reconstruction:

Hypothesis 1: When we are awake the central nervous system is in a state of continuous and 'spontaneous' activity which determines behavior.

Next in importance comes Hebb's special definition of motivated behavior:

Definition 1: Motivated behavior is organized and directioned behavior.

Very important, too, is Hebb's identification of motivation variables with cognitive variables which may be formulated in this way:

Hypothesis 2: Motivated behavior is determined by a cognitive (perception and/or insight) process in the cerebrum—called an 'organized phase sequence' —which has an organizing and directive function upon the 'spontaneous' continuous neural activity.

It is also important to formulate a hypothesis of the function of the learning processes:

Hypothesis 3: An 'organized phase sequence' is always determined by learning processes.

The different empirical variables by which this 'phase sequence' is determined may be summarized in the following important hypothesis:

Hypothesis 4: Organic conditions (lack of food, sex hormones, etc.) and emotional conditions determine originally unmotivated (unorganized, random) behavior. When a learning process has taken place organic and emotional conditions determine an 'organized phase sequence' and motivated behavior.

It is also important in a reconstruction of Hebb's theory to formulate a hypothesis about the existence of emotions:

Hypothesis 5: Positive emotions ('pleasure') are brain processes facilitating organization and determined by sensory stimulation below a certain intensity.

Hypothesis 6: Negative emotions ('unpleasure' and 'emotional disturbance') are brain processes which have a disturbing effect upon organization and which are determined by: 1) perceptual conflicts (including stimuli *above* the adjusted intensity), 2) perceptual lacks (in relation to what has been adjusted), and 3) changes in the supply of nutrition to the nerve cells.

And finally a definition or hypothesis about 'sleep' which plays a certain role in Hebb's theory:

Hypothesis 7: 'Sleep' is a condition which exists when there is an extreme lack of central-nervous-activity and motivated behavior.

Conclusion

Hebb's theory demonstrates that formal properties are not always the most important qualities of a scientific theory. Because of its originality it has already influenced psychological theory, and its influence may become still greater in the future.

Supplement

After this chapter was written Hebb published an important article in *Psych. Review* (1955 62, 243–54) where *he revised his previous theory of motivation.* Having described the pre-1930 opinion that the nervous system is *inactive*, which made activating motives necessary, he describes his view that the nervous system is an *activity* system resulting in this theory in 'Organization of Behavior' where motives are exclusively *directive*. Then he writes that 'it is still true that the brain is always active, but the activity is not always the transmitted kind that conducts to behavior' (p. 248). Based upon physiological examinations of 'the arousal system' in the brainstem and its function as a more indirect route which impulses can follow from the sense organs to cortex whereby they achieve an activating function, Hebb reaches the following conclusion (p. 249):

> Psychologically, we can now distinguish two quite different effects of a sensory event. One is the *cue function*, guiding behavior; the other, less obvious but no less important, is the *arousal* or *vigilance function*. Without a foundation of arousal, the cue function cannot exist... arousal in this sense is synonymous with a general drive state, and the conception of drive therefore assumes anatomical and physiological identity. ... the drive is an energizer, but not a guide ... Thus I find myself obliged to reverse my earlier views and accept drive conception...'

It should finally be added that this conception of 'drive' is in agreement with the conception now gradually dominating psychology.

Later Developments

Introduction. Hebb's book 'Organization of Behavior' has—since the preceding analysis was written—become a modern 'classic' in psychology. In the last few years Hebb has revised his own theory several times. We have already mentioned his revision of the concepts of motivation in his article in *Psychological Review* (1955). This revised theory of motivation is further elaborated in his '*Textbook of Psychology*', which appeared in 1958, and later in a revised and enlarged edition published in 1966. This book is one of the most original and outstanding introductory textbooks in modern psychology. It is not often that an *introductory* textbook contains the elaboration of an original and influenctial theory written by the creator of the theory himself[1]). The combination of abilities for theoretical

---

[1]) As a matter of fact, the present author only knows of one instance since *W. James*' 'Principles of Psychology'; namely, *B. F. Skinner*'s and *Holland*'s 'The Analysis of Behavior' (1961).

creativity and educational exposition is rare.

Besides this textbook Hebb has also written a systematic exposition of his theory: '*A Neuropsychological Theory*' in *S. Koch*'s 'Psychology: A study of a Science' (vol. I, 1959). This exposition is especially valuable for its comments on the *structure* of the theory, while the textbook goes into more detail about the *content* of the theory.

The Structure of the Theory. The formal development of the theory is still *not* a deductive system. Hebb writes explicitly about this problem in his 'Koch-paper' (p. 626):

'It seems obvious to me that overformalization can be sterile and cramping, both in thinking and experiment. But when is theory too formal? I don't know; clearly some formalization is necessary, and one must be definite and precise—up to a point.'

Hebb is also explicit about 'physiologizing' in his 'Koch-paper', and he elaborates his basic ideas about this in a very lucid manner (p. 632):

'What I mean by a psychological as opposed to a physiological construct, therefore, is that its referents are primarily in the behavior of the intact animal. One may name it, and hypothetically describe it, in physiological terms; but this is in the effort to maintain communication between different levels or universes of discourse. My theory is not an attempt to substitute physiology for psychology. No theory of the behavior of the whole animal could be, because in such a theory one is trying to deal with the functioning of the whole brain and nervous system, as influenced moment by moment by the whole internal environment, and the kind of construct one must work with '(learning', 'capacity', anxiety', 'intelligence') takes one at times completely out of the universe of physiological method and its concentration on the functioning of part systems rather than of the whole body over extended time.'

We have quoted so extensively because it summarizes the thinking of the leader of 'physiologizing' in contemporary psychology. He also elaborates it in connection with a discussion of the molar contra the molecuar theory (to which we shall return).

After re-analyzing Hebb's theory[2]), the present author thinks that the old classification into 'reductive contra constructive' theories should be replaced by *a new classification of theories.* This classification should contain *two main* categories: '*descriptive*' *and* '*explanatory*' *theories.* And the explanatory theories can further be divided into three *subcategories*: 1. '*Physiological* explanatory theories' (Corresponding to the old 'reductive'), 2. '*neutral* explanatory theories' (corresponding to the old 'constructive'), and 3. '*mentalistic* explanatory theories'[3]).

These three sub-categories are classified according to the category of hypothetical variables which are used in them. The present author thinks that this new classification should do justice to the fact that the so-called 'reductive theories'

---

[2]) And further by analyzing the theories of some of Hebb's followers (Berlyne, Bindra and others) who will be dealt with in a separate volume.

[3]) As main representatives for the categories could be mentioned: descriptive theory: Skinner; physiological explanatory: Hebb; neutral explanatory: Tolman and Hull; mentalistic explanatory: McDougall and perhaps Allport.

also use hypothetical *constructs*. The difference between the three sub-categories is only the sorts of constructs used (neuro-physiological, neutral-formal, or phenomenological respectively).

This new classification is only suggested here, but it is not used in the following chapters of this book[4]).

Turning to the next feature in the structure of Hebb's theory, it is still correct to classify it as a *behavioristic* rather than a mentalistic theory. Hebb is especially clear about this in his 'Textbook', where he writes (2. ed. pp. 4–6):

'the modern psychology began in 1913, when John B. Watson undertook a house-cleaning operation which consisted of discarding a lot of ideas about the mind that had been uncritically taken for granted. This was the founding of *Behaviorism*. Some of the ideas it rejected were brought back, but only when solid evidence was found to justify them.'

'This then is a bird's eye view of the reasons for the behavioristic direction that modern psychology has taken. Paradoxically it was the denial of mental processes that put our knowledge of them on a firm foundation. ... Today the evidence exists—behavioristic evidence—and all psychology has become behavioristic in the sense that it depends for its facts on the objective record.'

Except for the overstatement that 'all psychology has become behavioristic' the present author agrees with Hebb's evaluation of the role of behaviorism in the history of psychology. In spite of—or rather because of—its radical empiricism, behavioristic psychology has been responsible for a lot of reconstruction and reorganization in psychology in the first third of the century, and in the second third a less radically empirical' more liberal-theoretical, but still objective, scientific psychology has developed on this basis. But besides this scientific ('behavioristic') psychology there still exists a more philosophical ('phenomenological' or existentialist) psychology. And perhaps it is valuable to have this competition.

Hebb's comments on the different 'levels of analysis' are also very enlightening. After the exposition of his own theory he writes in his 'Koch-paper' (p. 630):

'It is clear that this theorizing is at several levels. ... the main part is molar.'

And in his 'Textbook' he compares the two levels of analysis in psychology with similar differences in levels of analysis in other sciences (his favorite example is meteorology), and he writes (p. 318):

'The situation is that we have, broadly speaking, two ways of knowing about the functioning of the brain and of mind as the highest level of brain function. One is physiological and anatomical, one is behavioral. The physiological tends to be *molecular*, or fine-grained dealing with units rather than the whole, concerned more with the trees than the wood; the behavioral tends to be more *molar*, large scale, looking at the wood rather than the single tree or small clumps of trees. Both kinds of information about brain function are essential. One adds to or may correct the other.'

From these quotations it can be seen that Hebb himself describes his own theory

---

[4]) This classification will be used in a new volume containing the analysis and comparison of ten new theories of motivation ('Modern Theories of Motivation' (in press)).

as '*mainly molar*' (cf. with the description in the first part of this chapter). It can also clearly be seen from the above quotations that Hebb thinks that analysis on the *molar* level *has to* be carried out with the application of 'psychological' or '*behavioral*' *constructs* (or 'neutral-formal hypothetical variables' as they are called in *this* book); and analysis on the *molecular* level can—or perhaps has to—be carried out with '*physiological*' *constructs* (or 'neuro-physiological hypothetical variables'). The main thing to keep in mind is that according to Hebb a '*physiologizing*' (or 'reductive') theory can be a *molar theory* using 'psychological', 'behavioral' or neutral-formal variables.

The last two features in the structure of Hebb's theory are easily described.

Hebb's theory may still be described as 'mechanistic'. Hebb is not explicit about this problem in his 'Koch-paper' or in the 'Textbook', but there are no changes in the discuourses which would furnish any reason for changing the original description.

Hebb's theory can still be classified as a *deterministic* theory. He is very clear on this point in the Koch-paper (p. 625):

'The "limits of prediction" in psychology, I would probably have said, are about the same as in any other science; that is, they are set by our own intellectual capacity. Maybe there are intrinsic limits to scientific prediction—that is, we may not be dealing with a fully deterministic universe—but it seems to me that the scientific method is to make the working assumption of determinacy up to the point at which it is conclusively refuted. Though it has *possibly* been reached by physics, in the so-called indeterminacy principle, this point is still far removed in biological research of any kind.'

Thus we can conclude this section of the chapter be describing Hebb's theory as *still being* '*classifying, reductive, behavioristic, molar mechanistic, and deterministic*'.

Although there have been no changes or developments in the structure of Hebb's theory, the present author thinks that the extensive quotations from Hebb's later expositions are justified because of the clear thinking Hebb exhibits concerning all these meta-theoretical problems.

The Content of the Theory. Turning to the content of Hebb's theory we find the material for our analysis in Hebb's 'Textbook'[5]).

Hebb classifies behavior as being '*sense-dominated*' ('reflexive') or '*higher*' ('voluntary'). This 'higher' or 'voluntary' behavior is determined by '*mediating processes*'. This is Hebb's term for the hypothetical variables (with physiological surplus meaning), which he formerly called 'cell assemblies' and 'phase-sequence'. It includes the processes which are equivalent to 'ideas' or 'thoughts' as well as 'attention' and 'sets' in older, mentalistic psychology.

'Mediating processes' thus are a *functional H-variable* with a *directing* function on behavior. It explains the direction and organization of behavior in learning and problemsolving. But what activates behavior? As we know from the preceding analysis of Hebb's first book, he thought at that time that special activating,

---

[5]) 'A Textbook of Psychology' (Saunders, Philadelphia, London, 2. ed., 1966).

dynamic or motivational variables were unnecessary. But in his 1955-paper he changed his theory about motivation, and in his 1966-book he has elaborated it in the light of research carried out in the past decade. In the last book there is a chapter (10) devoted to '*Motivational mechanisms*'. In this chapter he defines '*motivation*' in this way (p. 206):

'*Motivation* may be defined as a tendency of the whole animal to produce organized activity, normally varying from the low level of deep sleep to a high level in the waking, alert, excited animal, and varying also in the kind of behavior that results or the kind of stimulation to which the organism is responsive. Thus we may speak of a subject as being strongly (or weakly) motivated, meaning that he has a strong tendency to be active (or is lethargic); or we may speak of his having special motivation such as hunger motivation, sex motivation and so on.'

It is clear from this quotation[6]) that Hebb now uses the term 'motivation' in two slightly different—but *not* inconsistent—way: '*General* motivation' is the activation of behavior in *general*, while '*special* motivations' involve the activation of *special kinds* of behavior.

The '*special* motivations' dealt with in this chapter are: *hunger*, *pain*, *sex*, *maternal* and *exploratory* motivation.

In accordance with Hebb's physiological orientation he correlates these forms of motivation with '*motivational mechanisms*', about which he writes (p. 228):

'The main subcortical mechanism of motivation is that of that arousal system, in midbrain and thalamus; without it, all motivation ceases. The hypothalamus, however, also contains centers of special motivations, involving the control of eating, sex and maternal behavior, anger and fear, and further, the hypothalamus and neighboring structures contain regions which, when stimulated, give rise to apparently pleasurable motivational states.'

Besides discussing the experiments which formed the foundation for the general and the special motivational mechanisms (the arousal system and hypothalamic centers, respectively), Hebb also discusses the old '*homeostatic* concept' of motivation. Sex motivation in particular is *not* homeostatic, and Hebb therefore concludes that 'motivation may therefore be biologically primitive, and very powerful, without being homeostatic'. (p. 220).

In connection with 'motivational mechanisms' Hebb also discusses the problem of *reinforcement*, which he summarizes in these words (p. 228):

'In sum, this may be put as follows:
If arousal is very low, or very high, organized sequences of cortical activity are improbable for reasons given above; but if organized sequence does get started whose effect is to raise arousal from a low level or lower it from high level, that sequence has some chance of continuing without interference. Consequently, it has the best chance of being followed by consolidation (p. 124), and the next time the animal is in this situation that cortical process is most likely to be one that recurs: the animal will learn to do the things that raise or lower arousal to a moderate level. In this sense, an increase of arousal from a low to a moderate level is *reinforcing* and so is a decrease from a high to moderate level (p. 119).'

Although reinforcement in learning is not the main theme of this book, we have

---

[6]) Which the reader may compare with the definition of motivation in Hebb's first book.

quoted Hebb's hypotheses about reinforcement, because they show how the recent developments in motivational psychology have also contributed to the clarification of one of the main problems in learning theory[7]).

In addition to the function of the reticular arousal system, which is referred to in the quotation, Hebb refers in other connections to the function of the *septum* as revealed in the *Olds* and *Milner* experiments. Hebb concludes thusly (p. 232):

'The present experiments appear to show conclusively that excitation of the septum and certain other regions has a rewarding, or positively reinforcing, effect in a rat that has no discomfort. It therefore appears that a motivation may consist either of a tendency to escape from some stimulation (pain or discomfort), or of a tendency to seek other stimulation. The point parallels our earlier conclusion that an animal with high arousal avoids stimulation, but one with low arousal seeks it.'

The present author thinks that the demonstration of the existence of the motivational mechanisms—especially the rewarding mechanisms in the septum—is one of the main results of the 'neuro-psychological approach'.

The next chapter in Hebb's book deals with '*Emotion and Motivation*'. This relationship is also conceptualized in a new way as a result of the discovery of the arousal system. He summarizes it in the following way (p. 238):

'This discussion can be summarized as follows: Emotion in its general sense is directly correlated with arousal. Emotion, or arousal, is motivating up to the point at which conflicting activities in the cortex begin to interfere with one another, preventing the dominance of one activity that would produce *one* set of organized responses to the situation. How high arousal can be and still be motivating varies with the kind of behavior. It presumably varies also from one person to another.'

Thus 'emotion' in its *general* sense is correlated with arousal (and therefore with *general* motivation up to a certain point of arousal). But 'emotion' is also—like 'motivation'—used in a *specific* sense. 'Fear', 'anger', 'joy' and 'love' are emotions in the specific sense. These specific emotions can only be defined by referring to:

'the ideas that go with them, and the actions that these ideas (mediating processes) give rise to. No definition of emotion can omit reference to the cortical activity that gives any emotion its identity' (p. 239).

This relationship between cortex and emotion, which is expressed in the above quotation, has some other important consequences. The most general of these is the following (p. 239):

'Next we come to an important proposition: that an animal's susceptibility to emotional disturbance is directly related to the level of its intelligence. Man is the most rational animal, but also the most emotional; ... The correlation is so close that one can hardly avoid the notion that there is a direct causal relationship.'

Another important consequence of the relationship between cortical development

---

[7]) Hebb's view about the role of reinforcement in learning is that reinforcement does not seem to be necessary for the more 'cognitive' (mediating-process-involved) learning, but it seems to be necessary for the simpler S-R-learning.

and emotion or motivation is '*altruism*', in the higher animals. About this Hebb writes (p. 247):

'Among the distinctive features of behavior in the human species is the frequency of *altruism*, defined as intrinsically motivated purposive behavior whose function is to help another person or animal. In this definition, 'intrinsically motivated' means that the behavior does not depend on primary or secondary reinforcement: that the helper receives no benefit except the knowledge that he has helped; and 'purposive' implies that the behavior is under the control of mediating processes, thus excluding the reflexive cooperation of the social insects (ant, bee, termite).'

Thus Hebb explains altruism as a function of the cortex without postulating a special 'social' or 'altruistic motivation'.

In a similar way he explains the origin of 'play, which he defines as 'work done for the sake of doing it.' (p. 249).

And 'play' is not only physical or muscular but also 'mental', which occurs in man, apes, monkeys and other mammals such as rats. After referring to some experiments with rats, he concludes (p. 250):

'It is evident therefore that "mental play", involving the brain as much as the muscles, is a characteristic of the mammal and one that becomes more prominent in the higher mammals. . . . *Boredom* is a state in which the subject seeks a higher level of excitement, usually in some form of play, and the avoidance of boredom is a most important factor in human behavior.'

Hebb regards this play-motivation as a very important factor in shaping life in a modern, wealthy, 'overprotecting' society (as well as in ancient Rome, where circuses were needed as much as bread).

Hebb does not mention any other kinds of special motivations[8]).

We shall now therefore *summarize* the content of Hebb's theory of motivation:

Hebb only deals with *primary* motivations—no secondary motivations are mentioned or discussed in his book.

The primary motivations are all processes in—or activations of—some sort of '*motivational mechanisms*'. Besides the '*general* motivational mechanism' (the non-specific reticular arousal system) his theory contains the following '*special* motivational mechanisms':

The hypothalamic centers for *hunger*, *thirst*, *maternal motivation*, *sex-motivation* and *pain*.

He also explicitly mentions the hypothalamic centers for *anger* (rage) and *fear*. And the *septum* may be conceived as the organic mechanism for *love* and *joy*. But all these emotional *motivations* further have their organic bases in the interaction between the cortex, the arousal system and ANS.

Exploratory and *play-motivation* are regarded as primary, and the motivational mechanisms in these cases are apparently the arousal system and the cortex. *Altruistic* motivation is also regarded as primary and determined by the development of the *cortex* without other special mechanisms mentioned.

---

[8]) The rest of the book deals with perception, thinking and the scientific method—very valuable chapters, but outside the scope of this book).

In terms of the classifications used in this book, we can describe 'the motivational *mechanisms*' as *disposition variables* and their activation—the special *motivations*—are *functional variables*. Besides these *dynamic functions* Hebb's theory includes the organizing or *directing functions*, which in his latest book are called '*mediating processes*'. The corresponding *disposition* variables are the '*cell-assemblies*'.

All the variables in Hebb's theory are *hypothetical variables* with *physiological* 'surplus meaning'.

Conclusion. The reader may have guessed from this extensive analysis of Hebb's theory that the present author regards it very highly. The 'neuro-psychological approach' (or the physiological explanatory theories) is at the present time one of the most fruitful frames of reference for both motivational theory as well as general psychological theory. And Hebb has been the *leader of this approach*[9]).

---

[9]) In a supplementary volume about '10 Modern Theories of Motivation' (in press) some other 'physiological' theories (Berlyne, Bindra, Duffy, etc.) are analyzed.

Chapter 13

Tinbergen's Theory

The history of the word 'instinct' in psychology has been a strange one. After having been used for centuries as a hypothetical (explanatory) term parallel to 'reason' it was, according to many psychologists, misused around the turn of the century in ad hoc or pseudo-explanations (an 'instinct' was constructed for each inexplicable action). The term was therefore for some time—during the twenties and thirties—almost banished from scientific psychology; but now it is again accepted and used in a rather well defined way in psychology thanks to the Continental-European animal-psychologists working with the Austrian *K. Lorenz.* Lorenz is the main representative for the modern experimental study of instinct? but his work is mainly formulated in articles in periodicals, and he has not given any coherent and systematical presentation of his theory. This has been done, however, by Lorenz's best known student and assistant, the Dutch animal psychologist *N. Tinbergen,* who in '*The Study of Instinct*' (Oxford 1951)[1]) gives a coherent and systematical presentation of the main results of the study of instinct and of his own modification of Lorenz's theory. It is therefore only natural to include Tinbergen's theory in this study of modern theories of motivation.

THE STRUCTURE OF THE THEORY

Summary of the Theory

The content of Tinbergen's theory may briefly be summarized in the following way (mainly on the basis of Chapter V):

Instinctive responses can be divided into '*appetitive behaviour*' and '*the consummatory act.*' Appetitive behavior is the inquiring, striving, and purposive phase which can be of varying degrees of complication from species to species and also from individual to individual and from situation to situation, as it can consist of reflex movements, conditioned reflex movements and other acquired actions, and 'insightful' or intelligent behavior. The consummatory act is the final goal-phase of the instinctive response and the most simple and constant part, consisting of two

---

[1]) All references in this chapter are to this book.

components: '*taxis*' (orientating movements) and a stereotyped series of movements, typical of the species ('the fixed pattern').

As a whole the instinctive response is determined by both *external* and *internal* factors. The external factors are the stimuli to the exteroceptors and may be divided into 'directive' and 'releasing' stimuli. The last mentioned influence the stereotype component of the consummatory act, while the directive stimuli influence the orientating component (the taxis) and the whole appetitive phase. The internal or *motivating* factors are: hormones, internal stimuli to the interoceptors, and (maybe) automatic spontaneous nervous impulses. The motivating factors are co-ordinated in *a superior instinct center* in the central nervous system, from which impulses are sent to a hierarchy of sub-ordinated centers, each of which directs a series of movements which is part of the whole instinctive response. The connection to the sub-ordinated centers is blocked by an *innate release mechanism*, which can only be triggered by a certain kind of releasing signal-stimuli. The function of the instinct centers and the release mechanism co-ordinates the instinctive response to a behavior which is biologically practical under the conditions of existence normal for the species.

The presuppositions for Tinbergen's theory are mainly presented in the first chapter which has as its heading a definition of the field or object of his science: '*Ethology: the objective study of behaviour*' (p. 1). As problems special to ethology he mentions 1) 'the causal structure underlying behaviour' (p. 1), 2) 'the ontogeny of behaviour (p. 2), 3) 'the evolution of behaviour' (p. 2), and 4) 'the biological significance of behaviour' (p. 2). Then he points out that in the field of ethology 'I shall deal mainly with the causes of innate behaviour' (p. 2).

Tinbergen then compares ethology to other animal psychological schools and biological sciences. Ethology—in his and Lorenz's interpretation—differs from the comparative psychology of *McDougall* and *E. S. Russell* especially in that these scientists stress purposive behavior, whereas Lorenz's school stresses *the causality* of the behavior (and deduces purposefulness from this). Lorenz's school differs from theories of the well known Dutch animal psychologist *Bierens de Haan* in that it denies that subjective phenomena known from the introspective method of human psychology can be causal factors. The ethologists do not deny the existence of the subjective phenomena, they only deny their explanatory value.

Ethology differs from an other biological discipline, *physiology*, in that physiology mainly studies the function of the individual organs, whereas ethology deals with the behavior of the total organism. Ethology differs from the objective *behavioristic psychology* in that the object of ethological study is *innate* behavior, whereas behavioristic psychology studies non-innate behavior. These two disciplines also differ in their methods, as behavioristic psychology mainly uses standardized laboratory-experiments, whereas ethology especially uses experiments and observation in natural environments. Ethology differs from *introspective psychology* by using exclusively objective methods.

The presuppositions of Tinbergen's theory will be further discussed in the following analysis.

Level of Development of the Theory

With regard to level of development Tinbergen's theory must be classified as a *classifying theory*, since it consists of descriptions and classifications of different forms of innate (instinctive) behavior and an attempt at formulating explanatory hypotheses, yet without arranging them in primary and secondary hypotheses, as is done in deductive theories. Still, the theory is rather systematically and exactly formulated; Chapter V: 'An attempt at a synthesis', is especially well-arranged and clear, partly because of the excellent diagrams, which will be discussed later.

Constructive or Reductive Theory

Tinbergen's theory must be classified as *a reductive theory*, since he not only attempts to deduce behavior-theory from physiology, but even maintains that ethology is *a part* of physiology on the same level as neuro-physiology, sense-physiology, and muscle-physiology. He thus writes (p. 5):

'behaviour is always the outcome of a highly complex integration of muscle contractions ... it is our job to carry our analysis from these high levels down to the level of the neurophysiologist, the he sense physiologist, and the muscle physiologist.'

And he stresses especially the importance of the fact that all these disciplines use the same methods (p. 6):

'it certainly is important to be aware of the fact that the causal study of behaviour uses the same methods that are employed in the causal study of the functions of the three organ systems that play a part in behaviour. For it is this identity of method that will enable us, in the long run, to combine all these fields into one "physiology of movement".'

But even though Tinbergen's theory thus must be called a reductive theory, it also includes constructive elements in the form of hypothetical constructions (variables) as for example: IRM (innate releasing mechanism), and others which will be discussed later.

Mentalistic or Behavioristic Theory

Even though Tinbergen himself does not use the term 'behavioristic' there is no doubt that his theory is *a purely behavioristic theory*, since it exclusively uses behavioristic protocol statements ('objective methods') and physiologically interpreted, hypothetical variables. This is already pointed out in the definition of 'ethology' as 'the objective study of behaviour.' Besides, he writes in a comparison with psychology that (p. 6):

'In America most psychologists apply the "behaviouristic" method, which is fundamentally just another name for the "objective" method.'

And several places in the book Tinbergen argues for an 'objective' (behavioristic) theory and against a 'subjective' (introspective) theory. He writes (p. 4):

'Because subjective phenomena cannot be observed objectively in animals, it is idle either to claim or to deny their existence. Moreover, to ascribe a causal function to something that is not objectively observable often leads to false conclusions. It is especially dangerous in that the acceptance of the conclusion kills our urge for continued research.'

Even if Tinbergen is apt to identify 'objective' with 'scientific' he still grants that 'both the data gained by introspection and those found by objective study are facts' (p. 206). But although Tinbergen's more informal statements about the psycho-physical problem are somewhat unclear, his theory as such—especially as it is presented in Chapter V—is a systematic and purely behavioristic theory.

Molar or Molecular Theory

Tinbergen's theory must be described as *a relatively molecular theory*. He does not, however, use this description himself, and classification is also complicated by the fact that he—as previously mentioned—maintains that ethology studies the the behavior of the *total* organism, while physiology studies the function of the individual organs. But for practical reasons ethology has limited itself to include only the innate behavior of the simpler organisms and psychology to include only the more complicated forms of behavior. He thus writes (p. 205):

'But neurophysiology has been including higher and higher levels in its area of work, psychology is beginning to look at the lower, instinctive levels, and ethology has settled in between and so meets neurophysiologists at its lower levels and psychologists at its highest levels.'

According to this ethology must, then be described as being more molar than physiology and more molecular than psychology.

Field Theory or Mechanistic Theory

It is rather difficult to classify Tinbergen's theory with regard to this classification. Because of the frequent appearance of the term 'mechanism' it might seem most correct to characterize it as a mechanistic theory. But Tinbergen stresses that several 'causal factors' or variables can co-operate, as can be clearly seen from his figure 97, p. 124. He also points out directly several times in the text (for example p. 73) that:

'One thing is already evident: there is a mutual relationship between internal and external factors in the sense of an additive influence on the motor response.'

He also uses the designation 'configurational processes' and writes about this (p. 121):

'A few remarks may be inserted here on the configurational character of many processes involved in behaviour. Configurational processes may be found both on the receptor and on the motor side of behaviour.'

And although Tinbergen does not use the term 'field,' he is very close to doing so in the following quotation (p. 151):

'... a living organism is in an extemely unstable state. One of the main characteristics of the living organism is that it possesses an overwhelmingly complicated system of mechanisms that protect it against adverse influences of the environment and enable it to maintain itself as a living organism.'

So even if the theory cannot actually be described as a real field-theory, it seems most correct to classify it as *a rather dynamic theory.*

Statistical or Deterministic Theory

It is very easy to place Tinbergen's theory in this classification as *an extremely deterministic theory.* He maintains already on the first page that one of the two main objects of ethology is 'to determine the causal structure underlying the behaviour.' And the whole book is an attempt to summarize 'the causal factors' in a theory which can explain innate (instinctive) behavior. Especially in Chapter III on 'the "spontaneity" of behaviour' he argues against an indeterministic viewpoint, maintaining that 'spontaneous' behavior is not 'proof' of the existence of 'free will' or other indeterministic principles; 'spontaneous' behavior is caused by internal causal factors, among others by hormones, internal stimuli, and especially by impulses produced in the central nervous system. He writes about this (p. 72):

'the problem of spontaneity has now been made accessible to objective causal research, because it is now realized that internal factors are not necessarily of a purely subjective order. This view was the outcome of a confusion of "spontaneity" with the essentially subjective concept of free will.'

Also against the *teleological* point of view Tinbergen maintains that the deterministic viewpoint is primary and essential. He writes (p. 152):

'A description of the directiveness of life processes is not a solution of the problem of their causation. One the survival value of a process has been recognized and clearly described, the biologist's next rask is to find out how its mechanisms work; in other words, on what causal systems it is based.'

As can be seen from the quotations, Tinbergen's theory must be characterized as a *deterministic* theory in the broadest sense of the word.

The Model

Tinbergen uses an illustrative model in his theory, namely the diagrams 97 and 98, p. 124 and 125, which depict a hierarchy of instintive centers and releasing mechanisms. The diagrams are very clear and didactically valuable.

Summary

Tinbergen's theory is a classifying, reductive, purely behavioristic, relatively molecular, rather dynamic, and extremely deterministic theory.

MOTIVATION DEFINITIONS AND HYPOTHESES

Motivation in General

The word 'motivation' often appears alone and as an adjective in the expression 'motivational factors' in Tinbergen's book. This expression appears for the first time in connection with the discussion about whether behavior is a reaction or a spontaneous activity. He writes (p. 15):

'We are at present in a position to say that both opinions contain part of the truth. Behaviour is reaction in so far as it is, to a certain extent, dependent on external stimulation. It is spontaneous in so far as it is also dependent on internal causal factors, or motivational factors, responsible for the activation of an urge or drive.'

The meaning of the word 'motivation' can be found in the following quotations (p. 57 and 101):

'The effect of these internal factors determines the "motivation" of an animal, the activation of its instincts.'

'The internal causal factors controlling, qualitatively and quantitatively, the motivation of the animal may be of three kinds: hormones, internal sensory stimuli, and, perhaps, intrinsic or automatic nervous impulses generated by the central nervous system itself.'

As shown in the quotations there is a difference in meaning between 'motivational factors' and 'motivation', even more clearly apparent from the following quotation (p. 122):

'We have seen that the causal factors controlling innate behaviour are of two kinds, viz. internal and external. In most cases both kinds exert an influence and they supplement each other. Usually the internal factors do not themselves evoke the overt response; they merely determine the threshold of the response to the sensory stimuli. Therefore, the internal factors like hormones, internal stimuli, and intrinsic impulses determine what the psychologist calls the motivation; and I will call them motivational factors. As we have seen, it is highly probable that in many cases external stimuli may also raise the motivation, and some of them therefore also belong among the motivational factors.

Another category of external stimuli, viz. those activating releasing mechanisms, must be distinguished from the motivational factors; I shall call them releasing factors.'

Thus '*motivational factors*' means 'internal causal factors' including internal stimuli, hormones, and centrally produced nervous impulses. These factors must (in agreement with the terminology of the introductory chapters) be described as *empirical* variables—at least the first two—while the centrally produced nervous impulses should perhaps be classified as hypothetical constructions. '*Motivation*,' on the other hand, means '*an activation of certain centers of the central nervous system*.' This variable must be described as a physiologically interpreted, *hypothetical* variable—even if it is less hypothetical than most of the often more complicated variables in human psychology.

The Concept of Instinct

The concept ot motivatioin is closely related to the concept of instinct. As mentioned in the summary of the theory, Tinbergen uses the term 'instinctive behavior' or 'instinctive act' of both 'the appetitive behaviour' and 'the consummatory act'. In this he differs from *K. Lorenz* whose terminology he describes in the following way (p. 105):

'Lorenz, realizing that they (the consummatory actions) constitute the most characteristic components of instinctive behavior, that is to say those components that can be most easily recognized by the form of the movement, called them *Instinkthandlungen*, thereby greatly narrowing the concept of instinctive act. This use of the term gives rise to continuous misunderstandings and hence should be dropped.'

Regardless of which of the two terminologies is chosen, the description 'instinctive act' (or 'instinctive behavior') must be said to be *a descriptive term* or in accordance with the terminology of the introductory chapters—*an empirical variable*, namely a dependent behavior variable. The term 'instinct' is, on the other hand, *an explanatory term* or *a hypothetical variable*. This variable is defined by Tinbergen in the following way (p. 112):

'I will tentatively define an instinct as a hierarchically organized nervous mechanism which is susceptible to certain priming, releasing and directing impulses of internal as well as of external origin, and which responds to these impulses by coordinated movements that contribute to the maintenance of the individual and the species.'

When 'instinct' is thus defined as a system of 'nervous mechanisms' (including several superior and sub-ordinate centers with their releasing mechanisms—cf. Tinbergen figures 97 and 98), it must be described as a hypothetical *disposition* variable. The corresponding hypothetical function variable must be 'motivation', as this variable, as mentioned before, is defined as 'the action of instincts'.

The relation between instinct and motivation can now briefly be presented in the following way: 'Motivation' is an activation of instinct centers, of which the superior centers (in cats) have been localized (by electric stimulation) in the hypothalamus. This activation—the motivation—is functionally dependent upon 'motivational factors', internal stimuli from internal organs, hormones, and spontaneously produced nervous impulses (in the superior instinct centers). All these factors—and in certain cases also external stimuli such as changes in temperature—together influence the superior and the sub-ordinate instinct centers which are thereby activated or 'charged' with motivating impulses. These impulses are sent from the superior center to several subordinate centers which are thereby activated or charged with impulses, and to nerve paths which start 'the appetitive behaviour'. This behavior often brings the organism into contact with special external stimuli which have a releasing effect upon the innate releasing mechanism (IRM), whereby one of the subordinate instinct centers ceases to be blocked and a new 'appetitive behaviour' starts. This chain of superior and sub-ordinate appetitive behavior-acts is continued until a consummatory act is released, whereby the motivational factors in the organism stop activating the instinct centers, and the organism calms down for the time being.

As can be seen from this analysis of Tinbergen's theory of instinct, it is much more exact and systematical than older theories such as McDougall's. First of all the definition of instinctive behavior (and especially the distinction between appetitive behavior and consummatory act) is much more exact. Also the hypothetical variables and their inter-relations are much more exactly defined and formulated—especially because they are *physiologically* interpreted, and as a whole not very hypothetical, as they are often based upon direct neuro-physiological observations and experiments.

Hypotheses of Motivation

Besides the primary definitions and hypotheses already analyzed, some more or less explicitly formulated relatively special hypotheses of motivation can be found scattered throughout Tinbergen's book. They will be discussed in the following.

A rather important hypothesis is included in the following quotation formulated on the basis of Lorenz's observations (p. 61):

'A drive may even become so strong that its motor responses break through in the absence of a releasing stimulus.'

The behavior dealt with here is the so-called '*vacuum activity*.'

Later he discusses four possible hypotheses of the relation of hormones to instinctive behavior, formulated by *Lashley*[2]), and he mentions the following one as the most probable (p. 74):

'the hormone acts upon the central nervous system, thereby increasing the excitability of the sensorimotor mechanism specifically involved in the instinctive activity.'

A more general hypothesis of which the quoted hypothesis of 'vacuum activities' is a special case concerns the relation between motivation and external stimuli. He writes (p. 79):

'the level of the motivation determines the degree of sensory stimulation required to release the reaction. When the motivation is relatively strong, suboptimal external stimulation will still bring the total of factors above threshold value. Now, for many reactions the all-or-none law does not hold; they may appear in many different intensities.'

'The result of this situation is that, with a moderately strong motivation, incomplete external stimulation elicits incomplete reactions.'

'*Displacement* (or "substitute") *activity*' is a related phenomen about which the following (implicit) hypothesis has been formulated (p. 114):

'the conditions under which displacement activities usually occur led to the conclusion that, in all known cases, there is a surplus of motivation, the discharge of which through the normal paths is in some way prevented. The most usual situations are: (1) conflict of two strongly activated anatagonistic drives; (2) strong motivation of a drive, usually the sexual drive, together with lack of external stimuli required for the release of the consummatory acts belonging to that drive'.

Furthermore we have the following hypothesis of 'displacement activities' (p. 117):

'A comparative review of displacement activities reveals that they are always innate patterns, known to us from the study of other instinct.'

As shown by these quotations—and maybe even more clearly by the reconstruction in the next passage—almost all of Tinbergen's hypotheses belong to the type in Spence's modified classification which has at least one empirical variable. This shows the sound empirical basis of the theory.

Instinct in Man

Tinbergen's theory is formulated in such a way that it should be true of animal species of different degrees of development, from fish (and maybe even insects) to birds and mammals. Instinctive behavior is, however, less frequent in mammals, and in Man it is especially rare. (The only typical example is the instinctive sucking

---

[2]) In psych. Review, 1938, *45*, 445–471.

response of the baby). Instinctive *motivation*, on the other hand, can be found. As typical examples Tinbergen mentions 'the sexual drive' and 'the food-seeking drive'. There are also innate releasing mechanisms. Tinbergen (here following Lorenz) especially mentions the releasing mechanism of 'the parental instinct', which reacts to plump headshapes, etc. Displacement activities can also be found in Man in conflict-situations (for example scratching-oneself-behind-the-ear).

RECONSTRUCTION OF THE THEORY

As can be seen from the above analysis of Tinbergen's theory and from his definitions and hypotheses of motivation, the theory rests upon a sound empirical basis; but it needs formal reconstruction.

The first definition in this reconstruction of the theory of motivation can be formulated in the following way:

Definition 1: 'Behavior' means 'the totality of the movements made by the intact animal.'

Since it is very characteristic and essential that Tinbergen in his theory stresses the dependence of behavior upon both external stimuli and internal 'motivational factors', I suggest formulating this as a primary hypothesis:

Hypothesis 1: Behavior is both reactive and spontaneous as it is functionally related to both external stimuli and internal motivational factors: internal stimulation, hormones, and centrally produced nervous impulses.

Another important aspect of Tinbergen's theory is the mutual dependence and co-operation of the causal factors (empirical variables) determining the behavior of the animal. Therefore this is formulated in a second primary hypothesis:

Hypothesis 2: The empirical variables (external stimuli and internal motivating factors) form an inter-dependent totality, which determines the behavior of the animal via central nervous processes. However, the external stimuli determine mainly the release and orientation of the behavior, while the motivating factors determine the activation (the motivation) of the central nervous system and the behavior.

The above hypotheses and definitions are true of behavior in general. To be complete the reconstruction must also include some hypotheses and definitions dealing with instinctive behavior.

Definition 2: A. 'Instinctive behavior' is a generic term for both 'appetitive acts' and 'consummatory acts.' B. 'Appetitive acts' are very varying, purposive forms of behavior with very different degrees of complication (from simple reflex movements over aquired habitual acts to intelligent behavior). C. 'Consummatory acts' consist of two components: orientation movements (taxis) and innate, stereotype patterns of movements typical of the species.

Hypothesis 3: As a rule instinctive behavior is a pattern of several superior and sub-ordinate appetitive acts ending with a consummatory act which neutralizes the motivational factors.

Definition 3: An 'instinct' is 'an innate system consisting of a superior nervous center and several sub-ordinate centers with their releasing mechanisms.'

Hypothesis 4: The motivational factors activize the instinct centers from which nervous impulses are led to the muscles when external stimuli via innate releasing mechanisms have removed the blocking of the nerve paths from the instinct centers.

With regard to the more special hypotheses of motivation, the hypotheses about the relation between motivation and external stimuli will be dealt with first:

Hypothesis 5: The intensity of the motivation determines the intensity of the sensory stimulation necessary to release the behavior. The stronger the motivation, the weaker the external stimuli have to be (and vice versa).

Hypothesis 6: A motivation may be so strong that the behavior will appear without external releasing stimuli ('vacuum activity').

Hypothesis 7: Weak motivation combined with weak external stimuli will either release a smaller number of reactions or incomplete reactions ('intention reactions'). Strong motivation combined with strong external stimuli will release more reactions.

The hypotheses about 'displacement-activity' ('substitute acts') have been reformulated as follows:

Hypothesis 8: When impulses of a very intense motivation are blocked because two different motivations are in conflict or because the releasing stimuli are lacking, 'displacement-activity' will result often comprising movements belonging to an irrelevant (instinctive) act.

The hypotheses about the function of hormones as motivational variables can be reformulated in the following way:

Hypothesis 9: Hormones activate directly the instinct centers in the central nervous system.

Conclusion

Finally it should be stressed once again that Tinbergen's theory, in spite of the formal shortcomings which made a reconstruction necessary, is *one of the most valuable modern psychological theories*, because it combines so many neurophysiological research data with such a large number of comparative-biological research results whereby *Tinbergen's theory becomes a very useful link* between psychology and the rest of biology[3]).

---

[3]) W. S. Verplanck wrote after this chapter was finished in 'Annual Review of Psychology' (1958): 'instinct is once again dead' (p. 100) and 'Tinbergen's theory of instinctive hierarchies... is obsolete and largely abandoned (especially by Tinbergen who emphasizes the theory's inadequacies perhaps more than do others).' (p. 103).

Later References

1. Hinde, R. A.: Some recent trends in Ethology. (in S. Koch (edt.): 'Psychology—A Study of a Science'. Vol. 2, 1959, McGraw-Hill, N.Y.).
2. – Animal Behavior. (McGraw-Hill, N.Y. 1966).

Chapter 14

McClelland's Theory

The American psychologist *David C. McClelland* has contributed a series of experimental and theoretical papers to the psychology of motivation. The experimental papers have mainly dealt with *measuring* experimentally produced motivation by the use of a standardized group edition of Murray's T. A. T. The theoretical work began especially whith his book on '*Personality*' (1951). This is a very thorough and systematic book integrating different personality theories as as *Allport's* 'trait' theory, *Cattell's* factor-analytical theory, *Murray's* 'need' theory, and social-psychological role theories and culture-sociological theories. In the three chapters (forming the fourth part of the book) on 'Motive as a Personality Variable' he attempts to give an outline of the modern psychology of motivation, closing with his own 'Notes for a Revised Theory of Motivation' (p. 466–475)[1]). McClelland has developed this programme for a theory of motivation further in '*The Achievement Motive*'[2]) (1953), which he and his research assistants: John W. Atkinson, Russell A. Clark, and Edgar L. Lowell, have written. Eventhough this book—as other main works in modern psychology—is the result of teamwork, it is not unjust to describe the theory as 'McClelland's Theory'. As the theory in 'A. M.' is McClelland's last systematic presentation, it will form the main basis for the analysis to be given in this chapter.

THE STRUCTURE OF THE THEORY

Summary of the Theory

It is easiest to make a summary of *the content* of McClelland's theory on the basis of his 'Notes for a Revised Theory of Motivation'. Here he defines a motive as *an affective association* manifesting itself as purposive behavior and determined by previous association between signals and pleasure or pain. According to the definition *all motives are acquired* and all motivation is based upon emotions, not identical with emotions but rather *an expection of change in the affective condition.*

---

[1]) Later printed as an independent chapter in McClelland's work: 'Studies in Motivation' (1955).
[2]) This will in the following be abbreviated to 'A. M.'

Then McClelland presents the hypothesis that pleasure is from birth determined by every moderate increase in stimulus intensity, whereas further increase determines displeasure or pain. Thereby two kinds of motives become possible: *the positive* or *approaching* which is an expectation of pleasure or satisfaction (symbolized by an 'n' which is an abbreviation of 'need'), and *the negative* or avoiding, which is an expectation of displeasure or pain (symbolized by an 'f' for 'fear'). n Achievement and f Failure are, then, two different motives. But *no* distinction is made between primary, biogenic, and secondary, psychogenic, motives as *all* motives are acquired. But as biological needs almost always determine behavior which sooner or later results in satisfaction and thereby in pleasure (as the organism would otherwise die), *expectations* of increased pleasure in connection with the biological needs, i. e. motives are learned rather early. But other motives—for example n Achievement—are also rather universal in human beings in spite of the fact that they are determined by external stimuli, as stimuli may be so common in all cultures (for example in all forms of education) that the motive is learned just as early and remains just as intense for the rest of the life of the individual as the biologically determined motives.

The presuppositions of McClelland's theory are first of all the *empirical* studies made by himself and his assistants. As mentioned these consist of 'projective' measurements of experimentally produced motives. In the first study (1)[2]) *the hunger motive* was produced with different degrees of intensity by letting the subjects fast for different periods. In a later study (5) *the sex motive* was produced by letting the subjects sort pictures of naked women (and men) according to type of body. A third experimentally produced motive was *n Affiliation* (6) which was produced in two ways: One group of subjects wrote down which of the other members of the group they preferred (a sociometric study); another group of subjects were college students who were either admitted to or refused admittance to a fraternity[3]). The most extensive study is that of *n Achievement* which was produced experimentally by means of problem situations which were presented to the subjects as tasks of varying importance for their future careers. The motives produced were measured with a standardized group edition of Murray's T. A. T. As a rule only a few pictures (for example 4) were shown and a limited period (5 minutes) granted for writing a story answering four standard questions. The stories were then analyzed and evaluated according to a standardized scoring-system which proved to have a rather high degree of reliability (more than 0.90). The validity of the measurements (or the scoring-system) has been examined in connection with other methods of measuring and with other behavior variables.

On the basis of these original and valuable *experiments* on *human* motivation McClelland rejected the prevailing theories of motivation which in his opinion

---

[2]) See the list of references following this chapter.

[3]) Control groups are used in all experiments. The experimental technique and the statistical treatment is as a whole very exact and probably above criticism.

depended to much upon experiments with animals and were therefore unsatisfactory as explanations of the functions of the complicated non-biological motives. Since McClelland's criticism of other theories—together with his experiments—form the presuppositions of his own theory, the criticism will briefly be summarized here (based upon A. M. p. 12–27).

McClelland calls one type of motivation theory '*the survival model*'. All theories explaining motivation on the basis of 'biologically defined survival needs' (e. g. Hull, Young, etc.) belong to this group. The 'model' is criticized for the following reasons:

1) 'some survival needs produce a motive and some do not' (p. 15),
2) it is difficult to define the term 'survival needs,'
3) 'biological needs provide only a very partial basis for explaining how behavior is guided and controlled' (p. 16),
4) 'the extraordinary persistence and strength characteristic of learned human motives argues against their continued dependence on biological needs' (p. 17).

'*The stimulus intensity model*' is another type of motivation theory (e. g. N. E. Miller), so called by McClelland because it defines motivation as 'a strong stimulus . . . which impels action.' This model is criticized mainly for the following reasons (p. 20 in A. M.):

'What this evidence seems to add up to is that although strong stimulation often does give rise to pain or negative affect and thus provides a source of motivation, it does not always produce negative affect. And when it does not, it appears not to be a source of motivation. Therefore, negative affect would seem to be the causative motivational factor and not strong stimulation per se.'

Here—as in his criticism of the previously mentioned model—McClelland adds that his criticsm does not imply that he does not consider 'survival needs' and 'stimulus intensity' important conditions of motivation, but only that they are not *sufficient*.

The third type of model McClelland calls '*the stimulus pattern model*' because it states that motivation is determined by a stimulus pattern where there is a 'moderate discrepancy between expectation and perception.' Hebb's theory especially represents this group. McClelland criticizes it mainly for the following reasons (p. 24 in A. M.):

1) 'one must know the relationship between past learning and present perception in order to set up a motive.'
2) the theory is 'so general that the experimentalist trying to work with such a model is hard put to know when he is working with a motive or how to measure its effects.'

But in spite of this criticism, which is fully justified especially as far as the last point is concerned, McClelland adds (in A. M. p. 25):

'Still, Hebb's ideas have proved immensely stimulating to us, and our own theory in many respects picks up where he leaves off.'

Level of Development of the Theory

McClelland's own theory is mainly presented in the second chapter of A. M. (p. 27–96). Here twelve statements have been formulated which include the most important hypotheses of the theory. But no axiomatization of the theory has been made—let alone any symbolization or formalization. McClelland's theory must therefore be classified as a *type between classifying and really deductive theories.*

Reductive or Constructive Theory

It is rather difficult to place McClelland's theory in this classification. As can be seen from the above McClelland is rather critical in his attitude towards 'survival'-theories, which are mainly reductive; and he does not believe that all motivation can be explained on the basis of—or be reduced to—biological needs. But on the other hand he himself explains motivation as being based upon variables such as 'cues paired with adaption level discrepancies innately producing affect' (p. 14 in A. M.), and of these at least 'affect' can be interpreted as a hypothetical variable with physiological 'surplus meaning'. McClelland does not write anything about it explicitly in A. M., but he discusses it in 'Personality'[3]) where he writes (p. 88):

'a construct should not have properties which are inconsistent with the known characteristics of neural mechanisms. Neurophysiology may not always tell us what the 'surplus meanings' of our variables should be but it *can* eliminate certain properties as impossible, and it may suggest some useful additional ones. Psychologists have argued much about the usefulness of neurology to their science, but the fact remains that any hypothetical state attributed to the organism must operate within the limitations of the nervous system.'

Even if this quotation shows that McClelland is not anti-reductive in his attitude, his theory must be classified as being *a mainly constructive theory.*

Mentalistic or Behavioristic Theory

It can already be seen from the above that the hypothetical variables of the theory are not mainly neuro-physiological, so the theory cannot be extremely behavioristic but must either be mentalistic or neutral-formal, probably the latter. McClelland writes as follows about the protocol statements or methods of the theory (in A. M. p. 322):

'it is now clear to us that there is an opportunity here to reopen an almost discarded line of psychological inquiry, namely, the analysis of ideational content which appeared to have ended in a blind alley with the demise of introspectionism a generation ago.'

But he stresses explicitly the difference between the usual introspection and the method used by him and his assistants (A. M. p. 324):

'we are not dealing here with subjective reports in the traditional sense. A subjective report often involves what the subject thinks he is thinking *in terms of his own categories of content analysis.*'

---

[3]) In the following abbreviated to 'Pers.'

'Here we are collecting a thought sample under specified conditions and then applying to it a public system of content analysis which can be repeated by any observer who knows the system.'

After thus having pointed out clearly both the differences and the similarities between introspection and 'thought sampling'—as McClelland calls his method in order to distinguish it from an ordinary clinical projective method—he states its relation to behavioristic methods with the following words (p. 323 in A. M.):

'To the extent that we can develop a truly objective method of scoring "thought samples", we tend to close the gap between a psychology of "experience" and of "behavior". That is, the experimenter will be able to point to achievement imagery in a protocol with nearly the same degree of objectivity with which he can point to a "right turn" in a maze for a rat.'

Maybe McClelland is not the first to make use of the orally expressed thoughts of the subjects, nor is he the first to point out the difference between this method and ordinary introspection where the subjects give a phenomenological description of their experiences; but as far as I know McClelland is the first to point out the possibility that *the objective study of the written production of a subject can form a synthesis of behavioristic and introspective methods.*

As a consequence of the above McClelland's theory must—both with regard to hypothetical variables and protocol statements—be classified as *a neutral-formal theory.*

Molecular or Molar Theory

McClelland writes a good deal in Pers. about this problem: 'What Units of Analysis shall we use?' (p. 100). He maintains here that the problem cannot only be the simple choice between the alternatives: analysis or non-analysis, as scientific method must be analytic. Even the Gestalt psychologists analyze. The problem is which unit of analysis—or which variables—to choose. And the answer must be that one must use as many units of analysis as are necessary for an adequate solution to the research problem. On the other hand, one should avoid using too many and too microscopic and abstract units of analysis, as the resulting synthesis would be too complicated.

After having criticized the much too simple variables often used in the laboratories McClelland writes (p. 319):

'But we wanted to go beyond such simple variables in the conviction that, if we are to understand human nature, we must start operating in the laboratory with the kind of motives which actually are important in the lives of human adults.'

Based upon the above I find that McClelland's theory must be classified as *a mainly molar theory.*

Mechanistic or Field-Theoretical Theory

McClelland does not write anything explicitly about this problem in A. M. He writes, however, a good deal about it in Pers., especially in the last chapter, 'Interrelation, Among the Basic Personality Variables: Predicting the Concrete Act.' Here he points out that it is necessary to formulate hypotheses about interrelations between personality variables. He uses Lewin's fundamental formula:

B=f(P, E)'

which he expands, replacing 'P' with the symbols for the fundamental personality variables in his theory, namely: 'H' for '*trait*,' 'S' for '*schema*,' 'D' for '*need or motive*', and '*sS*' for '*self-schema*'. Thus the formula is as follows (p. 581 in Pers.):

B=f(H' S, D, sS)(E).

This fundamental formula is thus extremely field-theoretical in character. This is seen even more clearly in McClelland's diagram (Pers. 595) showing the functional interrelations between personality variables, situation factors, and behavior by means of arrows.

McClelland stresses, however, that this is only a program, and that so far only few hypotheses of this kind have been formulated. And if one studies the twelve hypotheses formulated in A. M. one will see that only about half of them (2, 4, 5, 6, and 12) deal with more than two variables.

Based upon the above McClelland's theory must, in my opinion, be classified as *a very dynamic, almost field-theoretical theory*.

Statistical or Deterministic Theory

This problem is only dealt with explicitly in Pers. where McClelland especially discusses it on p. 89–97. Here he deals with Allport's conclusion that only ideographic hypotheses can be used in the psychology of personality. McClelland formulates it in the following way (p. 90):

> 'Fortunately there is another approach to the problem. We need not conclude that we must have two different kinds of laws. We may need only to make an idiographic application of a nomothetic law or laws.'

And McClelland points out that this is in accordance with the practical application of the general or nomothetic laws of other sciences. Then he presents an interesting analysis of the reasons why everybody does not act in accordance with a general psychological law. (The three most important reasons are: 1) that one has failed to check whether or not the conditions preassumed in the law really are present in the case in question; 2) that a certain act is determined by more than one functional relation; 3) that the general law is really incorrectly formulated (and must therefore be changed)).

Furthermore McClelland maintains that it is often easier to get the idea to a general hypothesis (nomothetic 'law') by studying individual cases. But its generality must, of course, be tested through the study of the behavior of a large group of individuals.

Later McClelland discusses the classical problem of determinism in psychology more directly. Here he points out that it is in reality a question of *two* problems. The first is the problem of whether Man is free or determined. According to McClelland this is a pseudo-problem caused by a misunderstanding of the concept of causation in classical physics. McClelland joins the philosophers who maintain that 'increasing precision of predictions is the only valid meaning that causation has' (p. 96), and based upon this he points out that the problem of determinism 'is based partly on a misconception of the nature of the causation in theory construction' (p. 96). The second problem is the question of whether or not it is possible to predict human behavior with some degree of probability on the basis of a theory of personality. McClelland believes that we in real life—outside the situations in laboratories—very rarely have such a detailed knowledge of a person's personality or the external situation that a prediction can be reasonably exact. It is, however, possible to reach the point where an act which has already occurred can be *explained.*

As can be seen from the above summary of McClelland's excellent discussion, McClelland believes in the possibility of formulating deterministic hypotheses, even though it may often be difficult to use them in real-life situations.

The twelve general hypotheses in A. M. are all formulated as deterministic hypotheses. But the more special empirical results of McClelland's experiments are often formulated as statistical correlations. As a consequence of this—and of the formulations in Pers.—McClelland's theory must be classified as *a mainly deterministic theory.*

The Model

The already mentioned diagram p. 595 in Pers. is the only one which can be taken as an illustrative model of McClelland's theory. There is no diagram in A. M. The diagram in question is—as mentioned—a differentiation of Lewin's formula, B=f(P, E).

Summary

The above analysis of the structure of McClelland's theory can be summarized in the following description: *McClelland's theory is an almost deductive, mainly constructive, neutral-formal, mainly molar, extremely dynamic, and mainly deterministic theory.*

MOTIVATION DEFINITIONS AND HYPOTHESES

As already mentioned, the most systematic and thorough presentation of McClelland's theory of motivation can be found in Chapter II: 'Toward a Theory of

Motivation' (p. 6–96 in A. M.), which also includes the motivation definitions and hypotheses to be analyzed in this section. (The other chapters of A. M. deal with methods and empirical research results and will therefore not be analyzed here.)

Motivation Definitions

McClelland's fundamental definition of motivation is formulated as follows (p. 28):

> 'Our definition of a motive is this: *A motive is the redintegration by a cue of a change in an affective situation.* The word *redintegration* in this definition is meant to imply previous learning. In our system, all motives are learned. The basic idea is simply this: Certain stimuli or situations involving discrepancies between expectation (adaptation level) and perception are sources of primary, unlearned affect, either positive or negative in nature. Cues which are paired with these affective states, changes in these affective states, and the conditions producing them become capable of redintegrating a state (A) derived from the original affective situation (A), but not identical with it.'

According to this definition 'motive' in McClelland's theory must be classified as a *hypothetical* variable, as it is not a directly observable link between a signal ('cue') and behavior. It is, however, more difficult to decide whether it is to be classified as a neutral-formal, a neuro-physiological, or a phenomenological variable, but probably it must be interpreted as a *neutral-formal* variable, since no physiological or phenomenological 'surplus meaning' is mentioned.

On the basis of the definition 'motive' must be classified a sa function variable, taking part directly in the process determining behavior; the same is true of 'motive' in all the twelve hypotheses in A. M. In Pers., however, 'motivation' is a personality variable and thus a *disposition variable.* But McClelland uses the word 'motivation'—and 'need' or 'drive'—about both function variables and disposition variables, without, however, formulating the classification (or a similar distinction) explicitly. The only place where McClelland distinguishes between disposition variables and function variables in his terminology is in the above mentioned diagram (in Pers. p. 595). Here a distinction is made between 'Activated need pushes'[4]) and 'Need-system', which is a part of 'Personality-structure' (also including 'Schemasystem' and 'Traitsystem'). This lack of systematic distinction between motivation-function-variables and motivation-disposition-variables is not only characteristic of McClelland's theory. As already stated it also occurs in other theories of personality (Murray, Allport, etc.).

McClelland's definition of motivation is peculiar in two respects: 1) *all* motives are *acquired*, and 2) *motivation is based upon affect.*

With regard to the first point McClelland's theory resembles that of Hebb. In the above quotation (from p. 28) McClelland points to the importance of the

---

[4]) The terms are taken from Tolman's 'Psychological Model.'

learning process for motivation. The hypothesis may be reformulated simply thus: an *association* is formed between a *signal* ('cue') and *an affective state reproduced* by the signal. *This reproduction is the motive.* McClelland maintains that two possible hypotheses of acquisition of motives exist: 1) The association is only formed between a signal and a *changing* affective state. 2) The association may also be formed between a signal and a *static* affective state.

But it is strongly emphasized that (p. 28):

'*at the time of arousal* of a motive, the affective state which is redintegrated must be different from the one already experienced by the organism.'

Later McClelland points out that the signals (the cues) connected with the association 'may be unconnected with affective arousal or they may be response-produced cues resulting from the affective arousal.'

There are, in other words, two possibilities for the forming of association for both parts of the association ('cue' and 'affective state').

A consequence of McClelland's definition of motivation is that

'the traditional distinction between *primary* (biological need) motives and *secondary* (learned or social) motives has disappeared. Instead, we may speak of primary affect and secondary motives if we like.'

But later McClelland adds that in his opinion it is better to avoid the traditional distinction completely.

The other point which makes McClelland's definition of motivation peculiar is, as mentioned, *the dependence of the motivation upon affect.* McClelland gives several reasons for having chosen such a definition (or axiom). First of all he finds the general biological theories insufficient (cf. the criticism mentioned in the passage dealing with the presuppositions of the theory). Secondly, he finds that his theory can explain such widely different observations as *Young's* later experiments on the primary affect of 'palatability' in relation to 'need' and *Tinbergen's* experiment on releasing stimuli, and also everyday observations of the influence of emotions upon behavior. McClelland finds it particularly practical to compare instinctive behavior in lower animals to affective processes in Man. He writes about this (p. 31–32):

'in fact, the interesting possibility pursued there is that in man these specific overt reactions to 'releasing' stimuli are attenuated and occur instead as diffuse reactions of the autonomic nervous system signifying what we usually call 'affect'. Thus our motivational system for man has been constructed to parallel the analysis of instinctive behavior in lower animals made by Tinbergen (1959) and others. Certain types of situations innately release reactions which are diffuse and covert in man rather than specific and overt, but which are consummatory in the same sense in that they ultimately exhaust themselves. These diffuse reactions are what we mean by affect, and they can be observed either through verbal reports and autonomic reactions, or inferred from approach and avoidance behavior, as we shall see in the next section.'

Thus defining motivation as dependent upon affects, McClelland puts his theory up against 'the whole weight of psychological tradition' which 'supports the opposite view—namely that affect is the by-product or accompaniment of motives' (p. 87). But he presents several arguments which are meant to show 'how and why according to our theory affect apparently accompanies motives' (p. 89).

After this analysis of McClelland's fundamental definition (and axiom) of motivation it becomes evident that it is important for McClelland's theory to explain which empirical variables determine the existence of affect. Most of McClelland's hypotheses, however, deal with this subject.

Hypotheses on 'Affective Arousal'

In the section on 'Antecedent conditions for affective arousal' (A. M. p. 42–66) twelve hypotheses about the independent, empirical variables which determine the—more or less—hypothetical variable called 'affective arousal' are formulated. They are the only explicitly formulated hypotheses which can be found in the theory, and as they are also rather fundamental—probably the most fundamental hypotheses after the definition of motivation already quoted—they will all be quoted here:

Hypothesis 1: Affective arousal is the innate consequence of certain sensory or perceptual events.

Hypothesis 2: Positive affect is the result of smaller discrepancies of a sensory or perceptual event from the adaptation level of the organism; negative affect is the result of larger discrepancies.

Hypothesis 3: Natural adaptation levels for various sensory receptors differ.

Hypothesis 4: A discrepancy between adaptation level and a sensation or event must persist for a finite length of time before it gives rise to a hedonic response.

Hypothesis 5: Discrepancies from adaptation level will give rise to a positive-negative affect function in either direction along a continuum.

Hypothesis 6: Increases and decreases in stimulus intensity can be related to motivation only if adaptation level and learning are taken into account.

Hypothesis 7: Changes in adaptation level, with attendant hedonic changes, may be produced by somatic conditions.

Hypothesis 8: Changes in adaptation level, with attendant hedonic changes, may be produced by experience.

Hypothesis 9: Events can differ from expectations on a variety of dimensions.

Hypothesis 10: Frustration is a source of negative affect.

Hypothesis 11: The achievement motive develops out of growing expectations.

Hypothesis 12: In human adults adaptation levels are numerous and complex so that a single event may have several hedonic consequences.

Most of the hypotheses are, as can be seen, of *the* $S \rightarrow H$ *type* (cf. Spence's modified classification of hypotheses in Chapter 3) if 'affective arousal' is considered to be a *hypothetical* variable. Some of them are, however, more complicated as more than two variables are included (cf. the classification of the theory as an extremely dynamic theory). Hypothesis 2 may, for example, be symbolically presented in the following way:

$$AA = f(AL + S),$$

'AA' meaning 'Affective arousal,' 'AL' meaning 'Adaptation level,' and 'S' meaning 'Sensory or perceptual event.' 'Discrepancy' is symbolized by '+' in the formula.

As the hypotheses indicate, the variable '*adaptation level*' is a very fundamental variable in McClelland's theory. It must be considered a more exact and objective edition of the variable 'expectation,' which McClelland often uses in the informal text—and also in a few of the hypotheses. '*Adaptation level*' must, like 'expectation', be classified as *a hypothetical variable,* as it cannot be directly observed but is assumed—even though this cannot directly be seen from McClelland's theory, among other things because AL is not explicitly defined. But 'adaptation level' differs from 'expectation', which has a certain phenomenological 'surplus meaning', in that it must be said to be a mainly *neutral-formal* variable, although maybe with a certain physiological 'surplus meaning'. It is, however, very difficult to classify it as a *function* or a *disposition* variable; it seems to be *an in-between form,* a very slowly changing function variable.

Finally it should be pointed out that 'adaptation level' in McClelland's theory corresponds rather closely to 'homeostasis' or 'biological balance' in many other theories of motivation. McClelland's theory may therefore roughly be characterized as follows: There are only *two innate 'motives'*[5]): *striving for pleasure* and *avoidance of displeasure* and pain. *All other motives are acquired* and determine *striving for* or *avoidance of* everything that the individual on the basis of learning processes *expects* will cause pleasure or displeasure. In other words, it is a purely *hedonistic* theory, a modern reformulation of classical hedonism.

Definition of the Individual Motives

Since all motives are acquired it is difficult to distinguish between the individual motives. McClelland reaches the following conclusion (p. 76):

'So to be consistent, motives should be distinguishable primarily in terms of the *types of expectations* involved, and secondarily in terms of the types of action, in so far as they exist, which confirm those expectations in varying degrees and thus yield positive or negative affect.'

When different types of expectations determine different types of motives the conclusion must be that *universal human motives exist when the same conditions give universal human expectations.* These conditions may be both biological and cultural. McClelland summarizes it in the following way (p. 77):

'It is meaningful then to speak of motives "common to all men" (and animals) to the extent that conditions can be identified which will give rise regularly to affective change either through biological or cultural arrangements.'

And he reaches the following conclusion about the number of universal motives (p. 80):

'The number of motives possible then is determined by the number of expectations which psychologists can find which occur fairly universally and which frequently result in affective changes through confirmation or nonconfirmation. We will make no attempt to enumerate such common motives here, but it seems to us that with these two limiting criteria it should be possible to come out with not too long a list of motives common to all men.'

As an example of a universal, culturally determined motive the 'achievement' motive is mentioned. This motive is determined by universal expectations, which are again determined by universal conditions in all human development. McClelland formulates it in the following way (p. 78):

---

[5]) But they are not described as 'motives' in McClelland's theory.

'Clearly the expectations are built out of universal experiences with problem-solving—with learning to walk, talk, hunt or read, write, sew, perform chores, and so forth. The expectations also involve standards of excellence with respect to such tasks.'

The achievement motive has een studied in detail by McClelland and his assistants. In Chapter IX they have described their studies of the 'Origins of Achievement Motivation.' The results are summarized as follows (p. 328):

'The data we have to date strongly support the hypothesis that achievement motives develop in cultures and in families where there is an emphasis on the independent development of the individual. In contrast, low achievement motivation is associated with families in which the child is more dependent on his parents and subordinate in importance to them.'

Sex-determined differences exist with regard to the expectations determining the achievement motivation. This is summarized as follows (p. 330):

'The importance of such achievement expectations in the development of motivation is underlined by the striking difference we found in the way men and women reacted to our achievement arousal instructions. Women were left unmoved by references to leadership and intelligence; but if they were socially rejected, their achievement motivation increased, as measured in the standard way. The men, on the other hand, were unaffected by social rejection on the achievement dimension.'

McClelland points out that the above sex-differences can easily be explained on the basis of his own '"expectation" theory of motivation' when the cultural conditions which create different expectations in boys and girls are taken into consideration. In the same way the theory easily explains that some people are most strongly motivated by the expectation of *success*, others by the expectation of *failure*. McClelland calls the two sub-forms of the achievement motive '*need achievement*' and '*fear failure*'. A good deal of the empirical data can be easily explained if the existence of a positive and a negative motive is assumed.

Motivation and Learning Processes

McClelland finally presents a rather thorough analysis of how his theory is related to normal theories of learning (p. 89–96). He gives here the following hypothesis (p. 95):

'learning results from contiguity but it is especially influenced by the presence of a motivational association based on the past contiguity of cues and affective states.'

McClelland feels he has thereby solved the problem of whether there is one or two kinds of learning processes. His solution very much resembles Tolman's theory, probably because of the common basic principle, 'expectation.'

The function of motivation in the learning process is summarized by McClelland in the following statements (p. 93):

'To review the argument once more:

'Suppose we make the simple assumption that motivation is not necessary to produce an association (e. g., that associations are produced by contiguity or some other such principle). Then the problem is to explain why motivation often facilitates problem-solving or instrumental learning. This we have done by stating (1) that the organism seeks to maximize pleasure and minimize pain, (2) that responses which cue off anticipated pleasure will be made preferentially, (3) that in a problem-solving situation some responses will tend to be more closely associated with pleasure, and (4) that these responses will tend to be repeated since they cue off anticipated pleasure more dependably.'

RECONSTRUCTION OF THE THEORY

As can be seen from the above analysis McClelland's theory includes a number of explicitly formulated hypotheses. But they do not summarize the total content of the theory, and it is therefore practical to give a reconstruction with a larger number of explicitly formulated hypotheses.

The first step in the reconstruction of McClelland's theory of motivation must be his fundamental definition of motivation, and it is suggested that it should be formulated in the following way:

Definition 1: A motive is a reproduced affect determined by an associated signal ('cue').

The most important hypotheses concerning the forming of associations are as follows:

Primary Hypothesis 1: A signal which occurs simultaneously with a dynamic affect acquires a probability for being able to reproduce this affect later. This probability is proportional to the total number of simultaneous appearances of signal and affect. It is also proportional to the dynamic character of the affect.

In this last sentence both of the two possible hypotheses are summarized, since a *static* affective condition can be considered to be a borderline case of a *dynamic* affective process.

As 'affect' (affective condition and processes) is such a fundamental variable in McClelland's theory it is suggested that the reconstructed theory should include an explicit definition and a primary hypothesis about this variable.

Definition 2: 'Affect' comprises diffuse autonomous, endocrine, visceral processes which can be observed through verbal report or 'approach' and 'avoidance' behavior, or be measured through PGR, blood-pressure, respiration, etc.

As can be seen, this is a summary of the quotation from p. 31–32.

Primary Hypothesis 2: Affects are from birth a function of discrepancies between the adaptation level (AL) of the organism and the sensory or perceptual processes. Positive affects are determined by small discrepancies, negative affects by large discrepancies.

The above hypothesis is a summarizing reformulation of McClelland's first and second explicitly formulated hypotheses on 'affective arousal'. Three of the hypotheses (3, 7, and 8) will be summarized in a primary hypothesis which at the same time should be an implicit definition of the rather important variable AL.

Primary Hypothesis 3: The adaptation level (AL) of the organism is a disposition which especially characterizes sense-organs, nervous system, and muscles. AL may differ from one sense-organ to another. AL is a function of both somatic conditions and learning processes.

The other explicit hypotheses on affective arousal are suggested presented in the following way as secondary hypotheses:

Secondary Hypothesis 1: A discrepancy between adaptation level and a sensory-perceptual process must be of a certain duration before it determines an affect.

Secondary Hypothesis 2: Deviations from the adaptation level in either direction along a sensory continuum will determine positive and later negative affect.

Secondary Hypothesis 3: Changes in stimulus intensity can only determine motivation through the adaptation level and learning processes.

Secondary Hypothesis 4: Events may deviate from the adaptation level on a variety of dimensions.

Secondary Hypothesis 5: In human adults adaptation levels are numerous and complex so that a single event may determine several affects.

Secondary Hypothesis 6: Frustration determines negative affect.

Secondary Hypothesis 7: The achievement motive is determined by continuously growing expectations of achievement possibilities and demands.

As can be seen, the above secondary hypotheses are almost exact quotations of the corresponding hypotheses in McClelland's own formulation. Only a few minor changes have been made, the change in order, for example, to make the addition of a few more secondary hypotheses about the achievement motive more logical, namely reformulations of the quotations from p. 328 and 330:

Secondary Hypothesis 8: The intensity of the achievement motive is a directly proportional function of the education to independence and selfreliance.

Seeondary Hypothesis 9: In western culture sex-differences in the achievement motive are determined by different, culturally determined expectations. Men expect leadership and intellectual prestige, women social acceptance.

And finally a hypothesis which summarizes the relation between motivation and learning processes:

Secondary Hypothesis 10: Repetition of associated stimuli and reactions is a necessary and sufficient condition for learning, but motivation increases the speed of learning because the positive affect-increasing acts will be repeated most often.

Conclusion

It only remains to be said that McClelland's theory in my opinion is an original motivation theory based upon a pioneering experimental study of human, culturally determined motivation.

Later Developments

McClelland's main work from recent years is his book: 'The Achieving Society' which appeared in 1961[6]). This book is not a further development of his theory

[6]) Published by Van Nostrand, Princeton, N.J.

from 'Personality' and 'The Achievement Motive'; it is rather an *application* of his theory of achievement-motivation to the *economical* development of different societies at different times.

McClelland elaborates a hypothesis by the sociologist *Max Weber*, who postulated a causal relation between '*ideology*' and '*economical growth*'. As an example Max Weber pointed to the relation between the Calvinistic doctrines and capitalistic development.

McClelland accepts this hypothesis and elaborates it with the following psychological factors relating to the causal link between ideology and economical growth:

Ideology influences education and child-rearing, and education influences the development of *personality*. The personalities of the leaders in a society influence the *economical growth* of that society. If the ideology of a society stresses the importance of achievement (hard work, industriousness, initiative, responsibility, etc.) then the education and upbringing of children from earliest childhood should stress the importance of achievement. This sort of child-rearing and education in its turn will produce personalities with a strong achievement-motivation in accordance with the research of McClelland and his co-workers. And people with a strong achievement-motive prefer such jobs as leaders in business and industry. Their achievement-motivation and leadership qualities produce an economical growth in society.

McClelland verifies this hypothesis with evidence collected from different societies at different times; both modern and previous societies were investigated. He found a way of measuring for the ideology's content of achievement values. It simply consists of an application of his content-analysis of TAT-stories to the favorite literature in the society at the time in question. By this content-analysis he gets an achievement-score for the ideology. At the other end of the causal link McClelland measures the economical growth. This measuring process has to be different at different times. In modern societies he selects the production of electricity as the most valid criterion of economical growth. Then McClelland correlates the measurement of achievement values with the amount of economical growth, and he finds in his data a high degree of correlation. But there is a *delay* of 50 years between the time of highest achievement-valuation and the time of highest economical growth. This delay is explained by the fact that it takes time to produce leaders and for them to get leading positions, which often comes at an age of 40–50 years.

It would take us too long to go into greater detail concerning McClelland's research, and it is extremely difficult for an ordinary psychologist to give a critical evaluation of this research. It would seem to require a team of psychologists, sociologists, economists and historians to make a truly competent evaluation of McClelland's book. But this very fact shows McClelland's great achievement.

The present author thinks that this book is one of the main building stones in the bridge between psychology and the social sciences.

While McClelland himself thus has been busy with the *application* of his theory, his co-worker, *John W. Atkinson* has been developing independently the *theoretical foundation* of the theory of achievement-motivation, but this will be dealt with later in a special publication.

References

1. McClelland and Atkinson: The projective expression of needs I. The effect of different intensities of the hunger drive on perception. (J. Psych. 25, 1948, 205, 32).
2. McClelland: Personality (New York 1951).
3. McClelland, Atkinson, Clark and Lowell: The Achievement Motive (New York 1953).
4. McClelland (ed.): Studies in Motivation (New York 1955).
5. Clark, R. A.: The projective measurement of experimentally induced levels of sexual motivation (J. exp. Psych. 44, 1952, 391–99).
6. Shipley, T. E., Jr., and Veroff, J.: A projective measure of need for affiliation (J. expl. Psych. 43, 1952, 349–356).
7. McClelland: The Achieving Society (1961).

Chapter 15

Ten Other Theories

The previous chapters have contained a relatively thorough analysis of ten different theories of motivation. In order to achieve a comparatively exhaustive picture of, or at least a representative sample of the theories of motivation from the period, which can be used in the following comparative study, a less detailed analysis of ten other theories will be presented in this chapter, and in the following chapter an anlysis of articles in periodicals, etc., will be given.

The same general disposition that has been used in the previous chapters will also be used in the analyses in this chapter. The following changes will, however, be made: In the section on '*The Structure of the Theory* the theory will be placed in the usual six classifications, but the summary of the content and presuppositions of the theory will be left out, just as the section on '*The Model*' will usually be left out. The number of quotations will be limited. The second main section will, for the sake of brevity, be called '*The Content of the Theory*', and here—as previously—especially the definitions and hypotheses of *motivation* will be analyzed, but of course with due consideration of the other important variables when necessary for understanding the theory. The usual main section on '*Reconstruction of the Theory*' will be completely left out, and instead an attempt will be made to present the analyses in 'The Content of the Theory' in such a way that they at the same time give a *systematic presentation* of the content of the theories.

While the ten previous chapters have contained analyses of theories from the whole period from 1930 to 1955, the content of this and the following chapter will be centered around the last half of that period, especially the years from 1945 to 1957[1]).

The ten theories dealt with in this chapter are, chronologically: Frenkel-Brunswik (1942), Masserman (1946), Freeman (1948), Moore (1948), Maier (1949), Cattell (1950), French (1952), Stagner and Karwoski (1952), Skinner (1953), and Holt-Hansen (1956).

---

[1]) Theories from the period 1957–67, will be analyzed and compared in a new supplementary volume ('Modern Theories of Motivation'—in press). *About Freud's theories:* It might seem strange to leave out an analysis of Freud's theories in a work on theories of motivation, but it has been done for the following reasons: 1) Freud's production is mainly from the period *before* 1930. 2) It is difficult to choose one or a few of his works as representatives of his latest presentation of his theory (as has been done for other theories). 3) Freud's production forms (historically if not systematically) a coherent whole and would therefore call for a whole book if the analysis were to be just as thorough as the analyses of the other theories.

FRENKEL-BRUNSWIK'S THEORY

The Structure of the Theory

In 'Genetic Psychology Monographs' (vol. 26, p. 121–264) the Austrian-American psychologist *Else Frenkel-Brunswik* published a long article called '*Motivation and Behavior*', the result of year-long, empirical research-work.

The article contains many interesting empirical data and some implicitly formulated hypotheses of a comparatively low degree of abstraction. No attempt, however, is made to formulate general, explicit hypotheses, or to arrange these in a deductive system, for which reason the theory must be called *a classifying theory.*

Since no attempt is made to explain anything on the basis of physiological data or hypotheses, the theory must be classified as *constructive* (cf. p. 133).

The hypothetical variables are rather neutral-formal, and the protocol statements (the methods) are mainly behavioristic (namely 'rating' of motivation on the basis of behavior in a hundred adolescents observed in social situations). The theory must therefore be classified as a *neutral-formal* theory, very close to becoming behavioristic (cf. for example p. 125).

Since the subject is, as mentioned, behavior in everyday social situations, the theory must be classified as a *molar* theory.

Among the main results of the study are descriptions of complicated interrelations between different hypothetical variables and between the hypothetical variables and the behavior, for which reason the theory must be classified as an extremely *dynamic or field-theoretical* theory (see p. 126).

All research-results concerning the relations between variables are formulated as correlations (of different kinds), and therefore the theory must be classified as *mainly statistical.* No anti-deterministic presuppositions have, however, been formulated (cf. p. 127) just as there are very few explicit meta-theoretical formulations about the other classifications of the theory. Briefly the theory can be described as *a classifying, constructive, neural-formal, molar, extremely dynamic, and mainly statistical theory*

The Content of the Theory

'*Drive*' is the most important variable—and the only *motivation* variable—in Frenkel-Brunswik's theory. It is defined in the following way (p. 133):

> 'We are using the term, "drive" for consistent tendencies manifest in alternative and even inconsistent behaviors.'

It can be seen quite clearly from the above quotation and from the article in general that 'drive' is a *hypothetical* variable, or, as Frenkel-Brunswik expresses it (p. 125): 'motivation is inferred and has the character of an explanatory construct.' It is also quite clear that 'drive' is a hypothetical variable of the *neutral-formal* type (cf. p. 128). But Frenkel-Brunswik writes nothing explicitly about whether 'drives' are to be considered disposition variables or as function variables. As Murray, from whom she has taken quite a few things, she uses 'drive' partly as a motivation variable explaining a current action, partly as a permanent personality variable; therefore 'drive' must be classified as *both a function variable and a disposition variable* in Frenkel-Brunswik's theory.

In her study Frenkel-Brunswik works with the following nine- drives, taken from Murray's list. She defines (p. 141):

'1) "Drive for Autonomy" (independence and freedom).
2) "Drive for Social Ties" (social acceptance).
3) "Drive for Achievement" (a high standard of objective accomplishment).
4) "Drive for Recognition" (praise, commendation, respect, social approval, and prestige).
5) "Drive for Abasement" (self-depreciation, self-blame or belittlement).
6) "Drive for Aggression" (to deprive others).
7) "Drive for Succorance" (support from outside).
8) "Drive for Control" (dominance).
9) "Drive for Escape" (to escape all unpleasant situations).'

Besides 'drive' Frenkel-Brunswik in a single chapter uses the variable 'trait' which is not, however, considered a motivation variable by Frenkel-Brunswik. Still, it is interesting to see her distinction between them. She writes (p. 225):

'On general grounds three types of data should be distinguished... One of them involves specific behavior; another involves the dynamics behind behavior which our drive ratings attempt to approach the abilities necessary to bring them about... The ratings introduced for this purpose we propose to call ratings for general traits.'

It is, moreover, explicitly pointed out that motivation or 'drives' are hypothetical variables of an even higher degree of abstraction than 'traits,' which are only empirical generalizations of a rather low degree of abstraction.

Hypotheses of Motivation

Frenkel-Brunswik's studies have resulted in a variety of correlations between different 'drives,' between 'drives' and special actions, and between 'drives' and 'traits.' Only the most general hypothesis will be reformulated here (cf. p. 218–223 and p. 261):

The five 'drives' for: Social Ties, Recognition, Aggression, Control, and Escape, form a dynamic system which can manifest itself either in the behavior-pattern 'overt social activity' or in 'emotional maladjustment.'

Conclusion

Besides the many empirical motivation psychological correlations Frenkel-Brunswik's article also contains some methodical results concerning 'rating', its dependence upon the personality of the psychologists, and its agreement with other methods of the questionnaire-type and the projective type (T. A. T.). Even though 'Motivation and Behavior' is thus of more empirical than theoretical interest, its inclusion in this study is justified by the fact that there are relatively few experimental studies of human beings in the psychology of motivation and expecially few which have such an abundance of quantitative results.

MASSERMAN'S THEORY

The Structure of the Theory

Part I of the book '*Principles of Dynamic Psychiatry*' (1946) by the American psychiatrist *Jules H. Masserman* contains much empirical material in the form of 'cases' and also experimental studies of neurotic behavior in cats, which he has also reproted on earlier in articles in periodicals and in a single book; the second part of the book presents a systematically formulated '*bio-dynamic*' (i. e. biological-dynamic) *theory* and a subsequent refutation of criticism. Finally it contains some appendixes on more special subjects.

With regard to level of development the theory must be characterized as *a deductive theory* as it is formulated in 4 principles and 19 corollaries. These corollaries are, however, not deduced in a strictly logical way from the four principles, but the theory forms an *axiomatized* system to the same extent as does Hull's theory. Masserman's theory is, however, not as extensive (a total of 24 hypotheses as compared to Hull's 167), neither has any mathematization or other symbolization been attempted. But a meta-theoretical formalization has been made to the same degree—but not to the same extent—as in Hull's theory, as 6 'criteria of biodynamics' are formulated before the presentation of the theory is begun.

As indicated by the name 'biodynamic,' Masserman's theory is an attempt to construct a theory on the basis of biology. The first of the above mentioned criteria deals with this question (p. 100):

'1. Its theory must be firmly rooted in biologic observation and must be compatible with established biologic principles.'

For this reason the theory must be classified as *mainly reductive*.

None of the criteria describe the character of the theory as being purely behavioristic, however, but that can clearly be seen from the book as a whole. Maybe it is said most explicitly in the discussion of the psychophysical problem, formulated by Masserman in following way (p. 169–70):

'explicitly a definition which may already have been recognized as implicit in all of biodynamic theory: namely, *the "problem" of mind-body dichotomy vanishes when "mind", from an operational standpoint, is regarded essentially as body in action.* Even introspectively, we can be "aware" of our own "minds" only through observing our *acts.*'

Since the protocol statements of the theory (its methods) are behavioristic and its (few) hypothetical variables have a physiological 'surplus meaning' the theory must, as mentioned, be classified as purely behavioristic.

Masserman points out (p. 102) that in his experimental studies he has changed the general method from one consisting mainly of physiological experiments (internal stimulation of hypothalamus, etc.) into 'a study of the total behavior of the animal' (p. 102). It can be seen from this and from the theory in general (cf. for example 'criteria' 3 to 4) that the theory must be classified as a *molar* theory.

Masserman maintains explicitly in Criteria 2 (p. 100) that:

'2. Biodynamics must deal with empiric observations of behavior in their context. This mean that its approach must be holistic... Similarly, the theory must transcend the spurious dichotomy of "organism versus environment", and instead consider the latter as selectively integrated into the organism's field of reaction.'

Consequently the theory must be classified as being *rather field-theoretical* (cf. also the description 'bio-*dynamic*').

I believe, without being able to support the assertion by quoting explicit, meta-theoretical formulations on the subject, that the theory must be classified as *deterministic,* as all principles and corollaries are (qualitative) deterministic hypotheses.

As a summary the bio-dynamic theory can be described as *a deductive, reductive, purely behavioristic, molar, rather field-theoretical, and deterministic theory.*

The Content of the Theory

The first of Masserman's 'biodynamic principles' is called 'The principle of *motivation.*' It is formulated as follows (p. 104):

'*Principle I:* Behavior is actuated by the physiologic needs of the organism and is directed toward the satisfaction of those needs.'

The most important motivation variable 'need' is explicitly defined in the following way in the 'Glossary' (p. 286):

'*need.* A physiological (metabolic) deficiency or imbalance translated dynamically into behavior.'

It can easily be seen from this that need here is an *empirical function variable.* The *reductive* character of the theory is stressed by the most important variable in the first hypothesis being an empirical-*physiological* variable. Principle I is, with regard to its content a version of the usual principle of homeostasis, and formally it belongs to the rather rare type of hypotheses: S $\rightarrow$ R. A differentiated representation of this can be found in the five first corollaries which will be quoted here (without comments) for later use in comparisons (p. 107):

'*Corollary 1.* Physiologic determinants of behavior are mainly "unconscious", but enter awareness when the need becomes acute, or when complex and highly organized patterns of adaptation are required by the milieu.

Corollary 2. 'Physiologic' needs may serve race survial in apparent contravention to that of the individual.

Corollary 3. The forms of behavior evoked vary with the nature and interplay of needs, whereas their complexity and effectiveness are contingent on the perceptive, integrative and expressive capacities of the organism.

Corollary 4. Behavior patterns may persist as a function of biologic organization after the original, direct physiologic determinants are in abeyance.

Corollary 5. Socially adaptive patterns often represent complexly contingent expressions of relatively simple needs.'

The second biodynamic principle is called 'The principle of environmental evaluation' and is formulated in the following way (p. 107):

Principle II: Behavior is contingent upon, and adaptive to, the organism's interpretation of total milieu, as based on its capacities and previous experiences.'

It is the second principle which especially shows the field-theoretical character of the theory because it formulates the fundamental interaction between the organism and the environment. A few hypothetical variables appear in this principle, namely 'interpretation' and 'capacities.' They must further be classified as a function variable and a disposition variable, respectively, although they are not explicitly defined (but they can hardly be taken to be motivation variables). Principle II must therefore be classified as an H→R-hypothesis.

For use in the later comparison the five corollaries to this principle will also be quoted (p. 112):

'*Corollary 1.* This principle has no metaphysical bearing on the "ultimate" or "real" nature of the universe, nor does it have teleologic or eschatologic import.

Corollary 2. An organism "recognizes" and reacts to only those stimuli (1) to which it is physiologically sensitive, and (2) which concern its needs.

Corollary 3. "Masochistic" behavior may be manifested by an organism when such behavior mediates the accustomed satisfaction of concealed needs.

Corollary 4. The interpretations of stimuli may be spread by experiential association to related configurations and thus predetermine generalizations of "meaning" and attitude.

Corollary 5. This spread is manifested socially in the sphere of "interpersonal" relationships and in the clinical phenomena of transference.'

While the two first principles are fundamental, general-psychological and motivational-theoretical principles, the following one concerns abnormal psychology. It is called 'The principle of substitution' and is formulated in the following way (p. 113):

'*Principle III.* Behavior patterns tend to become deviated or fragmented under stress and, when further frustrated, tend toward substitutive and symbolic satisfaction.'

It can be seen from this hypothesis that 'stress' in the bio-dynamic theory equals 'frustration,' which is defined explicitly in 'Glossary' (p. 277) in the following way: '*Frustration.* Prevention of attainment and satisfaction.' Thus *frustration* is an external, *empirical variable*, and Principle III it therefore one of the rather rare S→R-hypotheses.

As the corollaries to this principles are of motivation-theoretical interest they will be quoted here (p. 121):

'The following corollaries may, then, be appended to the biodynamic principle of substitutive behavior:

Corollary 1. The substitution of behavior patterns is facilitated by the partial interdependency of bodily needs and interchangeability in their modes of satisfaction.

Corollary 2. The minimal hedonic level is contingent on variable personal, cultural and intercurrent factors.

Corollary 3. When end-goals are difficult of attainment energy is directed toward proximate or subsidiary goals.

Corollary 4. In circumstances of frustration, part-satisfactions may serve symbolically in lieu of total consummatory patterns.

Corollary 5. Under such circumstances conative energies may also be deviated into substitutive aggressivity. This phenomenon, however, cannot be directly translated into terms of group behavior.'

The fourth biodynamic principle is called 'Principle of conflict' and is formulated in the following way:

'*Principle IV: When, in a given millieu, two or more motivations come in conflict in the sense that their accustomed consummatory patterns are partially or wholly incompatible, kinetic tension (anxiety) mounts and behavior becomes hesitant, vacillating, erratic and poorly adaptive (i. e., neurotic) or excessively substitutive or symbolic (i. e. "psychotic").*'

As can be seen, this principle does not contain any hypothetical variables either, as '*conflict*' and '*anxiety*' must be regarded as *empirical* behavior variables or maybe rather: behavior-determined empirical variables ('response-produced stimuli'). This means that, with the exception of the few hypothetical variables in 'Principle II' (which were not motivation variables), *the four biodynamic principles are exclusively empirical hypotheses* (which proves that the classification of the theory as a reductive and purely behavioristic theory is correct).

Furthermore it is interesting to see that Masserman distinguishes in Principles III and IV between the effect of 'frustration' and the effect of 'conflict' on behavior. A clear distinction has not always been made between these two sets of conditions and their dependent behavior. Masserman bases the distinction—as well as Principles III and IV with their corollaries—upon his extensive experiments on cats.

The four corollaries belonging to Principle IV (p. 151) are only of interest for the theory and therapy of neuroses, and therefore they will not be quoted here.

Conclusion

Masserman's theory has been dealt with rather thoroughly because it is one of the theories which has reached the highest degree of formal development. It compares in this respect with the theories of Hull and Lewin. The theory is, however, less extensive and not as general-psychological as the other two theories. The bio-dynamic theory is also interesting as a conscious attempt to form a synthesis of reflexological and behavioristic ('bio-') theories and psychoanalytical ('-dynamic') theories. In other words, Masserman's theory is what I have previously called a 'unifying' theory[2a]).

FREEMAN'S THEORY

The Structure of the Theory

The American psychologist *G. L. Freeman*, who has previously written a textbook of 'Physiological Psychology' (1948) and made a series of experiments within this field, has made a summary of his more theoretical considerations in a book entitled: '*The Energetics of Human Behavior*' (1948)[2b]).

The book contains a number of explicitly formulated definitions and hypotheses (for example p. 220–221 and p. 221), but no attempt is made to axiomatize it. It must therefore, as many of the other theories, be placed *between classifying and deductive theories.*

The theory must, however, clearly be classified as a *reductive* theory. The title of the book and a large number of explicit formulations show this. Thus it is said (p. 32):

'*homeostasis* provide an essential integrating principle for tying psychology to physiology.'

It is easy to classify the theory as a *purely behavioristic* theory, as the hypothetical variables are interpreted with an exclusively physiological 'surplus meaning', and the protocol statements (the methods) used are purely behavioristic. The book contains many arguments against introspective, mentalistic psychology and against different forms of psycho-physical dualism, and there is also a very detailed argumentation in favour of 'somatic determinism' for the reason (p. 11):

'that somatic determinism is a philosophical view consistent with behavioristic theory, and that its adoption implies the availability of objective methods for attacking phenomena usually recognized by their conscious aspects.'

'The Psychosomatic Relationship' is discussed in an appendix (p. 310–24).

It is, however, a little more difficult to classify the theory as molar or molecular. On the one hand he accepts the definition of psychology as the science of 'the behavior of the organism as a whole' (p. 4), but on the other hand he maintains that macroscopic phenomena can most efficiently be solved through the study of 'the interaction of microscopically revealed parts' (p. 24). Most of the empirical

---

2a) Masserman's book appeared in a 2nd edition in 1961. The new edition contains a considerable amount of new illustrative material (among other things, an appendix about Ethology), but there are only very slight, stylistic changes in the principles and corrollaries of his 'bio-dynamic' theory. Therefore it is not necessary to deal further with the book here.

2b) Cornell University Press. New York.

material in the book is about individual muscular movements, so it must be most correct to classify it as a *mainly molecular* theory.

It can already be seen from the above that the theory emphasizes the 'interaction of part processes' (p. 21), for which reason it must be classified as being *extremely dynamic*. Freeman also finds (p. 5) that a theory of his type will make the 'field theories' of the Gestalt psychologists superfluous.

From the term 'somatic determinism' it can be seen that the theory is an *deterministic* theory.

The diagram p. 50 (and perhaps the diagram p. 267) can be considered to be *an illustrative model* of the theory.

In summary *Freeman's* theory can be described as an *almost deductive, reductive, purely behavioristic, molecular, extremely dynamic, and deterministic theory.*

The Content of the Theory

The theory is a rather exceptional, systematic utilization of '*the principle of homeostatis.*' Thus it is stressed already on p. 1 that the 'basic thesis' of the theory is:

'that all behavior is an attempt to preserve organismic integrity by 'homeostatic' restorations of equilibrium.'

And this is pointed out time and again in different ways (p. 321, 339, etc.). Freeman's classification of the organs of the body in two systems according to their function is also of motivation-theoretical interest: 1) 'the digestive-circulatory system as a source of energy' (p. 52), and 2) 'the neuromuscular system,' which is control mechanism' (p. 52).

The cooperation of these systems is stressed in a fundamental hypothesis (p. 66–67):

'the focal response discharge is always the product of stimulus induced excitation and the background energy condition already present.'

The book also includes a large number of general formulations of experimental studies on the transformation of energy in the organism in connection with behavior.

The following are the most important motivation variables:

'*The Arousal Index*,' defined (p. 101) as 'a construct dealing with excitability.'

'*The Discharge Index*,' which is 'a construct dealing with activity.'

Both are—as can be seen from the definitions—*hypothetical, physiologically interpreted function variables.*

Chapter V deals also with '*Motivations*' (p. 129–172). Here it is pointed out that 'all total behavior is motivated at least in the sense of relieving some organic displacement' (p. 132). But as the organism develops and learns to control the environment it reacts not only toward disturbances of the *internal homeostasis,* but also toward changes in the *external situation* which threaten the internal homeostasis. It is especially true that 'higher organisms at least tend to maintain constant states outside the body as well as inside' (p. 146).

In Chapter V problems such as 'compulsive behavior', 'reaction to frustration', and 'conflict in motivated behavior' are dealt with.

Freeman introduces an interesting distinction in Chapter VII (p. 202) in the following way:

'The homeostatic view-point concedes only two distinctly different types of total functional activity. One covers the non-discriminatory generalized emergency adjustments of emotion. The other cover the highly discriminatory specifically adaptive adjustments of perception and thought.'

Besides this fundamental classification Freeman distinguishes between two sub-groups within the last class. He writes (p. 213):

'We need to think of specific adaptive behavior as due to the interaction of two distinct central nervous factors, one (discriminative capacity) operating primarily on the sensory side, the other (discharge control) operating primarily on the motor side.'

A fundamental variable, 'set,' belongs to this last class, and it is defined in the following way (p. 220):

'Set-expectancies are tentative and antecedent homeostatic adjustment acts, developed in response to minimally displacing stimulus cues and preparing the channelization of discharge through some particular response outlets which, if not so prepared, would function only through a greater displacement to general equilibrium.'

As can be seen, this variable is also *a hypothetical function variable.*

Freeman's classification can be summarized in the following way:

Behavior {
a. *emotional reaction*
(strongly motivated, exclusively *autonomically* regulated reactions).
b. *discriminating reaction*
(motivated, but also cortically regulated through
1. sensoric processes (perception and thinking).
2. motoric-controlling processes (set-expectancy).

It would, however, lead to far to quote and analyze the more special hypotheses (p. 220–221 and p. 229) and Freeman's application of his theory to the psychology of personality (Chapter VIII) and psychopatology (Chapter IX).

Conclusion

I hope it is quite clearly indicated in the above—in spite of the brief analysis—that Freeman's theory is an original and systematic '*homeostasis*'*-theory*, which temporarily has only limited possibilities of application.

MOORE'S THEORY

The Structure of the Theory

The American psychologist and psychiatrist *Thomas Verner Moore* has given a revised synthesis of his earlier works in psychology and psychiatry in '*The Driving Forces of Human Nature*' (*1948*)[3]). The book is interesting because it differs widely from all the other books which have been analyzed here.

With regard to the level of development the theory is definitely a *classifying theory*, but its classifications are formed in an exceptionally systematical way.

The theory must be classified as being *constructive*, as it contains strong arguments against any attempt to reduce psychology to physiology (for example p. 6 and in the chapter on the development of psychology in America).

What makes the theory most remarkable is the fact that it must be classified as *extremely mentalistic*. Its hypothetical variables are explicit, with mentalistic 'surplus meaning' and its methods or protocol statements are mainly introspective. Moreover, a dualistic, psycho-physical hypothesis is explicitly presupposed. Thus he writes about *unconscious* concepts (p. 70):

> 'They cannot be chemical deposits in the nervous system. They are not physical but spiritual in nature. We may use the broad term "psychic" to designate them. When they are no longer present in consciousness they are unconscious. We may say that they exist as traces, but the term trace must be broadened to embrace psychic traces.'

The theory must be classified as being *molar*, as Moore will not study isolated 'states of consciousness' but 'mental mechanisms of behavior which are manifested by individual human beings' (p. 6), i. e. not 'microscopic' detail-processes, but 'macroscopic' units.

Being neither extremely mechanistic, nor extremely field-theoretical, the theory must be classified as being *mainly dynamic*; yet it may be more mechanistic than field theoretical, since 'elements' and their synthesis play an important part in the theory.

Moore's theory is also extraordinary with regard to the last classification. There is a whole chapter (the last chapter) about 'Formal Causality and the Philosophy of Nature'; moreover there is a chapter (Chapter 28) about 'The Philosophy of Will' which also mainly deals with the principle of causality.

Moore has several classifications of causality. 'Causes' are classified as:

a. 1) intrinsic, and 2) extrinsic.
b. 1) material, and 2 formative.
c. 1) efficient, and 2) final.
d. 1) mechanistic, and 2) psychic.

It is very difficult to understand the connection between these classifications because Moore does not give a combined classification. Only the three first ones are in Chapter 28 (p. 335–336) presented as being related in the following way:

a. intrinsic causes:
  1. material.

---

3) Grune and Stratton, New York 1948.

   2. formative (organizing).

b. extrinsic causes:

   1. efficient.
   2. final (= 'an end perceived by an individual which appeals to him as worthy of attainment).

But late (p. 339) the distinction between 'mechanistic' and 'psychic' is introduced without being placed in relation to the others. 'Psychic' is apparently used synonymously with 'final'; but in the last chapter it is apparently also used synonymously with 'formative' (at any rate when the discussion is about Man). But no matter how this is to be understood 'psychic' and 'final' causes are used in such a way that *a strict philosophical determinism can be united with a free will in Man,* because 'final' (and 'psychic') causes are being characterized in the following way (p. 336):

'The final cause is not an efficient cause and does not therefore force the choice by absolute necessity.'

Thus one cannot classify Moore's theory as deterministic or statistical, partly because his 'absolute necessity' is *not* identical with the determinism which characterizes the theories belonging to this class, partly because his 'final cause' and 'free-volition' are *not* identical with the statistical hypotheses which appear in some psychological theories. As a result Moore's theory cannot be classified as an intermediate class including both deterministic and statistical hypotheses, because his determinism is more speculatively absolute than are the hypotheses of these theories, and his 'final causes' are more indeterministic than the statistical hypotheses of these theories.

In summary Moore's theory can be described as *a classifying, constructive, mentalistic, molar, dynamic, and indefinable deterministic-indeterministic theory.*

The Content of the Theory

The extensive and differentiated system of classification in Moore's theory is of the greatest interest to this study. It can be presented (p. 106) in the following way:

'Elements of Mind'

I. Mental functions:

- A. Reception.
  - 1. Attention.
  - 2. Perception.
    - a. Sensory.
    - b. Intellectual.
- B. Construction.
  - 1. Association.
  - 2. Judgment.
  - 3. Reason.
- C. Conservation.
  - 1. Sensory.
  - 2. Intellectual.

II. Mental Products:

A. Representative, *actions* of consciousness.
  1. Sensory.
    a. External sensations.
    b. Internal images (phantasms).
  2. Intellectual-abstract ideas.

B. Appetitive, *reactions* of consciousness:
  1. Necessary.
    a. Affective.
      1. Feeling.
      2. Emotion.
    b. Conative.
      1. Impulsive.
      2. Desire.
      3. (Instinct).
  2. Free (act of will).

III. Mental dispositions:

A. General.
  1. Temperament (native).
  2. Character (acquired, result of voluntary action).

B. Special – Habits.
  1. Good – virtues.
  1. Indifferent.
  3. Bad – vices.

As can be seen from the above, the classification is to a high degree characterized by the mentalistic structure of the theory. This is first of all shown by the fact that the classification is divided into *three*, as he in addition to 'functions' and 'dispositions'—both corresponding to the classifications used in this book—includes 'products', which thus only contain the phenomenological manifestations of functions and dispositions—not the behavioristic. The classification is also extraordinary in its thorough separation of 'sensoric and 'intellectual' and in its unusual classification of 'habits' as good, indifferent, and bad habits. Thus an evaluati on based upon moral points of view is used as basis for the classification.

Moore points out in the text under the table that 'In dynamic psychology we consider only one group of these elements—the reactions of consciousness.' Of these the *conative* reactions (impulses, desire, and instinct) are of special interest for the present analysis, and they will therefore be dealt with in detail; the affective reactions are of less interest, and 'free acts of will' have already been dealt with sufficiently above.

Chapter 18 deals with 'Instinct and Impulse.' After a long analysis of the principle of instinct in which Moore—as in the other chapters—frequently quotes older philosophers, often from antiquity and especially from the Middle Ages, he reaches the following definition of instinctive behavior: '*the behavior of the individual acting as a unit organism*, directing itself to an end of importance but without conscious design or intentional adaptation of means to ends' (p. 233).

With the first part of the definition Moore wants to seperate instinctive behavior from pure reflex movements which are considered to belong to physiology. Moore adds that 'using the term in this sense there is no such thing as instinctive behavior in Man' (p. 233).

Later he writes (p. 235):

'The closest approach to it is a certain type of drive that is experienced and to which we give the term *impulse*.'

Later Moore defines this variable even more explicitly (p. 236):

'... define an impulse as a tendency that we experience in the presence of an actual opportunity, to make use of any one of our human abilities.'

It can be seen from the definition that 'impulse' must be classified as *a phenomenologically interpreted, hypothetical function variable.*

In the following chapter the variable 'desire' is defined thus (p. 243):

'The resultant of an impulse that is not or cannot be carried out is "desire".'

And later explicitly (p. 244):

'A desire is a craving that we experience to seek or produce a situation in which impulsive tendencies may be satisfied or natural wants may be supplied.' Maybe 'desire' can be redefined as 'a frustrated impulse.'

While 'impulse' is mainly used about tendencies to use our *sensoric* and *motoric* 'abilities', Moore introduces (p. 268) a new term for 'the tendency of the mind to adjust itself to pleasant and unpleasant situations', namely '*psycho-taxis*'. In other words, this variable is *an emotional impulse.* Moore classifies 'psycho-taxis' as positive and negative. Defense mechanisms are placed under psycho-taxis. If they develop in an abnormal or pathological way they are called '*parataxis*'.

There is not room here to attempt to formulate explicitly the many implicit hypotheses which can be found in the book.

Conclusion

As can be seen from the above, Moore's theory is very peculiar when compared to the other theories examined here. But is cannot be said that if is particularly original, because to a large extent it is a modern, systematical reformulation of an older, speculative-philosophical 'psychology'.

MAIER'S THEORY

The Structure of the Theory

In his book '*Frustration*—The Study of Behavior without a Goal' (1949) the American psychologist *Norman R. F. Maier* presents a summary of the results of year-long experimental studies of 'abnormal behavior in rats' earlier published in a long series of articles in periodicals. As the book contains some points of interest for motivation psychology it will be analyzed here.

The theory contains a number of implicit hypotheses in its definitions and classifications, but no explicit formulation or systematization of the hypotheses has been made, for which reason the theory must be described as *classifying*.

As the theory is an attempt to explain abnormal behavior (also neurotic symptoms) on the basis of experiments with animals and without the use of hypothetical constructions such as 'subconsciousness', etc., it must be classified as a *reductive* theory.

Maier writes (p. 154) about the experiments with animals that they are less repressed by 'mentalistic concepts and introspective reports, which are often vague and spotted with rationalizations'.—As this attitude to mentalistic, hypothetical variables and introspective method characterizes the whole theory, it must be described as being *purely behavioristic.*

As the behavior described and explained in Maier's theory is rather 'macroscopic,' it must be classified as being *rather molar.*

Maier writes (p. 166):

'Since the organism has a variety of needs and is stimulated by any objects with differing degrees of repelling and attracting properties (which vary with the needs of the organism), the behavior expressed on any given occasion is the resultant of many forces.'

As this fact characterizes the theory, it must be classified as being *extremely dynamic,* maybe even field-theoretical.

Without any doubt the theory must be described as being *deterministic.*

In summary *Maier's theory* can be described as a *classifying, reductive, purely behavioristic, rather molar, extremely dynamic, and deterministic theory.*

The Content of the Theory

In spite of the fact that Maier's book first of all deals with 'frustration'—it is, as far as I know, the most thorough experimental and theoretical analysis of this phenomenon—it also contains something about 'motivation' as these two factors are often closely related.

Maier's experiments with rats have led to the formulation of 'the hypothesis which states that motivation and frustration are qualitative different instigators of behavior and must therefore be described by different behavior principles' (p. 93).

It is therefore interesting to see how Maier defines these two variables.

He writes (p. 93):

'we shall use the term *motivation* to characterize the process by which the expression of behavior is determined or its future expression is influenced by consequencies to which such behavior leads.'

And later he writes in more detail (p. 96):

'According to the limited usage given the concept of motivation, it can be said that motivated behavior is controlled by both an internal and an external condition. Thus a need or a desire is always within the organism, whereas the incentive or goal is outside. Either condition may be present without the other and produce stimulus-response behavior, but both are essential for creating the state of motivation which selectively arouses behavior that may be called goal oriented. Behavior called forth by the state of motivation tends to relieve the internal condition and this in turn leads to satisfaction. So-called "adaptive behavior" is characterized by the fact that it leads to a reduction in need.'

As shown by the two quotations 'motivation' is either a description of a hypothetical variable ('the process' in the first quotation) or a generic term for those variables which determine motivated behavior (as in the second quotation). These variables are (cf. the second quotation) 'need' and 'incentive or goal.' They are not explicitly defined, but the connection indicates that they are *empirical function variables*.. As both—according to Maier's definitions—are necessary for the existence of *motivated or purposive behavior* this can only be *learned* behavior or *problem-solving behavior*. If only the goal (the external stimulus) is present, reflective behavior will be the only result, and if only 'need' is present, '*random behavior*' will occur. This last form of behavior together with *instinctive behavior* is by Maier not considered as being '*motivated behavior*,' which thus only includes learned and problem-solving behavior. The motivated or purposive behavior is further characterized by being *variable* or *plastic*, i. e. the consequences of the behavior modify future appearances of the same form of behavior.

The other important variable 'frustration' is defined in the following way (p. 94):

'We shall use the term *frustration* to characterize the process whereby the selection of behavior is determined by forces other than goals or mere neural connections. We have seen that availability is one of the basic forces that determines the behavior expressed in frustration.'

Later Maier gives a more direct description and explanation of 'frustration' as a sort of insoluble problem situation (p. 128):

'Thus the conditions leading to frustration are those which arouse behaviors which are directed away from objects but which fail to achieve escape. When positive incentives are present, however, an outlet for behavior is present, in that some specific positive activity, at least, is being stimulated. When only negative stimuli are present the motivation situation is such that it permits only a choice between the lesser of several evils. If the alternatives are strongly negative and the outlets for behaviors are sufficiently blocked, unresolved conflict is aroused. This type of conflict builds up tensions, and it is the accumulations of these tensions that institute the condition of frustration.'

In other words, Maier limits the frustrating *situation* to an *insoluble negative conflict situation;* and the state determined by frustration is defined as 'accumulation of tension', which must be classified as a *physiologically interpreted hypothetical function variable*.

As Maier has previously pointed out there is, as shown by his experiments, a qualitative difference between motivated behavior and *behavior determined by frustration*. The latter is described at different places in the book as *non-purposive* ('behavior without a goal') and *abnormally fixated*. That it is abnormally shown by *forced repetition*, and indifference to the *poor adjustment effectivity* of the consequences. The only effect or biological function of the frustrated behavior is that it is *tension-reducing*.

The only kind of frustration behavior which could appear in Maier's own experiment—because of the very limited experimental situation (Lashley's 'jumping apparatus')—was *abnormally fixated behavior*. But on the basis of the experiments made by other psychologists he generalizes his theory so it also includes *aggressive behavior* (Dollard et. al.: 'Frustration and Aggression' 1939), *regressive behavior* (Barker, Dembo, and Lewin: 'Frustration and Regression' 1941), and *resignation* and *neuroses*, which are considered *permanent final states* in a development determined by frustration (cf. p. 113–114). Also '*fear*' is explained as 'a conflict between the motivation and frustration processes' in Maier's theory (p. 133).

It would lead too far to deal with Maier's application of his theory to the therapy process here, or his interesting analysis of punishment and reward. The latter Maier sums up excellently in the following statement (p. 214):

'In general, reward has the effect of positive motivation. Punishment is its opposite only if motivation is maintained. Punishment also can serve as a frustrating agent...'

Conclusion

Maier's theory shows—as does Masserman's—that it is possible on the basis of *exact and objective experiments with animals* to formulate a theory, and that such theories can also be used to explain *human behavior*, even in a *practical and fruitful way*.

CATTELL'S THEORY

The Structure of the Theory

The American psychologist *Raymond B. Cattell* has—besides a few earlier books and a number of articles in periodicals—presented an extensive psychological theory in '*Personality—A Systematic Theoretical and Factual Study*' 1950—a synthesis of factor theories and psychoanalytical theories. After four chapters on methods—especially on statistical and factor-analytical methods—and one chapter on the influence of heredity and environment upon the personality follow four rather large chapters on 'Psychodynamics' dealing with motivation. Then come chapters on psychosomatics, personality and culture, abnormal and maladjusted development of personality, and stages of development. Finally there is a chapter which formulates 'Principles of Personality Formation'.

With regard to level and development Cattell's theory may be placed *between classifying and deductive* theories because—as mentioned—it formulates a number of explicit hypotheses ('laws'), but they are not logically systematized (axiomatized).

As the character of the theory is factor-analytical, it must be classified as a *constructive* (non-reductive) theory.

In the classification mentalistic versus behavioristic theories Cattell's theory may be characterized as an intermediate form: *a neutral-formal theory*, as he uses both introspective and behavioristic methods (protocol statements)—but mainly behavioristic—and also hypothetical constructions of explicitly neutral-formal character.

It is very difficult to classify Cattell's theory as molecular or molar as it includes the whole area from microscopic, physiological processes to macroscopic reactions between the individual and its (social) environment. But since most of the book is about the latter the theory may be characterized as a *mainly molar theory*.

The theory is, as mentioned, of psychoanalytical character, and it is therefore understandable that it should be classified as an extremely *dynamic* theory. (At several places Cattell stresses how dependent the individual *factors and sub-systems* are upon the whole: the personality).

It is more difficult to place it in the classification statistical versus deterministic theories; but, as or example indicated by the last hypothesis, it is probably most correct to characterize it as a theory which *in practice is statistical* (formulating statistical correlations), but *which in principle is deterministic* (the correlations are taken to be expressions of functional relations). Cattell's view upon this point is not very different from the one presented in Chapter 3.

Cattell's diagram (no. 27, p. 158) presenting 'a dynamic lattice' can be taken as an illustrative *model* of his theory. But his diagram (no. 41, p. 258) representing 'crossroads in the total adjustment process' is also important.

In summary *Cattell's theory* can be described as an *almost deductive, constructive, mainly molar, neutral-formal, dynamic, and mainly statistical theory.*

The Content of the Theory

Cattell classifies all psychological variables ('factors' or 'traits') in three groups: 'temperament-traits,' 'ability-traits,' and 'dynamic-traits.' Every action is an expression of or is determined by cooperation between all three kinds of 'traits', but to varying degrees. They can be defined by their methods of measurement. 'Ability-traits' vary especially with the complexity of the situation, 'dynamic-traits' vary especially with the incentives of the situation, and 'temperament-traits' vary very little with the external situation.

The dynamic traits can be classified as '*attitudes*', '*sentiments*', and '*ergs*' ('drives') which are structured in a 'dynamic lattice' in the following way (p. 176):

'In the dynamic lattice attitudes tend to be subsidiated to sentiments and sentiments to basic biological drives, but all subsidiation is divergent as well as convergent and includes many "instances" of "retrofluxion".'

As can be seen from the above 'basic biological drives' are the fundamental source of energy in the dynamic structure. Cattell calls them '*ergs*,' and he defines them in the following way (p. 199):

'An innate psycho-physical disposition which permits its possessor to acquire reactivity (attention, recognition) to certain classes of objects more readily than others, to experience a specific emotion in regard to them, and to start on a course of action which ceases more completely at a certain specific goal activity than at any other. The pattern includes also preferred behavior subsidiation paths to the preferred goal.'

When the above definition and McDougall's definition of 'propensities' are compared it is easily seen that Cattell has copied McDougall—and for explcit reasons. 'Ergs'—like 'propensities'—are *hypothetical* variables of the *neutral-formal* type manifesting itself both subjectively ('experience a specific emotion') and objectively ('a course of action'). And like 'propensities', 'ergs' are explicitly defined as *disposition* variables, but contrary to McDougall Cattell has no corresponding function variables (such as McDougall's 'tendencies'), because Cattell's other motivation variables or 'dynamic traits', namely 'attitudes' and 'sentiments', are also disposition variables. Furthermore Cattell has the same number of innate 'ergs' as McDougall has 'propensities, sixteen in all, appetitive and non-appetitive, in the mature human being, namely: 'escape, appeal, acquisitiveness, laughter, pugnacity, self-assertion, sleep, play, self-abasement, mating, gregariousness, parental drive, curiosity, construction, disgust, and hunger'. And Cattell maintains, in an attempt to make a synthesis of McDougall's and Freud's classifications, that these sixteen 'matured forms of drives' are differentiated (through maturation) from Freud's four 'instincts': hunger, libido, aggression, and anxiety.

Through learning processes and determined by unsatisfied 'ergs' (Cattell works with an extended 'law of effect' which also includes conditioning) a number of learned 'dynamic traits' develop, namely '*sentiments*' and '*attitudes*.' The variable 'sentiment' is defined in the following way (p. 161):

'For the present it suffices to define sentiments as major acquired dynamic trait structures.'

And the variable '*attitude*' is defined thus (p. 161):

'what we usually measure in attitude tests is a minor sentiment.'

The above definitions show that Cattell also on this point builds upon McDougall's (and Shand's) theories of sentiments. These are, as previously mentioned, *neutral-formal hypothetical disposition variables* according to the definition, and as Cattell does not define other than the three 'dynamic traits' mentioned here, his theory lacks function variables. This may partly be explained by the fact that Cattell's theory is a theory of personality and thus does not need function variables as much as does a theory of *behavior*. Maybe it is also partly explained by the fact that Cattell actually uses his terms 'erg,' 'sentiment,' and 'attitude' for both disposition variables, which they describe explicitly, and for the corresponding function variables.

In his theory Cattell also introduces the psychoanalytical terms 'id,' 'ego', and 'superego', using 'id' as a generic term for all 'ergs'; 'ego' and 'superego' are used to describe superior sentiment-structures.

In the last two chapters on 'psychodynamics' Cattell gives a very detailed and systematical presentation of the *adjustment-process* as a series of phases or 'dynamic crossroads,' each indicating the possible forms of reaction which arise when a 'drive' is activated, when it is frustrated, and when the frustration determines 'anxiety,' 'repression,' etc.

Hypotheses

Finally it should again be pointed out that Cattell in the last chapter has formulated 17 hypotheses ('laws') in which his whole theory is concentrated. Some of these hypotheses are motivation hypotheses. There is not room to quote or analyze them here, but the motivation hypotheses are listed below:

'Law 1. The law of innate goal tension patterns' (p. 633).

'Law 2. The law of satisfaction in rigidity' (p. 635).
'Law 3. Law of dispersion with excitement and deprivation' (p. 635).
'Law 4. Law of dynamic effect' (p. 635).
'Law 5. The law of alternating expression in naive conflict' (p. 637).
'Law 6. The law of suppressive mechanisms in permanent conflict' (p. 638).
'Law 7. Law of the nature and conditions of repression in permanent conflict' (p. 639).
'Law 8. Law of consequences of blocking complete failure of expression' (p. 640).
'Law 9. Law of combined expression' (p. 640).

The rest of the 'laws' are not special motivation hypotheses, rather hypotheses about the development of the personality structure and its dependence upon the biological and social context (Law 17).

Conclusion

Everything taken into consideration, Cattell's theory must be described as a rather systematical and exact theory which in my opinion is a theoretically and empirically fruitful synthesis of factor-analysis and dynamic psychology (Freud and McDougall)[4]).

FRENCH'S THEORY

The Structure of the Theory

The American psycho-analyst *Thomas M. French*, who has earlier published a long series of articles and contributions to symposia, began in 1952 to publish a larger work in four volumes with the common heading '*The Integration of Behavior*.' Only vol. I.: 'Basic Postulates', will be dealt with here. The other volumes are planned to more special subjects as for example dreams, neuroses, etc.

As the theory contains a number of explicitly formulated hypotheses ('a basic postulate' and some 'propositions'), and as moreover in one case (p. 64) a real logical deduction of one hypothesis from two others can be found, the theory must be described as being *partly deductive*. No real axiomatization or mathematization or other kinds of symbolization has been attempted, however, neither is there any formalized presentation of a meta-theory.

French writes about the importance of neuro-physiology in psychology (p. 11):

'most of us expect that a neurophysiological explanation of behavior will ultimately be found... It will be along time before we can describe in detail what happens in the brain while an animal is trying to achieve a particular goal. Fortunately, we can study this problem in two stages. We can make a dynamic analysis before we try to localize anatomically what occurs.'

---

[4]) *Cattell* has since this book first appeared produced several papers and two books: 'Personality and Motivation: Structure and Measurement (N.Y., 1957) and 'The Scientific Analysis of Personality' (1965). In order to deal with this important production in a fair and thorough manner the present author has decided to write a whole new chapter about Cattell's theory in the forthcoming book: 'Modern Theories of Motivation' (in press).

The two stages mentioned here are probably the constructive and the reductive stages. On the basis of this and the other statements in the theory I think that it it must be classified as a *constructive* theory.

About the methods of psychology French writes explicitly (p. 22):

'Subjective impressions may suggest valuable hypotheses, but they must be critically examined and tested before they can safely be accepted. However the resolute turning-away from subjective data has become a dogma in some circles is an overreaction against an earlier phase in the history of psychology.'

Thus French holds a positive attitude towards both behavioristic and introspective methods, although he most often uses the latter kind, and as his hypothetical variables are mainly neutral-formal, the theory must be classified as *neutral-formal.*

The only thing French writes explicitly which bears upon placing the theory in the next classification is the following (p. 38): 'these are primarily clinical studies', and as the theory mainly deals with the daily actions of the patients —and with their dreams about them—it must be described as *molar*.

It is explicitly stressed (p. 5) that a person's 'behavior is determined by two factors', namely the personality and the situation at hand. And further down the page it says:

'we attempt to resolve the determinants of behavior into components factors. We also try to reconstruct how these factors have combined to produce different kinds of behavior.'

As the hypotheses of the theory most often deal with several interacting variables, it must be described as an *extremely dynamic,* although not exactly field-theoretical, theory.

Although there are no explicit, meta-theoretical statements on the subject, there is no doubt that the theory must be classified as *deterministic*.

In conclusion, French's theory can be described as a *deductive, constructive, neutral-formal, molar, extremely dynamic, and deterministic theory*.

The Content of the Theory

French mentions and formulates a fundamental hypothesis several times. Already in the preface he writes (p. V):

'We assume as our working hypothesis that rational behavior and neurosis and dreams have much in common and that in irrational behavior we should find fragments of the integrative mechanism that we postulate to account for rational behavior.'

Even though the main purpose of the theory thus is to explain the processes of integration (cf. the title of the book) or 'insight'—as it is also more informally called—French is of course quite aware of the fundamental importance of motivation. Thus he writes (p. 6):

'it is impossible to understand most behavior unless we discover its motives'

and furthermore that

'like normal rational behavior, neuroses and dreams, too, are motivated by whishes.'

French also stresses the principle of 'homeostasis,' although he does not consider it the most fundamental. Thus writes (p. 10) that '"homeostasis" is the goal of a great many internal regulatory patterns of reaction.'

'Need' and 'hope,' French's most important motivation variables, are defined in the following way (p. 50):

'We should distinguish between motivating pressures according to the nature of their goals. Some motivating pressures have only negative goals... These states of unrest we call "needs" or "drives"; they are characterized by painful subjective "tension" which tends to seek discharge in diffuse muscular activity... Other wishes arise out of hopes... The goals of such wishes are positive. They are wishes for something, not wishes to get away from something.'

Thus French uses the word 'wishes' as a generic term for negative 'needs' and positive 'hopes.' (It is a distinction which strongly resembles McClelland's distinction between positive 'needs' and negative 'fears,'—but here 'need' is used with the opposite meaning.)

It is further quite clear that 'wishes,' 'needs,' and 'hopes' are *neutral-formal hypothetical* variables. French writes explicitly about this:

'The motives of another person cannot be observed directly. They have to be inferred from the observed person's behavior' (p. 44),

and later about motives:

'They happen to be theoretical constructs that even common sense uses, but they are, nonetheless theoretical constructs' (p. 45).

The motivation variables are for the most part *function* variables, but French writes (p. 45) that 'the basic motivational patterns underlying behavior do not change so frequently and so completely,' so there is also a tendency to regard them as disposition variables.

Later French makes another interesting distinction. He writes (p. 135):

'We can trace back the motives of behavior to two sets of interacting factors: (1) to the needs of the organism as a whole and (2) to delight in functional activity for its own sake.'

He adds that the biological needs are 'unpleasant,' while 'functional activity' is 'pleasurable'. Besides these explicit definition (and classifications) French's theory also contains—as mentioned —a number of explicit hypotheses. Only the most essential can be presented here, however.

The fundamental interaction between motivation and 'integration' (or 'insight') is formulated in the following way (p. 53):

'We summarize the process of activation of goal-directed behavior: First, the motivating pressure of a need seeks discharge in diffuse motor activity. Next, hope of satisfaction, based on present opportunity and on memories of previous success, stimulates the integrative mechanism to form a plan for realizing this hope. Finally, hope of satisfaction activates this plan so that it exerts a guiding influence, concentrating motor discharge on efforts to put the plan into execution.'

Later on French applies the same fundamental variables and hypotheses to the dream-process. He writes (p. 58):

'It is not only while we are awake that behavior is polarized between needs and hopes. The same polarization continues also in our dreams.'

French formulates two of his most important hypotheses about the interaction between motivation and integration in the following way (p. 62):

'1. Motivating pressure in excess of a certain maximum results in disintegration of the patterns of goal-directed behavior.'

'2. Hope of success increases the amount of pressure that can be withstood before disintegration of goal-directed efforts begins.'

About '*frustration*', which is defined as the 'realization that a goal to which one is commited is unattainable' (p. 125), the following summarizing hypothesis is formulated (p. 125):

'Reactions to an obstacle in the path of a goal-directed striving normally involve an integration of three factors: (1) the original goal-directed striving; (2) an aggressive urge to overcome the obstacle; and (3) an urge to avoid or flee from the obstacle.'

Finally a quotation which summarizes the essence of French's analysis of the influence of motivation upon the processes of sleeping and dreaming (p. 202):

'According to our hypothesis, disturbing pressures are at first absorbed by sleep itself. As this device begins to fail, the excess pressure is next absorbed by wish-fulfilling dream hallucinations. If this mechanism is successful, we expect the dream images to be of a pleasant, satisfying, and peaceful character. As still more pressure emerges from neutralization, the dreamer becomes aware of affects that become progressively more intense or more painful.'

Conclusion

French's theory is a good example of the fact that psychoanalytical theories have developed very much since Freud's first formulations—and this is true of both the formal structures of the theories and their empirical content. In both respects they are influenced by other psychological theories.

STAGNER'S AND KARWOSKI'S THEORY

The Structure of the Theory

In 1952 the American psychologists *Ross Stagner and T. F. Karwoski* published a book entitled '*Psychology*'. Contrary to the other theories studied in this book Stagner's and Karwoski's work is a textbook, even an 'introduction'. The reason for including it here is that it is representative of psychological textbooks which have made *motivation a basic principle in the psychological system.*

As the book is rather systematic and contains a number of explicit hypotheses but still—as is natural for an introductory textbook—is not actually axiomatized, it must be described as a theory belonging to *the area between classifying and deductive theories.*

The theory must be classified as a mainly *reductive* theory. For example it is said in the introductory chapter (p. 20) that:

> 'psychology is merely another science concerned with a specific system, namely, the brain.' . . . we find it expedient to assume that certain brain phenomena exist, because they provide a much-needed link between series of observations.'

The principle of homeostasis also plays a very fundamental part as a basis for explanation in the theory.

As the theory is mainly based upon behavioristic methods (protocol statements), and as the few hypothetical variables used are interpreted physiologically, the theory must be described as being *mainly behavioristic.* It is for example said that (p. 15):

> behaviorism is not too far out of line with the main trend of modern psychology.'

As there are several explicit formulations of the same content as the following (p. 20): 'psychology is concerned with the whole man', and as this point of view characterizes the whole presentation, the theory must be classified as *mainly molar.*

The theory maintains that it is very essential that all psychological theories deal with the 'man as a whole, and his adjustment to his environment' (p. 16); it must therefore be classified as *a mainly dynamic theory.*

Finally it must be classified as *extremely deterministic*, as several of the meta-theoretical formulations in the introductory chapter explicitly mention it.

The determinism is most clearly stressed in the following (p. 19):

'The concept of determinism implies that we can predict a person's actions. . . . When prediction proves inaccurate, we assume this to be a result of insufficient knowledge, not of inherently unpredictable human nature.'

In summary, *Stagner's and Karwoski's theory* can be described as *an intermediate form between classifying and deductive theories, a reductive, mainly behavioristic, rather molar, mainly dynamic, and extremely deterministic theory.*

The Content of the Theory

The importance of motivation is pointed out already in the beginning of the introductory chapter (p. 8):

'the key feature of modern psychology is the notion that motivation comes first.'

And motivation is based upon the principle of homeostasis, which is introduced in the following way (p. 16):

'The key concept which is used in this volume to tie the various aspects of psychology together is homeostasis.'

But if the principle of homeostasis is to be used as an all-explaining axiom, it must be extended in such a way that it 'appears to function on the social as well as the biological level' (p. 18).

But also the principle of homeostasis can be explained by the even more fundamental biological principle of evolutionary selection. It is formulated in the introduction to the first part of the book (dealing with 'Dynamics') in the following way (p. 33):

'organisms which mobilized energy and put forth vigorous effort to maintain these constances where those which survived.'

The principle of homeostasis as such is explicitly formulated as follows (p. 37):

'According to this principle, energy mobilization begins when an inner equilibrium is disturbed, and continues until this equilibrium is restored.'

As a consequence of the above it can be said that 'the unifying phenomenon in all forms of motivation is *energy mobilization* (p. 36).

The motivation variables are then divided into three classes: 1) 'biological drives', 2) 'emotions', and 3) 'social motives'.

About the first group it is said (p. 36) that:

'The most elementary forms of energy mobilization arise from definite biological needs of the organism.'

Even if it is not explicitly pointed out it can be seen from the above that 'need' describes an *empirical* and 'drive' a *hypothetical* variable (of the neurophysiological kind). Both are *function* variables.

Later it is stressed as fundamental that

'motivation cannot be ascribed to a specific set of inborn needs or drives. Motivation is a function of the total organism. . . the energies of the entire organism tend to be mobilized in active effort to restore the balance.'

Later (p. 41–42) the concept of '*tension*' is introduced as a description of that brain condition (and muscle condition) which is determined by 'needs.' Thus 'tension' must be equal to 'drive' (if 'drive' is not taken to include both 'need' and 'tension'—the presentation is not quite clear on this point. Tension may also be determined by an external stimulus, which is then called a '*valence*'.

Hunger, Thirst, Oxygen deficit, Maternal behavior, Sex, Excretory Needs, Pain, and Exploratory drives are classified as 'biogenic drives' (determined by 'heredity' and 'tissue needs'). It would, however, lead too far to quote all the empirical research results and hypotheses which are given in the chapter on 'Biological Drives.'

The chapter on 'Emotions' is opened with the statement that emotional behavior has the same characteristics as other kinds of motivated behavior ('goal direction, intensity, persistence, and variability'). It is then pointed out 'that emotion is a subordinate category of behavior—that emotions are secondary manifestations of drive' (p. 72).

The following reasons for this definition are given (p. 72):

'1. Emotion is generally a reaction to either drive frustration or drive satisfaction.'

'2. Emotions are generally serviceable to drive needs.'

'3. Emotion has a sign relationship to need satisfaction.'

In conclusion the following *definition of 'emotion'* is given.

'It refers to a group of actions and experiences based chiefly upon the biological drives and having an anticipatory or symbolic relationship to these drives.'

In other words, *'emotion'* is an *empirical behavior variable*, determined by 'needs' and 'drives'. It is unfortunately impossible, owing to lack of space, to discuss the many different research results and hypotheses concerning emotions.

In the chapter on 'Social Motives' it is also pointed out (p. 107) that:

'The *social motives* can also be related to the biogenec drives and to the emotions... Social motives resemble the emotions in that the goal objects are symbols.'

It is further maintained that these motives are *acquired* and that 'the key to this problem of learning social motives is found in the phenomenon of symbolic reward.'

The following are mentioned as the most important social motives (p. 108): 'Security, Dominance, Acquisitiveness, Group Identifications, and Values.' The second part of the book deals with '*Cognition*.' The relation between 'motivation' and 'cognition' is formulated in the following way (p. 132):

'Motivation provides the power which impels adaptive behavior, including learning, understanding the environment, thinking, and reasoning.'

These processes are called 'the processes by which man seek gratification of his motives'.

The third part of the book deals with 'Personality'. Motives and their conflicts play a fundamental role also here.

Conclusion

The above analysis shows that *it is possible to construct a simple systematic psychological system using 'motivation' as the most fundamental concept.*

SKINNER'S THEORY

The Structure of the Theory

B. F. Skinner, the American psychologist who became known through his very important work: 'The Behavior of Organisms' (1938), has published a book entitled '*Science and Human Behavior*' (1953). As the first work mentioned mainly deals with the psychology of learning while the latter is more general and also 'the latest systematic presentation by the author'[5]), the latter will be analyzed here.

It contains six parts:

I. The Possibility of a Science of Human Behavior (p. 2–44).
II. The Analysis of Behavior (p. 45–226).
III. The Individual as a Whole (p. 227–290).
IV. The Behavior of People in Groups (p. 291–332).

---

[5]) Cf. the criterion for selection in Chapter 4.

V. Controlling Agencies (p. 333–414).
VI. The Control of Human Behavior (p. 415–450).

Only the three first parts are, however, of interest in connection with the subject of this book.

As the presentation exclusively contains definitions, classifications, and more or less implicit hypotheses, but no attempt to systematize them, the theory must be described as *a mainly classifying theory.*

Skinner writes about the plan of his book (p. 39–40):

'The plan is obviously an example of extrapolation from the simple to the complex. No principle is used in any part of the book which is not discussed in Section II... The procedure is often referred to as reductionism.'

It might thus seem natural to classify the theory as a reductive theory. But the passage quoted is only valid for the later parts of the book which can be 'reduced' to or be explained by Part II. If then Part II: 'The Analysis of Behavior', is examined, one finds that the definitions and hypotheses give here *cannot* be reduced to physiology. Skinner writes (p. 28) that 'The causes to be sought in the nervous system are, therefore, of limited usefulness in the prediction and control of specific behavior', and he gives strong arguments against the use of hypothetical physiological variables as well as all other kinds of hypothetical variables. There is no attempt to reduce the variables to the hypotheses of some more fundamental science (for example to those of physics)—at the most a 'reduction' to a common scientific language. It therefore seems impossible to place Skinner's theory in this classification since it is neither reductive nor constructive as are other theories. At best Skinner's theory can be compared to physics, which is a 'fundamental' construction. But there is the difference that Skinner's theory is *not* hypothetical-deductive as it does *not* use hypothetical variables or theoretical hypotheses, only empirical variables and purely empirical hypotheses (of the S → R-type). Skinner's theory could maybe be characterized as *a radically empirical descriptive theory.*

In the next classification Skinner's theory also holds a special position in being the *most radical behavioristic theory* of the theories studied in this work. Therefore this aspect of the character of the theory will be made the object of a relatively thorough analysis. Skinner opens his argumentation against hypothetical variables, or 'inner "causes"' as he calls them, in the following way (p. 27):

'There is nothing wrong with an inner explanation as such but events which are located inside a system are likely to be difficult to observe.'

There are, however, some dangers connected with hypothetical variables, namely that:

'The practice of looking inside the organism for an explanation of behavior has tended to obscure the variables which are immediately available for scientific analysis. These variables lie outside the organism, in its immediate environment and in its environmental history. They have a physical status to which the usual techniques of science are adapted, and they make it possible to explain behavior as subjects are explained in science' (p. 31).

The quotation shows that Skinner wants to replace hypothetical variables with variables in the 'environmental history' of the organism. *Lewin's* argumentation *against* historical explanations and *in favour of* systematical explanations[6]) may be contrasted with this point of view. It can also be said against Skinner's argument that *other sciences—also physics—use hypothetical constructions in their theories.* Yet Skinner may still be right in that it might be more fruitful to avoid the use of hypothetical variables in psychology, but it can be said against this that one of the most exact and objective psychological theories—namely that of Hull—uses hypothetical variables.

Skinner's chapter on 'Private Events in a Natural Science' (p. 257–282) is the most logical argumentation in favour of a monistic (physicalistic) method in psychology. The argumentation is also unique in being based upon a very thorough analysis of 'verbal reactions upon own behavior'. Skinner concludes his analysis and argumentation with the following statement (p. 282):

The line between public and private is not fixed. The boundary shifts with every discovery of a technique for making private events public. Behavior which is of such small magnitude that it is not ordinarily observed may be amplified... The problem of privacy may, therefore eventually be solved by technical advances.'

It is more difficult to place Skinner's theory as molar or molecular. On the one hand 'the Analysis of Behavior' in Part II includes rather microscopic, experimentally produced reactions, but on the other hand the results of this analysis are used to explain the rather extensive macroscopic phenomena of behavior in the following parts ('The Individual as a Whole' and 'The Behavior of People in Groups'), so it is probably most correct to describe the theory as *an intermediate form between extremely molecular and extremely molar theories.*

It is also rather difficult to place Skinner's theory in the next classification. One would—on the basis of what is usually agreed upon by the opponents to behaviorism—expect that such a purely behavioristic theory would also be extremely mechanistic. Skinner also opens his 'Analysis of Behavior' with a section called 'Man a Machine' which shows that machines are more complicated to-day than at the time of Descartes when the principle of the reflex was discovered, and at the same time we have 'discovered more about how the living organism works and are better able to see its machine-like properties' (p. 47). He later writes, however, explicitly that 'we are not subscribing to a "conditioned-reflex theory" of all behavior' (p. 56).

Yet there are certain mechanistic characteristics in his analysis of behavior, thus, for example, his explanation of 'transfer' (p. 94):

'A more useful way of putting it is to say that the *elements* are strengthened whereever they occur. This lead us to identify the element rather than the response as the unit of behavior. It is a sort of behavioral atom, which may never appear by itself upon a single occasion but is the essential engredient or component of all observed instances.'

But there are also more dynamic aspects in the theory. There is, for example, a whole chapter (XIV) on 'The Analysis of Complex Cases' in which, among other things, it is said that (p. 205):

'Although a functional analysis begins with relatively isolated relations, an important part of its taks is to show how its variables interact.'

---

[6]) Cf. the chapter on Lewin's theory.

The sections on 'Multiple Effects of a Single Variable' and on 'Multiple Causes', etc., where the functional interrelations between variables are dealt with come next in the chapter. Consequently Skinner's theory must be classified as a *rather dynamic* theory (although bordering on mechanistic theories).

It might seem easy to classify Skinner's theory as extremely deterministic. Thus he writes in his introductory description of science (p. 13):

'it is a search for order, for uniformities, for lawful relations among events in nature.'

And later he writes directly on 'The Principle of Indeterminacy' (p. 17):

In our present state of knowledge, certain events therefore appear to be unpredictable. It does not follow that these events are free or capricious. Since human behavior is enormously complex and the human organism is of limited dimensions, many acts may involve processes to which the Principle of Indeterminacy applies. It does not follow that human behavior is free, but only that it may be beyond the range of a predictive or controlling science.'

But it soon becomes clear that Skinner's determinism at least is a determinism which is free from all the teleological, animistic, and rationalistic subprinciples of older philosophy. Skinner writes (p. 23):

'A "cause" becomes a "change in an independent variable" and an "effect" a "change in a dependent variable." The old "cause-and-effect connection" becomes a "functional relation".'

And when one considers the frequency with which Skinner uses the term '*probability*' in such connections as 'the probability of a response' doubt arises as to the correctness of classifying Skinner's theory as deterministic; the best description seems to be '*a probability-deterministic theory*'.

The Content of the Theory

In order to understand Skinner's theory of motivation, which is mainly presented in Chapter IX on 'Deprivation and Satiation', it is necessary to analyze his more general definitions first.

Skinner points out time and again that—apart from innate reflexes whose function is mainly to direct processes in the interior of the organism—'Behavior is the coherent, continuous activity of an integral organism' (p. 116).

And this involves that the independent variables do not 'cause' a reaction, but rather *change a continuous activity.*

Skinner formulates it in the following way (p. 62):

'It is a great advantage to suppose that the *probability* that a response will occur ranges continuously between these all-or-none extremes. We can then deal with variables which unlike the eliciting stimulus, do not "cause a given bit of behavior to occur" but simply make the occurrence more probable.'

By using the concept 'probablility of response' Skinner avoids the old, often criticised formulation of 'law and effect' in the following way (p. 64):

'A response which has already occured cannot, of course, be predicted or controlled. We can only predict that *similar* responses will occur in the future. The unit of a predictive science is, therefore not a response but a class of responses.'

This *increase in 'the probability of a response'* is equated with Pavlov's 'reinforcement'. Skinner nevertheless uses 'learning' for 'the reassortment of responses in a complex situation'. But even though Skinner thus borrows Pavlov's terminology it must be pointed out that Skinner does not use it with any physiological surplus meaning. It must also be said that Pavlov's 'reinforcement' and 'conditioning' only include stimulus substitution or '*respondent conditioning*', as Skinner calls it, while Skinner maintains that there is also an '*operant conditioning*' which is a 'reinforcement' of an 'operant', i. e. an action or movement which 'operates' upon the environments.

It seems evident from the above that it is of fundamental importance in Skinner's theory to answer the question '*Why is a reinforcer reinforcing?*' Several possible explanations are examined in the section in question (p. 81–84). One of the most acceptable is that 'reinforcement is effective because it reduces a state of deprivation' (p. 82). But Skinner points out several observations which show that (p. 82–83):

'it is not true that reinforcement always reduces deprivation. Conditioning may occur before any substantial change can take place in the deprivation measured in other ways. All we can say is that the *type* of event which reduces deprivation is also reinforcing.'

He adds that another explanation of the above may be found in 'the process of evolution'. This is a very fundamental explanation, but in Skinner's opinion it is not a particularly valuable explanation, as it is still necessary to find out which variables are 'reinforcing' in each species. And in addition it is necessary to provide for '*conditioned reinforcers*' in the individuals of a species.

From the above it can be seen that there is a relation between 'reinforcement' and motivation. '*Deprivation*' *is the most important motivation variable in Skinner's theory.* It is not defined explicitly, but that it is a pure *empirical* (independent) *function variable* can be seen from its relations to other variables. Its relation to 'homeostasis' is described as follows (p. 142):

'The notion of equilibrium is compatible with a functional analysis, but the two should not be confused. A study of equilibrium may enable us to predict the *direction* in which behavior will change as the result of a change in an independent variable, but it will not tell us much more. Equilibrium is hard to define and even harder to observe and measure. A much more clear-cut program is to show how deprivation affects the probability of relevant behavior, and this may be done without mentioning equilibrium.'

Skinner says that other motivation variables such as 'needs' and 'wants' are examples of 'inner causes' which he finds are impractical to use, because they are either deduced from an independent empirical variable, or from a dependent behavior variable, and 'so long as the inner event is inferred, it is in no sense an explanation of the behavior and adds nothing to a functional account' (p. 143–144).

Skinner speaks in favour of using 'drive' (p. 144):

'A need or want could simply be redefined as a condition resulting from deprivation and characterized by a special probability of response. Since it is difficult to lay the ghosts which hover about these older terms, there is a certain advantage in using a term which has fewer connotations. 'Drive' is sometimes used. A drive need not be thought of as mental or physiological. The term is simply a convenient way of referring to the effects of deprivation and satiation and other operations which alter the probability of behavior in more or less the same way. It is convenient because it enables us to deal with many cases at once.'

The above definition shows that '*drive*' (as well as the discarded 'need' and 'want') must be considered to be a hypothetical function variable, and it is the only hypothetical variable in Skinner's theory. But Skinner introduces it only to show after a short time that 'the simplicity of the concept of drive is only apparent' (p. 144), and in a whole section on 'The Practical Use of Drives' (p. 146–148) he writes that 'some examples of how behavior is actually controlled through deprivation and satiation will show how easily concepts referring to intervening states may be avoided.'

In the following chapter (Chap. X) '*Emotion*' is dealt with in the same way. Skinner says (p. 166):

'We define an emotion—in so far as we wish to do so—as a particular state of strength or weakness in one or more responses induced by any one of a class of operations.'

Skinner finds it most convenient to avoid using this hypothetical variable. He writes (p. 167):

'In the end, we find ourselves dealing with two events—the emotional behavior and the manipulable conditions of which that behavior is a function—which comprise the proper subject matter of the study of emotion.'

Finally it should be pointed out how Skinner defines a *disposition* variable as for example '*mood*' (p. 169):

'Moods and dispositions represent a kind of secondorder probability—the probability that a given circumstance will raise the probability of a given response.'

Because of lack of space a further analysis of the more special motivation variables must be left out.

Conclusion

Skinner's theory is interesting and *original* and very *simple* (few hypothetical variables) and it is very *systematic*. But it is only a collection of empirical generalizations (S→R-hypotheses) of a low degree of abstraction. There are few or no axioms which can form the basis for a deductive system. But it is a question what in the future will prove most practical in the development of psychology: a deductive theory with hypothetical variables (as for example Hull's) or a collection of purely empirical hypotheses as Skinner's[6a]).

[6a]) It is nearly a decade since the writing of this analysis of *Skinner's* theory. During these years Skinner has been very productive. He has written one book ('*Verbal Behavior*', N.Y., 1957) and in co-operation with others two other books ('*Schedules of Reinforcement*' with C. B. Fernster (N.Y., 1957) and '*The Analysis of Behavior*' with *Hollander* (N.Y., 1961)). Besides these books he has written several papers (some of which are collected in '*Cumulative Record*' (2nd ed., 1961). As none of these books or papers deal with the field of *motivation*, we shall *not* deal further with them in this book. But the present author cannot—in spite of his interest for *theories*—avoid expressing a very positive evaluation of Skinner's *empirical* approach and his application of his results in 'programmed learning'. I think that it is correct to state that Skinner is the most influentical contemporary psychologist in the field of *learning*.

HOLT-HANSEN'S THEORY

The Structure of the Theory

In an extensive experimental work '*After-Effects in the Behavior of Mice*' (1956) the Danish psychologist *Kr. Holt-Hansen* has presented an interesting theory which will be analyzed here because it deals with problems of the relation of motivation variables to the learning processes. The theory as such is presented in the last chapter of the book (p. 363–377). It is based upon a series of very detailed experiments with mice in a special experimental set-up, called a V-device (consisting of three parallel corridors connected at the ends. The mouse starts in the middle corridor and can go left or right and obtain food directly or indirectly). The results have been made the object of a very detailed *statistical study. The main result of the experiment* can shortly be described as 'a summary learning curve with a constant level of about 75% direct runs in the final period of the experiments'. In other words, *in 75% of the cases the mice will run left after a series of experiments where the food has been placed to the left*, and thus neither 50% which should be expected if the behavior was random (as was the case in the beginning of the experiment where the animal has 'learned' nothing) nor 100% which might be expected if the behavior was exclusively determined by one motivation variable (hunger).

Holt-Hansen's theory is an attempt to explain this result.

It must immediately be pointed out that the theory must be described as a '*miniature system*' (like Hull's first articles in Psychological Review in the thirties) because it only explains a very special behavior in a limited experimental situation. But there is a possibility that the theory can be generalized to behavior in general (just as has been done with Hull's theories). But the theory must with regard to level of development be classified as a *deductive theory*, as it consists of two primary hypotheses and a scheme from which the 75% experiment result and other results can be deduced. Besides this *axiomatization* there is also a *partly symbolic* presentation of the theory. But no systematic formulation of the meta-theory can be found.

The theory is inspired by Mendel's genetic theory, and the last chapter contains some physiological reflections, but no attempt is made to reduce psychology to biology, so the theory must be classified as a *purely constructive* theory. Several of the meta-theoretical formulations scattered in the last chapter show this clearly. Thus it is said of the hypothetical variables (p. 364):

'These factors are primarily to be regarded as mathematical constructs.'

Similar statements can be found elsewhere (p. 366, second paragraph, and p. 372, first paragraph).

It is a little difficult to place the theory in the next classification. As animal-experiments have been used exclusively, the protocol-statements of the theory (the methods) must, without any doubt, be described as being behavioristic. But in the largest part of the book the interpretation of the hypothetical variables is a little unclear, especially the use of the term 'phenomenal world' in relation to 'psychophysiological processes'. But in the last chapter it is quite evident that the hypothetical variables ('psychophysiological processes', 'factors', etc.) are to be interpreted as *neutral-formal variables*. Thus it is said in the final passage (p. 376):

'In other words, the factors may manifest themselves as behavior, or as biochemical processes, as neuroanatomical structures, as electrical phenomena, etc. Had humans been experimented upon under suitable analogous conditions, we might add that the factors may also manifest themselves in statements by the subjects concerning their experiences or phenomenal world.'

As a consequence of the above the theory must be classified as a *neutral-formal theory*.

In its present formulation the theory must be classified as a *molecular theory*, because the behavior described and explained is relatively 'microscopic'. (The book contains a very extensive chapter on the experimental analysis of different forms of 'micro-behavior').

The theory contains a number of statements about interrelations between variables. Thus it is said (p. 366) that 'no single factor is by itself capable of having effects'. And the two hypotheses of the theory deal exclusively with 'the interaction of the factors or chance processes' (p. 370). Consequently the theory must be classified as an *extremely dynamic* theory.

The theory must absolutely be classified as an *extremely statistical theory* (the only one belonging to this class among the theories examined here). Thus it is said in the first lines of the chapter on the theory (p. 363):

'The aim of this section is to present a probability model in explanation of important features of the learning process.'

And later (p. 372) the theory is characterized as 'an abstract probability model, that concerns stochastic processes'.

Furthermore all the hypotheses in the theory are formulated as *statistical* hypotheses. This does not imply, however, that the theory can be described as indeterministic. Several implicit formulations about this matter show that the opposite is the case. Thus it is said (p. 372):

'... the suggested probability model (may) be said to explain how the empirical results are *caused*.'

In summary, *Holt-Hansen's theory* can be described as *a deductive, constructive, neutral-formal, rather molecular, extremely dynamic, and statistical theory*.

The Content of the Theory

Since the theory, as mentioned, is a miniature-system and only deals with a special behavior in a rather limited experiment situation, it is only necessary to include two motivation variables.

They are described in the following way (p. 365):

'This discussion forms the basis for the use of the terms "need for food" and "hunger" when speaking of the animals' motivation or drive... Finally, it must be stressed that the experiments concerned in the present work led to the assumption of yet another need, the need "to be up and about".'

Further down the page the description of the last 'need' is presented as being synonymous with synonymous with another expression. It is said (p. 365):

'This need to be up and about—this need for activity—also showed itself in the maze experiments as a tendency towards action related to other alleys than that leading directly to the goal.'

The two motivation variables are probably to be considered *hypothetical function variables* and not empirical variables. It can especially be seen from the definition of the need for activity ('a tendency towards action . . .')—and also a later statement (p. 367): '. . . a brain process (e. g. a correlate to a need)' shows that we are dealing with a *hypothetical* variable.

These two 'needs' are the only motivation variables necessary to explain the behavior, as 'there is a certain probability for behaviour related either to the need for food, or to the need to be up and about.'

It is also necessary, however, to assume other variables, and in the 'model' 'needs' are placed in relation to some other hypothetical variables, namely 'factors.' These are defined in the following way (p. 366):

'By "factors" is understood: A necessary condition for the occurrence of a brain function.'

'Factors' are divided into two groups: 'activity factors' and 'engram factors'.

'Activity factors' include the following (p. 366):

'A factor that determines the brain process corresponding to the need for food will be called B. A factor that determines the brain process corresponding to the need to be up and about will be called b.'

'Engram factors' include two sup-groups:

1) 'Engram factors relating to needs.'
2) 'Engram factors relating to perception.'

The first sub-group includes another two 'factors,' namely an engram factor determined by *the need for food,* described as B^l because it will later determine behavior to the left (where the food is), and an engram factor determined by *the need for activity,* described as b^r because it later determines behavior to the right.

As summary, it can be said about these (p. 368):

'These engram factors are consequently regarded as being formed in connection with the function of "satisfaction" of the individual animal's needs, or "need reduction".'

In the second sub-group of engram factors there are also two factors, namely an engram factor determined by the perception of the route leading directly to the goal, called *A*, and an engram factor determined by the perception of the route leading indirectly to the goal, called *a*.

These 'factors' form the variables of the theory—or rather of the probability model. It has previously been mentioned that they must be classified as *neutral-formal hypothetical variables.* Their relation to the previously defined motivation variables (the two needs) is a little unclear, however. The relation between the double set of variables: 'needs' and 'activity factors', is not formulated explicitly in the theory. It is, however, probably analogous to the relation between function variables and disposition variables known from the third chapter of this book. In other words, 'factors' in Holt-Hansen's theory are a kind of *disposition variables* which co-determine the operation of function variables as 'needs' and 'perception'; these function variables are also determined by *empirical* variables (stimuli, etc.).

After the definitions of the above 'factors' the hypotheses on their 'interaction' are presented in the following way (p. 370):

'*The 1st hypothesis* concerns the rules regarding the interaction of the activity factors and each of the two factors in the two pairs of engram factors. This hypothesis asserts that: No matter whether one or the other of the two factors (in the pairs of factors mentioned) influences a run, the chances for interaction with each of the two activity factors are equal.

The 2nd hypothesis concerns the interaction between the two sets of engram factors, and is as follows: It is assumed that the two different pairs of engram factors are combined independently of each other. In other words, the probabilities for the 4 different combinations AB^l, AB^r, aB^l and ab^r are in the ratios 1 : 1 : 1 : 1.'

These two hypotheses give the following scheme (p. 371):

The 4 combinations of engram factors.	The two activity factors. B	b
AB^l	$A\,B^lB$	$A\,B^lb$
$A\ b^r$	$A\,b^r$	$A\,b^rb$
$a\ B^l$	$a\ B^lB$	$a\ B^lb$
$a\ b^r$	$a\ B\,b^r$	$a\ b^rb$

It can be seen that there are '8 factor-combinations and 8 resulting processes that lead to 8 behavioral results' (p. 371).

From the two hypotheses and the scheme it is possible to deduce the experimental result that 75% of the animals' runs were to the *left* in the following way: As each combination gives the probability $\frac{1}{8}$, the combinations AB^lB, AB^lb, aB^lB, and aB^lb, together give *the probability* $\frac{1}{2}$ for the occurrence of the behavior: run direct to the goal (i. e. left). The combinations ABb^r and aBb^r together give *the probability* $\frac{1}{4}$ for runs to the left, as B dominates br. *The total probability for runs directly to the goal, i. e. to the left, is thus* $\frac{3}{4}$ *or 75%, q.e.d.*

Conclusion

As can be seen from the above analysis, Holt-Hansen's theory is a very simple and exact theory. It would be interesting to compare it more thoroughly to two other 'miniature-systems' dealing with the same behavior, namely Tolman's two papers 'Determiners of Behavior at a Choice Point' and 'The Schematic Sowbug.'[7]) The result would probably be, that Holt-Hansen's theory gives a much more simple and more exact explanation, while Tolman's theory might give better possibilities for generalization to more complicated 'molar' behavior.

[7]) Both in Psychological Review—January 1938 and July 1939, respectively

Chapter 16

Other Literature about Psychology of Motivation

In order to make this book more usable to psychologists as a handbook of psychology of motivation, it will be necessary to give supplementary information to the analyses of 20 theories of motivation. The following supplement will give a summary of the latest literature about psychology of motivation published in books.[1)]

BOOKS OF MOTIVATION[1a)]

During the past years there has been a rising tendency in the number of published books about motivation. Those known to the author will be mentioned in brief and chronologically. Space forbids meta-theoretical analyses corresponding to the previously mentioned.

A. H. Maslow: Motivation and Personality (1954). The book is a collection of papers published in different periodicals In the papers Maslow's theories of motivation are put forward and dealt with, the main contents of the theories are stated in the following:

1. Certain 'higher needs' are as 'instinctive', constitutional, and specific of human species as are the organic needs for food, water, etc. These higher needs are for safety, social contact, self-assertion, for knowledge and understanding, esthetic values, and for self-actualization.
2. All the above needs constitute a 'hierarchy of needs' with a special order of precedence, the characteristic features of which are that the "higher needs" (e. g. the needs for esthetic values or selfactualization) will exist only if the "lower" ones (e. g. needs for food or safety) have been fairly satisfied. In conflicting situations the order of precedence will be perceptible in the way that a "lower" need (of medium strength) will always predominate a "higher" one (of medium strength).

Finally it should be emphasized that—as Murray's—Maslow's concept of 'need' is a hypothetic variable, a variable of function as well as of disposition.

---

1) In order to keep this book of manageable size the present author has decided to exclude from this edition the paragraphs which, in the earlier editions, dealt with papers in journal and symposia—especially the well-known *Nebraska Symposia on Motivation.* The reader interested in a more extensive survey of the literature about motivation is referred to *C. N. Cofer and M. H. Appley:* 'Motivation: Theory and Research' (Wiley, N.Y., 1964) which contains nearly 100 pages of references.

1a) This part of the chapter was written for the second edition which appeared in 1961.

Maslow is maintaining the consequences of his theory himself, for instance as regards psychotherapy. The theory is well-known to and has been used by educational psychologists.[2])

James Olds: The Growth and Structure of Motives (1956). James Olds is a student of Hebb. In the above mentioned book he quotes, after some interesting reflections upon the problem of theory construction, a number of experimental data concerning 'secondary reinforcement.' Olds then presents *a theory of reward,* mainly based upon Hebb, but also upon Tolman and Hull. From Hebb he has taken the hypothetical, neuro-physiological concept '*cell-assembly.*' Processes in such a hypothetical structure may be as well *motivating* as *cognitive* depending upon the strength of 'the intrinsic motive force.' *The learning process* consists of the forming of associations between two or more cell-assemblies. This 'backflow of motive force' is a purely hypothetical neuro-physiological construction which is to explain reinforcement. The book also contains some interesting chapters in which it is attempted to use Parson's system of concepts on these cell-assemblies. The formulations of the most important parts of the theory are very systematical (almost axiomatized)[2a]).

Harry Giles: 'Education and Human Motivation' (1957) contains an application of motivational theory to pedagogical problems.

C. S. Hall and G. Lindzey: 'Theories of Personality' (1957) contains in twelve chapters an analysis of seventeen theories of personality. There is also—besides the introductory chapter—a final comparative chapter. Four of the seventeen theories are identical with theories analyzed in this work; but the book is an introduction to the psychology of personality.

A book which in many ways is interesting is '*Perspectives in Personality Theory*' (1957), edited by *H. P. David and H. von Bracken* and published by 'The International Union of Scientific Psychology.' It contains many articles which are of interest in both motivational psychology and meta-theoretical psychology. Thus *G. W. Allport* makes an interesting comparison between 'European and American Theories of Personality,' maintaining that there are important differences in philosophical presuppositions and fundamental points of view. The European psychology has been more speculative and theoretical fruitful, whereas the Anglo-American psychology has maintained a more empirical-methodical attitude. A chapter written by *W. Luthe* on 'Neuro-humoral Factors and Personality' confirms the assertion made in Chapter 17 that a growing interest for physiological reduction experiments exists in psychology. A chapter of *J. Nutten* on 'Personality Dynamics' presents an outline and an original contribution to the psychology of motivation.

[2]) The present author intends to make a more thorough meta-theoretical study of *Maslow's* theory in the forthcoming book: 'Modern Theories of Motivation' (in press).

[2a]) It should be noted that Olds' and collaborators sensational experiments with intracranial stimulation having a rewarding function are *not* included in his theory. The reader may be referred to: J. Olds: 'Psysiological mechanisms of reward' (Nebraska Symposium on Motivation, 1955) or other later surveys.

McClelland analyzes the obstacles hindering a development 'Toward a Science of Personality Psychology.'

R. S. Peters: 'The Concept of Motivation' (1958). In his small book the author analyses types of explanation in psychology. He asserts that several types can be found and that they are mixed up in an inexpedient way in the theories of motivation. His principal objection is, however, that theories of motivation do not consider the fact that 'man is a rule-following animal'.

In my opinion most theories of motivation do, actually, explain this fact by referring to social motives (needs, drives).

Next, the author analyses the concept of motivation itself as it is used to-day' and he asserts that the concept is misused by psychologists when they use 'motive in the same way as 'drive', i. e. as a cause.

The author's principal thesis is that psychologists should not omit to study the psychological concepts of ordinary language, because they give the extensive knowledge about human behavior. As far as I can see, the psychological knowledge of ordinary language is most often inexact and distorted by direct misunderstandings. Therefore psychologists should wisely define their own scientific concepts independent of ordinary language.

In the following chapters the author analyses 'Freud's theory', 'Drive theories' (among others Hull's and Murray's), and 'The Regression to Hedonism' (especially P. Th. Young). In the last chapter Peters points out that psychology's lack of success is due to psychologists' attempts to make all-embracing theories and to lack of conceptual analyses. The author of this book cannot agree with R. S. Peters's many assumptions and conclusions, we are, however, in full agreement when the question arises of the necessity of conceptual and theoretical analyses in psychology. I find his book a very interesting and thought-provoking contribution to meta-theoretical psychology.

R. S. Woodworth: 'Dynamics of Behavior' (1958). The well-known American psychologist has in this book given a collective account of motivation, perception, and learning. Their interdependence is his reason for dealing collectively with these processes. In the first chapter he gives the 'point of view'. It can briefly be characterized as a 'functionalistic, molar behaviorism', which border on that of Tolman, and the majority of American psychologists.

In the second chapter he goes into details about the point of view by amplifying the classic S-R formula into:

$$S - O - R - R^{X}$$

When 'O' is symbolizing the intervening variables, existing in the organism, and 'R^{X}' is symbolizing 'retroflex' or 'sensory feed-back', a very important result of behavior with influence on future behavior (via O-variable).

In the third chapter he introduces 'drive' as the principal variable of motivation. 'Drives' are caused by 'needs' (peripheral, physiologic conditions) or by 'incentives'. (Thus Woodworth has accepted the same terminology of 'drive' and 'need' as has Hull). 'Drive' causes activation as well as direction of behavior. Woodworth also discusses the theory of 'non-directive drives', but finds that drives are at least determining the general direction of behavior, while incentives are determining the more specific direction.

In the fourth chapter he discusses several investigations of the motivation of exploratory behavior, motivation of achievement, and other kinds of non-organic motivation.

Freud's, Murray's, Hull's, and other psychologists' so-called 'need-primacy theories' are dealt with in the fifth chapter. Woodworth formulates his own 'behavior-primacy-theory' as a contrast, the principal of which is contained in the following (p. 133):

'The behavior-primacy theory regards the tendency to deal with the environment as a primary drive, and indeed as *the* primary drive in behavior. The various capacities for dealing with the environment afford outlets for the general behavior drive and give it different forms—given the necessary environmental opportunities. So the manifold human interests are predictable from the combination' It is the last sentence about 'interests' which rightly—as far as I can see—makes Woodworth add:

'Perhaps the behavior-primacy theory—will have practical value in education' (p. 133).

The following chapters of the book discuss as already mentioned 'perception' and 'learning', and will therefore not be dealt with here[3]).

By publishing this book Woodworth has once more shown his unique capability of estimating and giving surveys of psychology.

Gardner Lindzey (edt.): 'Assessment of Human Motives' (1958). As the title suggests this book does not deal with theories of motivation, the subjects are empiric methods for the registration and the measuring of motivation. Lindzey says about the relations between theory and empiricism (p. 15):

'A concern with the *assessment* of motives is fully as crucial as a concern with the *theory* of motives; in fact, the two are not to be clearly separated. Advance in one area automatically presupposes advance in the other.'

Lindzey has written the introductory chapter himself. Among other things he mentions the relations between theory and empiricism, analyses the relations as far as psychoanalysis is concerned, and makes an outline of the problems dealt with in the following chapters.

George Kelly argues in his chapter in favour of the redundancy of the concept of motivation and a pure cognitive approach to personality.

Leon Festinger also deals with a variable ('cognitive dissonance'), which is very

---

[3]) Woodworth's theory has later been analyzed more thoroughly and the results appear in the present author's forthcoming volume: 'Modern Theories of Motivation' (in press).

interesting from a psychological point of view, to problems of motivation as well as personality.

George Klein's chapter deals with attitudes or cognitive styles in thinking, perceiving, and expressions of drives.

Roy Schafer treats the psychoanalytic concept 'regression', and its importance to the adaptation and development of personality.

Irving Jani discusses 'The Psychoanalytic Interview as an Observational Method'.

Henry Murray treats problems connected with the results of his own research of thematic projective technique. Further, a number of general psychological (within motivation) and universal cultural problems are dealt with.

Raymond Cattell discusses other types of methods, viz. methods for measuring of motivation, i. e. 'objective factor analytical methods. This chapter as well as the previous and the following chapters may be read as a supplement to the analogous chapters in the present book.

Gordon Allport discusses the problems whether 'measuring units' or 'analysis level' should be used in psychology of personality. He asserts that the most fruitful concepts are those which can be used on the individual himself, being the object of research to psychology of personality.

John W. Atkinson: 'Motives in Fantasy, Action, and Society' (1958). As the title states the above book deals with the influence of motivation on the processes of fantasy, especially the kind of fantasy taking place under the test with McClelland's version of Thematic Apperception Test (cf. Chap. 11). In 46 chapters, written by nearly as many authors, the research made by McClelland, Atkinson and assistants has been collected. All the research work concerning the experimental testing of T.A.T. (also on other motives than 'achievement') is reported here. In other main sections the influence of motivation on other forms of behavior has been dealt with, especially those of achievement in the situation of testing. Finally, there are two large main sections about the social origin of motives and about the role of psychology of motivation in sociological, economic, and historical research. A very comprehensive, empiric research material has been collected, but it would lead too far to deal with it here.

Atkinson's definitions of different concepts of motivation (in chapter 42) present a special interest for the subject of the present book. In a foot-note he writes about the two terms 'need' and 'motive' (p. 596):

'These two terms have been used interchangeably throughout the book. The term, motive, however, is preferred because it does not imply that activation and direction of behavior is necessarily linked to conditions of deprivation. Of all the other alternatives available, the term motive seems most general in its connotation.'

Later on Atkinson introduces a distinction between 'motive' and 'motivation' (p. 601), thus 'the term motive refers to the more general and relatively stable disposition', while 'the term motivation refers to the arousal of a tendency to act to produce one or more effects.' These concepts are brought into relation with 'cognitive expectancy' in the following way (p. 603):

'This conception of motivation to perform an act as a joint function of the motives of the individual and the expectancies of motive-satisfying consequences elicited by situational cues.'

The terminology does not quite correspond to the one defined in the present book (cf. chapter 18). But Atkinson's and my own destinction between variables of disposition and function are concordant[4]).

Stanley Schachter: 'The Psychology of Affiliation' (1959). The small book contains the results of an exceptionally interesting and fruitful research concerning social motivation. On the basis of several theoretical considerations the author makes up his mind to investigate the relation between anxiety and affiliative tendency. The experimental subjects (college students) are placed in an anxiety-producing situation (by 'threats' of electrical shock), and are allowed to choose between loneliness and company while they are waiting for the anxiety-producing stimulus. Most people choose to be together with other people—even if verbal communication if prohibited. They prefer, however, to be together with persons (though unknown) who are subject to the same situation, rather than persons completely unknown, which indicates that company has anxiety-reducing effects. Great individual differences are characteristic features of the reactions, which prove to be dependent on the position among the siblings. An only child and the child first born will be more anxious, and will react more socially in the same anxiety-producing situation than later children. These facts are due to differences of child-rearing practices, which have been proved by several investigations.

The experimental principal results concerning the relation between position among the siblings, anxiety and affiliative tendencey are supplemented with other experiments (about the influence of hunger), and are supported by references to other psychologists' experiments of factual situations of life (e.g. fighter pilots' reactions during the Korean war).

Dalbir Bindra: 'Motivation—A Systematic Reinterpretation' (1959). As it is suggested in the title, the book is an attempt to make a systematic reinterpretation of the concept of motivation on the basis of the latest experimental results.

---

[4]) Atkinson has elaborated his theory further in his books 'An Introduction to Motivation' (1964) and 'A Theory of Achievement Motivation' (written with N. T. Feather, 1966). Atkinson's theory is one of the ten new theories analyzed in my book: 'Modern Theories of Motivation' (in press).

In the first chapter the author gives a critical account of the 'instinct-doctrine' and the 'drive-doctrine', and also of Nissen's and Hebb's hypotheses. Bindra asserts in connection with the latter that the main problem in psychology of motivation is not the driving force of behavior (which is the constant activity of the nervous system, merely) it is goal-directed aspect of behavior. The two main problems are:

1. 'the *origin* of directed activities', and
2. 'the *occurrence* of directed activities' (p. 18).

The two problems are, in Bindra's opinion, solved in the best way when a combination is made between Skinner's 'empty organism' and Hebb's neurophysiological approach.

In the second chapter it is maintained that 'emotional' and 'motivated' activities are undistinguishable, *every* kind of behavior being more or less goal-directed. Then a classification is put forward: 1) 'general activity and exploration', 2) 'withdrawal and aggressive activities', 3) 'eating, drinking, and sexual activities', 4) 'maternal behavior'.

The third chapter deals with 'Goal Direction'. The concept 'goal' is defined as follows (p. 54):

'A *goal* is thus an incentive that is chosen by the investigator as a reference point for describing observed behavior'.

Besides, 'goal direction' is defined as a 'multidimensional concept', which more or less includes such concepts as: 'appropriateness', 'persistence', and 'searching'. Bindra's analysis of 'goal-directed behavior' is an improvement of McDougall's and Tolman's well-known analyses of the same concept. Furthermore, two 'generalizations' are made concerning the origin of goal-directed behavior. The generalizations can be characterized as reformulations of 'the law of effect'.

In the fourth chapter the hypothesis is put forward that the 'development of motivational activities' always is a product of learning. There is no inherited ('instinctive'), goal-directed behavior in mammal. The only inherited basis of the learning of the so-called 'species-specific' behavior is certain simple, inherted reflexes and an inherited sensitiveness towards certain 'stimulus patterns'.

In chapter five 'An analysis of reinforcers' is made. The concept 'reinforcer' is defined, on the lines of Skinner, in a operationistic way (p. 116):

'*Reinforcer:* An event the occurrence of which changes the overall habit strength of a given response.'

After which the problem, 'why do reinforcers reinforcer?' is discussed. The various modern theories and many experimental data are discussed, but the author has not in any way committed himself to any definite hypothesis. A hypothetical mechanism called 'the positive reinforcing mechanism' is introduced. It is presumed to be effected by all the real, well-known reinforcers (drive reduction, stimulus increase etc.).

Chapter six treats 'Factors' determining habit strength', an interpretation of modern psychology of learning. Together with chapter seven, which deals with 'the role of sensory cues', it is a typical feature of Bindra's treatment of 'motivation'. When all (motivated) behavior is goal-directed, and this is the result of learning, then these subjects must be included in a psychology of motivation.

While the previous chapters have concentrated on modern psychology of learning (similar to Skinner's approach) thus the subjects of the subsequent chapters have been taken from the modern neurophysiological approach (similar to Hebb).

Chapter eight deals with 'Arousal and Behavior'. The author says about the concept 'arousal' that it refers to 'the energy' or 'excitation' level of an organism' (p. 210). And he says about its logical status (p. 213):

'Thus, the logical status of the concept of level of arousal is the same as that of the concepts of habit strength and goal direction. All these concepts serve as vague labels for a variety of specific and fairly exact measures, and it is these measures, rather than the global concepts themselves, that form the basis of empirical research.'

The measures, mentioned above, are 'electroencephalography', 'galvanic skin response', 'electrocardiogram' and others. The chapter also treats the causes of alterations in the level of arousal, viz.: environmental change, reduction in sensory variation, task performance, noxious stimulation, and certain drugs. All these factors have an effect on 'the reticular activating system' in the brain-stem, thus being the central mechanism for the level of arousal.

Chapter nine is about 'The role of blood chemistry', which is dependent on production of hormones, presence of nutritious substances, liquids, etc., and which influences behavior in various ways (among others by influencing the central nervous system, especially the brain-stem). The chapter gives a good summary of the latest research results in this field.

Bindra gives 'an overview' in the last chapter. Among other things he discusses the different froms of 'mediation variables', viz. 'intervening or transformation concepts' and 'hypothetical constructs'. His conclusions are the following (p. 289):

'Thus, in deciding upon an approach to the study of behavior, the question is not whether mediation concepts should have any excess meaning at all, but rather how much excess meaning a hypothetical construct can have and still be useful.'

Bindra characterizes his own point of view as 'between the positions of Skinner's and Hebb's point of view. As far as I can make out, it is more akin to Skinner's point of view than to Hebb's.

Then Bindra summarizes the contents of his book into 16 'tentative conclusions', he finishes with the following remarks: (p. 294):

'The above conclusions suggest that the traditional problem of "strength of motivation" is essentially a problem of the roles of different factors that determine the occurrence of a given response. The relevant sets of variables represent variations in habit strength, sensory cues, level of arousal, and blood chemistry'.

Out of the four mentioned factors it is only 'level of arousal' and 'blood chemistry' that are motivational variables according to the definition of 'motivation' which have been advanced in the present book (chapter 18).

At last Bindra outlines the consequences of his approach for the study of human motivational activities.

Bindra's book has been reported comparatively detailed here, being, in my judgment, an excellent systematic summary of experimental motivational psychology within three important psychologic branches: psychology of learning, comparative psychology, and physiological psychology. Only psychology of personality, the fourth branch, is lacking, if it should be characterized as a complete psychology of motivation. Thus Atkinson's and Bindra's books will supplement each other as summaries of empiric psychology of motivation[5]).

Frank A. Logan: 'Incentive' (1960). The book has a subtitle: 'How the conditions of reinforcement affect the performance of rats.' It may be of more interest to theory of learning than to theory of motivation, but the book will be mentioned here because Logan is a student of Hull and Spence.

It contains a temporary account about experimental results of 'incentives', and also a so-called 'micromolar theory' as an explanation to the results.

The experimental results can be summed up, as follows (p. 258):

'rats adjust to the various conditions of reinforcement in terms of the principles of maximization of reward and minimization of effort.'

The main thing about a 'micromolar theory' is that 'responses that differ quantitatively are considered to be different responses', and therefore 'a micromolar theory must make predictions in terms of probability of response' (p. 100). This basis brings back Skinner's theory to our mind; the constructs and the postulates of the theory, however, lean heavily on the Hull-Spence approach. The most important hypothetical constructs are: 'habit' (sHr), 'incentive' (sJNr), 'drive' (D), 'effort' (sFr), and 'temporary inhibition' (sTJr). The three first constructs have been directly borrowed from Hull's theory, only little changes have taken place in the definitions. The two last ones are partially new (although similar variables can be found in Tolman's and Hull's theories respectively). The three first mentioned work positively together for the increase of a reaction tendency ('excitatory potential,' sEr), while the two last mentioned work negatively for a decrease of the potential. Logan writes about 'primary motivation' (p. 104):

'There are five states of affairs which produce (D)', namely: 'hunger', 'thirst', 'sex', 'pain', and 'fear'. The different constructs are defined nearly as in Hull's theory. Logan's theory is likewise formulated in 17 postulates, and an example of deduction is given on the postulates. The very quantitative formulation of the theory has been influenced by statistics—in conformity with Skinner's and other late theories of learning.

---

[5]) *Bindra's* theory is treated in a whole chapter in my book 'Modern Theories of Motivation' (in press).

E. Tranekjær Rasmussen: 'Dynamisk Psykologi og dens Grundlag' (1960). 'Dynamic psychology and its basis', the title of the book, is in my judgment rather misleading, as the book deals with Ach's, Lewin's, and especially Murray's theories only, and not at all with dynamic psychology of the past three decades. I would have put the title rather differently: 'An epistemological analysis and reconstruction of Murray's theory', as the book contains many penetrating theoretical analyses and suggestions for improvements of Murray's theory. It is especially a very thorough enlargement of the theory concerning 'feelings' or 'affections' and their relation to 'need'. The book can be characterized as a theoretical development of Murray's work, when McClelland's work is considered an empiric development of Murray's work.

Walter Toman: 'Psychoanalytic Theory of Motivation' (1960). The above book consists of two parts: 'Part I: Conceptual Introduction' and 'Part II: The Theory at Work'. It is a systematic account of Freud's theory, the one not analyzed in the present book (cf. the foot note at the introduction to chapter 15). In Toman's book there is made no comparison with other theories, and further information will therefore not be given here.

Judson S. Brown: 'The Motivation of Behavior' (1961). The book gives, up to now, the most extensive and systematic account of a theory of motivation within the frame-of-reference, often called 'general behavior theory'. Brown's theory is, especially, an improvement of the motivational concepts in Hull's theory, and will therefore be described in some details here[6]).

In the first chapter the aim of psychology is discussed, i. e. description of behavior, ascertainment of empiric laws (S - R, S - O - R, and R - R - laws), and explanation of the laws by the aid of the physiological or the molar behavioral approach.

Regarding the last mentioned 'intervening variables' are needed, and they are gone through in the second chapter. It is done in such a pedagogical way that it will probably be intelligible to 'advanced undergraduates or beginning undergraduate students in psychology', for which students the book has been made. All methodological problems arising at the introduction of intervening variables are discussed, next the special category of intervening variables, called 'motivational' is introduced. As criterions with the particular purpose of delimitating this group the following suggestions are given: 1) energizing of responses, 2) reinforcement of responses, 3) function as punishment, 4) no chance of using other categories ('learning', 'perception', etc.). Finally, there is a discussion of the problems involved in the measuring of motivation.

Chapter three deals with 'primary sources of drive'. This terms is used instead of 'primary drives' owing to Brown's acceptance of Hull's 'single-drive-hypothesis',

[6]) A more extensive and thorough analysis will be presented in my book 'Modern Theories of Motivation' (in press).

according to which drive is caused by qualitatively different, primary 'sources of drive'. Among these primary sources of drive 'needs' are particularly emphasized, and are defined as 'bodily unbalance or departure from normality'. Brown argues strongly and cogently for the expediency of distinguishing between 'need' and 'drive' (in the same way as Hull and Woodworth). Moreover, he argues in favor of defining 'drive' as well as other concepts of motivation in such a way that they have 'function as the activating agents' only, while cognitive variables (perception and learning) have nothing but 'directive function'. This definition of 'motivation' as a merely dynamic or activating function corresponds exactly to the one suggested in chapter 18 of the present book. A similar definition has been made there, though on a pure conceptual analytic basis.

The rest of chapter three summarizes empiric results of research, that concern the correlation between 'primary sources of drive' and '*the* drive'.

Brown makes in chapter four a very interesting analysis of two different types of explanation used on 'motivated' behavior.

One type of explanation is 'the motivational interpretation', the principal representative of which is Hull's theory. Further Spence's, Tolman's, Duffy's, Morgan's, Hebb's second theory (1955), and other theories are mentioned.

The other explanatory type is 'the associative interpretation', which tries to explain motivated behavior without particular, activating, intervening variables, exclusively by 'associative variable as habit strength' and the like. These kinds of explanatory types are rather new. Brown goes through three imaginary versions of such an explanatory type, and also some typical, actually occurring, associative theories: Estes's, Bindra's, Hebb's first formulated (1949), McClelland's, and other theories.

Brown compares the two types' possibilities as to various experimental results, and concludes that 'the motivational interpretation' bears the greater impress of truth so far.

In chapter five 'Learned responses as sources of drive' are dealt with. The above formulation is analogous to the formulation: 'primary sources of drive', and it is especially here in the treatment of the problem about 'secondary drive' that the great advantages of Brown's theory are evident. A very simple theory it is, a theory that can presuppose the existence of a single, non-directive, multiplicative drive, activating all associative tendencies of behavior, and which may be determined itself by several different primary or learned sources of drive.

The most important learned source of drive is conditioned fear or anxiety. Brown maintains that this learned source of drive can explain 'the so-called acquired drives as those for money, affection, power, and security'.

In addition to anxiety other learned responses are discussed as possible sources of drive. Three possibilities are gone through:

1. *Hull-Spence's* 'fractional anticipatory goal responses'—understandable as a learned expectation of reward.

2. *McClelland's* 'affective-arousal model'—understandable as a combination of the anxiety- and the expectation-explanation.
3. *Brown's own hypothesis:* 'self-administered verbal commands might acquire, through a process of conditioning the power to affect overt reactions motivationally' (p. 193).

Brown's chapter about 'learned responses as sources of drive' is the most satisfactory treatment of the problem 'acquired drives' the author has ever met with.

The rest of the book contains few problems of theoretical interest, but it is an excellent summary of the empiric research within so widely differing branches as: 'Frustration and Conflict' (chapter 6), 'Human performance' (chapter 7), 'Motivation and perception' (chapter 8), and 'Miscellaneous motivational problems' (chapter 9)—dealing among other things with: Approach-eliciting stimuli, conditioning of emotional responses, and physiological studies related to the concept of general drive.

All things considered, Brown's book is in my opinion, the book that most comprehensively gives an account of the empiric results within the entire field of psychology of motivation. At the same time it is an interesting development and application of Hull's non-specific, multiplicative drive-theory, which is a very simple, consistent, and fruitful theory.

Latest Books[7])

The rapid development of motivational psychology in the last decade can be measured by the many 'books of readings' in motivational psychology. These books include parts of chapters from other books as well as papers from journals and symposia—especially the well-known '*Nebraska Symposium on Motivation*', which has been of enormous value in this field of psychology (originally edited by *Marshall R. Jones* and later by *David Levine*)[8]).

The many new textbooks and comprehensive handbooks of motivational psychology reflect this rapid development. We shall comment on those books which at the moment of writing (May, 1967) are known to the present author.

John F. Hall: Psychology of Motivation (Chicago, 1961). This is a textbook which stresses the biological foundation of motivation and the connection to learning theory. The same may be said about the next book:

John L. Fuller: Motivation—A Biological Perspective (N.Y., 1962). This is a small, but very well-written book which gives the reader a good introduction to the subject.

Dorothy Rethlingshofer: Motivation as related to personality (N.Y., 1963). As the title indicates this book is a combination of the psychology of motivation with the psychology of personality. This is as natural a combination as the combination between motivational psychology and the psychology of learning, but

---

[7]) This part of the chapter was written for the fourth edition (May, 1967).

[8]) In previous editions of the present book we made a rather thorough review of the volumes of the Nebraska Symposia covering the years 1954–1960, but lack of space makes it impossible to continue this work.

it is very rare that one person is able to intergrate all disciplines related to motivational psychology. That is the reason for team-work in writing the bigger handbooks on motivational psychology.

The largest among recently published handbooks is:

C. N. Cofer and M. H. Appley: Motivation: Theory and Research (N.Y., 1964). In the space of about one thousand pages (including 100 pages of references) this book covers the whole range of motivational psychology from 'bodily conditions' to 'social motivation'. The main emphasis is on empirical research but theoretical problems are also discussed within an empirical frame-of-reference, and there is very informative historical introduction as well as a theoretical synthesis. This synthesis takes the form of an explanatory sketch or theory of motivation. This theory defines 'motivation' as 'arousal' or 'invigoration'. According to this theory 'arousal' or 'invigoration' is determined by two mechanisms: a constitutional 'sensitization-invigoration-mechanism' and an acquired 'anticipation-invigoration-mechanism'. The present author thinks that these two mechanisms represent two hypothetical constructs, which succeed in integrating in a parsimonious way both the 'drive x habit-theories' as well as the 'value x expectation-theories' (to use Atkinson's terms).

From the view-point of the present author the most interesting handbook in the field of motivation comes to us from Germany:

Hans Thomae (Herausg.): 'Allgemeine Psychologie: II. Motivation' (Göttingen, 1965). This impressive handbook of close to one thousand pages forms the second volume of 'Handbuch der Psychologie in 12 Bänden', which at this writing is not completed. The book is the result of a considerable amount of team-work between many authors: R. Bergius, O. M. Ewert, H. Feger, W. D. Fröhlich, C. F. Graumann, H. Heckhausen, U. Lehr, P. Leyhausen, F. Merz, A. Mitscherlich, E. Mittenecker, H. Schmidtke, H. Thomae, H. Vogel and F. Weinert. All these contributors are German psychologists, but the book deals not only with German and continental psychology but with Anglo-American psychology as well. I think that the 'Handbuch' is a sign of an over-all up-to-dating in present day German psychology. In addition the 'Handbuch' shows the special German interest in systematic classifications and theory construction. Thus the book is divided in the following way:

'I Teil: Allgemeine Motivationslehre', 'II Teil: Differentielle Motivationslehre', 'III Teil: Spezielle Motivationslehre' and 'IV Teil: Ansätze zu einer Theorie der Motivation'.

The present author has not seen any other book with such a systematic and thorough treatment of the problems of motivation. This book may come to be regarded as a standard when making 'motivational classifications'. The present author finds that this 'Handbuch' contains a fruitful combination of both empirical research and theoretical (and meta-theoretical) analysis.

In this last respect it is comparable to the big American standard-work initiated by the American Psychological Association and edited by *S. Koch*.

Sigmund Koch (edt.): 'Psychology—A Study of a Science'. As the title states it is a meta-theoretical study of modern psychology, or rather a *meta-scientific* ('science of science') study, as it is not a meta-theoretical study of the structures of the theories, but also to some extent, a historical and sociological study of the development of the theories. The material comes from about 80 psychologists' writing about their own theories (or in some cases the late psychologists' theories). The account has been shaped in such a way that a meta-theoretical questionnaire formulated by S. Koch has been made the basis of it. Among the mentioned theories there are quite a number that have also been analysed in the present book, e. g.: Hebb's, Lewin's (written by D. Cartwright), Tolman's Hull-Spence's (written by Logan), Skinner's, Murray's, and R. B. Cattell's theories. To give an account of the above theories would take us to far, nor are there any essential changes, compared to the account of the theories used for the analyses in the present book. According to plans S. Koch is to summarize the result of the study of all the theories in seven volumes. They will undoubtedly turn out to be a 'gold-mine' in meta-theoretical psychology. Koch has made a temporary account at the end of the three volumes, formed as an article of about 60 pages. However tempting it might be to analyse and compare Koch's results with those of the present book I must resist from doing it, because space forbids detailed discussion[9]). It must be mentioned here, however, that one of the principal meta-theoretical results is that the logical Empiricism's 'model' of a scientific theory as an axiomatic, deductive system seems to be on the point of losing its value in psychology.

After these comments on textbooks and handbooks we shall turn our attention to some of the more specialized books about motivation.

Asger Langkjær: 'Contributions to a General Normology or Theory of Purpose-Setting. (Copenhagen, 1961). The Danish philosopher Asger Langkjær introduced the concept of 'need' into Scandinavian psychological literature in his book about 'Sales Psychology (1943). In a later book from 1961 he elaborates a comprehensive philosophy of values, which is based upon the concept of 'need'. But Langkjær does not conceive of 'need' as a biological state or biological processes in the organism. He criticizes the *homeostatic* theory of needs and also *Murray's* theory. Langkjær conceives of 'needs' as conditions established by 'purpose-setting'. This concept of 'need' as a deviation or deficiency compared to the 'norm' or 'purpose' of the organism resembles very much the 'expectation-theories' (Tolman, McClelland, Atkinson) and the 'cognitive dissonance-theory' (L. Festinger). But Langkjær has developed his theory without reference to the theories mentioned or to other modern psychological theories. The present author has had considerable difficulty in understanding and evaluating Langkjær's book, but perhaps it is because it is more philosophy (of values) than psychology (of motivation).

H. J. Eysenck (edt.): Experiments in Motivation (Oxford, 1964). This book contains material about experiments with human beings (part I) as well as with animals (part II). It includes 19 different papers about experiments with 'situation-produced motivation' and 'ego-involvement and attitudes as motivating factors' in human beings, besides 5 papers dealing with experiments with animals. The only general theme stressed in the book is the usefulness of *Hull's* formula: $sEr = sHr \times D$ as a guiding working hypothesis together with the *Yerkes-*

---

[9]) A review of Koch's works together with a synopsis of other meta-theoretical psychology have been written in: K. B. Madsen: 'Psykologien og videnskaben om videnskab', 1961. (Nordisk Psykologi, 1961, 13, 134–142). (Psychology and the Science of science).

Dodson law about the inverted U-shaped relationship between performance as a function of motivation and task difficulty. Lack of space makes it impossible to comment at greater length on the 24 individual experiments.

Elisabeth Duffy: 'Activation and Behavior (1962). This book contains a very parsimonious theory of motivation which is based to a large extent upon modern physiology. One of its most characteristic basic classifications is the distinction between 'activation' and 'direction' in behavior. This distinction was proposed by Elisabeth Duffy in *Psychol. Review* as early as the 1930's. It has later been observed in other theories. This book is therefore so important that it seems to deserve a more thorough analysis, which the present author has undertaken and which will appear in a supplementary volume, 'Modern Theories of Motivation' (in press). This is also the case with the next book:

D. E. Berlyne: 'Conflict, Arousal, and Curiosity' (N.Y., 1960). This book contains a very original theory of curiosity-motivation. Berlyne can be regarded as a student of Hebb and he bases his theory on his own experiments as well as on American and Russian neuro-psychological research. As the title of the book indicates curiosity-motivation is connected with a state of 'arousal' in the 'Reticular Arousal System', which is determined by conflicting stimuli or concepts.[10])

Berlyne's book has initiated a growing interest in explorative behavior among those Western psychologists who have looked to the Russian psychologists. Russian psychologists of recent years have been influenced by *Pavlov's* theory of the '*Orienting Reflex*' and have studied explorative behavior extensively. Some of the results of these experimental studies are collected in:

L. G. Voronin, A. N. Leontiev, A. R. Luria, E. N. Sokolov, and O. S. Vinogradova (editors): Orienting Reflex and Exploratory Behavior. (Moscow, 1958, English translation, Washington D.C. 1965). A smaller but very useful survey of theories and research by Western and Russian psychologists is collected in a small book:

R. Lynn: Attention Arousal and the Orientation Reaction. (Oxford, 1966). This book presents a short historical survey from Pavlow until the present time. Among the different theories or 'models' of orientation reaction presented is the neurophysiological model constructed by the Russian psychologist *E. N. Sokolov.* This model—like Berlyne's—conceives of the Reticular Arousal System as very important in orientation reactions. Also individual differences connected with the orientation reaction—especially the studies of *B. M. Teploy*—are dealt with in this book.

Finally we should mention a French book:

Werner Iff: 'La Motivation à L'Avancement Professionel' (Paris, 1962). This book contains an overview of the modern psychology of motivation and especially a presentation of McClelland's and co-workers study of the achievement motive. These theories and methods—together with other tests—are used by the author

---

[10]) The reader is referred to the chapter about Berlyne's theory in 'Modern Theories of Motivation' (in press).

in a study of attitudes and motivation in pupils at French military academies. The study is very through but it is impossible for us to treat it in detail here.

Summary

The present author has given an account of books and symposia about motivation from the last decennium. It shows the extent of the psychology of motivation, it is almost as extensive as is psychology itself, covering from biological borderlines to social scientific borderlines. As far as the present writer can see, however, three kinds of motivational theories are being crystallized:

1. *A physiological-oriented theory of motivation* with *Hebb's* theory as the chief representative and other later formulations, Bindra's, Morgan's, Berlyne's, etc. Close to this we find the comparative psychological and ethological theory with *Tinbergen's* theory as the chief representative.

2. *A learning theory of motivation* with *Hull's* theory as the chief representative, developed in a fruitful way by J. S. Brown, Logan, and other psychologists. Tolman's and Skinner's theories do not seem to be as important to the theory of motivation as Hull's theory.

3. *A Personality theory of motivation* with Murray's and McClelland's theories as the chief representatives, probably in keen competition with Cattell's theory. All these theories of personality show naturally many strong traces of the psychoanalysis, which has not been treated in the present book.

The present writer has tried to combine all the three types of theories of motivation in a synthesis on the basis of a comparative analysis in the last chapter of this book.

Part III

COMPARISON OF THE THEORIES

'*Meta-theory*' is often called a '*comparative methodology*,' and this is at least true about the last part of this book. A comparative study of the twenty theories which were analyzed one by one in the previous chapters will be presented in the following chapters. In the comparison I want especially *to find the common features or the dominating tendencies* in the theories, as they might be an example for future theory construction and form the foundation for *a synthesis* of the studied theories.

The comparative study will follow the same outline as the analytical study. Thus, the first chapter will deal with a comparison of *the structure of the theories*, the second chapter with a comparison of *the definitions of motivation*, and the third with *the motivation hypotheses*. Finally the last chapter will attempt to form *a synthesis* of the theories studied—corresponding to the reconstruction of the individual theories.

Chapter 17

Comparison of the Structure of the Theories

This chapter will present a comparative study of the structures of the theories. The outline used in the analysis of the structure of the individual theories will also be used here with the one exception that the first part, which gave *a summary* of the content of the individual theories, and the last part, dealing with *the models* of the individual theories, will be left out in the comparison. This chapter will, therefore, consists of the following sections:

a) The level of development of the theories.
b) Reductive and constructive theories.
c) Mentalistic, neutral-formal, and behavioristic theories.
d) Molecular and molar theories.
e) Mechanistic and field-theoretical theories.
f) Statistical and deterministic theories.

A final section will present an examination of possible *relations between the classifications.*

All the twenty theories will be included in the comparison in this chapter, but it will be divided so that the classification of the ten first theories will be compared to the classification of the ten last theories. The analysis of the last ten theories has not been as thorough as the analysis of the first ten theories regarding quotations. But the classification of the structure of the last ten theories may be considered more reliable and thus be used as '*control material*', because the analysis in the last ten chapters has been written in continuance within about two months while the analysis of the ten first theories has been made over a period of three years.

The theories which have been studied are mentioned in chronological order, and the below abbreviations will be used:

The first ten theories:

McDougall (McD), Tolman (To), Young (Y), Lewin (L), Allport (A), Murray (Mu), Hull (Hu), Hebb (He), Tinbergen (Ti), and McClelland (McC).

The last ten theories:

Frenkel-Brunswik (FB), Masserman (Mas), Freeman (Frm), Moore (Mo),

Maier (Mai), Cattell (Ca), French (Frh), Stagner and Karwoski (S-K), Skinner (S), and Holt-Hansen (H-H).

THE LEVEL OF DEVELOPMENT OF THE THEORIES

The first classification concerns the level of development of the theories. Each class includes several sub-classes, as the classifying theories—as mentioned in Chapter 3—can be divided into ad-hoc classifying and categorically classifying theories, whereas the deductive theories contain axiomatized, symbolized, and formalized theories.

This classification has, however, proved to be inconvenient for two reasons. First of all, only two of the sub-classes were needed, namely the *categorically classifying* and the *axiomatized-deductive* theories, as none of the theories could be characterized as ad-hoc classifying, only two of the theories (Hull's and especially Lewin's) could be characterized as being *partly* symbolizing, and none could be classified as formalized (even though several of them contain preliminary stages of a meta-theory in their more or less explicitly formulated premises). The analysis also proved that it was difficult to define the two main classes, since some of the theories ought to be placed in both of them. Thus it became necessary to make an intermediate class characterized by its content of classifying theories with some formulated explanations ('Laws' or hypotheses) which, however, are *not* systematized (axiomatized), but whose inter-relations are often presented in a clear diagram[1]).

The psychological theories which have been analyzed may be classified in three classes, the first ten being distributed in the following way:

1. *Categorically Classifying Theories:*
   McDougall, Allport, and Hebb.
2. *Explanatorily Classifying Theories:*
   Tolman, Young, Murray, Tinbergen, and McClelland.
3. *Axiomatized Deductive Theories:*
   Lewin and Hull.

It must, however, once again be emphasized that it is very difficult to draw any clear lines between the above mentioned classes, especially between class 1 and class 2, and therefore the classification of the individual theories is to some degree

---

[1]) After this had been written an article on the subject was published by F. A. Hayek: 'Degrees of Explanation' (in Brit. Journ. Philosophy of Science VI, 1955, 209–225). In this he says (p. 223) about a class of theories that 'in some fields the more generic theories are the more useful ones and further specification may be of little practical value,' and later on the same page: 'In some respects such theories may seem little more than schemes of classification, yet schemes which provide in advance only for such phenomena or combination of phenomena as the theories allow to occur.'

based upon personal judgement. Since no measure for the stage of development of the theories is to be found—except maybe in the number of explicitly and exactly formulated definitions and hypotheses—the following attempt to 'rate' the theories according to their level of development is even more personal. But in spite of these reservations I consider it possible to rate the theories according to their level of development in the following way:

McD He A	Y McC Mu Ti To	L Hu
classifying	explanatory	deductive

This rating of the ten analyzed theories according to their level of development is based upon an estimate of the number of explicitly formulated definitions and hypotheses ('laws,' 'principles,' 'postulates,' etc.) and upon the number of schematic and graphic presentations ('models') of each theory. It must, however, be stressed that the 'level of development' is exclusively a label for the formal-logical development of the theories, which, of course, is not the only factor determining their value. For comparison the rating of the other ten theories is presented here:

FB Mai Mo	S SK Frm Ca	Frh Mas H-H
classifying	explanatory	deductive

The result of the classification of the twenty theories according to their level of development is expressed by their distribution in the three classes: 6 classifying, 9 explanatory, and 5 deductive theories. *Thus the majority of the theories are explanatory.*

As can be seen the rating according to level of development does not follow the chronological order of the theories: some modern theories are placed among classifying theories, while some older theories are placed among deductive theories. It is, however quite likely that *the development of psychology historically will tend towards deductive theories.* Even though this hypothesis is not convincingly confirmed when only *the number* of deductive theories among those analyzed in this thesis is taken into consideration, it is, nevertheless, supported when *the importance* of the theories is also considered—measured by the number of empirical and theoretical studies they have started. In this respect Hull takes the lead—followed by Tolman and Lewin. It is quite interesting that Hull's theory both contains the greatest number of explicitly and exactly formulated definitions and hypotheses and is, at the same time, the most often quoted theory (at least in the United States). This shows clearly, in my opinion, that *an exact and systematical theory construction is of great value—also in psychology.*

There are only two classes in this classification, and only two classes are possible, since one of the classes is simply defined as the negation of the other. In Chapter 3 '*reductive* theories' were defined as theories the primary hypotheses of which can be deduced from the hypotheses of another more fundamental science, and '*constructive* theories' were, consequently, defined as theories the primary hypotheses of which *cannot* be deduced from the hypotheses of another science. Actually these definitions are only true about the *deductive* theories, but in the previous analysis they have been used as if the following had been added: 'or if the definitions, classifications, and maybe the hypotheses are (or are *not*) *related* to another science'. When we are talking about psychology this 'other science' must be physiology (or biology in its broadest sense). In psychology 'reductive theories' are therefore 'theories attempting to explain behavior on the basis of the hypotheses of physiological processes, or on the basis of physiologically interpreted, hypothetical variables', whereas the constructive theories explain on the basis of neutral-formal or mental, hypothetical variables.

Even though the classification itself—with this explicitly formulated extension—is simple and unambiguous, it was not always easy to place a theory in one of the two classes. Since not all theories have contained explicit formulations on the subject some cases of doubt have occurred. These cases of doubt could, of course, not be placed in an intermediate class, but have been characterized by adding 'mainly' in front of the classification (in the following symbolized by '?').

The first ten theories have been classified in the following way:

1. *Reductive theories:* Young (?), Hebb, Tinbergen.
2. *Constructive theories:* McDougall (?), Tolman, Allport, Lewin, Murray (?), Hull, McClelland (?).

As this classification is a classification in two complementary classes, it is not possible—as in the previous classification—to rate the theories according to their degree of constructivity or deductivity. But for the sake of clarity and later comparison with the results of the other classifications, it may nevertheless convenient to place the theories on a line with the extremely reductive and the extremely constructive theories at the ends and the cases of doubt closer to the middle. The classification of the theories then looks like this:

Ti He	Y	McD McC Mu	Hu A L To
extremely	mainly	mainly	extremely
reductive		constructive	

The classification of the ten last analyzed theories is as follows:

Frm Mai	Mas S-K	S (?) H-H	Frh C FB Mo
extremely	mainly	mainly	extremely
reductive		constructive	

The result of this classification may also be expressed in the following way: 7 of the theories are reductive, 13 theories constructive.

Thus *the majority of the analyzed theories are constructive*, but no clear psychology historical tendency of development stands out, as some of the more modern theories belong to the minority, the reductive theories.

Maybe the period mainly represented by constructive theory-building which began with Tolman's Purposive Behavior in 1932 *is now being followed by a new period of reductive theory-building* which began with Hebb's 'Organization of Behavior' from 1949[2]). But this development is not—as is often the case in cultural development—only an imitation of an earlier period, namely the behaviorism of Watson and the reflexological reductionism of Pavlov, but a kind of synthesis of the contradictory tendencies of earlier periods. The creators of the neo-reductive theories know—or ought to know— that even with the increased development of neurophysiology a reduction of psychological theories to physiological ones must be a deduction—or a less formal explanation—on the basis of physiological *hypotheses* with physiologically interpreted, *hypothetical variables* (the constructive 'element' in the reduction).

MENTALISTIC, NEUTRAL-FORMAL, AND BEHAVIORISTIC THEORIES

According to the definitions in Chapter 3 this classification contains three classes in which the theories are placed according to what kind of hypothetical variables and protocol statements they contain. The three classes are defined in the following way:

1. *Mentalistic theories*
are theories with hypothetical variables which are interpreted phenomenologically, and with introspective protocol statements.

2. *Behavioristic theories*
are theories with hypothetical variables which are interpreted neurophysiologically, and with behavioristic protocol statements.

---

[2]) This hypothesis about the future development of psychology has so far been confirmed by the appearance of a large number of articles of neuro-physiological character in periodicals, symposia, etc., during the last years (cf. the bibliography at the end of the book).

3. *Neutral-formal theories*
are theories with hypothetical variables which are interpreted as neutral-formal constructions, and with protocol statements which may be behavioristic and/or instrospective. (The diffuse mixed forms are included in this class).

This classification has been used on the first ten theories analyzed with results most clearly presented in the following way:

A	McD McC Mu L Y To Hu	He Ti
mentalistic	neutral-formal	behavioristic

The corresponding classification of the ten last analyzed theories is as follows:

Mo	Frh H-H C FB S-K	Mas Frm Mai S
mentalistic	neutral-formal	behavioristic

Thus the result of this classification of the twenty theories is: 2 mentalistic, 12 neutral-formal, and 6 behavioristic theories.

According to this *the majority* of the analyzed theories are neutral-formal. If the classification has been used correctly and if the selection of theories can be said to be fairly representative, this result shows that *the great contrast between behavioristic and mentalistic theories which* influenced psychology from about 1910 to 1930 *has been replaced by a higher synthesis*—the neutral-formal theories—mainly through Tolman's 'intervening variables' (or hypothetical constructions). It must, however, be added that the 'behavioristic element' in this synthesis is the dominant feature, as the behavioristic protocol statements (and methods) have received a certain 'privileged position' which they also must have epistemologically (cf. Chapter 3). And in spite of the six rather new purely behavioristic theories it is most likely that *the development in psychology will strengthen the tendency to form syntheses.*

MOLECULAR AND MOLAR THEORIES

This classification contains two classes which we in Chapter 3 defined in the following way:

1. '*Molar* theories' are 'theories the protocol statements of which describe phenomena of a *comparatively* low level of abstaction or *macroscopic* phenomena', in psychology: actions in everyday situations.
2. '*Molecular* theories' are 'theories the protocol statements of which describe phenomena of a *comparatively* high level of abstraction or *microscopic* phenomena', in psychology: movements and stimuli.

The classification has been defined in such a way that there is only a difference *in degree* between the two classes, so that intermediate forms can exist.

In the analytical part these intermediate forms have often been characterized by a 'mainly' in connection with 'molecular' or 'molar'. As a result of the classifications, the first ten theories may be ranked according to their degree of molarity (or molecularity) in the following way:

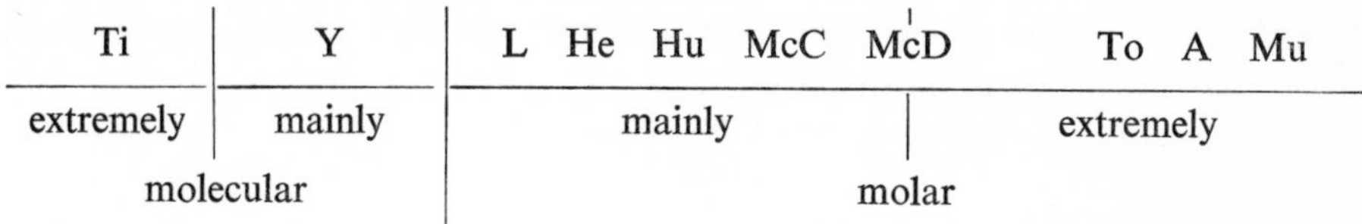

And corresponding to this the ten last analyzed theories may be ranked in the following way:

H-H Frm S | Mai Mas S-K FB Mo Frh C

extremely | mainly | mainly | extremely

molecular | molar

The twenty theories are distributed in the following way: 15 molar and 5 molecular theories. Thus *the majority of the analyzed theories are molar*. If—as in the previous cases—it is taken for granted that the classification has been used correctly and the selection of theories is representative, it seems likely that *the historical development of psychology has been in the direction of more molar theories*. To prove this statement would, however, demand a study of historical psychology and thus go beyond the subject of this book. It is, however, easy to accept that the development has taken this direction, as the Gestalt-psychologists in European psychology have critized 'atomistic mosaic-psychology' just as Tolman in American psychology critized 'the stimulus-response behaviorism'. Therefore it is likely that *in the future pure psychological theories will be molar* as compared to the pure neurophysiological theories which are more molecular, while 'physiological psychology' and ethology form an intermediate group. By adding the word 'pure' to 'psychological theories' in the italicized sentence this is changed from a more or less evident empirical ('synthetical') hypothesis of psychological historical content to a definitorical ('-analytical') statement of meta-theoretical content.

FIELD-THEORETICAL, DYNAMIC, AND MECHANISTIC THEORIES

This classification includes three classes (cf. Chapter 3), namely: *the mechanistic, the dynamic, and the field-theoretical*, between which there is only a difference *in degree*, namely a difference in the complexity of the functional relations. Since such a classification—just as the previous one—is difficult to use, I have—as hinted at in Chapter 3—tried to use the following criteria—mainly taken from the article by *v. Bertalanffy:*

1. *Mechanistic theories:* theories where the hypotheses normally contain *two variables* (as for example 'stimulus' and 'reaction').
2. *Dynamic theories:* theories where the hypotheses deal with *the interrelations of several variables* (as for example ${}_{S}E_{R} = f(D \times {}_{S}H_{R})$).
3. *Field-theories:* theories where especially inter-relations between '*the environment*' (empirical situation-variables) and '*the organism*' (empirical organical variables and hypothetical variables) are essential.

When analyzing the last ten theories I found it practical to divide the class of *dynamic* theories into two *sub-classes* named as '*mainly*' and '*extremely*', and bordering on the mechanistic and the field-theoretical theories, respectively.

Keeping this last addition in mind the classification of the first ten theories analyzed is:

He	Ti A	Hu McD Y Mu McC	To L
	mainly	extremely	
mechanistic	dynamic		field-theoretical

The corresponding classification of the last ten theories is:

	S Mo S-K	C Frh Frm H-H FB	Mai Mas
	mainly	extremely	
mechanistic	dynamic		field-theoretical

The above mentioned two classifications give the following distribution: 3 field-theoretical, 16 dynamic (of which the 11 are extremely dynamic) and 1 mechanistic theory. *The majority of the theories are thus dynamic, actually extremely dynamic,* and there are more field-theoretical theories than there are mechanistic theories.

Against this unsymmetrical classification-result the following criticism may be directed[3]):

1) The classification is not used correctly (or not practically).
2) The analyzed theories are *not* representative for the psychological theories of the period.

Ad 1. Of course I have tried to classify the theories according to the definitions in Chapter 3. But they are somewhat difficult to use, among other things because

---

[3]) The same criticism and counter-argumentation can maybe to some extent hold true with regard to the other classifications.

many of the major theories have very few explicitly formulated hypotheses which can be analyzed with regard to the number of inter-dependent variables. Therefore it has been necessary—as it has been with the other classifications—to take into consideration the presuppositions of the theories, that is, the more or less explicitly formulated meta-theoretical statements about the theory, among which some have often dealt with the classification in question. In this way we are exposed to a source of error, however, in that not all the theories follow their presuppositions to the same degree.

Ad 2. The theories have been selected so that they in my opinion should represent the general-psychological and/or motivation-psychological theories of the period. But I might be wrong, and some of the selected theories are maybe not as important as others which have not been selected. In order to achieve greater reliability of the results of the comparisons in this chapter, the number of the theories analyzed should have been larger. Finally it is far from self-evident that the theories must be distributed symmetrically in the classifications (or even 'normally distributed' in the statistical sense); but it might be said to be inconvenient to have a classification where one *main* class is almost empty.

If the result of the classification with the unsymmetrical distribution of the theories (most of them extremely dynamic) *is accepted* on the basis of this argumentation, there are *two possibilities:* 1) either the classification in question is without value, or 2) it has been of some importance, but is superfluous now.

As mentioned in Chapter 3, K. W. Spence speaks in favor of the first possibility. Personally I maintain the opposite view, that the other possibility is the one most likely to be true, but this can only be proved through a thorough *psychological historical* study of the development of psychology through a whole century, which is completely beyond the subject of this book. As a *hypothesis* it can be suggested that the discussion between the dynamic psychologists (the Gestalt-psychologists and the psychoanalysts) and the mechanistic psychologists (the older behaviorists and the reflexologists) *has influenced psychology in a field-theoretical direction.* If a detailed historical study of psychology could prove this hypothesis, it would exemplify that an old controversy in the history of science has come to an end because one form of theory construction has become dominant (while the controversy between behavioristic and mentalistic theories was brought to an end by the development of a synthesis (neutral-formal theories).

STATISTICAL AND DETERMINISTIC THEORIES

At the beginning (cf. Chapter 2 and 3) two classes were included in this classification: the *deterministic* and the *statistical* theories. During the analysis it turned out that many theories belonged to a logically possible *intermediate class* of theories containing both deterministic and statistical hypotheses. The classification used may therefore be explicitly formulated thus:

1. *Deterministic theories*
are theories which mainly contain explicit or implicit, *deterministic hypotheses* dealing with mathematical *functional* relations or qualitative, *causal or determining* relations.

2. *Statistical theories*
are theories which mainly contain explicit or implicit, *statistical hypotheses* including 'correlations' or other *quantitative probability-statements*, or *qualitative tendency-statements*.

3. *Mixed theories*
are theories which contain both statistical and deterministic hypotheses. This class also includes theories which have no explicit hypotheses and no meta-theoretical statements concerning the deterministic or statistical character of the theory.

On the basis of these definitions the classification of the first ten theories analyzed may be presented in the following way:

	Y Mu Hu McD	McC A To L He Ti
statistical	mixed	deterministic

And the corresponding classification of the last ten theories analyzed:

H-H FB	C S Mo (?)	Mai Frh Mas S-K Frm
statistical	mixed	deterministic

The sum of the above mentioned classifications gives the following distribution: 2 statistical theories, 6 mixed theories (— one which cannot be defined: Moore's theory), and 11 deterministic theories; thus: *the majority of the analyzed theories are deterministic.*

We find here an unsymmetrical distribution similar to that in the previous classification. But it can be stated with a rather high degree of probability that the distribution would have been different if the theories studied had been from other psychological areas, e. g. the psychology of personality, which presents many statistical hypotheses or correlations, and the psychology of learning, which now presents some statistical theories (or 'probability-models').

The following may be said about the relation of the results of the classifications to the problem of determinism:

None of the theories studied are indeterministic. Quite obviously an indeterministic theory is a logical impossibility as the function of a theory is to explain and predict phenomena, and this can only be done if a certain regularity or *invariance*[4]) *can be proved or presupposed.* Thus the examination has confirmed the statement made by *Højgård Jensen* and *I. C. Madsen:* 'The direct opposition to the physical determinism: that events are completely independent, that no regularity exists, has hardly ever been held as a serious philosophy by any normal human being' ('The Problem of Causality' p. 50)[5]).

Next the examination has proved that *none of the theories studied*, except those of McDougall and Moore, *are of a teleological or anthropomorphistic character.*

Finally it can be said that *the deterministic psychological theories do not presuppose any rationalistic principle of causation* (which assumes that causation is a 'necessary' or absolutely forcing relation). All the deterministic theories seem to presuppose that the behavior follows the independent (and hypothetical) variables with a certain probability. This is in agreement with the modern scientific principle of causation for example as it is presented by *M. Blegvad* (in 'The Problem of Causality', Nordisk Sommeruniversitet 1951).

About the *mixed* theories it is true that they as a rule presupposet hat behavior is causally determined, but the psychological hypotheses must be *'average-laws'* because of the constant variation of the hypothetical variables (Hull's $_SO_R$) or their complex interaction (Cattell's 17. 'law'), or because of the great individual differences (McClelland).

Only one statistical theory (that of Holt-Hansen) presupposes stochastic processes in the individual.

According to this study of the results of the classifications it seems likely that if psychological theories are to contain *quantitative hypotheses* they must either be *average-'deterministic'* hypotheses or *real stochastic-statistical* hypotheses (such as those of Hull and Holt-Hansen, respectively).

In my opinion it is, therefore, unnecessary to discuss whether or not statistical hypotheses are desirable in psychology. Moreover I think that as causal-deterministic hypotheses cannot be absolutely true anyway, but can only be of a relatively high degree of probability, there is in scientific practice *only a difference in degree in probability between deterministic and statistical hypotheses.*

Thus it might be said that the controversy between deterministic and statistical theories is also disappearing and that a higher synthesis is developing. This synthesis may be called, with the words of G. Rasch[7]): '*a statistical or stochastic causality*, as one of the essential characteristics of causality, *predictability*, in principle is possible when dealt with as a statistical problem'[8]).

This is the synthesis which is presented in Skinner's theory and which I described as *probability-determinism.*

---

[4]) cf. Kaila: Den mänskliga Kunskliga Kunskapen.

[5]) Nordisk Sommeruniversitet 1951.

[6]) Similar to what is happening to the controversy between behavioristic and mentalistic theories.

[7]) In 'Årsagsproblemet' (p. 248, Nordisk Sommeruniversitet 1951).

[8]) *Feigl* expresses the same view by the term 'predict-ability.'

RELATIONS BETWEEN THE CLASSIFICATIONS

After having compared the twenty theories with regard to the six classifications, it is now possible to study the *relations* between the classes. For the sake of clarity the six different rankings of the theories will be presented together.

McD He A	Y McC Mu Ti To	L Hu
classifying	explanatory	deductive

FB Mai Mo	S SK Frm Ca Frh	Mas H-H
classifying	explanatory	deductive

Ti He	Y	McD McC Mu	Hu A L To
extremely	mainly	mainly	extremely
reductive		constructive	

Frm Mai	Mas S-K	S (?) H-H	Frh C FB Mo
extremely	mainly	mainly	extremely
reductive		constructive	

A	McD McC Mu L Y To Hu	He Ti
mentalistic	neutral-formal	behavioristic

The corresponding classification of the ten last analyzed theories is as fellows:

Mo	Frh H-H C FB	S-K Mas Frm Mai S
metalistic	neutral-formal	behavioristic

Ti	Y	L He Hu McC McD	To A Mu
extremely	mainly	mainly	extremely
molecular		molar	

And corresponding to this the ten last analyzed theories may by ranked in the following way:

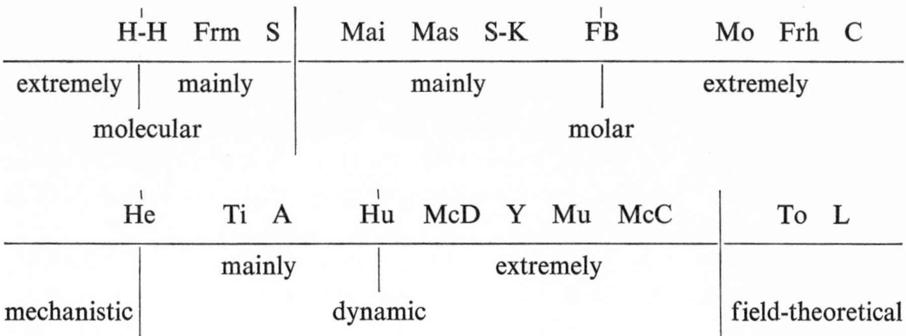

The corresponding classification of the last ten theories is:

	S Mo S-K	C Frh Frm H-H FB	Mai Mas
	mainly	extremely	
mechanistic	dynamic		field-theoretical

	Y Mu Hu McD	McC A To L He Ti
statistical	mixed	deterministic

And the corresponding classification of the last ten theories analyzed:

H-H FB	C S Mo (?)	Mai Frh Mas S-K Frm
statistical	mixed	deterministic

When possible relations between the above mentioned classifications are to be discovered and formulated, the ends of the scales must be of special interest as they present the extreme cases. Thus the number of the studied theories becomes still smaller, whereby the reliability of the results will be even less. Therefore the following general statements must be taken as *hypotheses* made to be tested by the study of still more theories.

If the first ten theories are compared it stands out that especially two of the theories, namely Tinbergen's and Hebb's, are often placed near the ends of the scales. Thus the theories of Tinbergen and Hebb prove to be the only extremely reductive and the only totally behavioristic theories. Moreover they are classified as the most mechanistic and the most deterministic theories.

On this basis the following *tentative* hypothesis can be made: that a correlation exists between the *four* classes: the reductive, the behavioristic, the mechanistic, and the deterministic, so that theories placed in one of the classes mentioned are very often placed in the other three classes, too.

To control of this tentative hypothesis one might check whether a similar correlation exists between the theories in the 'opposite' classes. It is apparent that the most constructive theories are those of Tolman, Lewin, Allport, and Hull, whereas those of Murray, McClelland, and McDougall are only 'mainly constructive'. The only totally mentalistic theory is that of Allport, whereas the theories of McDougall, McClelland, and Murray are neutral-formal theories with certain mentalistic 'sympathies'. The only actual field-theories are those of Lewin and Tolman, whereas the most dynamic theories are those of McClelland, McDougall, Murray, and Hull. No totally statistical theories exist among these theories. Two theories do appear together rather often, namely Tolman's and Lewin's. They are quite close to each other in their stage of development, both of them are constructive, both are neutral-formal (mainly behavioristic), both are relatively molar, they are the only real field-theories, and they are both deterministic.

If now these two paris of theories are compared (Hebb-Tinbergen and Lewin-Tolman) they prove not to be placed in different (or opposite) classes in all classifications. This is only the case in the reductive contra the constructive classifications and the mechanistic contra the field-theoretical classifications. Concerning the degree of development the theory of Tinbergen is much closer to that of Tolman than to that of Hebb (in my opinion). And in the classification mentalistic contra behavioristic, Tolman and Lewin are placed among the neutral-formal theories, even in the mainly behavioristic sub-class. Regarding the molar and molecular tendencies of the theories, that of Hebb is placed between Tolman and Lewin, whereas Tinbergen stands alone in the class of molecular theories. Finally all four theories are placed side by side in the class of deterministic theories.

As can be seen from the above mentioned comparisons the only comparatively reliable or probable correlation between the results of the classifications is the correlation between the classification 'constructive contra reductive' and the classification 'mechanistic contra field-theoretical,' in that the reductive theories (Tinbergen and Hebb) are also the most mechanistic theories, whereas the constructive theories (especially those of Tolman and Lewin, but also those of Hull, Murray, and McDougall) are also the most field-theoretical. If, then, the '*control-material*', the last ten theories analyzed is examined, it is easily seen that also here some of the theories are often placed together, namely those of Freeman, Maier, and Masserman. These theories are, like those of Tinbergen and Hebb, the most reductive ones. They are, however, *not* mechanistic (as were those of Tinbergen and Hebb), but field-theoretical. This disproves the tentative hypothesis (about the correlation between the second and the fifth classification), and it must therefore be abandoned.

The only relation between the classifications which can be seen directly from the table is *a relation between the reductive and the behavioristic classes:* The four extremely reductive theories (those of Ti, He, Mai, Frh) are also totally behavioristic theories; and if the mainly reductive theories (those of Mas, S-K, and Y) are considered, they, too, prove to be totally behavioristic theories, or in the mainly behavioristic half of the neutral-formal class. But this relation is probably of the logical kind, as it is a logical consequence of the definitions of these classes. This can also be seen from the fact that the mentalistic theories are extremely constructive. On the other hand, not all constructive theories are mentalistic, since the constructive theories are either mentalistic theories (A, Mo) or neutral-formal theories. Thus *no* complete connection (positive or negative correlation—or logical identity) can be found between second and third classification, only between the reductive and the behavioristic classes. But if a complete correlation had existed one of the classifications would have been unnecessary.

This negative result of the attempt to find relations between the classifications may, at least, be taken as a proof that *the classifications are not unnecessary, but describe six different independent theory-characteristics.*

Summary

This chapter has compared the classifications of the theories described in the previous chapters.

The classification of the theories according to their *degree of development* indicates that the development of psychology tends toward more exact and systematic theory construction (especially deductive theories).

The classification *reductive contra constructive* theories shows that the majority of the theories analyzed are constructive, but since several of the most modern theories are reductive it is possible that the future development will be towards reductive theories (although on a 'higher level').

The classification *mentalistic contra behavioristic* theories shows that most of the theories analyzed belong to an intermediate class, *the neutral-formal theories,* which is a higher synthesis of the two antitheses.

The classification *molecular contra molar* theories shows that the majority of the theories analyzed are molar, and it is likely that psychology will continue to develop in this direction.

The classification *mechanistic contra field-theoretical* systems shows that the majority of the theories analyzed belong to an intermediate class, *the dynamic theories.* Psychology will probably continue to develop toward increasingly field-theoretical systems.

The classification *statistical contra deterministic* shows that the majority of the analyzed theories are deterministic and only two of them statistical. Psychology will probably develop towards an intermediate form, a '*probability-determinism*'.

As a whole the results may be formulated in the following hypothesis: *Psychological theories are becoming more deductive, more neutral-formal, more molar, more field-theoretical, and probability-deterministic.*

No relations between the classes can be found, except for one single logically determined relation (between the classes reductive and behavioristic). Therefore the six applied classifications must represent six independent dimensions of theory-construction.

APPENDIX

OTHER META-THEORETICAL-PSYCHOLOGICAL STUDIES

In 'Principles of Systematic Psychology' (1943) *Coleman R. Griffith* has made a very thorough and comprehensive historical and philosophical study of psychological theories from the last century. He begins by defining some 'points of reference' which he divides into '*ontological*' and '*methodological*' points of reference. The following opposite points of view are included in the ontological points of reference: 1) the behavioristic contra the mentalistic, 2) the functional contra the existential, 3) the configurationalistic contra the analytical, and 4) the deterministic contra the indeterministic (the 'voluntaristic') point of view.

The following pairs are included in the methodological points of view: 1) the rationalistic contra the experimentalistic, 2) the genetic contra the static, and 3) the individualistic contra the social point of view.

Several of these different 'points of reference' correspond to the classifications of theories used in this and the previous chapters. Thus the first and fourth pairs of ontological points of view correspond closely to the classifications of the same names used here, but with the reservation that 'indeterministic' is not identical with 'statistical'. The third pair might be considered a combination of two classifications, so that 'configurationalistic' corresponds to a combination of molar and field-theoretical, whereas 'analytic' corresponds to a combination of molecular and mechanistic. The differentiation between functional contra existential points of view may be taken as a differentiation between a modern scientific and an older speculative-meta-physical point of view. The methodological differentiations do not correspond to any of the classifications used here, but taken as a whole they correspond more or less to the classifications 1) classifying contra deductive, and 2) reductive contra constructive theories.

After having defined these 'points of reference' he describes the different psychological systems (the '-isms', or 'schools') as '*patterns of points of reference*'. About the possible correlations or combinations of these 'points of view' into 'patterns' Griffith writes (p. 166):

> 'In theory, at least, there might be as many systems of psychology as there are possible combinations of points of reference. In practice, the theoretical limit has almost been reached.'

This quotation corresponds to the result of the previous analysis and comparison as Griffith has *no* classification corresponding to reductive contra constructive, defined in such a way that reductive theories cannot also be mentalistic. Moreover he describes the newer psychological '-isms' as follows:

'*Configurationism*' (Gestalt-psychology) is mentalistic, functionalistic, configurationalistic, deterministic, rationalistic, static, and individualistic.

'*Behaviorism*' is behavioristic, functionalistic, analytical, deterministic, experimentalistic, alternately genetic and static, and individualistic.

'*Psycho-analysis*' is mentalistic, analytical, existentialistic, deterministic, rationalistic, genetic, and individualistic.

These descriptions may be compared with the descriptions of the theories analyzed in this thesis. Even though these have not been classified according to the almost extinct 'schools' it is possible to point to some of the theories as having their roots in one of the three different schools.

Thus Lewin's theory is considered to derive from Gestalt-psychology. It was classified as a 'deductive, constructive, neutral-formal, mainly molar, field-theoretical, and deterministic theory.' If this description is compared with Griffith's description of 'configurationism' it is seen that there is agreement in all common classifications except at one point where Griffith describes configurationism as being mentalistic, while Lewin's theory here bas been classified as neutral-formal (moreover in the mainly behavioristic sub-class). But Lewin deviates in this respect from the more traditional Gestalt-psychologists (Wertheimer, Køhler, and Koffka), who were more anti-behavioristic.

Hull seems to be the most obvious representative for 'behaviorism'. His theory has been classified as a 'deductive, constructive, neutral-formal (mainly behavioristic), molar, dynamic, and deterministic theory.' The agreement with Griffith's description is even more obvious if *Tinbergen's* theory[10] is chosen to represent 'behaviorism' (quite unhistorically, of course). This shows how far away modern 'behavioristic' theories (Hull and Tolman) have developed from the original Watson-behaviorism, which Griffith has described.

Finally *Murray's* theory may be taken as an example of a theory which has its roots in psychoanalysis. His theory has been classified as 'explanatory, mainly constructive, neutral-formal (mainly mentalistic), molar, dynamic, and mixed statistical and deterministic'. This description agrees fairly closely with Griffith's description of psychoanalysis.

Griffith also predicts the development of psychology. He writes (p. 116):

> 'But already it is clear that the system of psychology is moving steadily toward the behavioral, functional, configurational, and determined goals, and away from the mental, existential, analytical, and voluntaristic goals.'

If this prediction is compared with the hypotheses stated in this book it is seen that there is rather close agreement, as during the study of the individual classifications it was predicted that psychology would develop towards the neutral-formal (but mainly behavioristic), field-theoretical, molar, and probability-deterministic

---

[10]) cf. the classification-scheme.

theories. This agreement between hypotheses by different writers working from different presuppositions confirms their probability.

Egon Brunswik has published a historical and meta-theoretical study of psychological theories and their development in 'The Conceptual Framework of Psychology'[11]). After having made an analysis of objectivity, complexity, and exactitude in science and especially in psychology, he gives the following psychology historical hypotheses (p. 50):

'1) There seems to be a continuous change-over from subjectivism to objectivism in psychology . . .

2) . . . a development from an emphasis on confined core events through perepheralism to functionalism, that is, broadly, from a static and molecular to a dynamic and molar type of approach . . .

3) Progress along one of these two perpendicular directions seems frequently accompanied by standstill or even a regression along the other, but in the end this standstill turns out to be only temporary.

4) The successive subjective phases appear as encapsulated, relatively causal miniature anticipations of the reference patterns found in their physicalistic counterparts.

5) There seems to be a time lag between these formally corresponding introspectionistic and objectivistic stages . . ., so that in many cases there is a spiral recurrence of analogous principles on more advanced levels of methodological perfection.'

If one compares these five hypotheses with Griffith's historical hypothesis and my hypotheses in the section on the six classifications, one finds an agreement which confirms the probability of the hypotheses. Brunswik assumes also the correlation between static and molecular and between dynamic and molar, respectively. This is a correlation which has *not* been confirmed by the study of these twenty theories, since for example Hebb's theory is molar and mechanistic at the same time. Moreover Brunswik emphasises in hypothesis number five 'a spiral recurrence of analogous principles on more advanced levels', and this is in agreement with what was pointed out in the section on reductive contra constructive theories. Brunswik formulates the dialectic development of psychology (cf. the synthesis of behavioristic and mentalistic theories in neutral-formal theories) in his description of the psychology in the thirties (p. 66):

'During a third phase of modern psychology, beginning in the 1930's there is a "convergence" of the predominantly Anglo-American tradition of empiricist rigor. . . with the predominantly Continental stress on complexity and richness of scope. This convergence possesses all the earmarks of a genuine "synthesis" of the preceding divergent, mutually "antithetical" movements (to apply Hegel's notions of the dialectics of the creative process). It is not an ecletic intercombination of selected fragments of existing schools; rather, abstract methodological features are united for the first time in formations of striking novelty of style.'

This synthesis of objectivity and molarity in psychology is by Brunswik called '*objective functional psychology*'.

In a 'Symposium on the probability approach in psychology'[12]) Brunswik points out that this objective, functionalistic psychology must be 'probalistic'

---

[11]) 'International Encyclopedia of Unified Science' vol. **I, no.** 10 (Chicago 1952).

[12]) Psych. Review, 1955, 62, 193–242.

rather than deterministic if it is to be satisfactorily molar, since the behavior of the organisms is adjustment reactions, in themselves probalistic because the organism simply has not enough possibility to react more regularly (deterministic) in a relatively unknown world. He contrasts 'probalistic functionalism' with nomothetic (deterministic), molecular, and reductive psychology. In the same symposium *Leo Postman* maintains, contrary to Brunswik, that deterministic theories can be both molecular and molar (which is in agreement with the correlations found here); *David Krech* also supports deterministic, reductive, molecular theory constructions (apparently there is a tendency to identify, or at any rate to correlate reductive with molecular, but such a correlation has *not* been confirmed by this study, as the theory of Hebb is reductive, but also molar). Brunswik answer, however, that 'probalistic functionalism' will increasingly influence psychology.

Addendum

Addendum: In recent years several meta-theoretical studies of psychological theories have appeared. The most comprehensive and thorough study is *S. Koch* (ed.): 'Psychology—A Study of a Science' (six volumes have appeared since 1959). Another very thorough and systematic meta-theoretical study of motivational theories can be found in *Hans Thomae* (Hrzgb.): 'Allgemeine Psychologie: II Motivation' (1965). Besides these the reader is referred to *Estes et al.:* 'Modern Learning Theory' (1954), *F. H. Allport:* 'Theories of Perception and the Concept of Structure' (1955), *S. Hall and G. Lindzey:* 'Theories of Personality' (1957), *E. R. Hilgard and G. W. Bower:* 'Theories of Learning' (3rd ed., 1966) and *B. B. Wolman:* 'Contemporary Theories and Systems in Psychology' (1966).

Chapter 18

Comparison of the Motivation Definitions of the Theories

This chapter will compare the most important definitions (and variables) of motivation in the twenty theories that have been analyzed. After the compariosn an attempt will be made to form *a synthesis* of the definitions which differentiates motivational variables from other psychological variables.

The final section will compare the different classifications or list of motivational variables.

THE COMPARISON OF DEFINITIONS

Tolman's classification of psychological variables was studied and revised in Chapter 3, and the classification was then used in the following chapters for the analysis of the definitions of motivational variables in the twenty theories. In this chapter a brief outline of the results of the classification will be given together with an attempt to combine the classifications. Therefore it will be necessary to be able to distinguish between the different psychologists' varying use of the same terms (for example 'drive'). To serve this purpose identical terms will be marked with an index consisting of the abbreviated name of the psychologist in question (cf. Chapter 17). To attain a further division between the same psychologist's varying use of the same term in two different books, these books will be marked by adding a number in the index (for example, 'To. 1.' means Tolman's first book (in this case 'Purposive Behavior') and 'To. 2.' means Tolman's second book (here: 'A Psychological Model').

Hypothetical and Empirical Variables

The most fundamental distinction between variables is that between *hypothetical* and *empirical* variables.

The *first* class includes both actual *hypothetical constructions* with 'surplus meaning' and the strictly reductively defined '*intervening variables*'.

The *empirical* variables include both *independent* (maybe experimentally controlled) variables and *dependent behavior variables.* This first sub-class includes both external *situation-variables* and, when they are empirical (i. e. directly observable), internal *organic variables.* In this connection behavior variables are all forms of behavior which are a function of motivation variables and which can therefore be used to formulate an operational definition or maybe to *measure* the motivation variables in question[1]).

The distinction between hypothetical and empirical variables can be supplemented by classifying the hypothetical variables according to their *interpretation* (their 'surplus meaning') i. e., according to whether they are *neutral-formal, neurophysiological,* or *mentalistic* variables.

By combining these classifications one obtaines the following classification of the motivation variables in the twenty theories:

I. *Hypothetical variables:*

a. *neutral-formal:*

Instinct (McD), Propensity (McD), Tendency (McD), Sentiment (McD), Demand (To-1), Drive (To-1), Need (To-2), Set (Y-1), Attitude (Y-2),Motivational trait (A), Instrumental trait (A), Force (L), Valence (L), Tension (L), Need (= Drive) (Mu), $_{S}E_{R}$ (Hu), r_G (Hu), Drive (Hu), Motive (McC), Erg (C), Drive (FB), Wishes (Frh), Need (H-H), Activity factors (H-H), Engram factors B^l and b^r (H-H).

b. *neuro-physiological:*

Drive (Y-1), Phase sequence (He), Motivation (Ti), Instinct (Ti), Arousal and Discharge index (Frm), Set (Frm), Drive (S-K).

c. *phenomenological:*

Desire (Y-2), Beta-press (Mu), Impulse (Mo).

II. *Empirical variables*[2]):

Initiating physiological state (To-1), Drive (To-2), Need (Y-1), Drive (A), Need (L), Alpha-press (Mu), Cathexis (Mu), Drive condition (= Need) (Hu), Drive stimulus (Hu), Motivational factors (Ti), Need (Mas), Need (Mai), Goal (Mai), Need (S-K), Deprivation (S).

In all: 15 empirical and 36 hypothetical variables (the last group consisting of 3 phenomenological, 8 physiological, and 25 neuro-physiological variables).

---

[1]) While behavior variables are descriptive, independent and hypothetical variables are explanatory.

[2]) There are only independent variables in this class, since no motivation variable is a dependent behavior variable.

Function Variables and Disposition Variables

Another fundamental classification of psychological variables, independent of the first one, is the classification *disposition variables* and *function variables*. This classification has been rather difficult to apply because many psychologists use the *same* term about a function variable and a disposition variable, and only a few use an explicit distinction corresponding to the one used here. Of course this might not always be necessary, depending upon what is the purpose of the theory. If it is *a theory of personality*, the purpose of which is primarily to describe and explain the structure of the personality and individual differences and their development, then the *disposition* variables are the most important ones, and the function variables will only be of secondary importance linking up the behavior which is regarded as a manifestation of the personality. If, on the other hand, it is *a general psychological theory*, the purpose of which is to describe and explain the behavior, the *function* variables are the most important. And then the structure in which the processes determining the behavior take place is a rather obvious condition for the existence of the processes, a condition which it is almost superfluous to discuss in the theory unless important individual differences (or differences typical of the species) in this structure makes it necessary to mention it. But even though a theory thus can deal mainly with the one kind of variable, it must necessarily take both kinds into consideration in order to be able to explain and predict with some degree of probability. The processes determining behavior (the function variables) are not only determined by the external situation and immediate organic state, but also by the structure in which they are taking place, a structure which can possess specific and individual characteristics (disposition variables) which take part in determining the development of the process (and which must therefore be included in quantitative hypotheses as rather *constant* 'variables'). It is to the same degree true that the psychology of personality cannot treat the function variables as only secondary connecting links to the behavior which is the manifestation of the personality (the disposition variables). These function variables are also determined by the actual external situation and internal organic condition, and these variables must be included if the theory of personality is to be used to predict the actual behavior of a certain person in a real situation.

Briefly: The classification in function variables and disposition variables is extremely useful in a psychological theory, and therefore the results obtained by using this classification in the analysis of the twenty theories are summarized in the following outline:

I. *Disposition variables:*

Instinct (McD), Propensity (McD), Sentiment (McD), Attitude (Y-2), Motivational and instrumental of trait (A)?, Need (Drive) (Mu), Instinct (Ti), Erg (C), Drive (FB), Activity factors (H-H), Engram factors B^l and b^r (H-H).

II. *Function variables:*

Tendency (McD), Init. phys. state (To-1), Demand (To-1), Drive (To-1), Drive (To-2), Need (To-2), Drive (Y), Need (Y), Set (Y-1), Desire (Y-2), Motivational and instrumental traits (A)?, Drive (A), Force (L), Valence (L), Tension (L), Need (Drive) (Mu), Press (Mu), Cathexis (Mu), $_SE_R$ (Hu), Phase sequence (He), Motivation (Ti), Motivational factors (Ti), Motive (McC), Drive (FB), Arousal and Discharge index (Frm), Set (Frm), Impuls (Mo), Need (Mas), Need (Mai), Goal (Mai), Wishes (Frh), Need and Drive (S-K), Deprivation (S), Need (H-H).

The result is as follows: 12 disposition variables and 41 function variables, each case of doubt being counted as *two* variables (one disposition variable and one function variable).

A New Classification

The two last classifications have been traditional (mainly based upon the suggestions of Tolman), and they have been used in the analysis of the motivation definitions in the twenty theories. But during this analysis I found that it would be convenient to use yet another classification of psychological variables. *Young's* definition of motivation in 'Motivation of Behavior' gave me this idea. The definition in question is as follows (p. 45):

'Motivational psychology may be defined as the study of all conditions which arouse and regulate the behavior of organisms.'

This definition points out more clearly than the definition in 'Encyclopedia of Psychology,' which was used as a temporary definition of 'motivation,' that *motivation variables,* according to Young's theory, *have two functions:* to *arouse* and to *regulate* the energy of the behavior. Young does not, however, go on to make any classification of motivation variables after having given this division of functions. Neither do any of the other theories explicitly make such a classification. But after having read the Nebraska Symposium, I found it still more practical to introduce a new classification. In the symposium in 1953 *Brown* proposed a distinction between 1) 'drive-function,' which should be named 'the energizing or activating properties of drives,' and 2) 'the property of directing or guiding behavior,' which is—it is added—'deliberately omitted from the group of drive properties'. In the symposium in 1954 *Farber* made use of the term '*dynamogenic*' about the '*energizing*' function, but maintained—contrary to Brown—that 'drive' can possess both the two different functions (which—as can be seen—are equal to Young's arousal-functions and regulating-functions).

At present I shall not remark upon Brown's statement that 'drives' have only energy-mobilizing functions and that the controlling function is exerted by other variables. It must, however, be pointed out that the problem is not (exclusively) an empirical one, but primarily a *semantic* problem, a fact which apparently has not been clearly understood by all the psychologists taking part in the discussion.

Based upon these considerations I find it useful to make a classification of the motivational variables of the twenty theories using the above mentioned distinction. Thereby, among other things, *the actual usage (the motivational definitions) of the psychologists* becomes clear, and this may later make it possible to decide how the usage *ought* to be (in order to be most scientifically fruitful).

The classification[3]) suggested can be defined in the following way:

I. '*Dynamogenic variables*' are 'all variables whose function is exclusively sensitizing, activating, or energy-actualizing or, in other words: *all variables determining the energy-characteristics* (intensity, persistence, etc.) *of the behavior*'.

II. '*Directive variables*' are 'all variables whose function is exclusively regulating, organizing, orienting, or direction-determining, or, in other words: *all variables determining directional characteristics of the behavior*'.

III. '*Vector variables*' are 'all variables whose function is *both dynamogenic and directive*.'

Applying this classification to the twenty theories one finds the following:

I. *Dynamogenic variables:*

Propensity (McD), Tendency (McD), Init. phys. state (To-1), Drive (To-2), Demand (To-1), Need (To-2), Need (To-2), Need (Y-1), Drive (Y-1), Drive (A), Motivational trait (A), Need, L, Tension (L), Press (Mu), Drive (Hu), C_D (Hu), Motivational factors (Ti), Motivation (Ti), Erg (C), Activity factors (H-H), Need (H-H), Deprivation (S), Need (Frh), Need (Mai), Impulse (Mo), Arousal index (Frm), Need (S-K).

II. *Directive variables:*

Set (Y-1), Attitude (Y-2), Valens (L), r_G (Hu), S_D (Hu), Phase sequence (He), Instinct (Ti), Instrumental traits (A), Set (Frm), Goal (Mai), Hope (Frh), Engram factors B^l and b^r (H-H).

III. *Vector variables:*

Instinct (McD), Sentiment (McD), Drive (To-1), Desire (Y-2), Force (L), Need (= Drive) (Mu), $_SE_R$ (Hu), Drive (FB), Motive (McC), Discharge index (Frm), Need (Mas), Wishes (Frm), Drive (S-K).

This classification of the variables in the twenty theories has been made in the

---

[3]) After having defined this classification I found that it resembled Duffy's categories of description, and later I found in Ps. Bull. (1955, 52, 331–28) an article written by *Farber* proposing a classification which resembles mine even more, namely his distinction between 'dynamogenic and directive aspects of variables'. But Farber fails to distinguish this classification from the distinction between disposition variables and function variables.

Classifications of psychological Variables

		Empirical Variables (Independent, Antecedent Variables)	Hypothetical Variables			Behavior Variables (Dependent, consequent variables)		
			Neutral-formal	Neurophysiological	Phenomenological			
Disposition Variables	Vector		*4 variables* (e.g. Murray's Need)				Vector	Disposition Variables
	Directive		*3 variables* (e.g. Young's Attitude)	Tinbergen's 'instinct'			Directive	
	Dynamogenic		*4 variables* (e.g. McDougall's Propensity Cattels Erg)				Dynamogenic	
Function Variables	Vector	*2 variables* (e.g. Masserman's Need)	*7 variables* (e.g. Murray's Need) Tolman's Drive (1932)	*3 variables* (e.g. Stagner's Drive)	Young's Desire		Vector	Function Variables
	Directive	*2 variables* (e.g. Hull's drive-stimulus)	*5 variables* (e.g. Young's Set)	*2 variables* (e.g. Freeman's Set)			Directive	
	Dynamogenic	*11 variables* (e.g. Tolman's Drive (1951)) Young's Need Hull's Need (CD)	*8 variables* e.g. Hull's Drive Tolman's Need (1951) Lewin's Tension	*3 variables* (e.g. Young's Drive)	*2 variables* (e.g. Moore's impulse)		Dynamogenic	

same way as the two classifications which have already been given in the previous chapters and which have only been repeated in this summary. It must be added that a few cases in doubt (for example Discharge index (Frm) and Need (Mas) have been placed in the third group (vector variable). Also a few compound variables, as for example 'Wishes (Frh)' consisting of a dynamogenic component ('need') and a regulating component ('hope'), which were not separated in the previous classifications, have been placed in the respective classes.

The result of the classification is as follows: 26 dynamogenic, 12 directive, and 18 vector variables.

Combination of the Classifications

The three classifications can be *combined*, whereby the scheme of classification p. 309 is produced.

THE SYNTHESIS

Limitation of 'Motivation'

The combined scheme of classification of all motivation variables in the twenty theories shows that there are often *many different motivation variables* under *the same heading*. If it is considered *practical that scientific terms are as precisely and as unambiguously defined as possible* 'motivation' should be defined precisely and unambiguously. The combined sheme of classification might serve this purpose, especially if it is assumed that *the most useful way of solving the problem of definition is to formulate precisely what is already common usage* (instead of introducing a new terminology)[4]).

The scheme shows that there are relatively few disposition variables. This means that *the majority of motivation variables in the twenty theories are function variables*. Except for McDougall's and Tinbergen's 'instinct' variables and Holt-Hansen's 'factors', the other disposition variables are all personality variables which are also used as motivation variables. This is a consequence of the lack of distinction between disposition and function. Holt-Hansen's theory is, however, an exception, as there is a set of disposition variables ('factors') corresponding to each set of function variables ('need' and 'perception'), and he also differentiates between dynamogenic variables ('needs' and 'activity factors' respectively) and regulating variables ('engram factors'). Also Tinbergen distinguishes in his theory between disposition ('instinct') and function ('motivation'). Even McDougall has in his last edition given up his vague and inclusive notion of instinct and made a distinction between disposition (propensity) and function (tendency).

---

[4]) *Carnap* points out that one of the tasks of meta-theory is to anayze the terms used in theories and formulate *suggestions* for more useful definitions.

If one wishes to develop a precise terminology it is necessary to avoid this ambiguous use of terms including both disposition variables and function variables at the same time. It is therefore suggested that the use of the word 'motivation' and of more special motivational terms (such as 'need' and 'drive') should be limited to the description of *function variables* so that all *motivation variables are defined as function variables.*

The scheme shows the distribution of *function* variables: there are 24 dynamogenic variables, but there are only 9 directive variables and 13 vector variables. Some of the doubtful cases have been classified as vector variables. One may ask whether it would be practical to make the word 'motivation' unambiguous by limiting its usage to include dynamogenic variables only and to exclude the directive variables (and vector variables). The problem has, as mentioned before, often been discussed during the past few years. Thus Hebb has pointed out in 'Organization of Behavior' (cf. Chapter 12) that the most important problem is not the activation of behavior (the dynamogenic component), but the organization of behavior (the regulating component). He therefore limits the usage of 'motivation' to include only acquired, directive variables. The problem is also discussed in the Nebraska Symposium mentioned previously. Thus *J. S. Brown* (1953, p. 6) points out that 'every case of directed behavior is to be ascribed, not to drives or motives, but to the capacities of stimulus cues, whether innate or acquired, to elicit reactions.' Both conceptions are supported by convincing arguments. There is, however, one argument which has not been presented, one which in my opinion is very essential: *It is easier to distinguish motivation variables from other psychological function variables if the word 'motivation' is limited to include only dynamogenic variables.* Thereby directive function variables are excluded—as for example 'sets'; vector variables are also excluded, though this conflicts with common usage because they include many variables which are usually considered to be motivation variables. They can, however, be understood (and defined) as *compound* variables consisting of a dynamogenic component (a motivation variable) and a directive component[5]). That this actually is in agreement with theory construction in modern psychology can be seen from an analysis of the most exactly defined variable in this group, namely Hull's reaction potential' which is defined as a product of a motivation variable ('drive') and a directive variable ('habit strength, $_SH_R$') plus a few more. But if one chooses *not* to limit 'motivation' to dynamogenic function variables it is very difficult to distinguish motivation variables from '*cognitive*' variables. How can the difference otherwise be defined between Young's 'sets' (which he considers a motivation variable) and cognitive variables such as 'thoughts'? Jørgen Jørgensen writes for example: 'It seems to me most reasonable to consider 'thoughts' to be a—very inclusive—kind of sets ...' (p. 449 in (121)).

As a consequence of the previous discussion I would suggest that '*motivation*

---

[5]) This is in my opinion a more practical solution to the problem than the one *D. Krech* suggested (cf. his article in 'Current Trends,').

variables' should be defined as synonymous with 'dynamogenic function variables,' and as a consequence of this I would define '*cognitive variables*' as synonymous with '*directive* function variables'.

Different Classes of Motivation Variables

A further limitation of the word 'motivation' is neither necessary nor practical. The scheme of combined classifications shows that the majority of motivation variables are distributed rather evenly in the row with *dynamogenic function* variables between the sections with *empirical* variables and *hypothetical* variables (11 and 15 respectively). It may thus be judged practical *to define 'motivation' as a common label for both empirical and hypothetical dynamogenic function variables*[6]).

But a new terminological problem arises with the above definition, namely: What kind of terms should be used for the empirical and the hypothetical motivation variables, respectively?

One might consider using the most frequent: 'need' and 'drive'. But the classification scheme shows quite clearly that the use of these terms is especially confused. They are used *synonymously* by Murray about a hypothetical variable (or rather about two: disposition and function). They are used about an empirical function variable (need) and a hypothetical function variable (drive) by Young and Hull, respectively. But they are used in exactly the opposite way by Tolman in his *last* work, while in his *first* work he had still another way of using 'drive'.

In my opinion *this terminological problem has three possible solutions:*

1) one could suggest an unambiguous definition of the very common, but now ambiguous terms 'need' and 'drive' and try to make it generally accepted among psychologists. Thus one might suggest Hull's terminology which is probably already the most widely used among American psychologists[7]). But Murray's terminology is also rather widely used, and it will be difficult to make a choice and even more difficult to eradicate the terminological confusion. This possibility will therefore be given up in spite of the fact that it is in most direct agreement with the basic principles of the present study (that it is practical to define precisely the most widely used terms).

2) *New terms might be suggested* (as for example Cattell's 'erg') with a precise, unambiguous definition of how to use them. But it is always difficult to gain general acceptance for such terms.

---

[6]) The distribution of *hypothetical*, dynamogenic function variables in the sub-classes neutral-formal (8) neuro-physiological (3) and phenomenological (2) is in agreement with the distribution of theories in the classes: neutral-formal, behavioristic and mentalistic theories found in chapter 17. But the distribution of hypothetical variables has no interest for the problem of definition, as it is a pure convention, which form of hypothetical variables one prefers (cf. chapter 3).

[7]) It is also accepted by Woodworth in his last edition of 'Experimental Psychology'.

3) *Older and well-known, but less used (and misused) terms might be given a precise and unambiguous definition.*

Since this *last* possibility is a compromise between the two first mentioned (both having their advantages and disadvantages) it seems to me to be *the most practical.* Therefore I *suggest* that the general term '*motivation*' should be used about *all dynamogenic function variables, both empirical and hypothetical.* The two last mentioned subclasses should be differentiated by adjectives used to modify 'motivation'. Instead of as previously just using the *meta-theoretical* terms 'empirical' and 'hypothetical', it is suggested that one should use the more *psychological* terms 'peripheral' and 'central' in the following way: '*peripheral motivation*' *designates* '*all empirical, dynamogenic function variables*', whereas '*all hypothetical, dynamogenic function variables*' are designated by '*central motivation*'. Furthermore, the following *distinction* between different types of '*peripheral motivation*' is suggested: '*Motivating stimuli*' *designates* '*all empirical dynamogenic function variables which are located outside the organism*' (situation variables, often called 'signals of danger', 'incentives', 'goal objects', etc.) while '*motivating impulses*' designates '*all empirical dynamogenic function variables which are located within the organism, but outside the central nervous system*' (including both actual nervous impulses from internal organs and hormonal effects directly upon the brain). It is expedient for practical-linguistic reasons to use the words '*motive*' and '*motives*'[8]) to indicate one and several kinds of '*central motivation*' respectively.

The definitions which have been suggested are definitions of classes of motivation variables and are based upon the combined scheme of classification. Operationalistic definitions can be given of a few concrete motives.

Affective Variables

This section will discuss a group of variables which has not been dealt with in the previous part of the chapter, but which is closely related to motivation variables in most psychological theories, namely the *affective variables* (emotions, affections, etc.). As far as I can see these variables have *two different definitions:*

1. *Affective variables are a kind of motivation* (cf. Leeper's article in Ps. Rev. 1948, 55, 5–21).

2. *Affective variables are conditions accompanying motivation* (cf. Young's theory).

In my opinion these two definitions are not contradictory, but they are applied to two different groups of affective variables: emotions and affections:

1. *Emotions are a kind of motivation.* This is for example true about 'fear' and 'anger'. Maybe they have an exceptional position in the different classifications of

[8]) 'Motive' is here used as a neutral-formal term without any of the phenomenological 'surplus meaning' which it has in ordinary daily usage.

motives (being partly innate, partly acquired), but they are still forms of motivation because they are *dynamogenic function variables.*

2. *Affections are conditions accompanying motivation.* This is true about 'pleasure,' 'delight,' 'satisfaction,' and perhaps 'joy,' 'unpleasure,' 'dissatisfaction,' 'dislike', and maybe 'grief.' These two groups of affections can also be described as '*positive or energy-producing variables*' and '*negative or extra-energy-mobilizing variables*'. Thus the 'positive (pleasant) affective conditions' can be defined as 'conditions determined by the completion of an action which reduces or satisfies a present motivation'; and in the same way the 'negative (unpleasant) affective conditions' can be defined as 'conditions determined by a present motivation which has not been reduced by an action'. The usual theory says that the positive (energy-producing) variables are parasympathetically determined internal processes, which accompany the satisfaction of a motive; whereas the negative (extra-energy-mobilizing) variables are sympathetically determined internal processes which accompany the rise of a motive and which are further strengthened by its frustration. According to the most common theory *affective conditions are determined by motivation.* But a few psychologists (Hebb, McClelland) maintain the opposite point of view: affective conditions determine motivation. This is, however, purely an empirical problem.

LISTS OF MOTIVES[9])

Principles of Classification

In the analytical chapters the different lists of the number of motives have been given. These lists will be compared in this section. First a summary of the principles of classification used in the theories will be given, forming the basis for the division of motives into different classes (as for example into 'primary' and 'secondary') made in the lists.

In the chapter on *McDougall's* theory three different editions of a list of *primary* or *innate* motives (instincts and emotions, or, in the last edition, propensities) are given. These lists have been the model for the lists given by many later psychologists. Except for these lists of innate propensities McD. does not give any lists of motives, because he maintains that all human actions are motivated by one or more of these primary propensities. A number of propensities can be organized into (acquired) *sentiments*, and as many of these may exist as there are combination-possibilities and objects which can serve as goals for these motivational systems. McD. gives two criteria for the innateness of a propensity, namely: *a comparative-psychological one* (the existence of propensities in other higher

[9]) In the following 'motive' and 'motives' will be used in accordance with the definition: '*motive*' = '*central motivation*' = '*hypothetical, dynamogenic function variable*'.

mammals) and *a psychopathological one* (the existence of an unnaturally strengthened propensity).

Tolman does not give a complete list of motives ('needs') in the last edition of his theory ('A Psychological Model'). But he divides them into three classes and mentions a few examples from each class. The first class is called '*primary* needs' and includes 'viscerogenic hungers' and 'fear,' 'aggression,' and 'exploratory need.' The second class is called 'secondary or socio-relational needs' (including for example 'need love, need approval, and need dominance,' etc.). This group is considered 'largely innate.' The third class is called '*tertiary* needs,' which are acquired, but still rather uniform in a given population. It is needs of cultural goals such as wealth, success, etc. The individual 'need' is defined as 'a readiness or tendency to persist toward and to perform a consummatory response relative to a certain more or less arbitrarily chosen "standard goal".' No other criteria are given for distinguishing between 'innate' and 'acquired' needs apart from the *comparative-psychological one* (the existence of the need in chimpanzees).

In the chapter on *Young's* theory a list is also given of '*primary drives*,' which are separated from '*secondary drives*' by 'reference to the physiological state of an organism.' This criterion of classification may—contrary to the comparative-psychological ones used by McDougall and Tolman—be described as the *physiological* criterion. Furthermore Young's list of 'primary drives' includes, besides the usual vital organic drives, a 'curiosity drive', which is based physiologically upon process in the sense organs, and some 'emergency reactions' (for example fear and aggression), the physiological basis of which is the production of adrenalin. All drives which are not physiologically based are for the present regarded to be 'secondary drives' of which Young does not give any list.

Allport has no list of motives which corresponds to the other lists analyzed here.

Lewin does not give a list of motives, either, but the distinguishes between 'needs' and 'quasi-needs' which largely corresponds to the previous classifications into primary and secondary needs.

Murray gives a rather extensive list of 'needs' which he classifies in many different ways; and in a later paper[10]) he revises and expands his classifications. From a motivation-psychological point of view his most important classification is the distinction between 'viscerogenic' and 'psychogenic' needs. The criterion of classification is the physiological criterion, as the 'viscerogenic needs' 'are engendered and stilled by characteristic periodic bodily events'.

Hull has 'hidden' a single list of 'primary drives' in the text in Prin. Behav. (p. 59–60). Besides he classifies drives as primary and secondary drives.

Hebb has not made any classification and only mentions in 'Organization of Behavior': 'pain,' 'hunger,' 'sex,' and 'sleep,' but in his later book he deals with several 'drives.' *Tinbergen* does not give any actual list of motives ('instincts')

---

[10]) In Parson and Shill: Toward a General Theory of Action' (1951).

either. He mentions, however, as instinctive motivation in man: 'food-seeking drive', 'sexual drive', and 'the parental instinct'. *McClelland* has no classification of motives, because he—like Hebb—defines all motives as acquired.

Cattell gives a list of 'ergs', or 'primary drives', including 16 motives which are similar to those in McDougall's list of 'propensities'. He also makes use of the same criteria of selection, but adds the hypothesis that these 16 'ergs' exist in adults as a development of Freud's four instincts: hunger, libido, aggression, and anxiety.

Stagner and *Karwoski* give a list of motives which, however, does not pretend to be complete. It includes three classes:

a. *Biological drives:* hunger thirst, oxygen deficit, maternal drive, sex drive, excretory needs, pain, and exploratory drives.

b. *Emotions:* anger, fear, and love.

c. *Social motives:* security, dominance, acquisitiveness, group identifications, and values.

The first group is considered to be exclusively *genetically* conditioned, the last to be exclusively *acquired*, whereas 'emotions' are considered partly genetically and partly acquired. The principle of classification used here is rather physiological.

The other eight theories in Chapter 15 do not give lists of motives. It is true that Frenkel-Brunswik gives a list of 'drives', but it derives from Murray's list and besides the list is only meant to be used in a specific study and is not at all considered complete.

The above mentioned lists are reproduced p. 317–18 to ease comparison. The classification-criterium is presented at the end of every list.

Comparison of the Lists

First of all, almost all lists include a classification of motives as *primary* (innate, physiologically determined) and *secondary* (acquired, socially or culturally determined). It is quite evident that the classification is preassumed in the lists, which do not mention the classification explicitly. The primary motives are then mentioned only, because the number of secondary motives is considered to be so large and individually varied that it would be impossible to mention them.

Secondly it may be mentioned that two criteria have mainly been used to distinguish between primary and secondary motives. One criterion is called *the physiological criterion*, as the primary or innate motives are defined in relation to a known physiological process in some organ. This criterion has the advantage that it is easy to give an operational definition of the motives in question on the basis of physiological processes. The other criterion may be called *the comparative-psychological criterion*, as the primary or innate motives are defined according to their existence in different animal species (especially among the higher mammals). This criterion has the advantage that it is more comprehensive and therefore does

Table for Comparison of Lists of Motives

McDougall's 'propensities' (1932).

1. Food-seeking p.
2. Disgust p.
3. Sex p.
4. Fear p.
5. Curiosity p.
6. Protective and parental p.
7. Gregarious p.
8. Self-assertive p.
9. Submissive p.
10. Anger p.
11. Appeal p.
12. Constructive p.
13. Acquisitive p.
14. Laughter p.
15. Comfort p.
16. Rest or sleep p.
17. Migratory p.
18. Coughing, sneezing, breathing, evacuation, etc.

Comparative-pathological criterion.

Young's 'primary drives' (1936).

1. Hunger.
2. Nausea.
3. Thirst.
4. Sex.
5. Nursing.
6. Urinating.
7. Defecating.
8. Avoiding heat.
9. Avoiding cold.
10. Avoiding pain.
11. Air hunger.
12. Fear and anger.
13. Fatigue.
14. Sleep.
15. Curiosity.
16. Social instinct.
17. Tickle.

Physiological criterion.

Tolman's 'needs' (1951)

I. Innate needs.

- a. *primary n.*
  1. viscerogenic hungers:
     food-hungers,
     palatability-hungers,
     thirst,
     sex,
     temperature control,
     oxygen intake,
     rest and sleep,
     etc.
  2. fear and aggression.
  3. exploratory n.
- *b. secondary, innate social n.*
  1. n. gregariousness.
  2. n. love.
  3. n. approval.
  4. n. dominance.
  5. n. submission etc.

II. Acquired, tertiary needs for culturally provided goals.

Comparative-psychological criterion.

Cattell's 'erg' (1950).

1. Escape.
2. Appeal.
3. Acquisitiveness.
4. Laughter.
5. Pugnacity.
6. Self-assertion.
7. Sleep.
8. Play.
9. Self-abasement.
10. Mating.
11. Gregariousness.
12. Parental drive.
13. Curiosity.
14. Construction.
15. Disgust.
16. Hunger.

Comparative-psychological criterion.

Murray's 'needs' (1938).

A. Viscerogenic needs:

1. n. Inspiration.
2. n. Water.
3. n. Food.
4. n. Sentience.
5. n. Sex.
6. n. Lactation.
7. n. Expiration.
8. n. Urination.
9. n. Defecation.
10. n. Noxavoidance.
11. n. Heatavoidance.
12. n. Coldavoidance.
13. n. Harmavoidance.

B. Psychogenic needs[1]*:*

14. n. Acquisition.
15. n. Conservance.
16. n. Order.
17. n. Retention.
18. n. Construction.
19. n. Superiority.
20. n. Achievement.
21. n. Recognition.
22. n. Exhibition.
23. n. Inviolacy.
24. n. Infavoidance.
25. n. Defendance.
26. n. Counteraction.
27. n. Dominance.
28. n. Deference.
29. n. Similiance.
30. n. Autonomy.
31. n. Contrarience.
32. n. Aggression.
33. n. Abasement.
34. n. Blamavoidance.
35. n. Affiliation.
36. n. Rejection.
37. n. Nurturance.
38. n. Succorance.
39. n. Play.
40. n. Cognizance.
41. n. Exposition.
42. n. Understanding.

Physiological criterion.

Stagner and Karwoski: 'motivations' (1952).

Biological drives:

1. hunger,
2. thirst,
3. oxygen deficit,
4. maternal drive,
5. sex drive,
6. excretory needs,
7. pain,
8. exploratory drives.

Emotions:

1. anger,
2. fear,
3. love.

Social motives:

1. security,
2. dominance,
3. acquisitiveness,
4. group identification,
5. values.

Physiological criterion.

[1]) Here Murray's presentation p. 80–84 in 'Expl. in Person.' is followed.

not exclude the many motives which exist in all humans (and in apes and other mammals) and which seem to be innate, but which cannot be proved to have a direct functional relation to certain physiological processes.

This classification has been discussed quite often in the more recent literature about motivational theory. *All three points of view are represented:*

1. *The classification* in primary and secondary motives is *necessary and/or practical.* This is presupposed in most theories of today.

2. *Only primary (innate, biogenic) motives exist.* The process of learning combines new signals or new goal-objects with the motives, or combines several motives with each other. This point of view was held by for example *Nissen* (in the Nebraska Symposium of 1954).

3. *Only acquired motives exist*, but innate emotions and organic conditions form the basis for the process of acquiring motives. This point of view was held by *Hebb* and *McClelland*.

The *first* of the three standpoints is *a compromise between the other two, and so far it has proved practical;* therefore I shall accept it in the following, but a certain synthesis with the second standpoint will be attempted, as I find it *appropriate to deal with as few acquired motives as possible.*

According to the usual scientific principle of economy it is *practical to presuppose as few motives as possible.* One must therefore avoid using a list of motives which is so long that the notion of motive does not explain anything. If the list becomes too long the result is that the explanations employing these motives as their basis do not really explain anything. I believe that Murray's list is close to the upper limit for the length which can be used if the above mentioned danger is to be avoided. But it would also be a mistake to try to explain everything from a single or a few motives. The explanations would then either be too vague and imprecise, or they would become too artificial and *speculative* because so many hypothesis would have to be assumed that simplicity would be lost. Thus I would take C. Bühler's 'expansion-tendency' as an example of an imprecise explanation; and many would maintain that Freud's libido-explanations are an example of this, too.

In accordance with the presuppositions leading to the suggestion of a 'synthesis'-definition of 'motivation' (cf. chapter 17), I maintain that the most appropriate list of motives must contain the motives which can be found in most of the lists published by other authors.

Suggestion for List of Motives

The human motives are in the following list classified into two groups: *primary* (innate, biogenic) and *secondary* (acquired, psychogenic) motives, according to the following definitions:

A primary motive is a central motivation which from birth (or maybe after process of maturation) is functionally related to peripheral, motivating impulses or stimuli.

A secondary motive is a central motivation[11]) *which is, after a learning process, determined by*[12]) *peripheral, motivating stimuli.*

The learning process spoken of in the definition will not be explained or further discussed in this chapter which exclusively deals with a comparison of definitions (and the classifications which are consequences of these). Temporarily it is

---

[11]) Maybe it is the same central motivation state (in the brain-stem) by all primary; differences between the motives are maybe caused by the different determining impulses or stimuli (cf. Nissen's point of view).

[12]) The term determined by will in the following be used as an abbreviated form of 'is functionally related to.'

presupposed. For the same reason no explanation will be given of the existence of 'motivating' impulses.

The *individual motives* in the following list *are defined* ('operational')—as in the general definition given above—on the basis of the peripheral, motivating impulses and stimuli, that is, *on the basis of independent empirical variables.* The other possibility, to define the individual motives 'operational' on the basis of the independent behavior variables, I consider less practical, because only a very few (or no) specific ('instinctive') patterns of behavior can be found in human beings; most of them are acquired, and moreover, even though determined by one and the same motive, the behavior of a certain individual may *change* if the milieu is changed. Besides the danger of pseudo-explanations is avoided. But even if one chooses to define the motives on the basis of the independent, empirical variables (motivating stimuli and impulses) it is still at the same time possible to *measure the force of motives* (of the central motivation) *through characteristics of behavior,* a method which might prove very practical (because the force (the intensity) of the motives is not only determined by the peripheral motivation, but also by other variables (among others the dispositions)).

It should also be pointed out that 'peripheral motivation' has previously been defined as including not only internal 'motivating impulses', but also external 'motivating stimuli', because in this way the problem of whether primary motives are exclusively 'homeostatic,' or whether 'external' primary motives also exist is solved, or avoided. Besides, in this way the definition of the secondary motives can be formulated analogously to that of the primary motives, since secondary motives are exclusively (?) determined by external stimuli.

According to the above definitions and basic arguments *a list of human* motives can be made; *first the primary motives:*

1. *The hunger motive* is a primary motive which is determined by motivating impulses caused by the metabolic processes (lack of nutriment in the blood and/or contractions of the stomach). Later on—after a learning process—it may be determined by motivating stimuli from the *food-objects.* In animals the hunger motive may from birth be determined ('instinctively') by motivating stimuli from a certain kind of food-object.

2. *The thirst motive* is a primary motive which is determined by motivating impulses caused by lack of liquid and/or dry mucous membranes in the throat.

3. *The sex motive* is a primary motive determined by motivating impulses caused by sex hormones in the blood and probably also by certain motivating stimuli[13]).

---

[13]) Cf. the discussion by Harlow in the Nebraska Symposium 1953.

4. *The nursing motive* ('maternal drive') is a primary motive determined by motivating impulses caused by certain hormones and probably also by certain motivating stimuli[14]) (round and plump shapes).

5 *The temperature motives* are primary motives which from birth (?) are determined by motivating stimuli acting upon the cold-receptors or warmth-receptors at tempteratures below and above the level of adaption, respectively.

6. *The pain-avoidance-motive* is a primary motive determined from birth by motivating stimuli acting upon the pain-receptors.

7. *The excretory motives* are primary motives determined by motivating impulses caused by a full bladder and/or rectum.

8. *The oxygen motive* is a primary motive determined by motivating impulses caused by an increase in the carbon dioxide content of the blood. It must, however, be said about this that under normal circumstances it is rare that a real motive (central motivation) arises, because the peripheral motivation directly determines innate reflex-regulating actions which are most often effective enough so that central motivation and actual behavior do not appear. This is, to some extent, also true about the motives of excretion, pain, and temperature.

9. *The rest and sleep motive* is a primary motive determined by motivating impulses from 'fatigue-substances' in muscles and maybe in other organs.

10. *The activity motives* are primary motives determined by motivating impulses maybe caused by metabolic processes in muscles (the muscle-activity-motive), sense-organs (sense-activity-motive), and the brain (brain-activity-motive).

Contrary to the previous motives which were primary according to both a physiological and a comparative-spychological criterion, a lack of direct physiological basis for the assumed *brain*-activity-motive is felt[14a]). But in the Nebraska Symposium in 1954 *Nissen* argued for the existence of a *brain*-activity-motive upon a comparative psychological basis. He writes (p. 300) that:

'among the requirements of all tissues is that they perform their normal functions', and that 'it is the function of the brain to perceive and to know'.

Later (p. 337):

'Capacity is its own motivation. A function or capacity of the senseorgans and brain is to perceive and to know, and this is one of the more important drives of all organisms'.

But it is also possible to give direct experimental reasons for the postulate of a 'brain-activity-motive'. Thus *K. C. Montgomery*[15]) has reported experiments with rats which give evidence that 'exploratory behavior' is not only independent of

---

[14]) Cf. Lorenz's argumentation given in the chapter about *Tinbergen's* theory of instinctive' motivating stimuli in man.

[14a]) Perhaps the function of the Reticular Arousal System could be conceived as the basis of the brain-activity-motive.

[15]) Jour. comp. physiol. Psychol. 1953, 46, 315–19 and 438–41.

hunger and thirst, but is also independent of 'the general activity drive'. This latter ought to be described as the muscle-activity-motive, however, since it was exclusively measured by an activity wheel.

Finally *the hypothesis of spontaneous, continual activity*[16]) *in the central nervous system might be used as basis for postulating a brain-activity-motive.*

The reasons for postulating an activity motive, especially a primary, brain-activity-motive, have been discussed in detail because *such a motive can explain much behavior* which is normally explained *by acquired* motives. Thus the number of necessary motives is reduced.

Two emotional motives which are partly primary, partly acquired[17]) must be added to the list (cf. the section on 'affective' variables).

11. *The security motive* ('fear') is an emotional motive which is determined by motivating stimuli ('signals of danger') which may partly be active at birth, partly only after a certain level of maturity has been reached and partly only after some learning has occured.

12. *The aggression motive* ('anger') is an emotional motive which is determined by motivating stimuli caused by frustrating situations.

The motivating stimuli of emotional motives are partly innate, partly acquired; but the autonomously-hormonal (adrenalin) regulated extra-energy-mobilizing condition which accompanies all the emotional motives is exclusively innate. In man, however, the emotional, expressive movements are partly innate (or maturated) and partly acquired.

The *secondary motives* most common in humans are as follows:

13. *The social-contact-motive* is a secondary (?) motive determined by (non-sexual) motivating stimuli from other human beings. Some will maintain that this motive is a primary one (that babies have an innate motive for 'physical' contact with others), and from a comparative-psychological principle of classification it might be taken to be a relatively primary (rather common) motive, but one can easily explain how it is acquired through the child's necessary life together with and dependence upon other people[17a]).

14. *The achievement motive* is a secondary motive determined by motivating stimuli from task-situations. This motive is very likely an acquired motive as it is far from being common (and is lacking completely in certain cultures). Research by McClelland and his assistants proves the dependence of the motive upon a certain form of education.

15. *The power motive* is a secondary motive determined by motivating stimuli from competition-situations. Some have maintained that this motive is a primary

---

[16]) Cf. the chapters on Hebb's and Tinbergen's theories.
[17]) Cf. Stagner's and Karwoski's classification of motives.
[17a]) *Harlow's* well-known experiments from the later years and mother-surrogates are indicaling a *primary* Social-contact-motive.

on (and Adler even postulated that it is the most important human motive), referring to the social class distinction ('pecking order') in lower animals. But it is not universal (in some cultures it does not exist at all) and it can easily be explained how it is acquired.

16. *The possession motive* is a secondary motive determined by motivating stimuli from property (all means to obtain directly the goals of other motives). Some have also maintained that this is innate by referring to the 'instinct' of acquisitiveness in some animals, but the motive does not exist in all cultures and it can moreover easily be explained how it is acquired; therefore it is most likely a secondary motive.

This list of 10 primary, 2 emotional, and 4 secondary motives is considered *sufficient* to explain human actions (when certain other psychological variables are also accepted). When an action cannot be explained using one of the above motives it is usually possible to do so *by using a combination of several co-operating motives* ('interests,' 'love,' etc.). Finally, a further *individual differentiation* of the above motives can take place through learning processes.

Murray's long list may thus be considered to be a differentiation of the motives mentioned in the above list. For example *the activity-motives* may be differentiated into: n Construction, n Cognizance, n Exposition, n Understanding, and n Play which all indicate different kinds of activity. In the same way *the possession motive* corresponds to: n Acquisition, n Conservance, n Order, and n Retention; *the achievement motive* corresponds only to n Achievement, whereas *the power motive* corresponds to: n Superiority, n Inviolacy, n Dominance, n Autonomy, and n Contrarience; and, finally *the social contact motive* corresponds to: n Affiliation, n Nurturance, n Succorance, n Blamavoidance, n Deference, n Similance, and n Abasement.

Summary

In the *first* part of the chapter the motivation variables of the twenty theories were classified as:

I. a) hypothetical and b) empirical variables.
II. a) disposition and b) function variables.

Then a *new* classification was given:
a) dynamogenic variables, b) directive (regulating) variables, and c) vector variables.

These three classifications were combined in one scheme of classification.

Based upon this scheme the following definitions were suggested in the second part:

'*Motivation*' = '*all dynamogenic function variables*, both empirical and hypothetical.'

All Psychological Variables

<table>
<tr><th colspan="2"></th><th>Empirical (Independent) Variables</th><th colspan="4">Hypothetical Variables</th><th>Behavior Variables</th><th colspan="2"></th></tr>
<tr><td colspan="2" rowspan="5">Disposition Variables</td><td rowspan="5">Species
Sex
Age
Genealogy
Life-history</td><td></td><td>Innate Dispositions</td><td>Acquired Dispositions</td><td></td><td rowspan="5">Individual Characteristic in the Performance of the Action (Characteristics of Intelligence and Personality, 'Style.')</td><td colspan="2" rowspan="5">Disposition Variables</td></tr>
<tr><td>Vec-tor</td><td>'Instincts'</td><td>'Sentiments,' etc.,</td><td>Vec-tor</td></tr>
<tr><td>Direc-tive</td><td>Intelligence Factors</td><td>'Habits'
'Engrams'
'Ideas'</td><td>Direc-tive</td></tr>
<tr><td rowspan="2">Dynamo-genic</td><td colspan="2">Personality Variables</td><td rowspan="2">Dynamo-genic</td></tr>
<tr><td>Temperament Dispositions</td><td>'character-traits'
'Attitudes'</td></tr>
<tr><td rowspan="3">Function Variables</td><td>Vector</td><td>Goal Objects
(Valences, etc.)
Incentives</td><td colspan="4">Compound Functions
(for example $_SE_R$ etc.)</td><td>Forms of Purposive Behavior
1. Instinctive
2. Acquired
3. Intelligent</td><td>Vector</td><td rowspan="3">Function Variables</td></tr>
<tr><td>Directive</td><td>Sensoric Reception of Directive Stimuli</td><td colspan="4">Perception, Reproduction, Production (Imagination and Thinking), Intention, ('sets' etc.)</td><td>Behavioral Criteria of Direction (Discrimination, etc.)</td><td>Directive</td></tr>
<tr><td>Dynamogenic</td><td>Peripheral Motivation
1. Motivating Impulses
2. Motivating Stimuli</td><td colspan="4">Central Motivation = Motives:
a) Primary Motives (10)
b) Emotional Motives (2)
c) Secondary Motives (4)
} Also Affective Accompanying Conditions.</td><td>Behavioral Criteria of Energy-Mobilizing (Intensity, Persistence, etc.)</td><td>Dynamogenic</td></tr>
<tr><td colspan="2"></td><td>Empirical Variables</td><td colspan="4">Hypothetical Variables</td><td>Behavior Variables</td><td colspan="2"></td></tr>
</table>

'*Central motivation*' = '*motive*' = 'all *hypothetical* dynamogenic function variables.'

'*Peripheral motivation*' = '*motivating stimuli and impulses*' = 'all *emperical* dynamogenic function variables.'

'*Affective variables*' are partly 'emotions' which are motives, partly 'affections' which are energy-producing and extra-energy-mobilizing, *accompanying conditions* of motivation.

In the *third* part the different lists of motives were compared, and *a list of motives* was suggested, including:

a. *primary* motives: 1) hunger motive, 2) thirst motive, 3) sex motive, 4) nursing motive, 5) temperature motive, 6) excretory motive, 7) painavoidance motive, 8 oxygen motive, 9) rest motive, 10) activity motive (sense-activity-motive, muscle-activity-motive, and brain-activity-motive).

b. *emotional* motives: 11) security motive, and 12) aggression motive.

c. *secondary* motives: 13) social-contact motive, 14) achievement motive, 15) power motive, and 16) possession motive.

I have modified the classification scheme in order to make it easier to understand the relationship between motivation variables and other psychologyical variables (p. 324).

Chapter 19

Comparison of the Motivation Hypotheses of the Theories

In the first part of the chapter the primary hypotheses or the axioms of motivation will be compared. It is thus a comparison of the statements which attempt to present an (implicit) definition or explanation of motivation based upon still more general hypotheses (about the organism).

In the second part of the chapter the hypotheses of the functional relations between different motives and between motives and other psychological variables the definitions and classifications of which were studied in the previous chapter, will be given.

Since several of the analyzed theories are formally rather incomplete, I find it practical in this comparative study to make use of the reconstructed theories which may be found at the end of each chapter. This chapter can therefore only deal with the first ten theories analyzed.

THE DIFFERENT AXIOMS OF MOTIVATION

Since only very few of the psychological theories are axiomatized (deductive) theories, only few explicitly formulated axioms (primary statements) about motivation can be found. Instead the most fundamental definitions and/or hypotheses of motivation in the (reconstructed) theory in question will be treated as motivation axioms; and to ease the comparative study an attempt will be made to summarize them in *one motivation axiom*. If none of the reconstructed definitions and hypotheses can be used as motivation axioms, an attempt will in each case be made to formulate one motivation axiom representing to as great an extent as possible the essence of what the theory says about motivation.

McDougall's theory contains in its reconstructed form two statements which may be taken as his motivation axioms. The first is *the principle of hormism*, and the other is the first hypothesis in the reconstruction (see Chapter 5). These statements may be summarized in *McDougall's motivation axiom:* 'All behavior is purposive and motivated[1]) by innate ·propensities' (in co-laboration with other variables).'

---

[1]) Here, and in the following, '*motivated by*' means the same as 'dynamically determined by', or shorter: 'activated by'.

In the reconstruction of *Tolman's theory* three hypotheses (1st, 2nd, and 3rd hypothesis, see Chapter 6) which may be considered axioms of a theory of motivation can be found. In order to ease the comparison they may be summarized in *Tolman's motivation axiom:* 'All behavior is determined by several co-operating hypothetical and empirical variables, ad it is motivated by 'drives', which are biological conditions of unbalance (in homeostasis)'.

Young's theory presents in the reconstruction two definitions (1st and 2nd definition, see Chapter 7) which may be considered motivation axioms. They may here be summarized in *Young's motivation axiom.* 'All behavior is motivated[2]) by a release of energy determined by 'needs,' which are biological conditions of unbalance.'

In the reconstruction of *Allport's theory* one of the definitions and one of the hypotheses (2nd definition and 1st genetic hypothesis, see Chapter 8) may be taken as motivation axioms and be summarized in *Allport's motivation axiom:* 'The behavior is motivated by dynamic, psychological variables ('motivational traits'), which in adults may be functionally independent of biological needs, but which are then influenced by external stimuli.'

Two statements in the reconstruction of *Lewin's theory* (1st definition and 2nd hypothesis, see Chapter 9) may be considered motivation axioms. They may here be summarized in *Lewin's motivation axiom:* 'The behavior is motivated by "tensions", which are determined by "needs", real (biological) "needs" as well as "quasi-needs" (intentions, etc.).'

Three statements in the reconstruction of *Murray's theory* may be taken as axioms of a theory of motivation (2nd definition, 2nd hypothesis, and 4th definition, see Chapter 10). They may be summarized in *Murray's motivation axiom:* 'All behavior is motivated by 'needs,' which are regnant brainprocesses determined either by physiological processes (outside the central nerve-system), or by press-situations, which may influence the bio-social conditions of life of the individual.'

In the reconstruction of *Hull's theory* several statements may be taken as motivation axioms (2nd hypothesis, 3rd hypothesis, and 6th hypothesis, see Chapter 11). They may be summarized in *Hull's motivation axiom:* 'All behavior is motivated by a few primary "drives" (determined by the needs of the organism) and by a large number of secondary, acquired motives'.

In the reconstruction of *Hebb's theory* three statements may be taken as axioms of a theory of motivation (1st hypothesis, 1st definition, 2nd hypothesis, and 3rd hypothesis). They may be summarized in *Hebb's motivation axiom:* 'All behavior is with regard to energy determined by the continual activity of the nerve-system, but it is organized and directed by cognitive, acquired variables'[2a]).

Two statements in the reconstruction of *Tinbergen's theory* (1st and 2nd

---

[2]) 'Motivated' is also here used according to the definition given in the last footnote and not in the same way as Young uses it including both energy-release and energy-directing.

[2a]) This axiom is only a summary of Hebb's theory from 1949 – the later versions are not included.

hypothesis, see Chapter 13) may be taken as motivation-axioms. They may therefore here be summarized in *Tinbergen's motivation axiom:* 'All behavior is motivated by hormonal processes, internal organic processes, and/or centrally produced nervous impulses'.

Several statements in the reconstruction of *McClelland's theory* may be considered axioms in a rather special kind of motivation theory (especially 1st and 2nd definition and 1st, 2nd, and 3rd primary hypothesis). They may here be summarized in *McClelland's motivation axiom:* 'All behavior is with regard to energy determined by primary affects (which are determined by differences between the level of adjustment of the individual and the perceived situation) or by acquired motives (which are expectations of changes in the affective conditions.'

Classification of the Axioms

The motivation axioms which have been formulated in the previous paragraphs may be classified in two classes according to the formal criterion of whether they are *constructive or reductive* (cf. Chapter 3). The reductive axioms may then be classified further in sub-classes according to the content of the hypotheses to which are being reduced (that is, from which motivation is deduced). Especially one class of axioms is found very often, namely *the homeostasis axioms,* that is axioms which reduce motivation to hypotheses of homeostasis-regulating processes. Other reductive motivation axioms may be brought together in a class which can be described as 'other biological motivation axioms'. I have also in the following classification to comparison placed the non-explicitly formulated motivation axioms of the ten last analyzed theories (based upon a rough estimation). The classification of the theories is as follows:

I. *Constructive motivation axioms:* McDougall, Allport, Moore, Cattell.
II. *Reductive motivation axioms:*
   a. *Homeostasis* axioms: Tolman, Young, Hull, Freeman, Massermann, Maier, Stagner-Karwoski.
   b. *Other biological* axioms: Lewin(?), Murray, Hebb, Tinbergen, McClelland, Frenkel-Brunswik, French, Skinner, Holt-Hansen.

Thus *the majority of motivation axioms are reductive (a total of 16)*, while only a minority (4) are constructive. In my opinion this result is not in conflict with the result arrived at earlier, that the majority of the studied theories are constructive with regard to structure. *A theory can very well be constructive as a whole, even though it attempts to reduce motivation,* since motivation—as a more biologically fundamental process—may be more easily deduced on a biological basis. (It would, on the other hand, have been contradictory if we had found that reductive theories contained *constructive* axioms about variables as fundamental as motivation). If the distribution of axioms in the two subclasses is examined, it will be seen that the number of homeostasis axioms (7) is almost the same as the number of other biological axioms (9). There is, however, the difference that 'older' theories have homeostasis axioms, while most modern theories have other biological motivation axioms. This result is in agreement with the immediate impression one receives when studying the newer (post-war) motivation theories. There is *a tendency to depart from the principle of homeostasis and to prefer other biological axioms.* Especially Hebb and McClelland[3]) have criticized the one-sided and speculative use of the principle of homeostasis.

On this basis I shall maintain that *it must be most practical to formulate motivation axioms with a broad biological basis*[4]), so that they explain motivation with reference to internal organic conditions ('motivating impulses') as well as to external situation-stimuli ('motivating stimuli'), even though the former may be the more important.

THE MOTIVATION HYPOTHESES

Classification of the Hypotheses

In Chapter 3 Spence's classification of psychological hypotheses was modified and simplified. During the analysis of the 10 first theories it became clear that there were three main classes of hypotheses: S→H, H→H, and H→R. Thus the two partly empirical classes and the completely theoretical class have been used the most, while the purely empirical class (S→R) has been without any real importance in this study[5]). It might, however—as already mentioned in Chapter 3—be wise to form a completely new class which includes the more complicated hypotheses of the following kind: $B=f(D \times H \times V \times K)$. In the following the very few hypotheses of this kind will instead be broken down into hypotheses of the kinds which are included in the three given classes (S→H, H→H, and H→R). Thus one of these hypotheses may be placed in more than one class.

Since many theories have not contained explicitly formulated hypotheses, it is necessary in the comparison always to make use of the reconstructions of the theories. (Therefore only the ten first analyzed and reconstructed theories can be included in this section).

The numbers in the following scheme of classification thus refer to the numbers of the reformulated hypotheses in the reconstructed theories. A number followed by a 'd' refers to a definition which has been included because it implicitly contains a hypothesis.

---

[3]) Cf. Harlow's criticism in his article in the Nebraska-Symposium from 1953.

[4]) Tinbergen's, Lewin's, and Murray's theories might be mentioned as examples.

[5]) Only Skinner's theory mainly contained purely empirical hypotheses (S→R). To some extent this is also true of Masserman's theory.

Classification of Hypotheses

The Psychologist's Name	S→H Hypotheses	H→H Hypotheses	H→R Hypotheses
McDougall	1 d. – 9.	2 – 7 – 8.	1 – 3 – 4 – 5 – 6.
Tolman	3 – 7 – 8 – 9.	1 – 2 – 4 – 5 – 6 – 7 – 8 – 10 – 11 – 12.	1 – 6 – 8.
Young	3 – 4 – 5 – 6 – 12 – 13 – 14 – 15 – 16.	7 – 8 – 9 – 10 – 11 – 17 – 18 – 19 – 20	1 – 2.
Allport	1 f.–h.	1 g.–h. – 2 g.–h.	2 f.–h.
Lewin	1 – 2 – 3.	2 – 4.	5.
Murray	2 – 3.	3 – 4 – 9 – 10 – 11.	1 – 5 – 6 – 7 – 8.
Hull[6])	1 – 3 – 4 – 6 – 7 – 9 – 10.	1 – 2 – 8.	1 *3* 5 *3* 8.
Hebb	3 – 4 – 5 – 6.	4.	1 *3* 2 *3* 4 *3* 7.
Tinbergen	2 – 4 – 9.	5.	1 – 2 – 3 – 6 – 7 – 8.
McClelland	1 d. – 1 p. h. – 2 p. h. – 3 p. h. – 1–8 s.–h.	9 s. h. – 10 s. h.	2 d. – 10 s.–h.
Total	47 Hypotheses	38 Hypotheses	32 Hypotheses

[6]) Hull's many secondary hypotheses are not included.

As can be seen from the above scheme *most of the hypotheses are S→H hypotheses*, there are fewer H→H hypotheses, and there is *a smaller number of H→R hypotheses*. There are, however, rather big differences between the individual theories contribution to these classes. It might therefore be of interest to find the relation between the number of hypotheses in the three classes from each of the ten theories, especially to find the relation between the purely theoretical hypotheses (H→H) on the one side, and the partly empirical hypothesis of both classes (both S→H and H→R) on the other, because this relation may be used as *a relative measure of the empirical basis of the theory;* it may be called '*theory-empiri-ratio*' (t/e), or the '*Hypotheses-Quotient*' (H. Q.), because *the larger the ratio, the more hypothetical the theory*, and the *smaller* the ratio, the more *empirical* the theory. In general terms the 'Hypotheses-Quotient' may be defined as '*the ratio between hypotheses of a 'higher' level of abstraction, and empirical, or partly empirical hypotheses*', as this formulation makes it possible to use the ratio in other sciences besides in psychology.

The hypothesis quotient of all the theories is thus: $\frac{38}{47+32}=0.48$. The quotients of the individual theories are:

McDougall $\frac{3}{2+5}=0.43.$

Tolman $\frac{10}{4+3}=1.43.$

Young $\frac{9}{9+2}=0.82.$

Allport $\frac{2}{1+1}=1.00$[7a]).

Lewin $\frac{2}{3+1}=0.50.$

Murray $\frac{5}{2+5}=0.71.$

Hull $\frac{3}{7+3}=0.30$[7b]).

Hebb $\frac{1}{4+4}=0.13.$

Tinbergen $\frac{1}{3+6}=0.11.$

McClelland $\frac{2}{12+2}=0.14.$

As can be seen from the above list there are great differences between the theories, Four theories have hypothesis-quotients above the average: Tolman, Young. Allport, and Murray; Lewin is about average[8]); and five theories are below average: McDougall, Hull, Hebb, Tinbergen, and McClelland. Even though these figures must be treated with reservation, I still believe that they can form the basis of *a new ranking of the theories according to their degree of hypothetical abstraction* (versus empiricism):

Ti	He	McC	Hu	McD	L	Mu	Y	A	To
Low H. Q.				H. Q. = 0.5				High H. Q.	

Average for the ten theories.

The ranks correspond very well to one's immediate impressions. I am, however, a little surprised to see the relatively high hypothesis-quotient for Young's theory, but maybe the reason is that a reductive theory containing neuro-physiologically interpreted, hypothetical variables at first glance seems to be more empirical than

---

7a) Uncertain because of the small number of hypotheses.
7b) If Hull's secondary hypotheses were included the quotient would most likely be lower.
8) A difference of 0.02 is not likely to be significant.

a constructive theory with neutral-formal (or phenomenological) hypothetical variables. Since neuro-physiologically interpreted variables are *hypothetical*, the rank of Young's theory is reasonable.

I cannot calculate the hypothesis-quotient for the last ten theories analyzed, but I will risk making a estimation of their ranking (based upon my immediate impression): *Skinner's* theory must have the lowest H. Q. (t/e being almost zero); *Masserman, Maier, and Frenkel-Brunswik* about the same as Tinbergen; *Freeman and Holt-Hansen* about average; *Cattell, French, Stagner and Karwoski, and Moore* above average. Thus we have:

S.	Mai	Mas	FB	H-H	Frm	C	Frh	S-K	Mo

Estimated H. Q.

The Comparison of the S→H Hypotheses

This class, which includes all hypotheses dealing with the functional relations between independent empirical variables ('S') and hypothetical variables ('H'), can furthermore be divided into two *sub-classes* according to whether the empirical variable is an internal variable ('impulses'), or an external variable ('stimuli').

The *first* of these sub-classes may be represented by *Si→H hypotheses*. The following hypotheses from the first ten theories will be included here:

Si→H Hypotheses:

McDougall	None.
Tolman	Hypotheses 3 – 7 – 8 – 9.
Young	Hypotheses 3 – 4 – 5 – 6.
Allport	Hypothesis 1 f. h.
Lewin	Hypotheses 1 – 2.
Hull	Hypotheses 1 – 3 – 7 – 10.
Hebb	Hypotheses 4 – 6.
Tinbergen	Hypotheses 2 – 4 – 9.
McClelland	Hypotheses 3 p. h. – 5 s. h.

The *second* sub-class may be represented by *Sy→H hypotheses*. To this class belong the following:

Sy→H Hypotheses:

McDougall	Hypotheses 1 d. – 9.
Tolman	Hypotheses 3 – 8 – 9.
Young	Hypotheses 12 – 13 – 14 – 15 – 16.
Lewin	Hypothesis 3.
Murray	Hypotheses 2 – 3.

Hull	Hypotheses 4 – 6 – 9.
Hebb	Hypotheses 3 – 5 – 6.
Tinbergen	Hypothesis 2.
McClelland	Hypotheses 1 d. – 1 p. h. 2 p. h., 1 – 2 – 3 – 4 – 6 – 7 – 8 s. h.

As can be seen from the above some hypotheses are classified in both subclasses, because they have a 'double content' (deal with the relation of both external and internal empirical variables to hypothetical variables). Thus the number of hypotheses in the two classes are: 22 Si→H hypotheses and 30 Sy→H hypotheses. (McClelland's theory especially increases the last number.) The figures show that *external empirical variables are just as important in a theory of motivation as are internal empirical variables*, (Cf. the section about axioms of motivation).

The Comparison of the H→H Hypotheses

This class of purely theoretical hypotheses can be divided into two subclasses according to whether the hypothetical variables are *exclusively dynamogenic*, or whether they are both dynamogenic and directive[9]).

The *first sub-class* may be represented by Hm→Hm hypotheses. Among the hypotheses which have been studied the following belong to this class:

Hm→Hm Hypotheses:

McDougall	Hypotheses 2 – 7 – 8.
Tolman	Hypotheses 7 – 10 – 11 – 12.
Young	Hypotheses 7 – 8 – 9 – 10 – 11.
Allport	Hypotheses 1 g. h. – 2 g. h.
Lewin	Hypotheses 2 – 4.
Murray	Hypotheses 3 – 4 – 9 – 10.
Hull	Hypothesis 8 (maybe).
Hebb	None.
Tinbergen	None.
McClelland	None.

If the hypotheses of this sub-class are closely examined it can be seen that they may be further classified in *three sub-groups:*

Sub-group 1 of Hm→Hm hypotheses deals with the facilitating and restraining effect of motives upon each other. Especially Tolman's and Young's hypotheses belong to this sub-group.

Sub-group 2 deals with more permanent relations between motives. Especially

---

[9]) The third possibility ('exclusively directive variables') should not be included in a theory of motivation.

Murray's hypothesis (and partly McDougall's hypothesis) belong to this sub-group.

Sub-group 3 deals with the functional relations between real motives and the accompanying affective conditions. Especially McDougall's theory provides hypotheses of this kind; but Murray also has some statements on this subject.

The *second sub-class* of purely theoretical hypotheses, which, as mentioned before, deals with the relations between *both dynamogenic* (motives) and *directive* (cognitive) variables, may be represented as *Hm⟷Hc hypotheses*. The following hypotheses belong to this sub-class:

Hm⟷Hc Hypotheses:

Tolman	Hypotheses 2 – 4 – 5 – 6.
Young	Hypotheses 17 – 18 – 19 – 20.
Murray	Hypothesis 11.
Lewin	Hypothesis 2.
Hull	Hypotheses 1 – 2 – (maybe) 8.
Hebb	Hypothesis 4.
Tinbergen	Hypothesis 5.
McClelland	Hypotheses 9 – 10 s. h.

Logically this sub-class can be divided into two sub-groups (as indicated by the double-arrow). The first *sub-group* included the *Hm→Hc hypotheses*, that is all hypotheses dealing with the influence of motivation upon cognitive variables. Most of the above mentioned hypotheses in the Hm⟷Hc class[10]) are included in this group (13 of a total of 17). The *second* sub-group includes *Hc→Hm hypotheses*, all hypotheses, that is, dealing with the influence of cognitive variables upon motivation. Relatively few hypotheses are included in this sub-group, namely Lewin's 2nd hypothesis, Hebb's 4th hypothesis, McClelland's 9th sec. hyp. (and maybe Murray's 11th hypothesis).

If the two sub-classes, Hm→Hm hypotheses and Hm⟷Hc hypotheses, are compared, we obtain the following result: 21 Hm→Hm hypotheses and 17 Hm⟷Hc hypotheses.

The comparisons of all hypotheses in the H→H class then show that *theories of motivation deal with both the inter-relations between motives and the relations between motives and cognitive variables.* Most of the hypotheses mentioned last have dealt with the influences of *motives upon cognitive variables,* and only a few have dealt with the opposite functional relation. Whether this is caused by the one-sided interest of the theory-makers, or whether it has empirical reasons only future investigations can show.

---

[10]) All hypotheses which are not mentioned in the next sub-group.

Comparison of the H→R Hypotheses

This class of hypotheses dealing with the functional relations between hypothetical variables and behavior variables cannot easily be divided into sub-classes on the basis of formal criteria; but the hypotheses may be classified in sub-classes according to the *contents* of the hypotheses.

Thus one sub-class of hypotheses deals with the functional relation between the behaviour and the hypothetical variable, of which the behavior is a *direct* function. These are often hypothetical variables, preciously described as *vector-variables.* Hull's '$_{S}E_{R}$' (cf. 5th hypothesis), and maybe *Tolman's 'locomotion'* (cf. 6th hypothesis) belong to this sub-class. This sub-class may therefore be called: *vector-variable-hypotheses.*

Another sub-class deals with the relation which Jørgen Jørgensen describes as the 'Law of Multi-Motivation.' McDougall's 4th hypothesis and Allport's 2nd f. hypothesis belong to this class.

Finally one sub-class deals with the conditions in cases of *conflict and frustration.* Tinbergen's 8th hypothesis and several of Hull's secondary hypotheses (theorems) belong to this sub-class besides his 8th hypothesis which may also be classified as an H→H hypothesis.

Summary

The first part of the chapter compared the *motivation axioms* of the theories. These could be classified as *constructive* and *reductive* axioms, and the last class could be divided into *homeostasis axioms* and *other biological axioms. Far the largest number of axioms were reductive, and there seems to be a tendency to prefer non-homeostatic biological axioms* in modern theories of motivation.

In the next part *the motivational hypotheses* of the theories were compared. They proved to be distributed in three main classes viz.: 47 S→H hypotheses, 38 H→H hypotheses, and 32 H→R hypotheses. A 'measure' of the hypothetical abstraction (versus empiricism) of the theories was defined and called the 'hypothesis quotient' $= \frac{H \rightarrow H}{(S \rightarrow H) + (H \rightarrow R)}$, or *the ratio between purely theoretical hypotheses and more or less empirical hypotheses.* The average hypothesis-quotient of the theories was calculated to be 0.48, and for the individual theories the results were as follows: Tinbergen = 0.11, Hebb = 0.13, McClelland = 0.14, Hull = 0.30, McDougall = 0.43, Lewin = 0.50, Murray = 0.71, Young = 0.82, Allport = 1.00, Tolman = 1.43. (Thus the first mentioned theories are the most empirical and the last mentioned the most hypothetical.)

The S→H *hypotheses* were divided into two sub-classes, Si→H hypotheses and Sy→H hypotheses, according to whether the empirical variable was an *internal* impulse, or an *external* stimulus. *External empirical variables proved to be just as important as the internal.* The H⟷H hypotheses were also divided into two sub-classes: Hm →Hm hypotheses and Hm →Hc hypotheses according to whether the hypothetical variables were exclusively dynamogenic, or both dynamogenic and directive. These sub-classes could be divided further into other sub-classes. The main result was that *the theories of motivation studied deal with the functional relations between different motives to the same extent as they deal with the functional relations between motives and cognitive variables. There were more hypotheses dealing with the influence of motives upon cognitive variables than vice versa. The H →R hypotheses* were classified in a few sub-classes according to the contents of the hypotheses.

'Good theory leads to its own destruction by making better theory possible.'

D. O. Hebb.

Chapter 20

Synthesis

SUGGESTIONS FOR A THEORY OF MOTIVATION

Introduction

My *reasons* for suggesting a theory of motivation in a comparative meta-theoretical study are the following:

First of all, one of *S. Kock's* four program points for Theoretical Psychology was the formulation of new theories[1]). Maybe this task is not included in my definition of *Meta-Theoretical Psychology:* The meta-theoretical study of psychological theories. But the formulation of new theories can be regarded as an application of meta-theory[2])—analogous with the applications of other sciences on solving practical problems.

Because of the enormous range of psychology and the complex character of the subject psychologists are today only able to carry out experiments suitable as a basis for 'miniature systems' (cf. Hull's first articles). *If a psychologist is to construct a more comprehensive theory*—as for example a theory of motivation—*he must base it upon empirical studies made by other psychologists,* as has already been done by many psychologists (Hull, Tolman, Lewin etc.). This is also true about the construction of theories in other sciences. And maybe it would even be easier for a specialist in meta-theory to formulate a comprehensive theory since it is possible for him to form a broader and especially a more neutral 'picture' which is not subjectively dependent upon partiality for his own experimental results. Furthermore, because of the character of the scientific method, *the essential criterion of the scientific value of a hypothesis or a theory lies in its testability* and *not* in that it is based upon research. Thus I feel justified in venturing an armchair theory.

The theory will be an attempt to form a *synthesis* of the most essential content

---

[1]) S. Koch's program includes the following four points:

1. 'Analysis of methodological or "foundation" problems that are more or less unique to psychology.'
2. 'Internal systematization og suggestive, but formally defective theoretical "formations".'
3. 'Intertranslation and differential analyses of conflicting „theoretical formulations.'
4. 'The construction of new theory.' (From S. Koch: 'Theoretical Psychology, 1950: An Overview.' Psych. Review. 1951, 58, 147–54).

[2]) A similar point of view has been expressed by L. L. Whyte in *Brit. –. Phil. Science* (1952, II p. 78).

of the previous chapters. Thus the section on '*the meta-theory of the theory*' will be a synthesis of the results of the comparisons made between the structures of the theories in Chapter 17; and the section on '*the definitions of the theory*' will be a summary of the suggestions for definitions arrived at through the synthesis in Chapter 18. Finally the part on '*the hypotheses of the theory*' will be a synthesis of the axioms and hypotheses compared in Chapter 19. As this chapter thus actually is a concluding synthesis, the statements will be formulated briefly and without explanations or many comments, as these can be found in the previous chapters. In the same way no *empirical* background for the formulated hypotheses will be given, as this can be found in the empirical basis of the 20 analyzed theories.

THE META-THEORY OF THE THEORY

1. The following motivation-theory is a *deductive theory*, as it consists of a logical system of definitions, primary hypotheses (axioms), and secondary hypotheses (theorems)[3]). The axioms will be *formulated in symbols*. The symbols might later be replaced by *quantitative* expressions. The hypotheses are *qualitative*.

2. The theory is *partly reductive and partly constructive;* as motivation will be deduced from *biological* hypotheses to as great an extent as possible, but a rather extensive use of *hypothetical constructions* will temporarily be necessary.

3. The theory is a *neutral-formal* theory as its hypothetical variables are to be understood as *formal constructions* which are *neutral* with regard to a theory of the psycho-somatic phenomena. Some of the hypothetical variables of the theory *might*, however, be interpeted neuro-physiologically (as brain-processes).

4. The theory is *mainly molar*, as its *dependent variables* are units of behavior which are every-day phenomena, *actions*, and not experimentally isolated movements.

5. The theory is rather *field-theoretical*, as its hypotheses deal with interrelations between variables, especially between external situation-variables and internal organic variables.

6. The theory is *probability-deterministic* as its hypotheses are about probabilities applicable only to the *average* of several individuals or of several actions of an individual. 'A functional relationship' between variables will often be expressed with the words 'determine' of 'is determined by' for linguistic reasons.

[3]) No logical proof of the deduction of the secondary hypotheses from the primary ones will be given.

THE DEFINITIONS OF THE THEORY

The theory deals with the following variables[4]*)*:

1. '*Motivation*' (M) $\underset{D}{=}$ all *dynamogenic* functions, i. e. functions which determine *the energy-characteristics of the behavior.*

2. '*Motives*' (Mc) $\underset{D}{=}$ *central motivation* $\underset{D}{=}$ all *hypothetical* dynamogenic functions. (This may neuro-physiologically be interpreted as processes in the brain-stem, specially hypothalamus and the reticular system).

3. '*Peripheral motivation*' (Mp) $\underset{D}{=}$ all *empirical* dynamogenic functions including:

a. '*motivating impulses*' (Mi) $\underset{D}{=}$ all *internal* empirical dynamogenic functions (both real nerve impulses from *internal* organs and effects of hormones on the brain).

b. '*motivating stimuli*' (Ms) $\underset{D}{=}$ all *external* empirical dynamogenic functions (all stimuli from the environment having a *dynamogenic* function).

4. '*Affects*' (Af) $\underset{D}{=}$ states accompanying motivation, including:

a. *positive* = energy-producing states accompanying reduction of motives.

b. *negative* = extra-energy-mobilizing states accompanying the rise of motives.

5. '*Cognitive processes*' (C) $\underset{D}{=}$ all *directive* functions, i. e. functions which determine *the characteristics of the direction and organization of the behavior.* (Neurophysiologically they can be interpreted as processes in the cerebrum.) These include:

a. '*peripheral cognitive processes*' (Cp) = all *empirical* directive functions (sensory perception) determined by *directive* or orientating (external) stimuli.

b. '*central cognitive processes*' (Cc) = all *hypothetical* directive functions. Included in these are: 1) perception, 2) reproduction, 3) production (fantasy and thinking), and 4) intention ('sets,' etc.).

6. *Dispositions* (d) $\underset{D}{=}$ relatively *constant hypothetical variables* which take part in determining the dynamogenic and directive functions in a way characteristic for each species and individual. They may be divided into:

a. *dynamic* dispositions (dyd).

b. *directive* dispositions (did).

Both these classes of dispositions include *innate* (id) as well as *acquired* (ad) dispositions so that four combinations exist: idyd, adyd, idid, and adid[5]).

---

[4]) The meta-theoretical term 'variable' will in the following be left out so that 'functional variables' equals 'functions' and 'disposition variables' equals 'dispositions.'

[5]) Cf. the scheme of classification in Chapter 18.

7. *The following motives are assumed* to exist in all human beings (with individual differences in frequency and strength because of dispositions):

a. *primary:* 1) hunger-m., 2) thirst-m., 3) sex-m., 4) nursing-m., 5) temperature-m., 6) pain-avoidance-m., 7) excretory-m., 8) oxygen-m., 9) rest-m., 10) activity-m. (muscle-a.-m., sense-a.-m., brain-a.-m.).

b. *emotional:* 11) security-m. ('fear'), 12) aggressions-m. ('anger').

c. *secondary:* 13) contact-m., 14) achievement-m., 15) power-m., 16) possession-m.

THE HYPOTHESES OF THE THEORY

The theory includes the following *axioms:*

Axiom 1: Behavior is a function of interacting motives (Mc), central cognitive processes (Cc), plus dynamogenic (dyd) and directive (did) dispositions; thus:

(1) $B = f((Mc \cdot dyd) \cdot (Cc \cdot did))$,
or (1a) $B = f(P_B)$,
as $P_B \overset{=}{_D}$ the probability of the existence of an action, defined in formula (1)[6]).

Axiom 2: Motives (Mc) are a function of interacting motivating impulses (Mi), motivating stimuli (Ms), plus central cognitive processes (Cc) and dynamogenic and directive dispositions; thus:

(2) $Mc = f((Mi \cdot dyd) \cdot (Ms \cdot dyd) \cdot (Cc \cdot did))$.

Axiom 3: Motivating impulses (Mi) are a function of organic conditions (O) which deviate from the organism's normal level of adjustment[7]) *and the latter is determined by both innate (id) and acquired (ad) dispositions;* thus:

(3) $Mi = f(O \cdot id \cdot ad)$.

Axiom 4: The dynamogenic function of motivating stimuli (Ms) is a function of the intensity of the stimulus (S) and of innate (idyd) or acquired (adyd) dynamogenic dispositions; thus:

(4) $Ms = f(S \cdot idyd \cdot adyd)$.

Axiom 5: Central cognitive processes (Cc) are a function of external directive stimuli (S) and directive dispositions (did) and simultaneously existing motives (Mc); thus:

(5) $Cc = f((S \cdot did) \cdot Mc))$.

---

[6]) Thus P_B is a vector-variable corresponding to e. g. Hull's $_SE_R$, with the difference, however, that P is only a logical symbol for formula (1).

[7]) Axiom 3 is thus a revision of 'the principle of homeostasis' as 'the level of adjustment'—an expression taken from McClelland—is a more useful term than 'homeostasis', biological balance', deprivation, etc.

These 5 axioms—together with the previous definitions—*imply the following theorems:*

Theorem 1: All behavior is more or less *motivated* and more or less *directed.*

Theorem 2: Adjusted, purposive actions[8]) will appear when the motivation is of an optimal intensity, such that the cognitive processes can direct and organize behavior, thus:

B adjusted, when $Mc = Cc$.

Theorem 3: If the intensity of the motivation increases and the effectivity of the cognitive processes decreases the result will be non-purposive, random behavior; thus:

B non-purposive, when $MC > Cc$.

Theorem 4: If the motivation increases beyond a certain intensity—*the frustration-tolerance of the individual*—the cognitive processes cease to function and *maladjusted, explosive actions* or *more permanent abreacting, neurotic symptoms* will appear; thus:

B maladjusted, when $Cc \rightarrow O$, *because* $Mc \rightarrow \infty$.

Theorem 5: When the intensity of the motivation is negligable, and when directive dispositions and functions dominate, *a non-persistent, automatized action* (instinctive intention-action or habit-action) will result; thus:

B automatic, when $Mc < Cc \cdot did$.

Axiom 2 implies:

Theorem 6: A motive may be determined mainly by internal motivating impulses; thus:

(2a) $Mc = f(Mi \cdot dyd)$[9]).

Theorem 7: A motive may be determined mainly by external motivating stimuli; thus:

(2b) $Mc = f(Ms \cdot dyd)$[10]).

Theorem 8: A motive may be determined mainly by a cognitive process, an intention ('set'); thus:

(2c) $Mc = f(Cc \cdot did)$[11]).

---

[8]) Which can be 'instinctive' or learned.

[9]) This is true of motives number 1 to 4, and 8 to 10 in the list of motives.

[10]) This is true of the rest of the motives in the list.

[11]) Such a motive equals what Lewin calls a quasi-need and Jørgen Jørgensen calls a need determined by a set.

Theorem 9: A motive may *originally* be determined by *motivating impulses*, later by motivating *stimuli*[12]).

Theorem 10: Such a motive may periodically be determined by motivating impulses and periodically by motivating stimuli[13]).

Theorem 11: The *intensity* of a motive is a function of several variables—for which reason it can only be *measured by the behavior*—and not only of *one* of the determining variables.

Theorem 12: Several motives may exist *at the same time*, each determined by its own variable (stimuli, impulses, or cognitive processes).

Theorem 13: Two or more co-existing motives *conflict* if the resulting actions exclude each other.

Theorem 14: A conflict can usually be resolved because some motives are apt to dominate others[14]).

Theorem 15: If the conflict-situation becomes *permanent* the intensity of the motivation will most often exceed the *frustration-tolerance* of the individual as a result of which *abreaction-behavior* will take place (cf. Theorem 4).

Theorem 16: Two or more co-existing motives may determine the same action. If the same motives often determine the same action they are called a 'motive-system' ('interests,' 'sentiments,' etc.).

Axiom 3 implies:

Theorem 17: Primary motives, such as hunger, thirst, sex-m., nursing-m., excretory-m., oxygen-m., rest-m., and activity-m., are mainly functions of motivating impulses determined by deviations from an *innately disposed level of adjustment*.

Theorem 18: Acquired changes in the level of adjustment ('habituation') *may determine special motives* (as for example 'hunger' for drugs, special kinds of 'appetite', 'need' of cleanliness, etc.).

Axiom 4 implies:

Theorem 19: The dynamogenic functions of external stimuli are, in human beings, determined by only a few innate dispositions, such as e. g. dispositions toward: sweet stimuli, sex-appealing stimuli, mother-appealing stimuli, intense

[12]) It is then a so-called 'externalized drive'.
[13]) Cf. Murray's 'phases': active, inducible, etc.
[14]) Cf. Maslow's hypothesis of hierarchy and the use of dominance in the obstruction-box-method.

heat and cold (in relation to a rather variable level of adjustment), and pain-stimuli.

Theorem 20: In lower animal-species there are more such innate dynamogenic dispositions toward external stimuli called 'innate releasing mechanisms' (by Tinbergen).

Theorem 21: Dispositions determining the dynamogenic function of external stimuli may be acquired through a learning process, which most likely occurs *when a 'neutral' (directive) external stimulus is often associated with a motivating external stimulus or a motivating impulse.* In this way dynamogenic dispositions for *secondary motives* are formed. In human beings[15]) this learning process *may* be more intelligent than it is in animals.

Axiom 5 implies:

Theorem 22: Motives have *a selective effect upon perception-processes,* may by means of acquired dispositions[16]).

Theorem 23: Motives have *a selective effect upon reproduction-processes.*

Theorem 24: Motives determine *thinking* and *intelligent behavior* in a *problem situation* which arises when instinctive or acquired actions do not lead to adjustment (the motive is not being reduced).

Theorem 25: Motives have *a dynamogenic and selective effect upon imagination* which may have a certain motivation-reducing function.

Theorem 26: Motives take part in determining the existence of 'intentions' ('sets') which direct actions towards motive-reducing objects ('goals') (cf. Theorem 8).

Conclusion

The twenty-six theorems are most likely not sufficient to explain the functional dependence of *all* actions upon motives (and maybe more theorems might be deduced from the five axioms); but, as mentioned in the introduction, the theorems are only meant to be suggestions for a theory of motivation, and, as all other scientific theories, it must be reformulated if theoretical and empirical studies disclose mistakes or omissions. As *H. Høffding* often stated, *scientific understanding will never cease to grow.*

---

[15]) Cf. *Wolfe's* well known experiment with chimpanzees learning to pay with chips.

[16]) Cf. *Postman's* article in the Nebraska-Symposium from 1954.

SUMMARY[1]

This book is a *meta-theoretical monograph on motivational theories.* This means that it contains the results of a philosophy-of-science study of modern theories of motivation. The book should therefore be useful for psychologists as well as philosophers of science. The book consists of three parts. *The first part* deals with the *frame-of reference* for the meta-theoretical study. *The second part* submits the *analyses* of 20 theories of motivation, and in addition, reviews more than 20 other books. *The third part* submits the results of a *comparative* study of the 20 theories and a synthesis of the theories.

Part I: 'Meta-theoretical Psychology'. The first part consists of four chapters.

Chapter 1 presents a systematic survey of '*Meta-Science*' or the 'science of science', which includes: Philosophy of Science, History of Science, Sociology of Science, Psychology of Science and some boundary disciplines. As the present book belongs (mainly) to the *Philosophy of Science*, this discipline is dealt with in greater detail. It can be divided into 3 sub-disciplines: Epistemology (the basic 'theory of knowledge'), Methodology (about empirical methods), and *Meta-Theory* or 'Systematology' (about scientific systems or theories). These sub-disciplines can further be divided according to the special sciences studied. Thus the present book belongs to the 'systematology of psychology' or 'meta-theory of psychology' category which for convenience could be labelled '*Meta-Psychology*' (= Meta-theoretical psychology).

Chapter 2 contains the description of *scientific theories* in general. A 'theory' is defined very broadly as being *any descriptive and/or explanatory text* (system of symbols). A scientific theory may—i. e. need not—be a *deductive system*—very much like a mathematical theory as to its systematical structure. The special problems of 'axiomatization', 'symbolization', and 'formalization' are discussed. The most fundamental requirement of a scientific theory is that its words and sentences must have a *meaning which can be tested through empirical observations*, directly or indirectly. The special problems of 'hypothetical terms', 'protocol statements', 'scientific hypotheses' ('laws'), and 'models' are dealt with.

[1]) A summary of the whole book, written in broad outline compared with the summaries of each individual chapter.

Chapter 3 gives a discussion of the special meta-theoretical problems in relation to psychological theories. The discussions conclude with some useful classifications of psychological theories. They are classifiable—by their systematic structure as a whole—into two classes: '*deductive*' and '*classifying*' (non-deductive) theories. They can also be classified in '*reductive*' and '*constructive*' theories, the classification of which depends on the theory as a whole, and the fact whether it is based on physiological hypotheses or not.
The 'terms', 'concepts' or '*variables*' of a psychological theory can be divided into empirical, independent *variables* (antecedent conditions), '*hypothetical variables*' (intervening, and frequently, hypothetical constructs), and dependent *behavior-variables.* Many special problems of psychological variables are discussed.

The age-old problem about the 'mind-body' or 'psycho-physiological' relationship is treated, and depending on the interpretation of the relationship the theorie (and their variables) can be classified as '*mentalistic*', '*behavioristic*', or '*neutral-formal*' theories.

As regards the *protocol statements* or the descriptive units 'used' in a psychological theory, they can be classified as a '*molar*' theory (with 'macroscopic' or 'real-life-like' behavior-units) or '*molecular*' theory (with 'microscopic' or 'experimental observable' behavior-units).

Depending on the number of variables in their hypotheses ('laws') psychological theories can be classified in '*mechanistic*' theories (with only two variables in every law) and '*field-theoretical*' theories (with several, interdependent variables in the laws).

The problems of interpretation of the functional relationships are discussed, and according to the character of the relationships the theories can be classified in '*deterministic*' theories (interpreting functional relations as *causal laws*) and '*statistic*' theories (interpreting functional relations as *correlations* or other non-deterministic laws).

The problems of 'models' in psychological theories are discussed, and a classification of definitions of 'psychology' is presented.

In *chapter 4* the frame-of reference, laid down in the preceding two chapters, is crystallized in a disposition for the analytical study of psychological theories. A *provisional definition of* '*motivation*' is given: 'all variables which arouse, sustain, and direct behavior'. A very brief sketch of the history of motivational psychology can also be found here.

Part II: Analyses of Theories. This part consists of 12 chapters. In the *first ten chapters* (chapter 5 to 14 incl.) 10 motivational theories are analyzed—one in each chapter. It is the theories of the following psychologists: *McDougall,*

Tolman, Young, Allport, Lewin, Murray, Hull, Hebb. Tinbergen, and McClelland.[1])

These 10 theories have been analysed in accordance with the disposition (given in chapter 4):

I. The *structure* of the theory:
   1. Deductive or classifying theory.
   2. Reductive or constructive theory.
   3. Mentalistic or behavioristic theory.
   4. Molar or molecular theory.
   5. Mechanistic or field-theoretical theory.
   6. Deterministic or statistic theory.

II. The *contents* of the theory:
   1. The definitions of motivational variables.
   2. The hypotheses about motivation.

III. The *reconstruction* of the theory:
   A critical and systematic reformulization of the theory's most fundamental definitions and hypotheses of motivation.

In *chapter 15*, ten other theories are analyzed, they have been made by the following psychologists: *E. Frenkel-Brunswik, J. H. Massermann, G. L. Freeman, T. V. Moore, N. R. F. Maier, R. B. Cattell, Th. M. French, Stagner and Karwoski, B. F. Skinner, and Holt-Hansen.* The analyses in this chapter are not very detailed, and no reconstruction has been made.

Chapter 16 gives a review of more than 20 books and symposia about motivation from the last few years. In this chapter a systematic, metatheoretical analysis has not been given, it is a summary of the contents of the books and the symposia. With this chapter the motivational literature from the period 1930–1966 can be said to be covered.[2])

Part III: Comparison of the Theories. This part consists of 4 chapters. In *chapter 17* the results of *the comparative study of the structure* of the 20 theories are presented. For this purpose the six classifications of theories are used (cf. the above mentioned disposition). They had to be modified with some intermediary grades so that the six classifications are now six dimensions of theory-characteristics. The 20 theories are placed along the dimensions as a sort of rank-order scales. The results of the classification are shown p. 347.[3])

After having observed the classification-scheme one can formulate some generalizations about some trends in the psychological construction of theories. These

---

[1]) A short summary of each individual chapter of this part cannot be given in other ways than the one already done after the chapters. (The reconstruction may also be read as a summary of the theory.)

[2]) Exactly till May 1967. In a new book 'Modern Theories of Motivation' (in press) 10 more theories will be analyzed.

[3]) The theories have been indicated by abbreviations of the psychologists' names, in cases of doubt—the list on p. 279 can be consulted.

FB	Mai	Mo	S	S-K	Frm	C	Frh	Mas	H-H
McD	He	A	Y	McC	Mu	Ti	To	L	Hu
classifying			explanatory					deductive	

Frm	Mai	Mas	S-K	S(?)	H-H	Frh	C	FB	Mo
Ti	He	Y	McD	McC	Mu	Hu	A	L	To
extremely		mainly		mainly			extremely		
	reductive					constructive			

Mo	Frh	H-H	C	FB	S-K		Mas	Frm	Mai	S
A	McD	McC	Mu	L	Y	To	Hu	He	Ti	
mentalistic			neutral-formal				behavioristic			

H-H	Frm	S	Mai	Mas	S-K	FB	MO	Frh	C
Ti	Y	L	He	Hu	McC	McD	To	A	Mu
extremely	mainly		mainly				extremely		
molecular						molar			

	S	Mo	S-K	C	Frh	Frm	H-H	FB	Mai	To
He	Ti	A		Hu	McD	Y	Mu	McC	Mas	L
	mainly				extremely					
mechanistic			dynamic					field-theoretical		

H-H	FB	C	S	Mo (?)		Mai	Frh	Mas		S-K	Frm
		Y	Mu	Hu	McD	McC	A	To	L	He	Ti
statistical				mixed				deterministic			

descriptive generalizations can be further generalized in the following meta-theoretical (and scientific-historical) hypothesis:

'Psychological theories are becoming more deductive, (perhaps) more reductive, more neutral-formal, more molar, more field-theoretical, and more probability-deterministic.'

In *chapter 18* the results of *the comparative study of the 'motivation' definitions* of the 20 theories are given. In the first part of the chapter the motivational variables of the 20 theories are classified in the following three classifications:

1. *Classification* (after Tolman):
   1. Empirical variables
      a. independent variables
      b. dependent behavior-variables
   2. Hypothetical variables
2. *Classification* (after Tolman):
   1. Function—variables
      (processes or temporary states)
   2. Disposition—variables
      (permanent structures or factors)
3. *Classification*[1])
   1. Dynamogenic (energizing or activating) variables.

[1]) A new classification—cf. foot-note on p. 301.

Classifications of psychological Variables

		Empirical Variables (Independent, Antecedent Variables)	Hypothetical Variables			Behavior Variables (Dependent, consequent variables)		
			Neutral-formal	Neurophysiological	Phenomenological			
Disposition Variables	Vector		*4 variables* (e.g. Murray's Need)				Vector	Disposition Variables
	Directive		*3 variables* (e.g. Young's Attitude)	Tinbergen's 'instinct'			Directive	
	Dynamogenic		*4 variables* (e.g. McDougall's Propensity Cattels Erg)				Dynamogenic	
Function Variables	Vector	*2 variables* (e.g. Masserman's Need)	*7 variables* (e.g. Murray's Need) Tolman's Drive (1932)	*3 variables* (e.g. Stagner's Drive)	Young's Desire		Vector	Function Variables
	Directive	*2 variables* (e.g. Hull's drive-stimulus)	*5 variables* (e.g. Young's Set)	*2 variables* (e.g. Freeman's Set)			Directive	
	Dynamogenic	*11 variables* (e.g. Tolman's Drive (1951)) Young's Need Hull's Need (CD)	*8 variables* e.g. Hull's Drive Tolman's Need (1951) Lewin's Tension	*3 variables* (e.g. Young's Drive)	*2 variables* (e.g. Moore's impulse)		Dynamogenic	

2. Directive (regulating or organizing) variables.
3. Vector-variables, which are combined dynamogenic and directive variables.

The results of the combined classifications are given in the scheme on page 348.

In the next part of the chapter there is made a comparative concept-analysis (an 'explication') of the motivational concepts in the 20 theories. The explication has resulted in the following suggestions of definitions:

'*Motivation*' = *all dynamogenic function variables, both empirical and hypothetical*'.
'*Central motivation*' = 'motives' = 'all *hypothetical* dynamogenic function variables'.
'*Peripheral motivation*' = 'motivating impulses and stimuli' = 'all *empirical* dynamogenic function variables'.
'*Affective variables*' are partly '*emotions*', i. e. motives, and partly '*affections*', i. e. energy-producing and extraenergy-mobilizing states, which accompany motivation.

In the third part of the chapter a comparison of the different lists of motives in the 20 theories has been made. The problems of classification of motives are discussed. and conclude in the following definitions:

'A *primary* motive is a central motivation which is from birth (or probably after processes of maturation) determined by motivating impulses or stimuli.'

'A *secondary* motive is a central motivation which is, after a learning process, determined by motivating stimuli.'

After the definitions a list of 16 motives are suggested. There is a special argumentation for the demonstration of an 'activity motive'.

In *chapter 19* the results of a comparative study of the hypotheses in the 10 theories are presented (analysed in chapters 5–14). First part contains a classification of the axioms (more fundamental hypotheses) of the theories in '*constructive*' and '*reductive axioms*'. The latter group is further divided into 'homeostatic' and 'other biological axioms'. *By far the largest number of axioms were reductive;* there seems to be a tendency to prefer nonhomeostatic biological axioms in modern theories of motivation.

The results have been supplemented with the results of the classification of the other hypotheses of the theories. They proved that motivating stimuli are just as important in modern theories as are motivating impulses.

As a non-intended by-product of the classification of the hypotheses the idea formed, of measuring the degree of 'speculativity' or abstraction (versus empiricism). This could be done by relating the number of pure theoretical hypotheses (H→H—hypothesis) with the number of more or less empirical hypotheses (S→H— and H→R—hypothesis). The relationship constitutes the so-called '*hypothesis-quotient*':

$$\text{H.Q.} = \frac{\text{H} \rightarrow \text{H}}{(\text{S} \rightarrow \text{H}) + (\text{H} \rightarrow \text{R})}$$

The H.Q. for the ten theories has been calculated as follows: Tinbergen = 0.11, Hebb = 0.13, McClelland = 0.14, Hull = 0.30, McDougall = 0.43, Lewin = 0.50, Murray = 0.71, Young = 0.82, Allport = 1.00, Tolman = 1.43, (which shows that Tinbergen's theory is the most empirical and Tolman's the most speculative). It is the present writer's hope that other philosophers of science will try to use the H.Q. in other fields of psychology or in other sciences to test its usefulness.

Chapter 20 presents the result of a *synthesis* of all the studied theories, in form of a *systematic theory* of motivation. The theory consists of some formal definitions, 5 axioms and 26 hypotheses of motivation. The theory attempts to combine the dominating trends of modern theories of motivation, especially the modern *physiological theories* (e. g. Hebb's theory), the modern *learning theories* (e. g. Hull's theory), and the modern personality theories (e. g. McClelland's theory). The main contents of the five axioms of the theory are that *behavior* is *determined by motivation (dynamogenic) and cognitive (directive) processes in combination. Central motivation* is interpreted physiologically as the 'arousal' or energy level of the brain-stem (especially the reticular system and the more specific 'motivational centers' in the hypothalamus). The central motivation itself is the result of the combined effect of *motivating impulses* from the organism's various organs, *motivating stimuli* from the environment, and influence of the on-going *cognitive processes* (probably in the cortex). The central motivation is als influenced by individually different dispositions (constitutional and acquired).

The contents of the 26 hypotheses which can be deduced from the 5 axioms cannot be summarized further than it have been done in the hypotheses (p. 334–37).

It is not the intention that this theory should be understood as 'the final word' in theories of motivation—it is intended to be a provisional, systematic summary of current theories of motivation.

K.B.M.

BIBLIOGRAPHY

Abbreviations:	An.Rev.	= Annual Review of Psychology
	B.J.Ph.Sc.	= British Journal for the Philosophy of Science
	Neb.Sym.	= Nebraska Symposium on Motivation
	Ps.Rev.	= Psychological Review
	Ph. Sci.	= Philosophy of Science
	J.Exp.Psych.	= Journal of Experimental Psychology

Adams, D. K.: The anatomy of personality (Doubleday papers in psychology 1954).

Adrian, Bremer, Jasper, and Delafresnay (eds.): Brain mechanisms and consciousness. A symposium (1954).

Alexander, F.: Three fundamental principles (Dialectica 1951, 5, 239–45).

Allee, Nissen, and Nimkoff: A re-examination of the concept of instinct (Ps.Rev. 1953, 60, 287–97).

Allport, G. W.: Becoming: Basic Considerations for a Psychology of Personality (Burns & MacEachern, Toronto, 1955).

Allport, G. W.: Pattern and Growth in Personality (Holt, N.Y., 1961).

Allport, G. W.: Personality – A psychological interpretation (Constable, London, 1956).

Allport, G. W.: Personality and Social Encounter (Beacon Press, Boston, 1966).

Allport, G. W.: Scientific models and human morals (Ps.Rev. 1947, 54, 182–92).

Allport, G. W.: The Individual and his Religion (Constable, London 1950).

Allport, G. W.: The Nature of Prejudice (Addison–Wesley, Cambridge, Mass., 1955).

Allport, G. W.: The nature of personality. Selected papers. (Addison Wesley, Mass. 1951).

Allport, G. W.: The Use of Personal Documents in Psychological Science (Social science research council 1942).

Amons, R. B. and C. H. Amons: Psychology of the scientist: I. Introduction (Percept. & Motor skills 1962, 15 (3), 748–50).

Andrews, F. M.: Creativity and the scientist (Dissertation Abstracts, 1963, 23, (9), 3524).

Andrews, T. G. (ed.): Methods of psychology (Wiley, N.Y., 1964).

Archambault, R. D.: The concept of need (Harvard, Educ. Rev. 1957, 27, 38–62).

Atkinson, J. W.: Motivational determinants of risk-taking behavior (Ps.Rev. 1957, 64, 359–72).

Atkinson, J. W. (ed.): Motives in Fantasy, Action and Society (Van Nostrand, N.Y., 1958).

Ayer, A. J.: Logical Positivism (Free Press, Illinois, 1959).

Ayer, A. J.: The problem of knowledge (Macmillan, London, 1956).

Baker, R. G.: Ecology and Motivation (Nebr.Symp. 1960).

Bawden, H. H.: The psychical as a biological directive (Ph.Sc. 1947, 1,4 56–57).

Beach, F. A.: Characteristics of masculine sexdrive (Neb.Symp. 1956).

Beach, F. A.: The descent of instinct (Ps.Rev. 1955, 62, 401–10).

Beach, F. A., and J. Jaynes: Effects of early experience upon the behavior of animals (Ps.Bulletin 1954, 51, 239–63).

Beck, L. W.: Constructions and inferred entities (Ph.Sci. 1950, 17).

Benjamin, A. C.: Is the Philosophy of Science Scientific? (Ph.Sci. 1960, 27, 351–58).

Benton, M.: Creativity in research and invention in the physical sciences. An annotated biblio-

graphy (USN Res.Lab.Rep. 1961).
Bergman, G.: Philosophy of science (Univ. of Wisconsin, 1958).
Bergman, G.: The logic of psychological concepts (Ph.Sci. 1951, 18, 93–110).
Bergman, G.: Theoretical psychology (An.Rev. 1953, 4, 435–58).
Bergman, G., and K. W. Spence: Operationism and theory construction (Ps.Rev. 1941, 48, 1–14).
Berlyne, D. E.: Conflict, Arousal and Curiosity (McGraw-Hill, N.Y. 1960).
Bindra, D.: Motivation – A Systematic Reinterpretation (Ronald Press, N.Y., 1959).
Björkman, H.: Psykologisk Forskning (Almquist, Stockholm, 1962).
Black, V.: Laboratory versus field research in psychology and the social sciences (B.J.Ph.Sc. 1955, 5, 319–30).
Blegvad, H. et al: Årsagsproblemet (Nordisk Sommeruniversitet, 1951).
Bloomfield, L.: Linguistic aspects of science (Internat. Encyclopedia Unified Sci. 1939, I (4)).
Böhr, N.: Atomfysik og den menneskelige erkendelse (Schulz, Copenhagen, 1957).
Böhr, N.: Atomteori og Naturbeskrivelse Univ. festskrift, Copenhagen, 1929).
Böhr, N.: Quantum mechanics and philosophy, in Survey of Philosophy in Mid-Century, 1958).
Bolles, R. C.: The usefulness of the drive concept (Nebr.Symp. 1938).
Boring, E. G.: A history of experimental psychology (Appleton-Cent. Co., N.Y., 2nd ed., 1950).
Boring, E. G.: History, Psychology and Science: Selected Papers (Wiley, N.Y. and London, 1963).
Boring, E. G.: Psychological factors in the scientific process, in Psychologist at large (Basic Books, N.Y., 1961).
Boring, Bridgman, Feigl, Israel, Skinner, and Pratt: Symposium on operationism (Ps.Rev. 1954, 52,5 m 241–94).
Braithwaite, R. B.: Scientific explanation (Cambridge Univ. London, 1953).
Brodbeck, H., A. Gewirth, and R. S. Rudner: Philosophy of the social sciences (Ph.Sci. 1954, 21, 140–65).
Bronfenbrenner, U.: Personality (An.Rev. 1953, 4, 157–87).
Brown, C. W., and E. E. Ghiselli: Scientific method in psychology (McGraw-Hill, N.Y., 1955).
Brown, J. S.: Acquired drives (Neb.Symp. 1953).
Brown, J. S.: The Motivation of Behavior (McGraw-Hill, N.Y., 1961).
Brown, J. S., and J. E. Farber: Emotions conceptualized as intervening variables (Ps.Bull. 1951, 48, 465–95).
Bruns, H. W.: Pragmatism and the science of behavior (Ph.Sci. 1960, 27, 58–64).
Brunswik, E.: Organismic achievement and environmental probability (Ps.Rev. 1943, 50, 255–72).
Brunswik, E.: The conceptual framework of psychology (Int. Enoc. Unif. Sci. 1952, II (5)).
Brunswik, Postman, Hilgard, Krech, and Feigl: Symposium on the probability approach in psychology (Ps.Rev. 1955, 62, 193–242).
Bühler, C.: Maturation and motivation (Dialectica 1951, 5, 312–61).
Buxten, C. E.: Learning (An.Rev. 1951, 2, 23–44).
Buytendijk, F., Pieron, H., Dell, P., Leary, G. C., Nutten, J. and Ancona, L.: La Motivation (Rapports et discussions). (Association de psychologie scientific de langue francaise. Symposium 5, Florence, 31. mars–3 Avr. 1958) (Presses universitaires, Paris, 1959).
Campel, N. H.: Foundations of Science (Dover, N.Y., 1957).
Campbell, David P.: The Vocational Interests of American Psychological Association Presidents. (American Psychologists 1965, 20, 636–44), Washington, D.C.).
Campell: D. T.: Methodological suggestions from a comparative psychology of knowledge processes (Inquiry 1959, 2, 152–82).
Carlsson, N. G.: Dimensions of behaviour (Gleerup, Lund, 1949).
Carnap, R.: Formal and factual science (Erkenntnis, 1934)
Carnap, R.: Testability and meaning (Ph.Sci. 1937–38).
Carnap, R.: The interpretations of physics, in H. Feigl and N. Brodbeck: Readings in the philosophy of science (Appleton, N.Y., 1953, pp. 309–18).
Carnap, R.: The two concepts of probability, in Feigl and Brodbeck: Readings in the philosophy of science (Appleton, N.Y., 1953, pp. 435–55).
Cartwright, D.: Lewinian Theory as a Contemporary Systematic Framework, in S. Koch (ed.): Psychology – A Study of a Science (McGraw-Hill, N.Y., Vol. II, 1959).
Cassirer, E.: An essay on man (Yale Univ. Oxford, 1944).
Cattell, R. B.: Personality (McGraw-Hill, N.Y., 1950).

Cattell, R. B.: The dynamic calculus: Concepts and crucial experiments (Nebr.Symp. 1959).
Catton, J. W.: On making prediction from Hull's theory (Ps.Rev. 1955, 62, 303–14).
Chambers, J. A.: Relating personality and biographical factors to scientific creativity (Psychol. Monographs, General & Applied 1964, 78 (7), No. 584).
Child, J. L.: Personality (An. Rev. 1954, 5, 149–70).
Clark, K. E.: America's psychologists: A survey of a growing profession (Washington, D.C., American Psychological Association, 1957).
Clark, R. A.: The projective measurement of experimentally introduced levels of sexual motivation (J.exp.Psych. 1952, 44, 391–99).
Cofer, C. N.: Motivation (An.Rev. 1959, 10, 173–202).
Cofer, C. N., and M. H. Appley: Motivation, Theory and Research (Wiley, N.Y., 1964).
Connor, D. J.: Determinism and predictability (B.J.Ph.Sc. 1957, 7, 310–15).
Cooley, W. W.: Research Frontier: Current research on the career development of scientists (Journal of Counseling Psychology, 1964, 11 (1), 88–93).
Datta, Lois-Ellin: Test instructions and the identification of creative scientific talent (Psychol. Reports 1963, 13 (2), 495–500).
David, H. P., and H. von Bracken (eds.): Perspectives in personality theory (Tavistock, London, 1957).
Davis, R. C.: Physical psychology (Ps.Rev. 1953, 60, 7–14).
Deese, J., and C. T. Morgan: Comparative and physiological psychology (An.Rev. 1951, 2, 193–216).
Diel, P.: Psychologie de la Motivation (Presses Universitaires de France, Paris, 1962).
Duffy, Elisabeth: Activation and Behaviour (Wiley, N.Y., 1962).
Duffy, E.: The psychological significance of the concept of "arousal" or "activation" (Ps.Rev. 1957, 64, 265–75).
Einstein, A.: Geometry and experience, in H. Feigl and M. Brodbeck: Readings in the philosophy of science (Appleton, N.Y., 1953, pp. 189–94).
Einstein, A.: Out of my later years (Philosophical Library, N.Y., 1957–58).
Einstein, A.: The fundamentals of theoretical physics, in H. Feigl and M. Brodbeck: Reading in the philosophy of science (Appleton N.Y., 1953, pp. 263–71).
Einstein, A.: The laws of science and the laws of ethics; in Feigl and Brodbeck: Reading in the philosophy of science (Appleton, N.Y., 1953, pp. 779–80).
Ellson, D. G.: The application of operational analysis to human motor behavior (Ps.Rev. 1949, 56, 9–17).
Eriksen, C. W.: Personality (An.Rev. 1957, 8, 185–211).
Eriksen, C. W.: Unconscious processes (Nebr.Symp. 1958).
Esper, E. A.: A History of Psychology as a Biological Science (Saunders, Philadelphia, 1965).
Estes, W. K.: A study of motivating conditions necessary for secondary reinforcement (J.exp. Psych. 1949, 39, 306–10).
Estes, W. K.: Learning (An.Rev. 1956, 1–38).
Estes, W. K.: Stimulus-response theory of drive (Nebr.Symp. 1958).
Estes, W. K. et al: Modern Learning Theories (Wym, N.Y., 1954).
Estes, Kock, MacCorquodale, Meehl, Mueller, Schoenfeld, and Verplanck: Modern learning theories (Appleton, N.Y., 1954).
Eysenck, H. J. (ed.): Experiments in Motivation (Pergamon, Oxford, 1963).
Eysenck, H. J.: Personality (An.Rev. 1952, 3, 151–174).
Eysenck, H. J., B. A. Farell, C. Crockett, and A. Moore: Philosophy and Psychoanalysis (Inquiry 1961, 4, 1–65).
Farber, J. E.: Anxiety as a drive state (Neb.Symp. 1954).
Farber, J. E.: Response fixation under anxiety and non-anxiety conditions (J.exp.Psych. 1948, 38, 111–31).
Farber, J. E.: The role of motivation in verbal learning and performance (Ps.Bull. 1955, 52, 311–27).
Feigl, H.: Notes in Causality, in H. Feigl and M. Brodbeck (ed.): Reading in the philosophy of science (Appleton, N.Y., 1953, pp. 408–18).
Feigl, H.: Principles and problems of theory constructions in psychology, in W. Dennis (ed.): Current trends in psych. theory (Prentice-Hall, N.J., 1951).

Feigl, H., and M. Scriven (eds.): Minnesota Studies in the Philosophy of Science, Vols. I and II (Univ. of Minnesota Press, Madison, 1956 and 1958.)
Fenstad, J. E.: Notes on the application of formal methods in the soft sciences (Inquiry 1959, 2, 34–64).
Fitch and Barry: Towards a formalization of Hull's behavior theory (Ps.Sci. 1950, 17, 260–65).
Flescher, R.: Instinct in man (Allen, London, 1957).
Flugel, J. C.: Men and their motives (Routledge, London, 1947).
Frank, L. K.: Feelings and emotions (Doubleday papers in psych. 1954).
Frank, Ph. G.: The Validation of Scientific Theories (Beacon Press, Boston, 1956).
Freemann, G. L.: The energetics of human behavior (Cornell Univ. Press, Ithaca, 1948).
French, Th. M.: Integration of behavior (Univ. of Chicago Press Vol. I, 1952).
Frenkel-Brunswik, E.: Motivation and behavior (Genetic Psych.Mon, 1942, 26, 121–264).
From, F.: Om oplevelsen af andres adfærd (Nyt Nordisk Forlag, Copenhagen, 1953).
Fuller, John L.: Motivation – A Biological Perspective (Random House, N.Y., 1962).
Galtung, J.: Notes of the differences between physical and social sciences (Inquiry 1958, I, 7–34).
Garrett, Henry E.: Great Experiments in Psychology (Appleton, N.Y., 1941).
Garwood, D. S.: Personality factors related to creativity in young scientist (Journal of Abnormal & Social Psychol. 1964, 68 (4), 413–19).
George, F. H.: Formalization of language systems for behavior (Ps.Rev. 1953, 60, 232–40).
Giles, H.: Education and human motivation (Philosophical Library, N.Y., 1957).
Ginsberg, A.: Hypothetical constructs and intervening variables (Ps.Rev. 1954, 61, 119–31).
Golann, Stuart, E.: Psychological study of creativity (Psych.Bull. 1963, 60, (6), 548–65).
Golightly, C. L.: Mind-body, causation and correlation (Ph.Sci. 1952, 19, 225–27).
Gregory, R. L.: On physical model explanations in psychology (B.J.Ph.Sc. 1953, 4, 192–97).
Griffith, C. R.: Principles of systematic psychology Univ. of Illinois 1943).
Guilford, P.: Factorial angles to psychology (Ps.Rev. 1961, 68, 1–20).
Hall, C. S., and Lindzey, G.: Theories of personality (Wiley, N.Y., 1965).
Hall, C. S., and S. J. Klein: Individual Differences in Aggression in Rats (J.comp.Psych. 1951, 371–83).
Hall, C. S., and P. H. Whiteman: The effects of infantile stimulation upon later emotional stability in the mouse (J.comp.physiol.psych. 1951, 44, 61–66).
Hall, J. F.: Psychology of Motivation (Lippincott, Chicago, 1961).
Harlow, H. F.: Learning (An.Rev. 1952, 3, 29–54).
Harlow, H. F.: Mice, monkeys, men and motives (Ps.Rev. 1953, 60, 23–32).
Harlow, H. F.: Motivation as a factor in the acquisition of new responses (Neb.Symp. 1953).
Hayek, F. A.: Degrees of explanation (B.J.Ph.Sc. 1955, 6, 209–25).
Hays, R.: Psychology of the scientist: III. Introduction to passages from the "idea books" of Clark L. Hull (Percept. & Motor Skills 1962, 15 (3), 803–6).
Hebb, D. O.: Animal and psysiological psychology (An.Rev. 1950, 1, 173–88).
Hebb, D. O.: Drives and the C.N.S. (Ps.Rev. 1955, 62, 243–54).
Hebb, D. O.: The organization of behavior (Wiley, N.Y., 1964).
Hebb, D. O.: A Textbook of Psychology (Saunders, London, 2nd ed. 1966).
Heider, F.: The gestalt theory of motivation (Nebr.Symp. 1960).
Hempel, C. G.: Analyse logique de la psychologie (Revue de syntese, Paris, 1935).
Hempel, C. G.: Fundamentals of concept formation in empirical science (Internat.Encycl.Unif.Sc. II (7), 1952).
Henle, M.: Some effects of motivational processes on cognition (Ps.Rev. 1955, 62, 423–32).
Henle, M.: Some problems of eclecticism (Ps.Rev. 1957, 64, 296–305).
Hess, E.: The relationship between imprinting and motivation (Nebr.Symp. 1959).
Hilgard, E.: Motivation in Learning Theory, in S. Koch (ed.): Psychology – A study of a science, Vol. V (McGraw-Hill, N.Y., 1963).
Hilgard, E. R.: Hull's: A behavior system (Ps.Bull. 1954, 51, 91–96).
Hilgard, E. R.: Theories of Learning (Appleton-Century-Croffts, N.Y., 3rd ed., 1966).
Hinde, R. A.: Animal Behavior (McGraw-Hill, N.Y., 1966).
Hinde, R. A.: Ethiological models and the concept of "drive" (B.J.Ph.Sc. 1956, 6, 321–31).
Hinde, R. A.: Some recent trends in ethology, in S. Koch (ed.): Psychology – A study of a science, Vol. II (McGraw-Hill, N.Y., 1959).

Holt–Hansen, Kr.: After effects in the behavior of mice (Munksgaard, Copenhagen, 1956).
Hook, S. (ed.): Psychoanalysis, Scientific Method and Philosophy (New Univ. Press, N.Y., 1959).
Hovland, C. J.: Clark Leonard Hull, 1884–1952 (Ps.Rev. 1952, 59, 347–80).
Hull, C. L.: A behavior system (Yale Univ. Press, New Haven, 1958).
Hull, C. L.: Conflicting psychologies of learning (Ps.Rev. 1935, 42, 439–516).
Hull, C. L.: Essentials of behavior (Yale Univ. Press, Oxford, 1951).
Hull, C. L.: Goal attraction and directing ideas conceived as habit phenomena (Ps.Rev. 1931, 38, 487–506).
Hull, C. L.: Knowledge and purpose as habit mechanisms (Ps.Rev. 1930, 37, 511–28).
Hull, C. L.: Principles of behavior (Appleton, N.Y., 1943).
Hull, C. L.: Psychology of the scientist: IV. Passage from the "ideas books" of Clark L. Hull (Percept. and motor skills, 1962, 15 (3), 807–82).
Hull, C. L.: Stimulus equivalence in behavior theory (Ps.Rev. 1939, 46, 9–30).
Hull, C. L.: The goal gradient hypothesis and maze learning (Ps.Rev. 1932, 39, 25–43).
Hull, C. L.: The problem of intervening variables in molar behavior (Ps.Rev. 1943, 50, 273–91).
Hull, C. L.: A proposed quantification of habit strength (Ps.Rev. 1945, 52).
Hull, Hovland, Ross, Hall, Perlins, and Fitch: Mathematical-deductive theory of rote learning (Yale Univ. Press, Oxford, 1940).
Hunt, C. L.: Mind. mechanism, and adaptive behavior (Ps.Rev. 1937, 44, 1–32).
Hunt, J. McV. et al: Studies of the effects of infantile experience on adult behavior in rats (J. Comp. Psych. 1947, 40, 291–304).
Hutten, E. H.: Explanation in psychology and physics (B.J.Ph.Sc. 1956, 7, 73–85).
Hyman, R.: The Nature of Psychological Inquiry (Prentice-Hall, N.J., 1964).
Iff, Werner: La motivation a l'avancement professionel (Centre national de la recherce scientifique, Paris, 1962).
James, J.: Principles of Psychology (Dover, N.Y., 1950).
Janis, I. L.: Motivational factors in the resolution of decisional conflicts (Nebr.Symp. 1959).
Jones, M. R. (ed.): Current theory and research in motivation (The First Nebraska Symposium on Motivation, 1953).
Jørgensen, J.: Filosofiske forelæsninger (Munksgaard, Copenhagen, 1962).
Jørgensen, J.: Hvad er psykologi? (Munksgaard, Copenhagen, 1955).
Jørgensen, J.: Psykologi på biologisk grundlag (Munksgaard, Copenhagen, 1941–45).
Jørgensen, J.: Remarks concerning the concept of mind and problem of other people's mind (Theoria 1949, 15, 116–27).
Jørgensen, J.: Sandhed, virkelighed og fysikkens metode (Munksgaard, Copenhagen, 1950).
Jørgensen, J.: The development of logical empiricism (Intern. Encycl. Unified Sci. II 9, 1952).
Kaila, E.: Den mänsliga kunstskapen (Natur og Kultur, Stockholm, 1939).
Kaila, E.: Personlighedens psykologi (Nyt Nordisk Forlag, Copenhagen, 1948).
Kaila, E.: Physicalismus and phänomenalismus (Theoria 1942, 8, 85–125).
Kaila, E.: Tankens oro (Natur og Kultur, Stockholm, 1945).
Kantor, J. R.: Interbehavioral Psychology (Principia Press, Indiana, 1958).
Kausler, D. H. and E. P. Trapp: Motivation and cue utilization in intentional and incidential learning (Ps.Rev. 1960, 67, 373–79).
Koch, S.: Behavior as "intricately" regulated (Neb.Symp. 1956).
Koch, S. (ed.): Psychology – A study of a science, Vols. I, II, III (McGraw Hill, N.Y., 1958 and 1959).
Koch, S. (ed.): Psychology – A study of a science, Vols. I–VI (McGraw-Hill, N.Y., 1959–63).
Koch, S.: The current status of motivational psychology (Ps.Rev. 1951, 58, 147–54).
Koch, S.: Logical Character of motivation concept (Ps.Rev. 1941, 48, 15–37, 127–54).
Koch, S.: Theoretical psychology 1950: An overview (Ps.Rev. 1951, 58, 295–301).
Koch, S.: Clark L. Hull, in Estes et al.: Modern learning theory (Wyn, N.Y., 1954).
Køhler, W.: Dynamics in psychology (Grove Press, N.Y., 1960).
Køhler, W.: Gestalt psychology (Liveright, N.Y., 1947).
Kohn, W.: Satiation of hunger from food injected directly into the stomach (J.comp.physiolog. psych. 1951, 44, 403–12).
Krech, D.: Cognition and motivation in modern psychological theory, in W. Dennis (ed.): Current trends in psychological theory (Pittsburg, 1951).

Kreck, D.: Dynamic Systems as open neurological systems (Ps.Rev. 1950, 57, 345–61).
Krech, D.: Dynamic Systems, Psychological Fields and Hypothetical Constructs (Ps.Rev. 1950, 57, 283–90).
Krech, D., and G. Klein (ed.): Theoretical models and personality theory (Duke Univ. Press, Cambridge, London, 1952).
Kriedl, P. H.: Differential interest patterns of psychologists. (Unpubl. doct. diss., Univ. of Minnesota, 1949).
Lachman, Roy: The model in theory construction (Ps.Rev. 1960, 67, 373–79).
Langkjær, Asger: Contributions to a general wormology or theory of purpose-setting with particular reference to imperatives and definitions of serviceability (Dansk Videnskabs Forlag, Copenhagen, 1961).
Langkjær, Asger: Hvad er behov? (Handelsvidenskabelig tidsskrift 1954, 18, 152–72).
Langkjær, Asger: Normer og behov (Erhvervsøkonomisk tidsskrift 1955, 19, 102–21).
Langkjær, Asger: Salgspsykologi (Harck, Copenhagen, 1943).
Langkjær, Asger: Vore drifter og behov (Vinding, Copenhagen, 1949).
Lashley, K. H.: Experimental analysis of instinctive behavior (Ps.Rev. 1939, 45, 445–72).
Leeper, R. W.: A motivational theory of emotion (Ps.Rev. 1948, 55, 5–21).
Lehman, H.: The creative production rates of present versus past generation of scientists (Journal of Gerontology 1962, 17, 409–17).
Lesche, C.: Psykosomatiske problem, in V. Valpola (ed.): Människan-Forskningsobject (Nordiska Sommeruniversitet, 1960).
Leverell, H. W.: The mind we measure and its dimensions (Phi.Sci. 1948, 15, 39–46).
Levin, H., and A. L. Baldwin: Pride and shame (Nebr.Symp. 1959).
Lewin, K.: A dynamic theory of personality (McGraw-Hill, N.Y., 1935).
Lewin, K.: Behavior and Development as a Function of the Total Situation (1946), reprinted in G. W. Allport: Pattern and Growth in Personality (Holt, N.Y., 1961).
Lewin, K.: Das Problem der Willensmessung (Psych. Forschung 1921–22, 1–2, 191–302 and 65–140).
Lewin, K.: Die psychische Tätigkeit bei der Hemmung von Willensvorgängen (Zeitschr.f.Psych. 1917, 77, 212–48).
Lewin, K.: Field theory in social sciences, ed. by B. Cartwright (Harper & Row, N.Y., 1951).
Lewin, K.: Formalization and Progress in Psychology (1940), reprinted in G. W. Allport: Pattern and Growth in Personality (Holt, N.Y., 1961).
Lewin, K.: Principles of topological psychology (McGraw-Hill, N.Y., 1936).
Lewin, K.: The conceptual representation and the measurement of psychological forces (Duke Univ., Durham, 1938).
Lewin, K.: Vorbemerkungen über die seelichen Kräfte (Ps.Forsch. 1928, 7, 294–329).
Lewin, K.: Vorsatz, Ville und Bedürfnis (Psych.Forsch. 1928, 7, 330–85).
Lewis, C. I.: An analysis of knowledge and valuation (Paul Carus lectures 7, ser. 1945) (Open Court Publishing Co., La Salle, Illinois, 1946).
Lindsley, D. B.: Psychophysiology and motivation (Nebr.Symp. 1957).
Lindsley, D. B.: Physiological Psychology (An.Rev. 1956, 323–48).
Lindzey, G. (ed.): Assessment of Human Motives (Grove Press, N.Y., 1958).
Littmann, R. A.: Motives, history and causes (Nebr.Symp. 1958).
Littmann, R. A., and E. Rosen: Molar and molecular (Ps.Rev. 1950, 57, 58–65).
Lockman, R. F.: Characteristics of APA members in the 1962 "National Scientific Register' (Amer. Psychologist 1962, 17 (10), 789–92).
Logan, F. A.: Incentive (Yale Univ. Press, New Haven, 1960).
Logan, F. A.: Micromolar approach to behavior theory (Ps.Rev. 1956, 63, 63–73).
Logan, F. A.: The Hull-Spence Approach, in S. Koch (ed.): Psychology – A study of a science, Vol. II (McGraw-Hill, N.Y., 1959).
London, I. D.: Psychologists measure of the auxilliary concepts of physics and mathematics (Ps.Rev. 1944, 51, 266–91).
Lynch, W. W.: An approach to the study of motivational problems in education (Bull. School of Education, Indiana University 1955, 31, 5–46).
Lynn, R.: Attention, Arousal and the Orientation Reaction (Pergamon, Oxford, 1966).
McClelland, D. C.: Personality (An.Rev. 1956, 7, 39–62).

McClelland, D. C.: Personality (Holt, N.Y., 1960).
McClelland, D. C.: Some social consequence of achievement motivation (Nebr.Symp. 1955).
McClelland, D. C. (ed.): Studies in motivation (Appleton-Century, N.Y., 1955).
McClelland, D. C.: The achieving Society (Van Nostrand, N.Y., 1961).
McClelland, D. C.: The psychology of mental content reconsidered (Ps.Rev. 1955, 62, 297–302).
McClelland, D. C., and J. W. Atkinson: The projective expression of needs (J.Psych. 1948, 25, 20, 5–32).
McClelland, Atkinson, Clark, and Lowell: The achievement motive (Appleton-Century-Croft, N.Y., 1953).
MacCourquodale, K.: Learning (An.Rev. 1955, 6, 29–62).
MacCourquodale, K., and P. E. Meehl: On a distinction between hypothetical constructs and intervening variables (Ps.Rev. 1948, 55, 95–107).
McDougall, W.: An introduction to social psychology (Methuen, London, 1963).
McDougall, W.: An Outline of Abnormal Psychology (1926).
McDougall, W.: An Outline of Psychology (1923).
McDougall, W.: Psychology, the study of behavior (1912).
McDougall, W.: The Energies of Men (Methuen, London, 1950).
McGuigan, F. J.: Formalization of psychological theory (PsRev. 1953, 60, 377–82).
McGuigan, F. J.: The logical status of Hull's principle of secondary reinforcement (Ps.Rev. 1956, 63, 303–9).
MacKay, D. M.: Mindlike behavior in artefacts (B.J.Ph.Sc. 1951, 2, 105–21).
MacKinnon, D. W.: Personality (An.Rev. 1951, 2, 133–36).
Madden, E. H.: A logical analysis of "psychological isomophism" (B.J.Ph.Sc. 1957, 8, 177–91).
Madden, E. H.: The philosophy of science in gestalt theory (Ph.Sci. 1952, 19, 228–38).
Madsen, K. B.: Behov og emotioner (Unpublished thesis about Shand and Murray, 1950).
Madsen, K. B.: Dyr og mennsker (Gad, Copenhagen, 1952).
Madsen, K. B.: En videnskabsfilosofisk analyse og sammenligning af nogle dyslexi-teorier (Nord. Tidsskr. f. Specialpedagogik, April 1961).
Madsen, K. B.: Komplementaritet i psykologien (Nordisk Psykologi 1958, 10, 1–14).
Madsen, K. B.: Moderne motivationspsykologi (Nord. Psykologi 1960, 12, 325–34).
Madsen, K. B.: Moderne psykologiske Teorier (Munksgaard, Copenhagen, 1960).
Madsen, K. B.: Motivations-teorier (4. Nordiske Psykologmødes Kongresberetning 1956–57).
Madsen, K. B.: Psykologi (Munksgaard, Copenhagen, 1949).
Madsen, K. B.: Psykologi og videnskaben om videnskab (Nord. Psyk. 1961, 13, 134–42).
Madsen, K. B.: Teoretisk psykologi (Nordisk Psykologi 1954, 6, 160–75).
Maier, N. R. F.: Frustration (McGraw-Hill, N.Y., 1949).
Malmo, R. B.: A neuropsychological dimension (Ps.Rev. 1959, 66, 367–86).
Malmo, R. B.: Measurement of drive (Nebr.Symp. 1958).
Maltzman, L.: The process need (Ps.Rev. 1952, 59, 40–48).
Mandler, G., and W. Kessen: The Language of Psychology (Wiley, N.Y., 1959).
Marx, M. H.: Intervening variables or hypothetical constructs? (Ps.Rev. 1951, 58, 235–47).
Marx, M. H.: Motivation, in C. W. Harris (ed.): Encyclopedia of Educational Research (Macmillan, N.Y., 1960, pp. 888–901).
Marx, H.: Some relations between frustrations and drive (Neb.Symp. 1956).
Maslow, A. H.: Deficiency motivation and growth motivation (Nebr.Symp. 1955).
Maslow, A. H.: Higher needs and personality (Dialectica 1951, 5, 257–64).
Maslow, A. H.: Motivation and Personality (Harper & Bros., N.Y., 1954).
Maslow, A. H.: The Psychology of Science (Harper, N.Y. and London, 1966).
Maslow, A. H.: The theory of threat (Ps.Rev. 1941, 48, 264–66).
Massermann, J. H.: Principles of dynamic psychiatry (Saunders, Philadelphia, 1961).
Mav, M. H.: Experimentally acquired drives (J.exp.Psych. 1948, 38, 66–77).
Maze, J. R.: On some corruptions of the doctrine of homeostasis (Ps.Rev. 1953, 60, 405–12).
Meisner, W. W.: Intervening constructs-dimensions of controversy (Ps.Rev. 1960, 67, 51–72).
Melton, A. W.: Learning (An.Rev. 1950, 1, 9–30).
Miller, N. E.: Comments on theoretical models, in Krech and Klein (ed.): Theoretical models and personality theory (Duke Univ. Publ., Cambridge, London, 1952).
Miller, N. E.: Learnable drives and rewards, in S. S. Stevens (ed.): Handbook of experimental

psychology (1951, pp. 435–72).
Miller, N. E.: Studies of fear as acquirable drive (J.Exp.Psych. 1948, 38, 89–101).
Moore, O. K., and D. J. Lewis: Purposes and learning theory (Ps.Rev. 1953, 60, 149–56).
Moore, Th. V.: The driving forces of human nature and their adjustment (Grune & Stratton, N.Y., 1948).
Morgan, D. N.: Creativity today. A constructive analytical review of certain philosophical and psychological work. (Journal of Aesthetics and Art Criticism 1953, 12, 1–24).
Morgan, C. T.: Physiological mechanisms of motivation (Nebr.Symp. 1957).
Mowrer, C. H.: Learning theory and personality dynamics (Ronald Press, N.Y., 1950).
Mowrer, O. H.: Motivation (Annual Rev. of Psych. 3, 1952).
Mowrer, O. H.: Motivation and neurosis (Nebr.Symp. 1953).
Mowrer, O. H.: Two-factor learning theory reconsidered (Ps.Rev. 1956, 63, 114–28).
Murphy, G.: Historical introduction to modern psychology (Harcourt, N.Y., 1951).
Murray, H. A.: Drive, time, strategy, measurement, in G. Lindzey (ed.): Assessment of Human Motives (Grove Press, N.Y., 1958).
Murray, H. A.: Explorations in personality (Oxford Univ. Press, Oxford, 1938).
Murray, Henry A., Bibliography of, in R. W. White (ed.): The Study of Lives (Prentice-Hall, N.Y., 1963).
Murray, H. A.: Preparations for the scaffold of a comprehensive system, in S. Koch (ed.): Psychology – a study of a science, Vol. III (McGraw-Hill, N.Y., 1959).
Murray, H. A.: Some basic psychological assumptions and conseptions (Dialectica, 1951, 5, 266–92).
Murray, H. A.: Toward a classification of interaction, in T. Parsons and E. A. Shils (eds.); Towards a General Theory of Action (Harvard Univ. Press, Cambridge, Mass., 1951).
Murray, H. A., and C. Kluckhohn: Outline of a conception of personality, in Murray and Kluckhohn (eds.): Personality in nature, society and culture (Knopf, N.Y., 1948, 2nd ed., 1953).
Murray and Morgan: A Clinical Study of Sentiments (Genet. Psychol. Monogr. 1945, No. 32.
Murray, H. A. et al.: Explorations in Personality (Oxford Univ. Press, N.Y., 1938).
Næss, Arne: Erkenntnis und Wissenschaftliches Verhalten (Skrifter udg. av det Norske videnskabs akademi II. Oslo 1936).
Næss, Arne: Science as Behavior, in Metapsykologi (Universitetsforlaget, Oslo, 1962).
Nagel, E.: Teleological explanations and teleological systems, in Feigl and Brodbeck: Readings in the philosophy of science (Appleton, N.Y., 1953).
Neff, W. D.: Physiological psychology (An.Rev. 1953, 4, 255–72).
Nelson, T. M. and S. H. Bartley: Numerosity, number, arithmetization, measurement and psychology (Ph.Sci. 1961, 28, 178–203).
Neurath, O., N. Böhr, J. Dewey, B. Russell, R. Carnap, C. W. Morris: Encyclopedia and unified science (Internat. Enc. Unif. Sci. I (I), 1946).
Nissen, H. W.: The nature of the drive (Nebr.Symp. 1954).
Nissen, H. W., and J. Semmes: Comparative and physiological psychology (An.Rev. 1952, 3, 232–60).
Nuttin, J.: Consciousness, behavior and personality (Ps.Rev. 1955, 62, 349–55).
Nuttin, J.: Personality (An.Rev. 1955, 6, 161–86).
Olds, J.: Physiological mechanisms of reward (Neb.Symp. 1955).
Olds, J.: The growth and structure of motives (Burns and MacEachern, Toronto, 1956).
Olds, J., and P. Milner: Positive reinforcement produced by electrical stimulation (J.comp. physiol.psych. 1954, 47, 419–27).
Parsons, Talcott, and E. Shils (ed.): Toward a general theory of action (Harvard Univ. Press, Cambridge, Mass., 1951).
Patton, R. A.: Physiological psychology (An.Rev. 1954, 5, 247–321).
Pelz, D. C.: Freedom in research (International Science and Technique, 1964, No. 31, 54–66).
Pelz, D. C.: Social factors in the motivation of engineers and scientists (School Science and Mathematics, 1958, 58, 417–29).
Pepper, S. C.: The sources of value (Univ. of Calif. Press, Cambridge, 1958).
Peters, R. S. (ed.): Brett's History of Psychology (Allen & Unwin, London, 1953).
Peters, R. S.: The Concept of Motivation (Routledge, London, 1958).
Peters, R. S., and H. Tajfel: Hobbes and Hull – metaphysicians of behavior (B.J.Ph.Sc. 1957, 8, 30–44).

Plant, H. C.: Condition, cause, freewill and the directions of time (Br.J.Ph.Sci. 1960, I, 212–13).
Popper, K. R.: The logic of scientific discovery (Harper & Row, N.Y., 1965).
Post, H. R.: Simplicity and scientific theories (Br.J.Ph.Sci. 1960, XI, 32–41).
Postman, L.: Motivational factors in perception (Nebr.Symp. 1953).
Postman, L. (ed.): Psychology in the Making (Knopf, N. Y., 1962).
Pratt, C. C.: The logic of modern psychology (Macmillan, N.Y., 1940).
Rapaport, D.: On the psychoanalytic theory of motivation (Nebr.Symp. 1960).
Rasmussen, E. Tranekjær: Berkeley and modern psychology (B.J.Ph.Sc. 4, 2–12).
Rasmussen, E. Trankjær: Bevidsthedsliv og erkendelse (Munksgaard, Copenhagen, 1956).
Rasmussen, E. Tranekjær: Dynamisk psykologi og dens grundlag (Munksgaard, Copenhagen, 1960).
Razran, Gregory: Russian Physiologist's Psychology and American Experimental Psychology: A Historical and a Systematic Collation and a Look into the Future (Psychol. Bulletin, 1965, 63, 42–64).
Reichenback, H.: The rise of scientific philosophy (Univ. of Calif. Press, Los Angeles, 1957).
Retlingshofer, D.: Motivation as related to personality (MacGraw-Hill, N.Y., 1963).
Ritchie, B. F.: Laws of motivation (Nebr.Symp. 1954).
Roe, Anne: The making of a scientist (Dodd-Mead, N.Y., 1955).
Rosenthal, R.: On the social psychology of the psychological experiment (Amer. Scientist 1963, 51, 268–83).
Rozebook, W. W.: Do stimuli elicit behavior? (Ph.Sci. 1960, 27, 159–70).
Rozeboom, W. W.: Mediation variables in scientific theory (Ps.Rev. 1956, 63, 249–64).
Russell, B.: An inquiry into meaning and truth (Allen, London, 1940).
Russell, B.: Human knowledge (Allen, London, 1948).
Russell, B.: Our knowledge of the external world (London, 1927).
Russell, B.: The analysis of mind (London, 1922).
Russell, E. S.: The "drive" element in life (B.J.Ph.Sc. 1950, I, 108–16).
Ryle, G.: The concept of mind (Penguin, London, 1963).
Schachter, S.: The Psychology of Affiliation (Stanford Univ. Press, Palo Alto, 1959).
Scheffer, J.: Explanation, prediction and abstraction (B.J.Ph.Sc. 1957, 7, 293–309).
Schneirla, T. C.: An evolutionary and developmental theory of biphasic processes underlying approach and withdrawal (Nebr.Symp. 1959).
Scriven, N.: Views of Human Nature, in Wann (ed.): Behaviorism and Phenomenology (Univ. of Chicago Press, Chicago, 1964).
Sears, R. R.: Personality (An.Rev. 1950, 1, 105–18).
Seward, J. P.: A neurological approach to motivation (Nebr.Symp. 1956).
Seward, J. P.: Drive, incentive and reinforcement (Ps.Rev. 1956, 63, 195–203).
Seward, J. P.: How are motives learned (Ps.Rev. 1953, 60, 99–110).
Seward, J. P.: Hull's system of behavior: An evaluation (Ps.Rev. 1954, 61, 145–59).
Seward, J. P.: Introduction to a theory of motivation in learning. (Ps.Rev. 1952, 59, 405–13).
Seward, J. P.: Reinforcement and expectancy (Ps.Rev. 1956, 63, 105–13).
Seward, J. P.: The sign of a symbol (Ps.Rev. 1948, 55, 277–96).
Shipley, T. E., and J. Veroff: A projective measure of need for affiliation (J.exp.Psych. 1952, 43, 349–56).
Skinner, B. F., and J. G. Holland: The Analysis of Behavior (McGraw-Hill, N.Y., 1961).
Skinner, B. F.: Science and human behavior (Macmillan, N.Y., 1960).
Smedslund, J.: Studies in psychological theory (Oslo, 1951).
Smith, F. V.: Critical notice and appreciation of the work of the late Professor Clark L. Hull. (Brit.J.Psych. 1954–65, May).
Smith, F. V.: Psychological concepts and linguistic restraints (Br.J.Ph.Sci. 1959, X, 223–27).
Smith, F. V.: The explanation of human behavior (Constable, London, 1960).
Smith, F. V.: The System of William McDougall, in The Explanation of Human Behavior (Macmillan, London, 1952).
Snygg, D.: The need for a phenomenological system of psychology (Ps.Rev. 1941, 48, 404–24).
Spence, K. W.: Behavior theory and learning. Selected papers (Prentice-Hall, N.J., 1960).
Spence, K. W.: Behavior theory and selective learning (Nebr.Symp. 1958).
Spence, K. W.: The methods and postulates of "behaviorism" (Ps.Rev. 1948, 55, 67–68).

Spence, K. W.: The nature of theory construction in contemporary psychology (Ps.Rev. 1944, 51, 47–68).

Spence, K. W.: Theoretical interpretations of learning, in S. S. Stevens (ed.): Handbook of experimental psychology (Wiley, N.Y., 1951).

Stagner, R.: Homeostasis as an unifying concept in personality theory (Ps.Rev. 1951, 58, 5–17).

Stagner, R., and T. F. Karwoski: Psychology (McGraw-Hill, N.Y., 1952).

Stellar, E.: Physiological psychology (An.Rev. 1957, 8, 415–36).

Stellar, E.: The physiology and motivation (Ps.Rev. 1954, 61, 5–22).

Stephenson, W.: Postulates of behaviorism (Ph.Sci. 1953, 20, 110–20).

Stevens, S. S. (ed.): Handbook of experimental psychology (Wiley, N.Y., 1958).

Stevens, S. S.: Psychology and the science of science (Ps.Bull. 1939, 36, 221–63).

Stevens, S. S.: The operational basis of psychology (Amer.J.Psych. 1935, 47, 323–30).

Stevens, S. S.: The operational definition of psychological concepts (Ps.Rev. 1935, 42, 517–27).

Symonds, P. M.: What education has to learn from psychology (Teachers College Record N.Y. 1955, 56, 277–85).

Tegen, Einar: Amerikansk psykologi (Tiden, Stockholm, 1949).

Teuber, H. L.: Physiological psychology (An.Rev. 1955, 267–96).

Thomae, H. (ed.): Handbook der Psychologie. Bd. 2. Allgemeine Psychologie. Motivation (Verlag für Psychologie, Göttingen, 1965).

Thomae, H. (Herausg.): Die Motivation menschlichen Handelns (Kieperheuer u. Witsch. Köln, Berlin, 1965).

Thompson, R., and W. Slucken: Cybernetics and mental functioning (B.J.Ph.Sc. 1953, 4, 130–46).

Tinbergen, N.: The study of instinct (Oxford Univ. Press, N.Y., 1951).

Tolman, E. C.: A cognition-motivation model (Ps.Rev. 1952, 59, 382–400).

Tolman, E. C.: A psychological model, in A. Parson and F. Shils (eds.): Towards a general theory of action (Harvard Univ. Press, Cambridge, 1951).

Tolman, E. C.: Collected papers in psychology (Univ. of Calif. Press, Los Angeles, 1951).

Tolman, E. C.: Kurt Lewin, 1890–1947 (Ps.Review V, 55, 1948).

Tolman, E. C.: Operational behaviorism and the current trends in psychology, in Collected Papers (Univ. of Calif. Press, Los Angeles, 1951).

Tolman, E. C.: Principles of performance (Ps.Rev. 1955, 62, 312–26).

Tolman, E. C.: Principles of Purposive Behavior, in S. Koch (ed.): Psychology – A study of a science, Vol. II (McGraw-Hill, N.Y., 1959).

Tolman, E. C.: Purposive behavior in animals and men (1932).

Tolman, E. C.: The nature and functioning of wants (Ps.Rev. 1949, 56, 357–69).

Tolman, E. C., and L. Postman: Learning (An.Res. 1954, 5, 27–56).

Toman, W.: On the periodicity of motivation (Nebr.Symp. 1960).

Toman, W.: Psychoanalytic Theory of Motivation (Pergamon Press, Oxford, 1960).

Törnebohm, H.: A logical analysis of the theory of reativity (Almqvist & Wiksell, Stockholm, 1952).

Törnebohm, H.: Discourse Analysis (Theoria 1955, 21, 42–54).

Törnebohm, H.: Fysik och Filosofi (Univ. Gotenburg, 1957).

Toulmin, S.: The philosophy of science (Hutchinson, London, 1953).

Turner, M. B.: Philosophy and the Science of Behavior (Appleton, N.Y., 1957).

Underwood, B. J.: Learning (An.Rev. 1953, 4, 31–58).

Valpola, V., and P. Törnudd: Vetenskapeligt samarbete och inter-disciplinäre problem (Nordisk Sommeruniversitet, Helsinki, 1963).

Verplanck, W. S.: A glossary of some terms used in the objective science of behavior (Ps.Rev. Supplement nov., 1957).

Vorogin, L. G., A. N. Leontiev, A. R. Luria, E. N. Solokov, and O. S. Vinogradova (eds.): Orienting Reflex and Exploratory Behavior (Moscow 1958, English translation, American Psychological Ass., Washington, D.C., 1957).

Walker, E. L.: Learning (An.Rev. 1957, 8, 113–38).

Wall, W. D.: The wish to learn – research into motivation (Educat. Research 1958, I, 25–37).

Watson, G.: Apparent motion and mind-body-problem (B.J.Ph.Sc. 1957, 8, 113, 138).

Watson, I. R.: The Great Psychologists: From Aristotle to Freud (Lippincott, N.Y., 1963).

Watson, J. B.: Behavior: an introduction to comparative psychology (1914).

Watson, J. B.: Psychology from the standpoint of a behaviorist (1919).
Webb, W. B.: Responses in absence of acquisition motive (Ps.Rev. 1952, 59, 54–61).
White, R. W.: Competence and the psycho-sexual stages of development (Nebr.Symp. 1960).
White, R. W.: Motivation reconsidered: The concept of competence (Ps.Rev. 1959, 66, 297–333).
Whithers, R. F. J.: Epistemology and scientific strategy (Br.J.Ph.Sci. 1959, X, 89–102).
Whiting, J. W. M.: Sorcery, Sin and the Superego (Nebr.Symp. 1959).
Whitrow, G. J.: The study of philosophy of science (B.J.Ph.Sc. 1956, 7, 189–205).
Wittenborn, J. R.: Inferring the strength of drive (Nebr.Symp. 1957).
Wisdom, J. O.: A new model for the mindbody relationship (B.J.Ph.Sc. 1951, 2, 295–301).
Wolman, B. B.: Contemporary Theories and Systems in Psychology (Harper, N.Y., 1960).
Wolpe, J.: Need-reduction, drive-reduction and reinforcement (Ps.Rev. 1950, 57, 19–26).
Woodger, J. H.: Physics, Psychology and Medine (Cambridge Univ. Press, London, 1956).
Woodger, J. R.: The technique of theory construction (Internat. Encycl. Unif. Sci. II (5), 1939).
Woodworth, R. S.: Contemporary schools of psychology (Menthuen, London, new ed., 1965).
Woodworth, R. S.: Dynamics of behavior (Menthuen, London, 1958).
Woodworth, B. S., and Mary Sheehan: Contemporary Schools of Psychology (Ronald, N.Y., 3rd ed., 1964).
Woodworth, R. S., and H. Schlosberg: Experimental psychology (Menthuen, London, 1958).
Wright, G. H. von: Den logiska empirismen (Natur och Kultur Stockholm, 1943).
Young, P. T.: Appetite, palability and feeding habit (Ps.Bull. 1948, 45, 289–320).
Young, P. T.: Emotion as a disorganized response (Ps.Rev. 1949, 56, 184–191).
Young, P. T.: Emotions in man and animals (Wiley, N.Y., 1943).
Young, P. T.: Food-seeking, drive, affective process and learning (Ps.Rev. 1949, 56, 98–121).
Young, P. T.: Hedonic Organization and Regulation of Behavior (Ps.Rev. 73 (1), 59–86).
Young, P. Th.: Motivation and Emotion – A survey of the determinants of human and animal activity (Wiley, N.Y., 1961).
Young, P. Th.: Motivation, in P. L. Harriman (ed.): Encylopedia of psychology (1946).
Young, P. T.: Motivation, in W. S. Monroe (ed.): Encyclopedia of Educational Research (1950).
Young, P. T.: Motivation of Behavior (Chapman, London, 1959).
Young, P. T.: The experimental analysis of appetite (Ps.Bull, 1941, 38, 129–64).
Young, P. T.- The role of affective processes in learning and motivation (Ps.Rev. 1959, 66, 104–25).
Young, P. T.: The role of hedonic processes in motivation (Nebr.Symp. 1955).
Young, P. T.: The role of hedonic processes in the organization of behavior (Ps.Rev. 1952, 249–62).

INDEX OF NAMES AND SUBJECTS